THE BEST BUSINESS STORIES
OF THE YEAR: 2004 *Edition*

Andrew Leckey, nationally syndicated investment columnist for the Chicago Tribune Company, is director of the
Donald W. Reynolds National Center for Business Journalism at the American Press Institute. He was previously
a CNBC anchor and contributing editor for Quicken.com.
Leckey was director of the Business Journalism Program
at the University of California, Berkeley, and a visiting
professor at Boston University. He received the National
Association of Investors Corporation's Distinguished Service Award in Investment Education. Leckey has been
the author or editor of nine financial books. He was a
Knight-Bagehot Fellow in Economics and Business Journalism and a fellow of the Media Studies Center, both at
Columbia University.

John C. Bogle, guest editor and founder of The Vanguard
Group Inc., was named by *Fortune* magazine as one of the
investment industry's four Giants of the Twentieth Century. In 1974 he created Vanguard, now one of the world's
two largest mutual fund organizations, serving as chairman
and CEO until 1996 and senior chairman until 2000. A
tireless advocate for investor rights and sound business
ethics, Bogle is a bestselling financial author whose books
include *Bogle on Mutual Funds* and *Common Sense on Mutual
Funds*. He is a magna cum laude Economics graduate of
Princeton University and has received honorary degrees
from seven universities. He is president of Bogle Financial
Markets Research Center.

THE BEST BUSINESS STORIES

OF THE YEAR: 2004 *Edition*

THE BEST
BUSINESS STORIES
OF THE YEAR

2004 *Edition*

Edited by *Andrew Leckey*

with guest editor *John C. Bogle*

VINTAGE BOOKS

A DIVISION OF RANDOM HOUSE, INC.

NEW YORK

A VINTAGE BOOKS ORIGINAL, JANUARY 2004

Copyright © 2004 by Andrew Leckey
Introduction copyright © 2004 by John C. Bogle

Permissions to reprint previously published material can be found at the end of the book.

Library of Congress Cataloging-in-Publication Data is on file.

ISBN: 1-4000-3146-X

Book design by Christopher M. Zucker

www.vintagebooks.com

Printed in the United States of America
10 9 8 7 6 5 4 3 2 1

CONTENTS

FOREWORD

Difficult periods bring out the best in business journalism. Previous editions of *The Best Business Stories of the Year* have included dramatic events such as the dot-com tumble, economic fallout from the 9/11 terrorist attacks, the collapse of Enron, the tragic death of *The Wall Street Journal* reporter Daniel Pearl, social inequities in the business world, and disturbing financial and ethical lapses by Wall Street and accounting firms. Yet the series has also been great fun, profiling larger-than-life business personalities and providing humorous, sometimes quirky, glimpses into intriguing companies and the less-traveled roads of business. The quality writing of diverse publications and web sites is always the driving force of this anthology. Initial guides for this unpredictable journey were the respected journalists Marshall Loeb, Ken Auletta, and Allan Sloan, each taking a turn as an annual edition's guest editor.

We are pleased to have John C. Bogle, founder and former CEO of The Vanguard Group Inc., as guest editor for *The Best Business Stories of the Year: 2004 Edition.* With leadership of corporate America under siege, fingers pointing, and indictments flying, it is an excellent time to get a top businessperson's take on quality business journalism. The possibility of an edition with a corporate executive rather than a business journalist as guest editor was first brought up when the series was hatched several years ago. There had initially been some concern about whether a CEO might toss the extensive reading and critiquing process to a public relations staffer, be too much of an advocate for business to view it critically, or have personal skeletons in the closet. Corporate leadership is under fire, with even Jack Welch, once the patron saint of CEOs, losing his halo when his extravagant General Electric severance package was revealed in divorce proceedings.

Enter Bogle, who in addition to his management credentials is a successful author of books and magazine articles, a crusader for investor rights and ethical business standards, and an occasional book reviewer in publications such as *The Wall Street Journal*. He is a voracious, critical reader of all things financial, able to rattle off names of the top journalists at major publications and comment on strengths and weaknesses of coverage. Rather than wink at CEO indiscretions, he considers them an insult to his convictions. The 75-year-old Bogle's passion seems to have grown even stronger since February 26, 1996, when he became the recipient of a heart transplant. He now keeps a breakneck pace of speaking engagements around the country that totaled nearly 70 events in 2003, and is often called upon to testify before congressional and professional hearings on investment and economic policy.

"Brings tears to my eyes," Bogle wrote in a note after reading the story of a Seattle couple that lost the American dream. "This is a story that *must* be told," he wrote about the fall of Arthur Andersen accounting. "A must!" he wrote about Qwest's demise. His comments ran the gamut from "great stuff" and "this is an urgent topic that will increase in importance," to "others covered this issue much better" and "simply doesn't dig deep enough." He often sounded more like a hard-nosed managing editor than a former mutual fund CEO.

The Best Business Stories of the Year: 2004 Edition therefore takes an unflinching look at business, warts and all. Smarting from criticism that it should have been more aggressive in regard to the dot-com bubble and a number of major corporate scandals, business journalism has become more sophisticated and investigative, with the important tools of accounting and financial analysis added to the reporter's arsenal. No one simply accepts a company's party line anymore, but carefully runs all the numbers, asks informed questions, and snoops behind the scenes. This approach is demanded by readers and investors alike. Many young people have also entered the field of business journalism, some attracted by Enron headlines much as an earlier generation of political reporters was lured by Watergate. I've been privileged to teach some of these up-and-coming business journalists at the University of California, Berkeley, and Boston University, and am convinced that they have the talent to take reporting and editing to a higher level. As they take their places at publications of all types and sizes, I've found their work to exhibit depth and flair that was missing from business stories a decade ago.

This anthology admires and respects business writing. There are many different types of great business stories being produced by publications and web sites. While many of these are longer stories, some are columns or shorter pieces. Not all deal with weighty issues. Few readers regularly see all the business and general publications whose stories we have included here. Besides looking through hundreds of articles in print and on web sites, we consulted editors, writers, and contest officials for additional recommendations. We especially appreciated editors who proudly sent us their staffs' best work. Our hope is that with the publication of *The Best Business Stories of the Year: 2004 Edition* even more people will join us and give further suggestions so that we can present as diverse a mix as possible.

Sincere thanks to the writers of the pieces in this anthology. I also wish to thank Edward Kastenmeier, senior editor at Vintage Books, who has been a joy to work with throughout this series, and my literary agent Nat Sobel, an ongoing source of encouragement and advice.

The stories in *The Best Business Stories of the Year: 2004 Edition* were originally published between July 1, 2002, and June 30, 2003. Selections for next year's anthology will be made on that same "fiscal year" basis. Editors or writers who wish published or online business stories to be considered for next year's edition should throughout the year send copies to Andrew Leckey, c/o *The Best Business Stories of the Year,* Vintage Books, 1745 Broadway, New York, NY 10019. We look forward to reading the next group of stories as we continue on the unpredictable journey of the financial world.

—*Andrew Leckey*

INTRODUCTION

The history of business is, in many respects, the history of our times—our values, our aspirations, our hopes, and our fears. And if business history can be drama, surely the players on the stage—the stars, the supporting cast, the extras—and the workers behind the stage—the set designers, the scene changers, even the grips—are all part of that history.

The twelve-month period from which *The Best Business Stories of the Year: 2004 Edition* were drawn includes some of the most remarkable dramas—personal and corporate—in the long and checkered history of U.S. business. The signature events of the year clearly revolved around corporate and financial malfeasance—unethical, if not always illegal, behavior in the executive suite, mirrored on Wall Street and among accounting firms that were ostensibly representing the public. These betrayals of trust were not only the backdrop, but a cause, of the loss in investor confidence that helped drive stock prices down to an October 2002 low some 50 percent below their bull market high, reached just two and a half years earlier. The result was one of the two greatest bear markets since the depression of the 1930s.

Under the surface, our economy was changing, too. Not only did the long prosperity of the Nifty Nineties fade, but the distribution of wealth among our citizens changed in ways that raised serious questions about whether our American system of democratic capitalism was working properly. Specifically, the gap between our wealthiest families and those in the lower regions of our society expanded to its widest ever. In their successive articles in *The New York Times Magazine*, Paul Krugman ("For Richer") and Michael Lewis ("In Defense of the Boom") have created wonderful—and contradictory—word pictures of this aspect of our society.

While many of those who were the winners in this distribution of wealth surely created wealth for others, any society that does not concern itself with the least-favored of its members—especially a society that holds that all men are created equal, that assures each one of its citizens of the right to life, liberty, and the pursuit of happiness, and that promises to promote the general welfare—owes itself some serious self-examination about whether it is measuring up to the high standards and values established by the Founding Fathers.

OWNERS' CAPITALISM BECOMES MANAGERS' CAPITALISM

The excesses of executive compensation—and of executive behavior—are also smartly chronicled. James B. Stewart's *New Yorker* profile ("Spend! Spend! Spend!") of the poster boy for these excesses—Tyco's Dennis Kozlowski—presents a character whose deeds defy our imagination. Like Al Capone, Kozlowski seems likely to be punished, not for what was, arguably, the looting of the Tyco treasury, but for tax evasion. (In his case, this budding art collector failed to pay New York sales taxes on five paintings valued at tens of millions of dollars.)

Other examples of these excesses were more subtle. "Rich Man, Poor Company," the story by Chris O'Brien and Jack Davis of the *San Jose Mercury News,* describes massive sales of stock to the public by executives in forty companies shortly before their stocks' prices dropped at least 99.5 percent. (Insider sales totaling $2.5 billion by executives in two other companies were excluded from the study; one stock had fallen "only" 98.7 percent, the other by 97.1 percent.) The failure of corporate compensation committees to rein in excessive pay is vividly documented by Diana Henriques and Geraldine Fabrikant in *The New York Times* ("Deciding on Executive Pay").

In a phrase I've come to use often, this was the era of "the imperial CEO." That phrase is iterated in Jerry Useem's fine *Fortune* piece, subtitled "How Corporate Leaders Lost Our Trust," and reiterated ever more recently by no less a figure than Securities and Exchange Commission chairman William E. Donaldson. When CEOs turned their focus from the hard work of building the long-term value of the corporation to the far easier task of hyping the short-term price of the stock (and then selling their optioned shares), it reflected a shift—indeed, what has been called a "pathological metamorphosis"—from the traditional *owners'* capitalism to *managers'* capitalism for which we are paying the price today.

"Earnings guidance" quickly became part of this concentration on stock price rather than corporate value. Executives promised a certain level of earnings each quarter, as if business conditions never fluctuated. And when they couldn't "meet expectations" the old-fashioned way—with new markets, new products, greater productivity, heightened efficiency— they did it the new-fashioned way, by taking advantage of every loophole that "generally accepted accounting principles" (GAAP) could provide.

CO-OPTED ACCOUNTANTS

In the process, accountants were co-opted, and became partners of management rather than independent auditors. Max H. Bazerman, George Loewenstein, and Don A. Moore chronicle this issue in "Why Good Accountants Do Bad Audits," from the *Harvard Business Review,* in which they lay out a plan to reduce the auditor's interest in pleasing the client. Rebecca Blumenstein and Carol Hymowitz chronicle an especially messy example of this co-option in "Troubling Options." Their article from *The Wall Street Journal* describes how Ernst & Young, auditors for Sprint, offered the firm's chief executive and its president a tax shelter offering staggering savings estimated at $100 million each on their stock option gains. Both of the executives then paid $2.9 million to the company's so-called independent auditors, an even larger aggregate than the company's audit fee of $2.5 million. The Internal Revenue Service then challenged the tax dodge, and Ernst & Young, once these executives' partner, because their adversary. Sprint stock has tumbled, and both executives, now terminated by the board, may face personal bankruptcy. "Oh, what a tangled web we weave when first we practice to deceive."

As independent auditors became accessories to earnings guidance, nowhere was the fallout more severe than in the case of Arthur Andersen, accountants to Enron. The result, as Flynn McRoberts of the *Chicago Tribune* and his associates report ("The Fall of Andersen"), was the firm's failure. In its drive to boost profits, Andersen diluted its own lofty standards, rewarding partners who generated hefty consulting fees, and forced out its elite corps of in-house ethics watchdogs. As one client after another pushed the numbers to the edge of the envelope, and then beyond, the firm's reputation shrank, other clients terminated its services, the Justice Department sued, and the firm went under—an ironic fulfillment of the words of one of the eulogies given at founder Arthur Andersen's 1947 funeral: "He would rather the doors be closed than that the firm should continue to exist on principles other than those which he established."

WALL STREET LAYS AN EGG

Investment banking firms, brokers, security analysts, and money managers were also not only willing but eager partners in the happy conspiracy to raise stock prices. "Wall Street Lays an Egg," the classic 1929 headline from *Variety*, could have been an equally apt headline as the 2000 stock market bubble continued into early 2003. The Street's excesses are brilliantly chronicled in John Cassidy's *New Yorker* article "The Investigation," describing how New York State attorney general Eliot Spitzer and his staff unearthed the shoddy practices of modern-day investment banking, forced the firms to pay $1.4 billion in fines, and instituted a series of long-overdue reforms.

Included in these reforms were steps designed to assure the independence of Wall Street "sell side" research analysts from the IPO process, and at least one firm promptly took even more severe action. Prudential Securities jettisoned its investment banking operation and embraced truly independent research, a story ("Inside the Rock") covered by Loch Adamson in *Worth*. But the "buy side" was hardly free from blame. As the financial shenanigans accelerated, pension fund and mutual fund managers simply didn't do their homework. As chronicled in Edward Robinson's "Alliance Capital's Bad Bets" in *Bloomberg Markets*, the firm's clients paid a high price for its frequent reliance on bizarre investment concepts rather than on detailed research.

As the investment shortcomings of so many institutional money managers doing their work "the old-fashioned way" became evident, hedge fund managers, doing their work in quite a different way, moved into the mainstream of investing. "Where the Money's Really Made," by *Fortune*'s Andy Serwer, analyzes how hedge funds work, explains why they often implode, and describes the staggering compensation raked in by their entrepreneurial managers. Is a hedge fund bubble now in the making? Only time will tell.

Even the SEC's attempt to squash the use of inside information about stocks by brokers and fund managers through a new "Fair Disclosure" rule (Regulation FD) was frustrated. According to Bob Drummond ("Unfair Disclosure," in *Bloomberg Markets*), the rule is "not working," and cries out for more vigorous enforcement. Other peculiar anomalies also remain in the financial markets, illustrated in Noelle Haner-Dorr's story, "Big Bucks, Small Town, Bond Haven." Her surprising saga describes how tiny Moore Haven, Florida, became a powerhouse in bond underwriting.

While many of the past excesses were found in the stock market, some important warnings signs for the future are currently found in the bond market—especially in the growth in debt incurred by America's corporations, governments, and consumers. In "The Debt Bomb" (published in *Barron's*), Jonathan R. Laing describes how total debt outstanding rose to $31 trillion, three times our GDP, the highest ratio in history. The consequences? Again, we can only watch and wait, and hope for the best.

BUSINESS FAILURES—AND SUCCESS

The tinsel and glitter of the market bubble led astray even seasoned business leaders who should have known better. The champion failure, later resulting in a write-off of $100 billion in asset values, was the merger of AOL Time Warner, whose downfall is covered by *Newsweek*'s Johnnie L. Roberts. (Time flies. When he wrote his story, "How It All Fell Apart," CEO Gerald Levin and Chairman Steve Case were "locked in a fierce power struggle." Both of them would soon lose their jobs.)

In a similar merger of a rock company (one that makes real things) with a paper company (one that counts things yet to come), telephone giant U.S. West was acquired by telecom upstart Qwest. In the boom and bust that followed, as described by Lou Kilzer, David Milstead, and Jeff Smith in the *Rocky Mountain News* ("Wild, Wild Qwest"), all too typically, shareholders and employees were impoverished, but the option-engorged Qwest executives sold their shares early in the game and were bountifully enriched.

Two other business stories offer important lessons. In "The Year the Music Dies" (from *Wired* magazine) Charles C. Mann worries about the impact of internet technology on record labels and CDs and delivers a requiem for the music industry. And in *Red Herring,* Julie Landry expresses concern that technology in the schoolroom is doing more to enrich tech companies' wallets than it is to enrich student learning. Her attention-getting title is a memorable quotation from President Bush: "Is Our Children Learning?"

Despite the many business failures of the recent era, there were notable successes. Starbucks is a classic story of entrepreneurship, and the remarkable growth and profitability of this, well, purveyor of high-priced coffee, is told in *BusinessWeek* ("Planet Starbucks" by Stanley Holmes). Another success story, "The Monopolist," is told by Connie Bruck in *The New Yorker,* a profile of MCA's Lew Wasserman, whose shrewd and tempestuous career (abetted by a measure of corner-cutting) transformed television entertainment. Yet another success story, the rise of search engine Google to preeminence in its field, is chronicled by Stefanie Olsen on CNET News ("The Google Gods").

Management consultants played an important role in many of the business successes—and some of the failures, too. Giant consulting firm McKinsey & Co., described as the "world's most prestigious" in John A. Byrne's *BusinessWeek* article "Inside McKinsey," gained unwanted attention as the principal adviser to Enron, one of the greatest business failures of the era.

In all, the forces that inflated the bubble—corporate managers and management consultants, our flawed system of corporate governance, accountants, the Wall Street sell-side, and the institutional buy-side, and of course individual investors themselves—constituted a happy conspiracy of those who reveled in stock prices that soared far above intrinsic corporate values. And so "The Decline and Fall of the Cult of Equity" inevitably followed, as chronicled in Andrew Hill's column in *Financial Times,* a tongue-in-cheek description of the foolishness of the era.

HUMAN BEINGS

The boom and the bust sadly took its toll not only on people and companies with high profiles, but also on the human beings who perform the day-to-day tasks required to make our economic system work. Jeffrey Kosseff's "Amid Telecom Ruins, a Fortune Is Buried" about lost jobs, vanished investments, and thousands of miles of unused fiber-optic cable from *The Oregonian* describes the sweeping problems in the aftermath of the telecom boom. Steve Huettel's "Flight into the Red" from the *St. Petersburg Times* describes a remarkably similar parallel in the airline industry. And Shirleen Holt describes the devastation at an intimate personal level in her story "The Death of One American Dream" from *The Seattle Times.*

The year also gave us stories of individuals who were, one way or another, making a difference. Joanne Kimberlin's story of shoplifter Chrystine Anne Kelly ("The New Face of Shoplifting") in *The Virginian-Pilot* describes a profession, as it were, that most of us have not even thought about. Similarly, *The Wall Street Journal*'s Lucette Lagnado describes the case of Rebekah Nix in "Full Price: A Young Woman, an Appendectomy, and a $19,000 Debt," the story of one person's attempt to cut through our bizarre system of health care pricing and trace the source of $19,200 in medical bills. Writing in *Mother Jones,* Karen Olsson tells the story of Jennifer McLaughlin ("Up Against Wal-Mart") and her campaign to form a trade union and enhance working conditions at the giant retailer.

Another human interest story is Meg James's "Big Battle for a Silly Old Bear," chronicling the lawsuit against Walt Disney Company by Shirley Slesinger Lasswell, an heir of Winnie the Pooh creator A. A. Milne's American literary agent. The stakes are enormous, for in just four years Disney's annual Pooh revenue has risen from $100 million to $1 billion. So, too, are the stakes for the family of Jay Pritzker, whose $15 billion empire, as described by Suzanna Andrews in *Vanity Fair* ("Shattered Dynasty"), has resulted in a torrent of anger, greed, and betrayal (and, of course, a lawsuit) among his heirs.

THE BIG PICTURE

Even though the overpowering secular trend toward globalization began to falter during the past year, its impact remains profound. Yes, some nations have been winners and some losers, but every nation has some of each, a pattern described in an extensive report by William Finnegan in *Harper's Magazine* ("The Economics of Empire"). His report raises the question of whether what is called "market fundamentalism" (or, using the kinder formulation, "free trade"), described as the cornerstone of the Bush administration's view that "the *real* freedom [is] the freedom for a person or nation to make a living," a commercial freedom compared to which "free speech, a free press, religious freedom, political freedom are secondary at best." No matter what their political stripe, thoughtful citizens owe it to themselves to consider the implications of this philosophy for our society and for our neighbors around the globe.

It was not by accident that we chose "A Virtuous Cycle," written by James Surowiecki in *Forbes,* as the concluding story for this volume of business stories. It is a reminder that at the roots of capitalism are trust, honesty, and decency, and that the recent era in which managers' capitalism superseded owners' capitalism need be only a temporary aberration in a system that has been the engine of world economic growth for more than two centuries. "The value of trust and fair dealing," Surowiecki writes, "is a lesson that capitalists periodically need to learn all over again." Forewarned is forearmed.

The stories in this volume remind us that when we depart from that commonsense standard, trouble lies near at hand. As citizens, and especially as investors, each one of us has an obligation to help take capitalism back to its proud roots, firm in the conviction that its principal role is to benefit society as a whole. We are citizens of the world. For our own collective good, we must not forget that it is never too late to build a better world. "Press on, regardless."

—John C. Bogle

THE BEST BUSINESS STORIES

OF THE YEAR: *2004 Edition*

Dennis Kozlowski is the poster boy for CEO extravagance and mis-
conduct. Writing in *The New Yorker,* James B. Stewart personalizes the
man behind the reputation. He follows him from humble origins to the
extraordinary personal riches he extracted from Tyco International
and his eventual ouster as CEO. Kozlowski was scheduled to go to
trial on conspiracy and fraud charges in fall 2003, with a separate trial
on tax avoidance charges to follow. Meanwhile, Tyco discovered more
than $1 billion in accounting problems and had to restate several years
of earnings.

James B. Stewart

Spend! Spend! Spend! Where Did Tyco's Money Go?

ON A FRIDAY AFTERNOON last May, Mark Belnick, the
general counsel of Tyco International, the giant industrial conglomerate,
hurried into the Boca Raton office of the company's chairman and chief
executive officer, L. Dennis Kozlowski. Belnick had with him a copy of
a grand-jury subpoena that had just been served on the company and
that named Kozlowski personally.

Kozlowski stared at the text, which called for documents "reflecting
all transactions between Tyco International . . . and Alexander Apsis or
Alexander Apsis Fine Arts, LLC from 1999 to the present." The subpoena evidently concerned some paintings that Kozlowski had bought
the previous year, after he had decided to become a serious art collector.
They included a Monet and a Renoir. For the Monet, he had paid $3.95
million; for the Renoir, $5.5 million.

After studying the subpoena, Kozlowski picked up the phone and
called Christine Berry, who worked for Fine Collections Management, in
West Palm Beach, and was Kozlowski's art adviser. She had taken him to

various galleries and negotiated the purchase of the paintings. According to Kozlowski, the following conversation ensued:

"Who did we buy the Monet from?" he asked. Berry answered that the seller was Alexander Apsis, a dealer and former specialist for Sotheby's in London and New York. Without mentioning that he'd just received a subpoena, Kozlowski began questioning Berry about the purchase of the painting and the details of its delivery to his office at Tyco's headquarters, in Exeter, New Hampshire. "Do you mind if my lawyer gets on the phone?" Kozlowski asked.

Berry didn't answer immediately. By having the art shipped to New Hampshire, Kozlowski had avoided paying New York State's 8.25 percent sales tax—some $325,000 on the Monet alone. She told Kozlowski that she didn't want to talk to the lawyer, and needed to check her records and get back to him.

Three days later, on Monday, May 6, Berry sent Kozlowski a fax:

> I know you were inquiring about the shipment of the Monet to New Hampshire, so I dug up the paperwork associated with the delivery. Following this page is the bill of lading for the delivery. This is the only paperwork associated to these pieces . . . Best, Christine

The accompanying bill of lading, dated January 2, 2002, on the letterhead of the Southern Trucking Company of Brooklyn, identifies the "consignee" as Dennis Kozlowski, 1 Tyco Park, Exeter, New Hampshire. The shipper's signature is Christine Berry's, and under "received by consignee" is the signature of an assistant at Tyco in New Hampshire. A list of five works was attached: the Monet, the Renoir, another Impressionist painting, an Old Master, and a 1920 British hunting scene.

In other words, the paperwork supported the notion that the art had been shipped and duly received outside of New York state. Neither Kozlowski nor Belnick felt it necessary to alarm Tyco's board by mentioning the subpoena.

But Berry had been mistaken. The bill of lading she sent Kozlowski was not the only document pertaining to the shipping. In a memo to

Chris Hanson at Southern Trucking, dated December 21, 2001, she had written, in her own hand:

> Happy Happy Chris! Here is a list of the five paintings to go to NH (wink, wink) . . . Please make cardboard boxes or use crates to match the piece count. Cheers & thanks.

In New Hampshire, as Berry must have known, the assistant had signed for the delivery of empty boxes. One painting, the Monet, had simply been moved up the street from Apsis's apartment, at 930 Fifth Avenue, to Kozlowski's at 950 Fifth, where Berry had hung it in the living room.

Kozlowski had taken command of Tyco ten years earlier and transformed it from an obscure former government laboratory with $3 billion in revenues to an industrial conglomerate with $36 billion in revenues. The company's products range from security systems and industrial valves to medical equipment. Tyco's market capitalization was $1.5 billion when Kozlowski took charge; by 2001, it was $106 billion. Most of Kozlowski's compensation came in Tyco stock and options, and he was worth more than $400 million.

In the weeks after the subpoena was issued, other Tyco executives began to notice that Kozlowski, uncharacteristically, was rarely in the firm's New York office, and often couldn't be reached. He retained a leading criminal lawyer, Stephen Kaufman. He canceled meetings and business trips. Then, on Friday, May 31, Kaufman informed Kozlowski that he was about to be indicted for tax evasion. The following Monday, Tyco announced that the board had demanded and received Kozlowski's resignation as chairman and CEO.

In September, a second indictment charged Kozlowski with personally defrauding Tyco of more than $300 million. Belnick was indicted for falsifying records. As details emerged in the media, Kozlowski, more than any other executive who had prospered in the great bull market of the '90s, came to personify an epoch of corporate fraud, executive greed, and personal extravagance. It was a role that almost no one would have predicted for him.

I first met Dennis Kozlowski in December 2002, at his lawyer's offices. I had spoken to him once before, in a brief telephone interview for a Talk of the Town item in February 2000, about short sellers; he had insisted on personally taking my call and had answered all my questions with refreshing directness. Since then, I'd bought a thousand shares of Tyco stock, at a price of $40.59, and watched it rise in value ($63.21), and then plummet ($6.98). I'd become familiar with Kozlowski's business strategy, his dedication to shareholders, and his reputation for thrift and charm. Overweight and unprepossessing at the age of fifty-six, he certainly didn't look the part of one of America's most successful executives. Once, according to a Tyco executive, after a television appearance with Carleton Fiorina, the sleek, poised CEO of Hewlett-Packard, Kozlowski asked, "What am I doing here? I'm just a dumb Polish guy who can barely talk."

His disinclination to put on airs was part of his appeal. He told the audience at a Goldman Sachs conference in Manhattan in November 2000, "I grew up in Newark, New Jersey, right across the river. I was probably the first generation in my family to go to college. . . . But the real basis for everything I learned about acquisitions I learned from my Polish grandmother."

At our first meeting, Kozlowski, wearing a suit and tie, initially seemed uncomfortable and somewhat restless. He is bald, with a fringe of light-reddish hair, and his face colors easily. Perhaps because he isn't polished or articulate, he doesn't appear to be especially self-aware. He seemed bewildered by the intensity of the public outcry against him.

But, as he described Tyco's business operations, he had a sure command of even the smallest details, and was relaxed and eager to discuss them. His defense of Tyco's growth strategy—that is, his practice of frequently acquiring competitors in Tyco's disparate business lines—is persuasive even today. He does not seem naive or unsophisticated about nonbusiness subjects that interest him, such as wine and yachting, even though he is largely self-taught.

In the next few months, I interviewed Kozlowski on several occasions. Kaufman, his lawyer, was present, either in person or by phone. I agreed not to quote Kozlowski without Kaufman's authorization. Kozlowski spoke without inhibition about his former life—about his career, his youth in Newark, and his increasing forays over the years into the rarefied worlds of sailing, the art market, Fifth Avenue real estate, charitable boards, and Manhattan society.

Dennis Kozlowski grew up in a small apartment building in west-central Newark, a Polish and Italian Catholic working-class neighborhood that was largely demolished for urban-renewal projects in the late '60s. His father, Leo, was a member of the Polish American Republican Club in New Jersey and the local chapter of the Polish Falcons of America. Leo held a variety of jobs—professional boxer, reporter, and investigator for the New Jersey transit system. In the course of his work, he was shot twice; one bullet remained lodged in his neck for the rest of his life.

Kozlowski saw himself as strictly average, unlikely to achieve much beyond what his father or his uncles had. According to a recent *Business-Week* investigation, friends remember him as "an easygoing, even comical kid." At Newark's West Side High School, a history teacher praised him for having a logical mind, and encouraged him to join the debate team. Debating in front of school assemblies gave him confidence, and during his senior year, on the day when students and teachers reversed roles, Kozlowski was named the school principal. His history teacher made him feel that "I could be a leader, if I applied myself," Kozlowski says.

After graduating in 1964, Kozlowski lived at home while working to put himself through college at Seton Hall University, in South Orange. During his freshman year, he played basketball there. ("Not very well," he has said. "But good enough to get a couple of hundred dollars off my tuition.") He worked at a car wash, waited tables, and played guitar in a five-man band called the Hi-Tones. He joined two fraternities, did a fair amount of drinking, majored in accounting, and graduated in 1968 with a B-minus average. In his spare time, he dreamed of sailing and flying, two interests he'd had since childhood, and spent afternoons on Barnegat Bay on a Sunfish.

Kozlowski's first job after college was as an auditor for the SCM Corporation, formerly the Smith-Corona typewriter company. He began dating a company secretary named Angeles Suarez, originally from the Bronx, and they married a few years later.

While visiting an SCM operation outside San Francisco in 1969, Kozlowski discovered the Napa Valley, and visited the Robert Mondavi winery. Though he says he had never seen anything but Manischewitz at home, he began to acquire a taste for fine wine. In 1974, he followed his boss at SCM to Nashua Corporation, a New Hampshire office-equipment manufacturer, where he was made director of auditing. That year, Kozlowski won an auction conducted by Boston's public-television affiliate for a wine-study course in Cambridge, where he earned a "master mixologist" certificate. On business trips to Europe, Kozlowski began dropping in on estates in Burgundy and Bordeaux. By the mid-'70s, he had a collection of nearly a thousand bottles of wine.

In 1975, a headhunter asked Kozlowski if he would be interested in a position as assistant comptroller and head of auditing at a company called Tyco Laboratories. The chairman of Tyco was Joseph Gaziano, a burly, garrulous former engineer. Emulating Harold Geneen, who built the conglomerate ITT, Gaziano had acquired a number of small companies in his years as chief executive. Now he was seeking bigger targets. The notes from Kozlowski's first job interview at Tyco survive: "A strong candidate but lacks judgment."

Still, Kozlowski got the job and was happy to leave Nashua Corporation, which was faltering. His wife was pregnant, and they moved to Waltham, a suburb of Boston. The child, a daughter, was followed by a second daughter a few years later.

Gaziano couldn't read a balance sheet, but he was ambitious and loved the trappings of corporate power—he had the use of three houses and a private plane. Shortly after Kozlowski arrived at the company, Tyco bought an ITT subsidiary, Grinnell Fire Protection Systems, which was barely breaking even, and Gaziano made Kozlowski a vice president of what was now Tyco's largest division. Kozlowski slashed bureaucracy, firing large numbers of people, decentralized decision making, and bid aggressively on new business. Within six months Grinnell showed a million-dollar profit.

Gaziano was less interested in operations than in acquisitions. Sometimes he barely knew what businesses his targets were in, let alone how he would integrate them into Tyco if his bids succeeded. He was one of the earliest corporate raiders, and among the first to take "greenmail"—multimillion-dollar payments from takeover targets who pay inflated prices to buy their own stock back from a hostile bidder.

Gaziano liked to say that acquiring companies was like being infected with a social disease: "The fun is in the getting it." For three years, Kozlowski watched as Gaziano pursued a hostile bid for Ludlow Corporation, a manufacturer of packaging and carpet backing. In 1982, the bid succeeded, but Gaziano died shortly afterward, of cancer. John Fort, another engineer, became Tyco's new CEO.

Abstemious almost to a fault, Fort could hardly have been more of a contrast to Gaziano. At Tyco's headquarters in Exeter, the company bought land and built three modest, shingled low-rise office buildings that lacked even a cafeteria. From trees that were felled to clear the land, Fort had the builder set aside the hardwood, which he offered to employees for firewood and used to heat his own home. His company car was an old Chevy. Fort sold the company plane and flew coach, as did Kozlowski and other Tyco executives. Fort was a champion of shareholder value, often declaring, "The reason we were put on earth was to increase earnings per share."

At Grinnell, Kozlowski acquired many of its competitors without drawing antitrust attention. He raised the unit's revenues from $212 million in 1983, when he was named president of the unit, to $700 million in 1987. That year, Kozlowski joined Tyco's board. He was named Tyco's president and chief operating officer in 1989. During these years, he honed the principles that later surfaced in his "Polish grandmother" speech—among them "Only hire people who are smart, poor, and want to be rich" and "Have fun and change your commandments as often as necessary."

Kozlowski was now earning nearly a million dollars a year, enough to afford a New Hampshire beach house for his wife and two daughters and expand his wine cellar. In 1987, he paid $250,000 for a 51-foot Baltic sailboat, and joined the Corinthian Yacht Club, in Marblehead, Massachusetts. Shortly before the 1991 recession, he commissioned a $1.5 million racing sloop, putting up a $500,000 down payment. The shipyard went bankrupt before the boat was completed, and Kozlowski never got his money back.

At the Corinthian, Kozlowski met Dan McDougall, the club's commodore, who ran an advertising agency outside Boston. Kozlowski hired McDougall to oversee Tyco's corporate advertising, and they became

friends. McDougall also collected art, mostly American Impression-
ists, and dabbled in art dealing. He entertained often at his home, in
Gloucester, and Kozlowski showed a growing interest in his paintings,
especially marine art. He was smitten by an 1879 painting by W. G.
Yorke of a Maine coastal schooner passing Sandy Hook, New Jersey,
which Kozlowski knew from his own sailing, and McDougall agreed
to sell it to him for $35,000. Kozlowski bought a painting by another
marine artist, W. E. Norton, and asked for McDougall's guidance in
acquiring more. Kozlowski also liked Depression-era paintings of street
urchins; he told McDougall that he could identify with the subjects of
the paintings.

The 1991 recession hurt Tyco's earnings. The company was not as
diversified as it seemed. Much of its revenue came from supplying sprin-
kler systems for the commercial construction industry, which is vul-
nerable to business cycles, and both earnings and stock price suffered.
Fort's reaction was to focus on operating efficiencies in the businesses
Tyco already owned, and back off from growth through acquisitions.
Kozlowski says he pushed for the opposite course: seize on economic
weakness to acquire even more and bigger companies at bargain prices.
In 1992, Fort retired, though he remained on the board of directors.
Kozlowski was named chairman and CEO.

Now fully in charge, Kozlowski revealed a fierce ambition to transform both himself and Tyco, which took some directors by surprise.
"One thing we found out after he was CEO is that he really had a big
pair of balls," a board member says. "By God, he was not afraid of risk.
He took risks and he made it work." Kozlowski launched into a deal
frenzy that took Tyco shares from $32.38 when he became chairman to
a high of nearly twice that in 2001. Kozlowski ultimately owned three
million shares and options covering ten million more. With an aggressive incentive-pay plan that closely tied Kozlowski's earnings to Tyco's
earnings and cash flow, his own annual compensation went from
$950,000 in 1992 to $26 million in 1997, $70 million in 1998, and
$137 million in 2000. At an investor conference in 1999, he was asked
why he kept working. "The money is a way to keep score," he replied.

When Kozlowski's options vested, enabling him to buy large

amounts of Tyco stock at very low prices, he owed income tax on the difference between what he paid for the shares and what they were worth. Kozlowski and other top executives had often emphasized that they were so confident in Tyco's future that they would rarely, if ever, sell their Tyco stock. But how could they pay the taxes on their gains without selling off some of the shares? The Tyco board decided to institute a Key Employee Loan (KEL) program "to encourage ownership of Company common stock on favorable terms," according to company documents. "Loan proceeds may be used for the payment of federal income taxes due on the vesting of Company common stock," the plan reads. Such loan programs became standard at large corporations as stock prices soared.

No one at Tyco begrudged Kozlowski his income or spent much time wondering what he did with it. He traveled constantly, often from Sunday night until Friday, and worked long hours. He estimates that 70 percent of his time was spent traveling on business. He was a demanding boss, with a short attention span and scant patience for lengthy meetings. At the same time, he had trouble refusing requests, whether it was someone at a subsidiary asking him to attend a local function or one of his lieutenants asking for a raise. But in the late '90s friends like McDougall saw less and less of him, and when they did see him they felt pressured to get to the point. McDougall thought that he'd never encountered a chief executive who worked harder.

The company hired a Manhattan-based corporate-image consultant, Robert Dilenschneider, to burnish Kozlowski's image and enhance the company's reputation. Dilenschneider's firm prepared a detailed plan for Kozlowski to emerge as the next Jack Welch, the then-much-admired chairman of GE. The plan, submitted to Kozlowski in a bound notebook that was still in his office last summer, called for him to give conspicuously to charity, join corporate and charitable boards of directors, and seek out speaking opportunities at such visible venues as the Economic Club of Chicago and the World Economic Forum, in Davos, Switzerland.

In the course of all this, Kozlowski's marriage deteriorated; by the time he was named chairman, he and his wife had moved into separate houses, though they remained married. He subsequently became involved with Karen Mayo, a waitress at Ron's Beach House, in North Hampton, New Hampshire. The affair became public when Kozlowski and Mayo were shown on national television holding hands at the U.S. Open.

On the surface, little changed at Tyco's headquarters in Exeter, which retained the austere aura of the Fort years. Kozlowski initially seemed every bit as frugal as Fort, declining, at one point, to replace the offices' worn carpeting. But as Tyco's revenues and profits rose, Kozlowski began to spend more freely. In 1995, Tyco opened a New York office on Fifth Avenue, and in 2001 moved to 9 West Fifty-seventh Street, a skyscraper with a swooping glass facade. The office has Oriental carpets, antiques, an executive chef, and expansive views of Central Park. The building commands among the highest rents in Manhattan. The renovation of the office cost $7 million, but Kozlowski saw it as an insignificant incremental cost for a company that now had $36 billion in revenues. As he explains it, "We were all about growth. It took thirty-seven million dollars in expenses to affect our earnings by even one cent per share." This became a recurring theme: No matter how expensive in absolute terms, the cost was insignificant as a percentage of Tyco's revenues and profits.

In connection with the move to New York, the compensation committee of Tyco's board approved, according to a company document, a plan to "cover the transfer of applicable employees" as part of a "relocation of the company's corporate headquarters to New York City." Under the program, Kozlowski rented an apartment at 817 Fifth Avenue, and Tyco paid $264,000 in annual rent. But no public announcement that Tyco's U.S. headquarters had moved was ever made, and Kozlowski went to great lengths to maintain the appearance that the headquarters remained in New Hampshire. All calls to Tyco's U.S. headquarters were routed through the Exeter switchboard, and Kozlowski insisted on meeting fund managers, other investors, stock analysts, and reporters in New Hampshire, even if he had to travel there expressly for that purpose.

One of the largest of Kozlowski's acquisitions was ADT Security Services, in 1997, at a cost of $5.6 billion. This gave Tyco ADT's tax-advantaged Bermuda incorporation and its primary U.S. offices, in Boca Raton, Florida. ADT's chief executive was Michael Ashcroft, a self-made, British-born billionaire whose urbane manner and lavish lifestyle made a big impression on Kozlowski. He especially admired Ashcroft's yacht, the *Atlantic Goose*. Ashcroft joined Tyco's board in 1997, and Kozlowski toasted him after he was made a life peer by Queen Elizabeth in 2000.

In Boca Raton, Tyco expanded ADT's offices, leasing a building and renovating it to include a gym and an executive dining room. After acquiring ADT, Kozlowski had given ADT's employees the choice of staying in Florida or moving to New Hampshire; 90 percent had chosen to stay in Florida. Kozlowski and Karen Mayo began spending more time there themselves, especially during the winter. Eventually, Kozlowski designated Florida as his primary residence, and Mayo opened a New American cuisine restaurant, called Zemi, in Boca Raton. Kozlowski bought five adjoining lots in the Sanctuary, a gated community there, and built and furnished a sprawling Spanish colonial-style house. He financed the purchases with a $30 million interest-free "relocation loan" from Tyco, even though the board never approved a relocation plan for Florida. Kozlowski maintains that since the rationale was the same, he and other employees were entitled to the benefits offered in the New York relocation plan.

In Florida, the company also kept a doctor on the payroll and hired Mayo's personal trainer as a full-time fitness consultant. To facilitate Kozlowski's and other executives' travel among the now far-flung operations, the company owned or leased six aircraft and a helicopter.

Kozlowski, who had been renting a summer place on Nantucket, bought a large shingled house on the island, on Squam Road, in 1997. He financed the purchase through the Key Employee Loan program. An entry in Kozlowski's KEL account dated December 29, 1997, indicates he repaid $5.96 million for "Nantucket property" and borrowed $14,725 for "Nantucket wine cellar."

These expenses seem far removed from any payment of federal tax due on vested stock options, which was the stated purpose of the loan program, but Kozlowski reasoned that he would otherwise have had to sell Tyco stock, which would be publicly disclosed and might shake investor confidence. Thus, he insists he was complying with the spirit of the program. And, in any event, he says he always intended to pay the money back, as he did with the Nantucket loans. This rationale, of course, could be extended to virtually anything Kozlowski bought that he might otherwise pay for by selling Tyco stock.

In 1998, Kozlowski spent millions of dollars on a 130-foot J-Class sloop called *Endeavour,* which had been built in the 1930s for the British industrialist Sir T. O. M. Sopwith and competed in the 1934 America's Cup race. It had a crew of nine, which Kozlowski retained, and a working marble fireplace. The boat was extremely costly to maintain, even for someone with Kozlowski's income, but he saw it as a legitimate business expense, some of which could be charged to Tyco. With the move to New York, the line between Kozlowski's personal interests and Tyco's corporate interests had already blurred, and the use of a yacht to promote Tyco's image seemed justifiable. Tyco has its own racing boat, with which Team Tyco competed in the around-the-world Volvo Ocean Race; the company also reimbursed Kozlowski $110,000 for the use of *Endeavour.*

Kozlowski had also embarked on a campaign of charitable activities. He and Mayo were active in AIDS charities on Nantucket and in the United Way campaign in New Hampshire, and they chaired a dinner for the Christopher Reeve Paralysis Foundation in New York. People involved in these and other organizations praise Kozlowski's generosity and compassion, especially toward underprivileged children.

He made these contributions out of his own money; Tyco made many other corporate contributions, and three employees evaluated proposals. Though the company gave generously, Kozlowski limited charitable gifts to no more than 1 percent per share. Here, too, the line between Kozlowski's personal donations and Tyco's corporate donations blurred. Tyco made contributions to Seton Hall, his alma mater ($1 million); Middlebury College, where he was on the board of trustees ($500,000); Berwick Academy, a Maine prep school attended by his daughters ($300,000); the Shackleton Schools, a Boston-based private institution for youth with disciplinary problems ($200,000); and the Babies & Children's Hospital of New York ($200,000). A million-dollar check toward a $10 million pledge to the America's Cup effort at the California International Sailing Association also came from Tyco, as did $1.3 million in donations to the Nantucket Conservation Foundation, which bought land next to Kozlowski's Squam Road property, thereby limiting development.

Tyco's lawyers ultimately determined that, beginning in 1997, Kozlowski handed out $43 million in personal donations that actually came from Tyco.

Despite the company's success and increasing visibility in the financial community, it had received scant national publicity. But in 1999 Tyco was contacted by a *Barron's* reporter, Jonathan Laing, who interviewed Kozlowski in Tyco's New Hampshire offices. In April 1999, *Barron's* put Kozlowski on its cover, with the headline "Tyco's Titan: How Dennis Kozlowski Is Creating a Lean, Profitable Giant." Noting that "he grew up in the tough Central Ward of Newark" and "clearly he hasn't forgotten where he came from," the article declared that Tyco "is purposely kept decentralized and lean near to the point of anorexia. . . . Perks for senior management like first-class travel, country club memberships, fancy severance packages and the like are anathema. Offices are Spartan." This may have been true in New Hampshire, but not in Manhattan or Boca Raton. There was also no mention of the fleet of corporate aircraft.

Although the comparison to Jack Welch had been an explicit goal of the Dilenschneider campaign, and the article was overwhelmingly positive, Kozlowski says he was embarrassed. He felt uncomfortable in the spotlight, and worried that the article heightened public scrutiny. When *Forbes* followed with a cover story in 2000, it showed Kozlowski posing in front of Tyco's corporate helicopter. The photograph angered him, because the helicopter suggested a corporate extravagance that was at odds with the frugal image Tyco wanted to project.

That year, Kozlowski's compensation from Tyco jumped to $137 million, in part because, without consulting the board, he decided to "forgive" a large portion of the company's relocation loans, including $19.4 million he borrowed to buy his house and land in Florida. He also gave special bonuses to top executives to mark Tyco's successful public offering of shares in its TyCom undersea-cable subsidiary and the divestiture of ADT's automobile-auction division. The TyCom bonuses amounted to $76.5 million, of which Kozlowski's own share was $33 million. The ADT bonuses totaled $56 million; his own share of this bonus pool was $25.6 million.

Again, Kozlowski insists that the bonuses, and his forgiven loans, however large, represented a relatively small percentage of the proceeds of deals like ADT Automotive, which sold for $300 million more than its appraised value three years earlier, when it was acquired, or TyCom, which generated a onetime gain of $1.76 billion even after the bonus payments. Still, the bonuses weren't disclosed, either to shareholders or to the board. According to Tyco's lawyers, the ADT bonuses were buried in the company's accounting records as "direct selling costs." Most of the TyCom payments appear as "TyCom offering expenses." Moreover, recipients signed a confidentiality agreement, promising not to reveal the bonuses on pain of forfeiture.

Although Kozlowski was not extraordinarily wealthy, he remained curiously stingy, at least with his own money. "Dennis was always cheap, no matter how much he earned," one Tyco executive who worked closely with him recalls. Beginning in 1998, according to court filings, his expense records indicate that he charged the company for $72,042 in jewelry, $155,067 in clothing, $96,943 in flowers, $52,334 in wine, and $60,427 in club-membership dues. One expense receipt recently obtained by prosecutors is said to show that Kozlowski left a $5,000 tip on a roughly $8,000 tab at Karen Mayo's restaurant. Kozlowski denies this. Other expenses were covered by the Tyco relocation-loan program or the Key Employee Loan program. Account ledgers indicate that Kozlowski used these loans to make substantial payments for Oriental rugs, interior decorating, landscape design and services, wine cellars, a $90,000 automobile, a "yacht stylist," home-fitness equipment, and swimming pool maintenance. They also reflect unexplained payments of more than a million dollars to Mayo. Kozlowski maintains that, with the exception of loans he forgave, or reclassified to other accounts, he repaid all loans by the end of Tyco's fiscal year. Company records suggest that he repaid only $21.7 million of $61.7 million in relocation loans.

Kozlowski was also generous to other employees. Mark Swartz, the chief financial officer, received more than $21 million in relocation loans, and Kozlowski forgave $9.8 million in loans. Mark Belnick, the general counsel, got a $12 million bonus and used $10.4 million in relocation loans to buy property in Park City, Utah, the ski resort. Kozlowski forgave large loans to a secretary, a corporate party planner, and a human resources employee, among others. In total, he forgave $56.4

million in relocation loans. And Kozlowski used a $7 million relocation loan to buy an apartment at 610 Park Avenue, which he gave to his wife, Angeles, as part of a divorce settlement that enabled him to marry Karen Mayo, in 2000. (Kozlowski later repaid $5.2 million of the loan and forgave the balance.)

In 2001, Kozlowski was searching for a New York apartment for Tyco to buy rather than rent. He was convinced that high-end Manhattan real estate would continue to appreciate, and thus would be a good investment for the company; it would give him a discreet place for meetings with investment bankers. Tyco was doing so many deals that he worried the stock would be affected every time investment bankers were spotted going to Tyco offices. But after looking at properties with various real estate agents, Kozlowski had been rejected by boards at 817 Fifth Avenue and 927 Fifth Avenue. Then Swartz introduced him to Dolly Lenz, a broker at Insignia Douglas Elliman.

Even in a field of cutthroat competition, Lenz was notable. In an article in *Gotham* entitled "Hello, Dolly!" Lenz took credit for representing Barbra Streisand, Mariah Carey, royalty, and heads of state. Kozlowski was initially wary of her aggressiveness, and sometimes referred to her as Jaws, but he let her show him some condominiums and co-ops. Kozlowski liked an apartment at 950 Fifth Avenue, a duplex overlooking the park. It was owned by Stephen Schwarzman, a prominent investment banker and the president of the Blackstone Group. Lenz said that she knew many of the owners of the building, which had only seven apartments, and that Kozlowski would pass muster with the board. To smooth the board-approval process, Kozlowski spoke with two other apartment owners, Jonathan Tisch, the chief executive of Loews Hotels, part of the Tisch-family-controlled Loews Corporation, and Robert Hurst, a vice chairman of Goldman Sachs, one of Tyco's investment banking firms.

Like many co-ops, 950 Fifth did not allow corporate ownership of any of the apartments, but Kozlowski thought that this wouldn't be a problem: The co-op shares would be held in his name, even if Tyco paid for the apartment.

During Kozlowski's interview with the board, he says that no one asked him who was paying for the apartment, and his application was approved. Tyco subsequently paid $16.8 million for it, and another $3 million in construction costs. Kozlowski chose his Nantucket decorator, Wendy Valliere, for the interiors, in part because she offered to lower her commission on purchases for the apartment. Kozlowski gave her a budget of $5 million, or 30 percent of the purchase price, which Valliere told him was a rule of thumb for interior decoration. He met with her only two or three times during the project. As for the furniture and antiques she was to acquire, all he said was, "Make sure they will hold their value." The project came in $700,000 over budget. Kozlowski loved giving tours of the renovated apartment, showing off what looked like wallpaper patterns but were actually hand-painted designs by two craftsmen from Germany.

Kozlowski saw little of his neighbors, but Hurst invited him to join the board of the Whitney Museum of American Art. Chronically short of money, the Whitney was exactly the kind of institution that Robert Dilenschneider recommended as likely to confer prestige. It was also an opportunity, in Dilenschneider's words, to "network him more deeply into the city." Kozlowski disclaimed any art expertise and told Hurst he brought only a willingness to work. Still, he gave $5,000 a year to the museum personally. Tyco, for its part, pledged $4.5 million.

Later that year, Kozlowski's steward on *Endeavour* introduced him to Mark Lessard, who was in charge of fine wine sales at a West Palm Beach company, Fine Collections Management. Kozlowski bought two shipments of wine through Lessard—mostly California Chardonnay. Lessard mentioned that Fine Collections could also help Kozlowski acquire art, and introduced him to Christine Berry, the head of Fine Collections' art advisory program.

Berry impressed Kozlowski as soft-spoken and scholarly. She had a master's degree in art history from the University of North Texas, in Denton, and had worked at the Whitney, where, as an assistant registrar, she handled routine paperwork, such as documents related to works lent to the museum. The following Saturday, Lessard arranged for Kozlowski and Karen Mayo to visit William I. Koch, an heir to the Koch oil-and-gas fortune, at his home in Palm Beach and view his extensive art collection, which includes works by Cezanne, Monet, Winslow Homer, and Frederic Remington. They also toured his wine cellar, custom-built by

Austrian stonemasons. Kozlowski and his wife dressed casually for the visit, and seemed dazzled by the Koch estate, which had been featured in an architectural magazine. Lessard was on hand as well. No one mentioned that Koch had provided the capital to start Fine Collections and partly owned the business, or that Berry was not his art adviser. Koch was an expert collector and made all his own decisions, which, he now says, he assumed Kozlowski knew.

Over a bottle of white Burgundy, a 1985 Montrachet, Kozlowski indicated that he'd like to expand his art collection, and Koch recalls offering some advice: "Don't buy something because someone recommends it. Buy it because you love it."

Christine Berry began sending Kozlowski slides and photographs of various works, and that summer, in London, the Kozlowskis and Berry went to the Richard Green Gallery, on New Bond Street, one of London's largest dealers, where they met with Penny Marks, Richard Green's sister. Kozlowski and Mayo admired several paintings, including a fall landscape by the English artist Atkinson Grimshaw; a painting of a horse and groom by Sir Alfred Munnings, a noted British equestrian painter; and a romantic work by Adolphe-William Bouguereau. Berry handled the negotiations, and eventually Kozlowski bought the three works for nearly $2 million. He was impressed, he says, that Berry was able to talk the gallery down in price, more than earning her 8 percent commission.

Although the paintings were destined for the Kozlowskis' apartment on Fifth Avenue, they were flown to Newark, trucked to Exeter, where Kozlowski's secretary signed for them, and delivered to New York City the next day. No New York sales tax was paid. (Because the Richard Green Gallery does business in New York, it is required to withhold sales tax on goods destined for New York.)

That fall, Berry again got in touch with Kozlowski, telling him that representatives of the Richard Green Gallery were going to be in Florida and could bring some paintings to his house in Boca Raton. Penny Marks arrived one afternoon with about twenty paintings, which she had her associates uncrate in Kozlowski's living room. There was an array of Old Master and European Impressionist works, including paintings by Sisley, Caillebotte, Fantin-Latour, and Renoir. These artists represented a major leap for Kozlowski in both quality and price. He felt he needed art for his large new homes in both Florida and New York, and to an extent he felt obligated to buy something, given the trouble that Marks was going to. He also admired several of the paintings, especially a Renoir still life, *Fleurs et Fruits.* But the price, $5.5 million, gave him pause.

According to Kozlowski, Berry explained that he needed some "flagship" paintings that would establish his reputation as a serious collector. This would in turn enhance the "provenance" of any work he acquired, and thereby raise the value of all his works. She felt that the Renoir and the other paintings were fairly priced and would be "money well spent."

Kozlowski recalls asking, "If I sold tomorrow, would I do as well or better at auction? Or would I be leaving money on the table?"

Berry's response, according to Kozlowski, was to assure him that, at a minimum, he'd "break even."

In a statement issued by Berry's lawyer, Alan S. Futerfas, she says, "The idea that I would tell someone they need a 'flagship' painting is ridiculous." According to her, it was Kozlowski who "was interested in buying works of art by extremely prestigious artists." She insists that she never encouraged him to buy paintings he didn't want. ("We will not act as a sounding board for Mr. Kozlowski's defense ideas and respond to every false assertion," Futerfas says. "Ms. Berry looks forward, if called, to testifying about what actually occurred.")

In any case, Kozlowski couldn't make up his mind. One of his favorite adages from his Polish grandmother was, "If there is ever the slightest bit of doubt, don't get married," and he had often invoked it to reject a proposed takeover candidate. But in December Berry called again, urging him, as he recalls it, to "rush over" to an apartment just two blocks away on Fifth Avenue. When he arrived, Berry was there, along with Alexander Apsis, the apartment owner and the seller of a Monet seascape, *Pres Monte Carlo,* showing a view of the Mediterranean off Cap Martin. Kozlowski was captivated by it, because he had sailed there.

By the next day, Berry had got Apsis to drop his price of $4.5 to $4 million. Kozlowski refused to pay more than $3.95 million. With just $50,000 separating them, Kozlowski says Apsis agreed to the lower price provided the deal closed in January, presumably for tax reasons. The invoice for the purchase, dated December 14 and sent to Kozlowski in care of Fine Collections in West Palm Beach, contained this caveat: "Sales tax is not applicable as the painting is being sent to New Hampshire. Proof of shipment will be required."

Kozlowski's doubts about the other works seemed to vanish. Berry quickly negotiated the purchase of the Renoir for $4.7 million, about 15 percent less than the asking price, as well as three other works: an Impressionist landscape by Caillebotte for $1.3 million (asking price: $1.6 million); a Dutch Old Master still life for $2 million (asking price: $2.6 million); and a hunting scene by Munnings for $800,000 (asking price: $1 million)—a total of $8.8 million. Berry's lawyer maintains that Kozlowski was in such a rush to get the paintings that he "flatly rejected" her offer to compare prices for similar works. Fine Collections took a $704,000 fee, in addition to the $316,000 for the Monet. After the transactions, Berry herself received a "gift" of $10,000 from the Green Gallery, which she didn't disclose to Kozlowski or report to Fine Collections.

The paintings were intended for Kozlowski's home. Nonetheless, he paid for all of them with Tyco's money in the form of interest-free loans from the KEL program, since otherwise he would have had to sell Tyco stock. (He says he repaid the loans by the end of January.)

Two months after hanging the paintings in his apartment, Kozlowski suffered an attack of buyer's remorse. He rarely entertained at the apartment, and few people would see them. He says he felt guilty about paying so much. Perhaps he had a premonition. He called Berry and asked if she could sell them "quickly and quietly." She said she didn't think it would be a problem; she'd ask some clients in Palm Beach. A month later, he called again. She was "looking into it," she said, but he sensed a certain coolness in her voice.

Had Kozlowski done the due diligence used for any of his corporate acquisitions, he would have known that the paintings probably could not be quickly resold for anything close to what he'd paid for them. Three of the paintings had been acquired at auction in recent years by the Richard Green Gallery for far lower prices than Kozlowski paid: the $4.7 million Renoir had gone for $3.6 million; the $1.3 million Caillebotte for around $800,000; and the $800,000 Munnings for less than $500,000.

The summer that Kozlowski visited the Richard Green Gallery in London was also Mayo's fortieth birthday, and in anticipation Kozlowski had mentioned to Barry Sternlicht, the chief executive of Starwood Hotels, that he wanted to throw a birthday party for her in an exotic location. Kozlowski had been a Starwood director, and Sternlicht suggested that he consider the Hotel Cala di Volpe, in Sardinia, one of the company's luxury resort properties in the Mediterranean. Kozlowski was planning to spend most of that July in Europe, attending the Paris air show and visiting European customers of Tyco's electronics division. He had no trouble construing the birthday party for his wife as partly a business function.

That spring, the invitations went out:

> *Ottima Festa*
> *Ottimi Amici*
>
> Our summer party is moving from Nantucket to Sardinia. Please join us in the celebration of friendships and Karen's 40th birthday in the scenic Costa Smeralda.
>
> Accommodations have been arranged at the Hotel Cala di Volpe Resort. We look forward to seeing you there—the fun begins the evening of June 10th.
>
> *Buon viaggio e felice arrivo—a presto!*
> Karen & Dennis
> The best present for my birthday is your company so please, no gifts.

The invitation hardly prepared guests for what awaited them. The planned festivities were described in an e-mail dated April 23 from a Tyco employee to its corporate event coordinator, Barbara Jacques:

> Guests arrive at the club starting at 7:15 p.m. The van pulls up to the main entrance. Two gladiators are standing next to the door, one opens the door, the other helps the guests. We have a

lion or horse with a chariot for shock value. The guests proceed through the two rooms. We have gladiators standing guard every couple feet and they are lining the way. The guests come into the pool area, the band is playing, they are dressed in elegant chic. Big ice sculpture of David, lots of shellfish and caviar at his feet. A waiter is pouring Stoli vodka into his back so it comes out his penis into a crystal glass. Waiters are passing cocktails in chalices. They are dressed in linen togas with fig wreath on head. A full bar with fabulous linens. The pool has floating candles and flowers. We have rented fig trees with tiny lights everywhere to fill some space. 8:30 the waiters instruct that dinner is served. We all walk up to the loggia. The tables are all family style with the main table in front. The tables have incredible linens with chalices as wineglasses. The food is brought out course by course, family style, lots of wine, and it's starting to get dark. Everyone is nicely buzzed, LDK (L. Dennis Kozlowski) gets up and has a toast of K (Karen).

Everyone is jumping from table to table. E Cliff has continued to play light music through dinner. They kick it up a bit. We start the show of pictures on the screen, great background music in sync with the slides. At the end Elvis is on the screen wishing K a happy birthday and apologizing that he could not make it. It starts to fade and Elvis is onstage and starts singing happy birthday with the Swingdogs, a Nantucket band often hired for Tyco events. A huge cake is brought out with the waiters in togas singing and holding the cake up for all to see. The tits explode. Elvis kicks it in full throttle. Waiters are passing wine, after-dinner drinks, and there is dancing. 11:30 light show starts. HBK (Happy Birthday Karen) is displayed on mountain, fireworks coming from both ends of the golf course in sync with music. Swingdogs start up and the night is young.

Among the sixty or so guests were a number of Tyco executives and directors and their spouses, including Mark Swartz, Barbara Jacques, and Lord Ashcroft. Also on the list were Dan McDougall, the decorator

Wendy Valliere, and the *Endeavour* crew. Some guests were initially puzzled by the invitation. They barely knew Karen Mayo and rarely socialized with Kozlowski. The timing of the party was also awkward. Tyco had recently completed a $9 billion acquisition of the CIT Group, a large financial services company, and, in keeping with Tyco's strategy of sharply cutting costs at the companies it acquired, Tyco planned to announce the termination of numerous CIT employees the same day as the party.

When Michael Robinson, Tyco's treasurer, said he didn't think he could make it to the party, he was pressured to attend. One of the company jets was assigned to fly him to Sardinia. Upon boarding the plane, Robinson saw that Kozlowski's daughter was on board, along with her boyfriend. It occurred to Robinson that he was the business excuse for using the Tyco jet and that the cost of the trip could therefore be charged to the company. (Robinson returned the next day on a commercial flight.) Several other executives were also asked to attend, though not all of them did. They were told that their presence would "help Dennis out."

Reaction to the party ranged from enthusiasm to embarrassment. A videotape of the event dwells on guests squealing over the anatomically detailed, vodka-spouting David and the moment that the breasts on the birthday cake, shaped like a life-size female nude, did in fact explode. No one denied that the event was memorable.

Kozlowski says he volunteered to pay for a portion of the party's expenses out of his own funds, "whatever was fair." Only later did the Tyco executives learn that Kozlowski was reimbursed based on a formula—a ratio of Tyco executives and directors to other party guests—for allocating a share of the costs to Tyco. According to court records filed this past fall, Tyco paid for "more than $1 million" of the party's cost of $2.1 million.

Not long after the Monet and the Renoir were delivered to Kozlowski's Manhattan apartment, in January 2002, New York state banking authorities referred an investigation of suspected money laundering to Manhattan district attorney Robert Morgenthau. The case focused on an account into which millions of dollars were being deposited before being wired to offshore accounts. The pattern looked particularly suspicious because the account address, an exclusive building at 930 Fifth Avenue, was supposed to be strictly residential. The account belonged to Alexander Apsis.

Morgenthau handed the case over to one of his senior investigators, John Moscow. Moscow subpoenaed Apsis's account statements, books, invoices, and shipping records. He learned that the former Sotheby's curator worked as a self-styled "art expert," advising clients, often acting as an agent for buyers and sellers. Despite the large cash flow, Moscow found no evidence of any money laundering.

But the statement "Sales tax is not applicable" on the copy of the invoice sent to Kozlowski for the Monet painting leaped out. Moscow's investigators soon learned that the painting had never gone to New Hampshire but had been moved two blocks uptown. Moscow had just been handed a high-profile investigation of one of America's top corporate executives.

At about the same time, in December 2001, Kozlowski had been reviewing a draft of Tyco's annual proxy statement, which disclosed that a Tyco director, Frank Walsh—the former chairman of Wesray Capital, the hugely successful leveraged-buyout firm—had been paid a $20 million "finder's fee" for helping bring about Tyco's acquisition of CIT earlier that year. (All payments of more than $60,000 to directors must be publicly disclosed.) Walsh had first suggested that Tyco acquire a finance arm, and had then introduced Kozlowski to CIT's chairman, which ultimately led to Tyco's $9 billion acquisition of the company. Kozlowski felt that the CIT deal was a "home run" for Tyco, and that it wouldn't have happened without Walsh, but he was having second thoughts about the payment. Indeed, Kozlowski had agreed to the fee only after Walsh promised to give half of it to charity.

But now, in the wake of Enron and other corporate scandals, Kozlowski wondered if the payment would be interpreted as self-dealing by a director, and render his own involvement as suspect. He'd never mentioned it to the other directors, but now he had Mark Swartz, the chief financial officer, call a board member named Joshua Berman, a lawyer, and read him the paragraph about the payment. Berman recalls that the information left him speechless.

Within an hour, Berman was in Kozlowski's office on West Fifty-seventh Street. He said it was "a blatant conflict of interest," and "unheard of" for a director to propose, advocate, and vote on a deal from which he expected a fee. Berman had ordered a search for other reported instances of a director receiving a fee of this magnitude. He found none. This was also likely to be a public relations disaster, which Tyco could ill afford. "I screwed up," Kozlowski conceded. "We've got to fix this."

"Get the money back," Berman said, offering to speak to Walsh himself. When he did, Walsh maintained that it was Kozlowski who had said, "I suppose you'll want a fee," adding that they had been told that a $20 million fee wasn't "material" in the context of a $9 billion deal, so it didn't have to be disclosed. "Why do you need it?" Berman asked. (Walsh was already a wealthy man.) "Everybody would be better off if we just undid it."

Over the next week, various board members urged Walsh to return the fee. (Walsh maintained that some board members told him to stand his ground.) Kozlowski thought he was on the verge of returning it, but then he balked. Walsh argued, according to Kozlowski, "I deserve this fee. If I give it back, it looks like I did something wrong. How could I look myself in the eye in the mirror each morning?"

"Perception, perception, perception," Kozlowski says he replied. "This will go down badly. The world has changed." But Walsh wouldn't budge. The matter was added to the agenda of a January 16 board meeting in Boca Raton that had already been called to discuss a radical new plan Kozlowski was proposing for Tyco.

After a decade of promoting spectacular growth through acquisitions, Kozlowski had suddenly embraced a plan orchestrated by investment bankers at Goldman Sachs to break up Tyco into four separate companies and thereby "unlock" shareholder value. At the end of 2001, the price of Tyco shares was $58, about where it had begun the year, bringing an end to the decade of dramatic price increases that had propelled the value of Kozlowski's options. Still, Tyco had done much better than many other high-growth companies in a year when the Nasdaq index dropped more than 17 percent.

Tyco directors, executives, and friends like Dan McDougall say it is hard to overestimate the effect the stagnant stock price had on Kozlowski. The fact that he was "making shareholders rich" and that

Tyco's profit and revenues were surging had long been both the business rationale and the moral underpinning of Kozlowski and Tyco's spending and compensation policies. As Kozlowski had said in countless speeches, he believed in rewarding management performance. But, when that performance faltered, then what? He didn't even know exactly what his real estate and other fixed expenses were per year, but he did know, as he put it, that his lifestyle "had become awfully expensive."

In 2001, for example, Kozlowski had received grants of stock worth more than $50 per share, and roughly half of that was immediately due in tax. If the stock price dropped, he not only made no money on the stock but stood to suffer a substantial after-tax loss if the stock price fell into the twenties. Moreover, most of the directors had chosen to receive their $75,000 annual director's fee in Tyco stock options, so they, too, wanted the stock to rise. Kozlowski concedes that he felt intense pressure to get the stock price up. "We said, 'Let's live or die by the stock price,'" Kozlowski says, "and we did. Management created its own pressure. But this is what shareholders were clamoring for, too." So when investment bankers at Goldman Sachs gave Kozlowski an analysis that valued the parts of Tyco in a range of $127 billion to $148 billion, or $65 to $75 a share, he leaped at the breakup plan. CIT alone, they argued, was worth between $13 billion to $17 billion. (Goldman Sachs stood to earn a large portion of an estimated $140 million in fees from the breakup.)

The January 16 meeting was the board's first at the offices in Boca Raton, which had a fitness center, executive dining facilities, and a palm-lined driveway. Some directors were upset by what they saw. "It was ridiculous," one director says. "It was overdone, lavish. It didn't look like an office. It looked like a luxury hotel." When Lord Ashcroft greeted Kozlowski, he said, "Dennis, you've been a naughty boy."

Before the meeting began, Berman again confronted Walsh. "Let me be absolutely clear," he told his fellow director. "What you did was wrong. Even if it had been disclosed, it was wrong. Think about your position."

The board spent most of the day discussing the breakup plan, reaching no decision. Then Kozlowski gave Walsh an opportunity to speak. "I think I contributed a lot and the amount I got was low," compared with what investment bankers got, Walsh said. "I'm entitled to it." He was excused, and the director Richard Bodman spoke. He said that Walsh had "betrayed" members of the board. Berman was dispatched to break the news of the board's vote: "It was unanimous" that Walsh return the money, Berman told him. "And I mean unanimous." Walsh called his wife, then walked back to the room and gathered his papers. "Adios," he said, and walked out. He and his wife did not show up that evening for the directors' dinner at Kozlowski's house.

Just two days later, Kozlowski called an emergency board meeting for Sunday in Bermuda to approve the breakup plan, saying the directors had to act immediately. Perhaps distracted by the Walsh issue, no one on the board had raised serious questions about whether the Goldman Sachs valuations were realistic, or how Tyco's abrupt change in corporate strategy might be perceived in a market that was already on tenterhooks in the wake of a succession of corporate scandals. Though some directors worried that Kozlowski was moving too fast, they backed the plan, and news of the breakup was announced the morning of January 21. Kozlowski and other Tyco executives eagerly awaited the opening of the market, expecting Tyco's shares to soar. Instead, after a brief rally, investors assumed that such a radical, sudden change had to have been motivated by the kind of accounting irregularities that had felled Enron, and the shares soon started to slide.

In this environment, the timing of the proxy statement disclosing the Walsh payment, which was made public on January 29, couldn't have been worse. As the directors had feared, there was a heated public reaction. The stock plunged more than $8 that day alone. By February 6, Tyco stock had dropped more than 50 percent, to $25 a share. Kozlowski was stunned by the market's reaction. No one would listen to the breakup valuations; he felt that the market was in the grip of an irrational panic. On April 25, Tyco called off the ill-fated breakup plan, but to no avail. By the end of April, Tyco shares were at $18. (When CIT was finally divested by Tyco last year, it brought not the $13 billion to $17 billion that Goldman Sachs had estimated but $4.6 billion—barely half of what Tyco had paid for it.)

The directors were also shocked by the reaction to the Walsh disclosure. Suddenly, Tyco board membership was perceived as a business and social liability. One director complained to Kozlowski, "I'm being embarrassed at my country club." Several directors demanded that Tyco sue Walsh to get the money back. Kozlowski had done nothing to stop them when they ousted Walsh from the board, but now he drew the line. "If you go after Frank, you're going after me," Kozlowski insisted. The issue was discussed, but no immediate action was taken.

The board also began to see Kozlowski in a harsh new light. As the stock plunged, the man they knew as impulsive, decisive, and a confident risk taker now seemed paralyzed. "He was frozen," one director recalls. "He was afraid to change direction. He was not leading."

As rumors of accounting fraud circulated, the board's corporate-governance committee—Joshua Berman, Lord Ashcroft, Richard Bodman, and John Fort—undertook an extensive review of Tyco's books and compensation practices. Unknown to Kozlowski, the four had already virtually concluded that he had to be replaced; the only question was when. The board asked the chief financial officer, Mark Swartz, for records detailing, among other things, the company's charitable contributions, loans to and stock transactions involving top management, and use of company-owned apartments and planes. Increasingly suspicious, the board also hired an outside law firm, Boies, Schiller & Flexner, to investigate the same matters. When Berman spoke with David Boies, the mood was grim. Berman described the circumstances of the Walsh payment, and added that the directors had become suspicious of Kozlowski himself.

By May, when Kozlowski received his grand jury subpoena, his relations with the board were tense and rapidly deteriorating. Even as he was hiring Stephen Kaufman as his personal lawyer, he was reluctant to tell the Tyco board about the subpoena. Nor was he told that he was the target of the investigation; he thought it was an inquiry into the Monet painting's provenance. He hoped that somehow his lawyers would "make it go away." This, in any event, is what he told Bill Koch after Fine Collections Management received its own subpoena, on May 10. Over the phone, Koch read Kozlowski the text, which called for the production of all documents related to "dealings with L. Dennis Kozlowski," Alexander Apsis, and the Richard Green Gallery.

"They're just checking into the legal title" of the Monet, Kozlowski said. "My lawyers will take care of it."

Koch was dubious. "Dennis, it looks like they're after you for tax reasons," he said.

Koch was worried about bad publicity, and says he was shocked when he saw the shipping invoices and the handwritten memo from Christine Berry with the notation "wink, wink." As he put it, "If you're going to do something illegal, you don't say 'wink, wink.'"

After Berry, too, was subpoenaed in the sales-tax case against Kozlowski, Koch said he would stand behind her, get her a lawyer, and pay her legal expenses. But "don't lie," he instructed. "Tell the truth, no matter who it hurts. We're turning over the documents as they are and we're not altering anything. It's not worth lying over."

In her testimony, Berry stated that in their phone conversation on the day Kozlowski received the first subpoena, he said, "I guess I owe sales tax," and Berry replied, "I think you do." She also testified that Kozlowski had told her to have empty boxes shipped to New Hampshire. Kozlowski denies mentioning sales tax to Berry and giving orders to ship the boxes.

On Friday, May 31, at 7:30 p.m., Kozlowski learned from his lawyer that he was going to be indicted for nonpayment of sales tax. From his office, he began calling his directors. Kozlowski felt that they were supportive; several said they would stand by him. But by Saturday evening they were unanimously demanding his resignation. Kozlowski agreed to step down, but only after the board had assured him it would consider paying his salary and give him access to company planes, cars, and the New York apartment—in other words, treat him as a respected former chairman. At one-thirty in the morning on Monday, June 3, the board conferred by phone and accepted his resignation. John Fort, Kozlowski's predecessor, became Tyco's interim chief executive. One of his first measures was to dismantle the fleet of corporate planes and repossess Kozlowski's cars.

By September, the lawyers from the Boies firm had completed their investigation, which went far beyond the Walsh payment or the issue of unpaid sales tax. Based on their findings, on September 17 Tyco filed a report with the Securities and Exchange Commission concluding that Kozlowski, Mark Swartz, and the general counsel, Mark Belnick, "engaged in a pattern of improper and illegal conduct by which they enriched themselves at the expense of the company with no colorable benefit to the company and concealed their conduct from the board." In an accompanying civil suit against the three, Tyco accused Kozlowski of an "egregious violation of the trust reposed in him by the Board and its shareholders." Tyco said the total amount of damages caused by Kozlowski "is not yet known," but it asked for repayment of all compensation and benefits since at least 1997, as well as more than $100 million that he allegedly misappropriated—a total of more than $400 million. And, based on substantially the same facts, the Manhattan district attorney filed another indictment, accusing Kozlowski and Swartz of transforming Tyco into a "criminal enterprise" for their own enrichment. Last week, Belnick was indicted again, on charges of grand larceny, for allegedly stealing more than $12 million in unapproved bonus payments. All three have pleaded not guilty.

Tyco's SEC filing revealed that among the invoices from Wendy Valliere, the Nantucket interior decorator, paid by Tyco were $15,000 for a "dog umbrella stand"; $6,300 for a sewing basket; $17,000 for a "traveling toilette box"; $2,200 for a gilt wastebasket; two sets of sheets for $5,960; and $6,000 for a shower curtain.

The press leaped on these revelations; the *News* called Kozlowski the "Tyco Pig." "It was horrible," he told me. "I felt like I was reading about a person I didn't know. I didn't recognize myself." He said that he had never realized he owned a dog umbrella stand or other such high-priced objects, and he had gotten Valliere on the phone and demanded an explanation. She insisted that most of the items were antiques, well worth the price and a good investment. And the notorious shower curtain was not a curtain at all but an upholstered partition used to screen off an antiquated servant's bath. She argued that the partition had actually saved money, by making it unnecessary to replace two dilapidated windows. Valliere told *The Wall Street Journal,* "It's not just some stupid dog umbrella stand. It's a very unique, beautiful piece." She said the items were "perfectly normal accoutrements" in a Manhattan luxury apartment, and "I was hired to do a job, and I did a beautiful job."

Kozlowski's trial on the conspiracy and fraud charges is scheduled for this June; trial on the tax-avoidance charges will begin after the first trial ends. On the conspiracy and fraud charges, Kozlowski faces fifteen to thirty years in prison and forfeiture of up to $600 million.

In December, Frank Walsh pleaded guilty to failing to disclose his $20 million fee to the board. Walsh told one friend, "I feel I've lived through the French Revolution of corporate governance." He agreed to repay the fee and a $2.5 million fine but was spared a prison term. Fine Collections Management no longer exists; Bill Koch dissolved it after concluding that it had turned into "a bloody nuisance," as he puts it. Christine Berry is expected to testify under a grant of immunity. It's not yet clear whether Penny Marks or anyone from the Richard Green Gallery will testify. For the first time in many years, the gallery did not show up last month at the Winter Antiques Show in New York. The gallery also withdrew from the Palm Beach International Art and Antique Fair.

Whether or not Kozlowski is ultimately acquitted, the fact remains that the richer he became, and the less he actually needed Tyco's money, the more he felt entitled to take it. He may simply have become the most visible example of something that was epidemic in the bull market: a chief executive who couldn't separate himself from the company he ran, the corporate equivalent of *"L'état c'est moi."*

Since his indictment, Kozlowski's assets have been frozen; he has been granted a $14,000-per-month allowance by the New York Supreme Court overseeing his case. Among Kozlowski's assets subject to the court's freeze is the Monet painting, which still hangs in the Manhattan apartment, now a Tyco property, from which Kozlowski is barred. He hasn't seen the Monet since June, and says, "I wish I'd never laid eyes on it."

Despite Kozlowski's extravagance, there is an important distinction between Tyco and other corporate scandals. Unlike Enron, Global Crossing, WorldCom, and Adelphia, Tyco has not turned out, so far, to be another massive corporate accounting fraud. Though the company remains under investigation by the SEC, the Boies firm recently concluded that Tyco's accounting, though aggressive, generally conformed to accepted accounting principles and required only a relatively modest restatement of earnings (about $380 million). Tyco's accountants, PricewaterhouseCoopers, have vigorously defended the integrity of the firm's audits. Tyco has new senior management and will soon have an entirely new board of directors, led by Edward Breen, a respected former Motorola executive. The company avoided bankruptcy and has moved quickly to stabilize its financial structure. As of early 2003, my thousand shares of stock, after rising from $40,590 to $63,210 and then dropping to $6,980, were worth $15,750.

Civilization may one day unearth a time capsule containing a message that explains what really went on in the boom-to-bust period of the 1990s. Andrew Hill, columnist for the *Financial Times,* would be a fine author for that message. Here he delivers a tongue-in-cheek, yet dead-on, eulogy for a unique time in history when new paradigms were showered down upon unsuspecting investors.

Andrew Hill

The Decline and Fall of the Cult of Equity

MEDIA COMMENTATORS have declared the death of the Cult of Equity. But few have cared to dig deeper into the phenomenon. Until now.

Equity, Cult of (1991–2002). The cult swept the developed world in the late twentieth century, for a time eclipsing longer-standing religions (cf Christianity; Islam; gold; bank accounts, high interest), before fading quickly in 2000 and 2001.

Key attributes. The cult shared many of the principal elements of other primitive religions. It was founded on naturally occurring desires—principally the urge to make an enormous fortune with little or no effort; it often required of its adherents a profound suspension of normal rational thought (for more detailed analysis of this phenomenon, see pet product retailers, internet *passim*); and, once involved, its followers became its chief proselytizers.

As in many cults, "true" disciples were required to pledge large sums to individual sects, organized through the powerful but as yet little-understood network of mutual funds, brokerages, and investment banks (qqv), uncovered by financial archaeologists. Followers were then bound into its rituals with regular homilies called Research (qv).

Places and forms of worship. Disciples of the cult sometimes congregated in its temples and other places of worship (see NYSE: Nasdaq MarketSite). But part of the attraction of the movement was that it did not demand social contact. Worshipers could as easily participate in its ceremonies by phone or computer, as appear in person.

As the cult developed, key rituals (see Bell, opening; Bell, closing; Testimony, Humphrey-Hawkins) were frequently made available to disciples via television, print, and online media.

Clergy: Unlike most primitive religions, the cult's high priests and priestesses were not ordained; they emerged through the popular will of its adherents. Some led mass worship (see CNBC). Others, by virtue of their position and pronouncements, became the witting or unwitting objects of vulgar idolatry (see Blodget, Henry; Greenspan, Alan). The reputations of these senior clerics depended on the constantly recurring "Miracles of the New Economy" (qv), involving issues of precious "securities" (see Netscape, IPO of; Amazon.com, IPO of; eBay, IPO of). Of these, "equities" and "options" in particular were treasured, traded, coveted, and worshiped in their own right (cf Mammon; Midas; Sins, Seven Deadly).

Foundations and early history. The cult was built on a groundwork of existing, solid institutions, called corporations. In this precult era, the people learned to live with regular cycles of feast and famine. But in the mid-1990s a so-called New Paradigm school of clerics emerged, fostering a belief that the Cult of Equity would last and prosper for all eternity (see Dow, 100,000). Followers were said to "get it"; opponents or skeptics "did not get it" and were ridiculed or driven from the community (see Investors, fixed-income; Economy, Old).

On the cult's fringes, fetish items developed and were idolized (see Pets.com sock puppet). Adherents began to build their own shrines to the promise of life after work (cf Nest egg, retirement).

Decline and fall. Simultaneously, however, the seeds of disaster were being sown. "Wall Street" and "the City" (qqv), nexuses of the power and mystery of the cult, were riven by conflict. Congregations began to doubt the powers of the priests and priestesses. Their fabulous promises were exposed as a sham, following the period of the so-called False Miracles (2000–2001) (see AOL and Time Warner, merger of; online retailers, profitability, or lack thereof; telecoms licenses, 3G).

Disillusionment bred contempt. It emerged that the earlier promises of an infinitely comfortable afterlife had proved too tempting for some of the cult's most prominent followers. They were crushed as the religion's demise accelerated (see Kozlowski, Dennis; Lay, Kenneth; etc.)

Demands for further tithes, known as Margin Calls (qv), bankrupted other disciples, as much of the precious "equity" of the late 1990s was revealed to be worthless. In the Massacre of Silicon Valley (April 2000), billions of stock options were ritually drowned.

Death and burial. In due course, the cult's priests and priestesses turned on one another. Many former enthusiasts for, and beneficiaries of, the cult renounced its ways and were reborn as opponents (the so-called Bear Market Conversions of 2002).

New, powerful critics of the cult's excesses emerged—Eliot Spitzer (cf Inquisition, Spanish), George W. Bush (see above, Bear Market Conversions).

They made frantic efforts to revive the cult using codes of practice, industry-wide settlements, and the ordination of new clergy who it was thought would inspire the confidence of their disillusioned flock (see Pitt, Harvey; Financial crimes SWAT team). But the effort was futile. The mighty religion's places of worship had already crumbled; its disciples had dispersed. The Cult of Equity was no more.

Life was beautiful for Doug and Sue Irvine, with large paychecks and comfortable retirement savings their ticket. But, as with many families caught in the economic downturn, good times ended once a steady job disappeared. In this story from *The Seattle Times,* Shirleen Holt chronicles a sad fall from financial grace.

Shirleen Holt

The Death of One American Dream

FOR DOUG AND SUE IRVINE, this house atop a bluff in Fall City is the toughest loss of all. For 24 years they'd raised their children here, entertained business associates, celebrated the holidays with friends over meals as expansive as the views.

In the old days, Sue Irvine would have been chatting happily as she sat with guests, admiring the Cascade Mountains and the Snoqualmie River that spread out below them. Doug Irvine, soft-spoken and intense, might have been locked in a conversation about politics or international business.

That was before.

Before Doug lost his job as a vice president for an export company. Before their finances crumbled and their social circle shrank. Before the tension started pulling at the edges of their close-knit family and middle-class dreams.

Before Doug, now 63, accepted the only position he could find: a

$7.50-an-hour job selling cameras and clock radios at the local Target store.

This is after.

After a FOR SALE sign has been planted in the front yard and after half of their belongings have been moved elsewhere. After their retirement account has been reduced to nothing. After they fell into debt. Visiting the house after all that, Sue Irvine is uncharacteristically quiet.

"I get sad coming here." She runs her fingers over a box of books saved for her future grandchildren. "It reminds me of what's happened to us."

What happened to the Irvines is part poor planning and part misplaced optimism—a combination gone sour through bad timing. What happened to them is happening to more and more aging Americans who rode the giddy economic wave of the 1990s and thought their careers could go only one way—up. Doug Irvine was earning nearly $93,000 a year as a marketing executive when his career faltered. The export operation he was heading overseas shut down, and in 1998 at age 58 and with very little in savings, he was out of work. It seemed a small setback at the time. Things were booming back home in Washington. He had made career leaps before, and always landed well. A lifetime of experience and can-do confidence would surely serve him again. He had experience, optimism, energy—and years to save for old age.

But this time, Doug Irvine was shoved not into a new opportunity but into a crack in the economy that soon split into the most stubborn recession in decades.

THE RISE

This wasn't the future Sue Irvine expected. Growing up in the 1950s, when most married women stayed home, she aspired to a life like that of the woman she baby-sat for, the doctor's wife.

"She ordered her clothes from Boston," says Sue, now 60, "read books, played bridge, and looked pretty."

Sue met Doug in 1968 at a party on Mercer Island. She was a research nurse at the University of Washington. He was an aeronautical engineer for Boeing who had come to the United States from Scotland two years earlier.

"He was so interesting and so gentle," she says.

"Keep going," Doug prompts.

"And so sexy."

They married a year later. They had two children, John and Jill. Piece by piece, they built the world they would come to love.

In spirit, Doug was always more entrepreneur than engineer. He found Boeing's hierarchy too rigid, so he left in 1970 to try marketing, first in the seafood industry and later for an engine distributor. He specialized in opening risky foreign markets, willing to trade job security for the excitement of building something from the ground up.

That is what he loved about America. Work hard. Take chances. Get ahead.

By 1979, their family in place and nothing but promise ahead, the Irvines bought the last piece of their dream: a 3,400-square-foot raised-ranch-style house in Fall City just south of Snoqualmie for $118,000. Doug's career would advance. Sue would quit working. They would put the kids through college and then put money away for retirement.

But there always seemed to be plenty of opportunity and plenty of time. And Doug was never keen on the retiring part. "If I keep my health, knock wood . . ." he says. "I've got lots of energy and I'm raring to go."

They rode the boom of the 1990s in comfort. Doug became vice president of exports for a Portland-based construction and distribution company. When he was assigned to open a market for marine engines in Vietnam, he and Sue left the house in the hands of their grown son, John, and moved to Ho Chi Minh City. The assignment satisfied Doug's entrepreneurial drive and his social conscience. He would sell the engines and generators that would power a struggling nation's fishing fleets, ferry boats, and coast guard.

"In our own tiny way we were going to help this country get on its feet again," he says.

But doing business in Vietnam proved tougher than the company had expected. In 1998, the division shut down. The Irvines came home, and Doug expected to soon find work.

"I'M OVERQUALIFIED"

With his neatly combed graying hair and athletic build, Doug could be mistaken for a country-club retiree enjoying a post round break at Starbucks. Having just ended his shift at Target, though, he's still in his work clothes: khakis and a red Polo shirt.

"I just feel like I need a boot up my ass," he says, taking a gulp of coffee.

His job search has stalled while he's been working the electronics counter at the Issaquah store. His paycheck doesn't cover half the $2,200 mortgage payment on the Fall City house, but the health benefits are good—a crucial consideration for a couple in their sixties.

For Doug, having a job—any job—feels better than the futile whiplash of search-and-rejection. He had landed a couple of other jobs since returning from Vietnam but nothing permanent and nothing that paid what he used to earn. His odds of replacing his old salary and status slipped along with the economy. A survey last summer by the Chicago outplacement firm Challenger, Gray & Christmas found that one in four executives—25 percent—fails to find new work that pays at or above his or her old salary. It's the biggest drop-off in the 16 years the firm has tracked executive pay. A few years ago, only one in ten executives failed to bounce back.

Worse, the average job search now takes four months, compared with three months in 2000. And for 1.7 million Americans, joblessness has lasted six months or longer.

Doug isn't stuck behind a sales counter for lack of effort. He reads the want ads and knows—*knows*—he could do those high-flying jobs, even if he's never worked in this or that specific industry. He knows how to negotiate deals, build teams, troubleshoot. These are transferable skills.

"But if I submit this," he says, holding his two-page résumé, "Whoosh! It'll go right over their heads."

He used to churn out résumés daily, tweaking the text to suit the position and making sure recruiters saw his skills before they saw his age. He hired a career counselor to help him market himself. He joined international trade groups to network with people.

He's applied for more jobs than he can remember—with a tooth-brush company, a housing developer, an electronics manufacturer, the British Consulate. He has seldom received the courtesy of a response. In the rare interviews he's had, the message was the same: He's overqualified.

The excuse prompts rare indignation from Doug:

"If I'm *over*qualified, by definition I have to be qualified. You know damn well it's age discrimination." And in that opinion, too, he's part of a growing trend. The number of age-discrimination complaints filed with the U.S. Equal Employment Opportunity Commission rose 14.5 percent in 2002, a larger percentage increase than race, gender, and disability complaints combined.

DEAR MOM AND DAD

These days, Doug can barely muster the energy to scan the classifieds.

"The defeatism is insidious. You don't really feel depressed . . ." his voice trails off. "It's hard to describe."

It's a chilly night in January, and Doug and Sue live in a contemporary apartment in Snoqualmie while they ready the Fall City house for sale.

Sue Irvine had gone back to work, reluctantly, as a school nurse. But even with that, there's no way they can cover the mortgage, make the $1,175-a-month apartment rent, and pay for the remodeling to get their $399,000 asking price on the house.

"Financially it didn't make any sense to move into this apartment," Sue says. "But emotionally, it made a huge amount of sense."

For her, the house holds too many memories. That is where the kids, John and Jill, had water fights in the backyard (and once, when their parents weren't home, inside the house).

It's where they shouted their Christmas lists up the chimney.

It's where Doug tucked Jill into bed every night with a different stuffed animal. He maintained the ritual even when he was away on business trips, listing what animals she was to sleep with on what nights. It's where they thought Jill would get married.

"I think you've been down a lot more than you think you have," Sue tells Doug now. She knits furiously, as if to distract herself. A lively woman whose thoughts tumble out unedited, she's promised to let her husband do most of the talking tonight.

But not before she makes one more point.

"You didn't want to take a job like Target, because you were afraid it's what you would be doing for the rest of your days," she says.

"I don't think I felt bad about working at Target," Doug counters. "Target is an excellent company. But in terms of working your way up . . ."

He thought customer service would be a foot in the door. He thought he'd advance through the ranks back into management. He applied for two promotions, but they went to younger people with more seniority.

"That's when I realized this is not feasible for me," he says.

Like his mother, 32-year-old John Irvine finds it hard to accept his father's fall from middle-class executive to clock-puncher.

"There are lots of nights when I go to bed thinking about it and I can't go to sleep," he says. "He's a person who should be adding value to this society and imparting wisdom to others, and this economy doesn't allow it."

His father's situation does not compute: Doug is driven to work hard; he's a man of high integrity and equally high intelligence. He taught his children to share his faith in the American dream: Hard work is rewarded with steady progress in career and income.

"Now that's totally shattered," John Irvine says.

John, a former stockbroker now working toward an MBA, admired his father's unshakable optimism, but now he wonders if it's become a form of denial.

Why is he wasting eight hours a day working at Target when he could invest that time looking for a real job?

Why didn't his parents save more? Why, after five years, haven't they dug themselves out of this hole?

Someone had to take charge. So on Mother's Day of last year, John Irvine presented his parents with a typed letter:

"I am convinced that opportunity exists in the middle of this debacle," he wrote. "Good things will happen to us but we have to make them happen. Change is doing something different. What are we doing differently?" Taking a lesson from business school, he scheduled weekly goal-setting meetings with his parents, complete with printed agenda items: Doug's job search, financial security, climbing out of debt. "I was trying to force my parents to be accountable," he says.

Doug and Sue agreed to sell the Fall City house to pay off their debt and to take out term life insurance in case something happened to Doug. They agreed that while Doug needs to look for something beyond Target, the top jobs are probably out of reach.

"I could get $150,000 a year as a marketing manager," Doug says. "My son makes me see that it isn't realistic. I certainly think I'm way above Target level, but maybe between $40,000 and $50,000 is attainable."

MONEY WOES

By early February, the Fall City house has been on the market for five months. The couple's finances—and their relationship—is stretched to snapping.

Sue, the worrier, says they are one month from disaster: "We are not that far from being street people."

Doug, the optimist: "We are not one month away. We're two or three months away from having a significant problem."

The couple earns a combined $54,000, well above the average household income in Washington. But their expenses—the mortgage, rent, a car loan, insurance, utilities—leave them short every month. Their credit-card debt has swelled to $52,000.

"It wasn't too many years ago that I bought a Coach handbag," Sue says, almost in wonder. "I would never do that today."

At one point they had $70,000 in various retirement accounts. But Sue cashed out her pension when they left for Vietnam; Doug used up his 401(k) while he was between jobs.

It's another trend: Nearly two-thirds of Americans cash out their

401(k) plans between jobs, according to a 2001 survey by Hewitt Associates. At least 15 percent of working Americans have no retirement savings; nearly half who do have saved less than $50,000.

Without a financial cushion, the Irvines welcomed the small miracles that come in times of financial crisis—an unexpected refund from their escrow account, a forgotten check from an old job. And the precipitous drop in income forced changes in their expectations, if not their desires.

They no longer go to restaurants, and rarely entertain at home. Their once-expansive dinner parties have succumbed to Doug's schedule (if he wants to work 40 hours each week, he has to take whatever schedule Target gives him) and to a shrinking social circle.

"Our phone does not ring," Sue says. "It's like cancer. People don't want to be around people who have cancer."

They do have some loyal friends and old business connections who Sue thinks could help Doug find a suitable position. If only Doug would pick up the phone.

"He does not want to be somebody who is using someone."

Doug shoots back: "Once again you are overstating the case. There's a huge difference between using people and networking."

Sue: "I don't know anyone who doesn't think highly of you, but you have not contacted them. You don't make phone calls. You never make phone calls."

They fall into an awkward silence.

Doug: "I believe you can only go to the well so often."

RELIEF AND A NEW START

"Did you hear?" Jill Irvine asks. "They got an offer on the house."

It's a Sunday afternoon in late February. Jill is taking a rare day off from her two jobs and college, where she's studying to be a nutritionist. Her schedule gave her less time to attend her brother John's family meetings. She has inherited her father's optimistic personality, and is convinced he'll bounce back.

But she inherited her mother's love of her childhood home, and the cost of losing it is steep.

"It sucks that they've remodeled it for somebody else to buy," she says. "The thought of other people living there is just sad."

Yet the sale, which closed last week, eases the financial burden that had been tugging at the Irvines. The house sold for $375,000—about $25,000 less than the asking price, but enough to net $92,000. They'll use half to pay off their credit cards. The rest will provide a down payment on a $225,000 condominium they found in a new development in Snoqualmie.

John Irvine shakes his head. "They haven't even done a spreadsheet on what their budget is, what they can afford," he frets. "And they won't do it."

But Sue Irvine is done making sacrifices for a while. The condo is a downsized but gracious home base where Doug can work out of his funk and together, perhaps, they can regain some of what has slipped away. Doug, too, seems reenergized, the old salesman in him coming back to life. He's too young to give up on his career. He knows what he needs to do. He'll quit Target and reinvest in his search for a real job. Forget the old shotgun approach; answering newspaper ads, blasting out résumés, and competing with hundreds of younger candidates is a recipe for failure. He's going to take the rifle approach: identify promising companies, develop the right contacts, get introductions to the decision makers.

He has experience, optimism, and energy.

What he's running out of is time.

The world's wealthiest families avoid the economic insecurities of average folks in recession. However, their family feuds over pieces of the financial pie indicate that they do understand the value of a dollar. Suzanna Andrews, in *Vanity Fair* magazine, describes the contentious dismantling of the $15 billion Pritzker business empire after its leader, Jay Pritzker, died. The battle continues, with additional lawsuits and document requests filed since this article appeared.

Suzanna Andrews

Shattered Dynasty

IT IS A SIMPLE MOMENT that stands out most vividly in the memories of Jay Pritzker's friends—a moment during his funeral which did not seem to them remarkable at the time, but which in retrospect was the last time they saw his family united. "It was a very cold day and there was snow," one friend recalls. Because of the weather, many guests had not been able to make it to Chicago that day in January 1999; still, nearly one thousand mourners had shown up at the Emanuel Congregation to pay their respects, forcing the police to barricade part of North Sheridan Road to make way for the limousines. Chicago's mayor, Richard Daley, had come, as had the former congressman Jack Kemp, the real estate billionaire Sam Zell, and the advice columnist Ann Landers, along with scores of investors and businessmen with whom Pritzker had dealt in the decades during which he amassed one of the largest fortunes in America. The former director of the National Gallery of Art, J. Carter Brown, who, before his death last year, chaired the jury of the famed Pritzker Architecture Prize, was there. And so were representatives of the countless hospitals, cultural groups, and charities to which Pritzker had, before he died at the age of 76, given hundreds of millions of dollars. "The temple was filled," says one of Jay Pritzker's friends.

At the front of the synagogue, taking up several rows of seats, were almost all of the 52 living members of the Pritzker family. For many of the mourners, it was the first time they had seen so many of the publicity-shy clan in public. Intensely private, they are rarely photographed or interviewed, almost never seen. Marian "Cindy" Pritzker, Jay's wife of 51 years, and his younger brother and business partner, Robert, were seated in the front row, flanked by Jay's three sons, Thomas, John, and Daniel, and his daughter Gigi. With cousins surrounding them in a protective phalanx, they formed a tableau that Jay Pritzker, friends say, would have loved. In life, they say with sadness now, nothing was more important to him or gave him more joy than his family.

All three of Jay's sons spoke at his funeral that day. They spoke about his passions for skiing and buying companies, and about how much they loved him. "I've lived a privileged life, and truly the greatest privilege was getting to know Dad in my adult years," said Daniel, a rock musician, who is now 43. "Growing up was kind of like having Chuck Yeager and John Glenn for a dad," said John, now 49 and an entrepreneur in San Francisco. And then Tom, Jay's oldest son, stood up to speak. It was Tom, now 52, to whom Jay had passed the torch; Tom controlled the family's empire—including its crown jewel, the Hyatt Hotels Corp., the Pritzkers' web of more than two hundred privately held companies, vast tracts of real estate, and some one thousand family trusts, all of which, taken together, are said to be worth $15 billion, if not more. His father, Tom told the crowd, "believed a man's only immortality comes from the values he instilled in his children. The country has lost a great man. I've lost my father. I've lost my partner. I've lost my best friend." As he spoke, Tom began to cry.

The day of his funeral was the last time that many of Jay Pritzker's friends saw his three sons together. The moment that sticks in their memories is how lovingly his sons spoke of their father—because what they did next would surely have destroyed him.

The first hint of trouble came last November. Just before Thanksgiving, Robert's 19-year-old daughter, and Jay's niece, Liesel Pritzker—a Columbia College freshman and an actress who starred alongside Harrison Ford as the president's daughter in the 1997 movie *Air Force One* and who is currently appearing in the Broadway play *Vincent in Brixton*—filed a lawsuit in Chicago against her father and all the Pritzker cousins. Setting off an explosion of publicity, she accused her family of looting her trust funds and those of her 20-year-old brother, Matthew, in a way that was "so heinous, obnoxious and offensive as to constitute a fraud." The amount of money that Liesel claimed was taken from her was staggering—$1 billion—and she not only demanded it be returned, but asked the court to award her $5 billion in punitive damages. It was a stunning lawsuit, not just because of the money involved, but also for the questions it raised about the Pritzkers. What could have happened within a family, people asked, that would lead a young woman to sue her 76-year-old father and go public with such ugly accusations?

As Liesel's case moved forward, it brought to light something more disturbing. In a confidential agreement made in 2001, Jay Pritzker's children, his nieces and nephews, and his cousin Nicholas had decided on a ten-year plan to break up the family's business empire and split the assets among themselves. Each of those who participated in the agreement would reportedly get an equal share—estimated at $1.4 billion. Liesel and her brother were the only cousins not included in the secret pact.

If outsiders were shocked by the family's decision to rip apart one of the great American fortunes and dismantle a business empire that had taken four generations one hundred years to build, they have been horrified by the bitter feuding within the family that led to the agreement. Led by Jay's two younger sons, John and Daniel, they say, one group of cousins turned on the other, pitting brothers against sisters, cousins against cousins, and forced them to do what Jay Pritzker had expressly told his family he did not want them ever to do: grab the family's money for themselves. "It's sad and a little bit disgusting," says one old family friend. "As far as I'm concerned, the kids are assholes," says another close friend of Jay's. "Jay agonized over the last ten years of his life how he was going to leave this, [and] all I can say is he would be spinning, *spinning,* with embarrassment in his grave if he knew how these children have handled it."

Other wealthy families have struggled over the fortunes built by their fathers and grandfathers—the Rockefellers, the Binghams, the Kochs, among them—but few people expected that the Pritzkers would fight, and certainly not so "viciously," in the words of a family friend. Few families had been as close as the Pritzkers. They were each other's best friends, people who knew them say, and their fortune was built on this closeness. "The family was kind of The Family—one for all, all for one," says Bruce Leadbetter, a Dallas investor who worked with Jay for nearly thirty years. They shared an 860-acre family farm, pooled their money, and their trusts were interlinked. They really liked one another. Even after he married, Daniel lived close to his parents, and one investor recalls how Jay would sometimes be an hour late for meetings because, he'd say, "Danny wanted to talk, and I felt I wanted to do that." "Jay used to joke that the family operated like a kibbutz," says Sugar Rautbord, a Chicago socialite and novelist who had known Jay since she was a teenager.

There are some people who say that greed, pure and simple, is what drove the Pritzkers to tear apart what the patriarch had built and is what keeps them fighting bitterly even now over how the money will be distributed. But close friends say that would be easier to take than the real reason. "It's not money," says one. "It's just this personal, vicious anger they have," a friend says. "It is so emotional, you can't believe it. It's what hate does."

It was a Friday in June 1995, a friend recalls, when Jay Pritzker phoned him early in the morning and asked if he would go with him for a drive. "We went for a ride that day, but it turned out that isn't why Jay had called me," this friend says. "He wanted to talk. He was worried." Jay had decided that the time had come for him to announce to the family his plans for the future, and he had called a meeting for that afternoon. He was slowing down. He had heart problems that would soon force him to give up his great passion, heli-skiing. It was time, Jay believed, to prepare for his succession, and he was nervous. He wanted to be fair, and he wanted his children to be happy, but he also wanted to ensure that the family business and fortune were in the best hands.

Jay's four children gathered that afternoon at Tom's magnificent Lakeview Drive apartment. They were joined by Robert and Nicholas and six of Jay's nieces and nephews. Liesel, who was then 11, and Matthew, then 13, were not invited. As everyone took their seats, Jay prepared to speak. He was worried, as was Cindy, about how his plan would be received. His family had grown; there were so many adult members now, with such different interests. After making a few opening remarks, he handed each person a copy of a letter. Two pages long, typewritten and single-spaced, it was signed by Jay and Robert, and, reading much like a last will and testament, it laid out their instructions to the family. "We are writing to clarify some of the confusion that may exist about Family wealth and the Family Trusts," the letter began. Most of the family's wealth, it explained, was in corporations owned by trusts. "From time to time," the letter continued, money from the trusts would be distributed to family members "to meet their reasonable needs." However, after those needs were met, "the Trusts were not intended for and should not be viewed as a source of individual wealth." What they were primarily designed for was to accumulate wealth to invest in the family's business and enhance the family's position through its philanthropic donations—not to make billionaires out of individual Pritzkers. "Our generation and our forebears," the letter said, "were raised with the concept that we not spend more than we, as individuals, earned or contributed to the Family and society."

Jay Pritzker was a man who detested conspicuous consumption and who feared the effect of too much wealth on individuals and on society. "He felt that was the greatest risk [to society], too much separation between the haves and the have-nots," Bruce Leadbetter says. Although he lived well, he did not live luxuriously. He never had bodyguards, nor did Robert, who always flew coach, despite the fact that the family owned a Falcon 900 jet, which Jay had bought reluctantly, says a family friend, to use for business travel. As with Robert, "you wouldn't notice Jay in a crowd at all," says Leadbetter. "You'd go into a Hyatt hotel and you'd see him standing in line and checking in with everyone else." Jay

tried to teach his children not to expect to have money "just because
you are born a Pritzker," says one friend. He drove a Ford Taurus, says
another friend, because he was part owner of a Ford dealership, but
also because "he didn't want his children to think about Rolls-Royces
and Mercedeses." Jay, says Mel Klein, who was a business partner for
thirty years, "believed that anything that went to individuals should be
based on productivity and contributions, *not* just because you were in the
bloodline."

In his and Robert's letter, Jay made clear that the family trusts were not
to be broken up until the law governing trust perpetuities required it,
which one source suggests might not be until 2042. Jay also made
explicit his plans for succession. Tom would take his place at the head of
the family business. A published expert on eleventh- to fifteenth-century
Tibetan art and a close friend of the Dalai Lama's, Jay's oldest son had
worked in the family business since getting law and business degrees
from the University of Chicago in the late 1970s.

Penny and Nicholas would work with Tom as, in effect, vice chairmen of the Pritzker operations. The daughter of Jay and Robert's
younger brother, Donald, who died in 1972, Penny is the first female
Pritzker to rise to the top of the family empire. Now 43, Penny is a
triathlete and a Harvard graduate, with law and business degrees from
Stanford. Nick, now 57, is probably the most charming and outgoing of
any Pritzker, after Jay. Although he was Jay and Robert's cousin—their
uncle Jack's son—he was closer in age to Jay's children and had started
to work for the family business in 1975. As Jay saw it, this was the triumvirate that would lead the Pritzkers into the new century.

Jay made it clear that he expected his children and nieces and
nephews to "feel morally bound" to follow his wishes. "Since our generation primarily created the wealth our Family possesses, within the limits imposed by the law, we are entitled to express our wishes as to the
disposition of that wealth," Jay wrote.

Attached to the letter was a separate memo. It was, some say, Jay's
peace offering, a gesture he hoped would help keep the family happy. In
it, he outlined a series of lump-sum payments and allowances that would

be given to each member of the fourth generation and to Nick. The pay-outs had been put in place around 1990, but Jay increased the amounts. Starting when they graduated from college, each of the cousins would now get a yearly stipend—paid retroactively—that would begin at $100,000, after taxes, and climb to $1 million a year at the age of 40. On top of that, there would also be lump-sum payments for having passed key points in their lives—graduating from college, reaching the age of 30, and so on. By their 45th birthdays, it is said these payments would add up to a tidy $25 million per cousin, also after taxes.

One doesn't have to read between the lines to understand that Jay was worried about giving this kind of money to the next generation. "We earnestly hope that providing [this] money from the Trusts will not destroy the family ethic," he wrote in the letter, "and it is our belief that in some circumstances making excessive amounts available could have that effect."

After Jay spoke and the letter was read, everyone seemed happy. No one raised any objections. "There was *no* dissent," says a friend of the Pritzkers'. It appeared that Jay's gambit to buy peace in the family had worked.

In the history of American business, there are probably few men who were as pragmatic about making money as Jay Pritzker. He did not buy companies out of ego, or because they were in fashionable industries, or because they were well-known names. He bought them only if he believed they could make him a profit. In a career spanning nearly fifty years, Jay bought and sold more than two hundred companies and financed the start-up of many others. Most of these were companies that few people have ever heard of—nuts-and-bolts manufacturing compa-nies such as the Amarillo Gear Co. and Darling Store Fixtures. He would buy them if he thought they were undervalued by the market, or if their tax structures were such that, when combined with other companies in his empire, they would help him reduce—and sometimes eliminate—the taxes to be paid to the federal government.

"Jay was always looking for an *angle*," says one banker who knew him well. "A tax angle, or a value angle. Something that others didn't see." He was the kind of man who could sit in a hotel coffee shop near Los Angeles International Airport, as he did one day in 1957, see that it was bustling, discover that the hotel had no vacancies, and see a deal. The coffee shop was called Fat Eddie's, and the hotel was Hyatt, named after its owner, Hyatt von Dehn, and Jay bought both that afternoon for $2.2 million, writing his offer price on a Fat Eddie's napkin. His bet was that business executives would want to stay at luxury hotels near major airports, and he turned out to be right. Today the Hyatt chain is said to be worth anywhere from $5 billion to $7 billion.

Among hard-core financiers, Jay is considered to have been perhaps the greatest deal-maker of his day, although he was almost completely unknown to the general public. Few people, for example, knew that he controlled Braniff Airlines for a time in the 1980s, or *McCall's* magazine, which he bought in 1973 and then sold in 1987, or Ticketmaster, which he bought in 1982 and sold in 1993, or Levitz Furniture. Or that his family owns a quarter of Royal Caribbean Cruises and helped found Tenet Healthcare Corporation, the second-largest hospital owner in the country. Jay hated publicity and managed to avoid it even when involved in wildly controversial deals—using a partnership called Resource Holdings for an unsuccessful hostile run at the ITT Corporation in 1984, for example, and a partnership called GKH to represent him in 1989 in a failed bid by First Boston to break up RJR Nabisco.

Jay was color-blind, but if someone didn't lay out his socks in the morning he didn't mind going to business meetings wearing mismatched ones. At the opera or the symphony he would run to a phone during intermission to call his business partners. "Once, he lost a tooth when he was visiting Tom in Nepal," Sugar Rautbord recalls. Too busy to do anything about it on his return home, "he just went to the opera with a big gap in his teeth." He lived for business. "He was a deal nymphomaniac," says Leadbetter.

Unlike many investors of his stature and wealth, Jay did most of his own deals. "He'd be out there himself," says one prominent investment banker, meeting people, sniffing around for opportunities. Older investment bankers recall how awed they were as young men to pick up the phone and have Jay Pritzker tell them he was downstairs and could he come up for a chat? He'd sit in their offices and pepper them with questions and listen intently. And he would do them little favors. It was how he won loyalty and why they brought him deals before they showed them to anyone else.

To many of those who invested with Jay over the years, there was no financier who was more honorable. "You could play cards with Jay over the phone," says Leadbetter. "You could absolutely trust him." Not everyone felt this way, however. In the early 1990s the Pritzkers were sued by Donald Trump, who charged that the family had used "fraud, extortion and money laundering" in an attempt to force him out of his 50 percent share of the Hyatt next to Manhattan's Grand Central Terminal. In his lawsuit, Trump said the Pritzkers had, among other things, extracted $60 million in unearned management fees from Hyatt, used other Pritzker companies to bilk the hotel, and siphoned off even more money through "improper bookkeeping" in order to force him to sell his interest to them. The suit was eventually settled. Similar allegations were made in another lawsuit, filed in 1988, that was even more bitter and protracted. Paul Dopp, a New Jersey businessman, accused Jay of using "deceit and duress" in an attempt to force him out of his share of a deal he'd made with Jay to buy two casino hotels in Puerto Rico. The case went to trial, and eventually Dopp won a judgment of $15 million. "Jay Pritzker thinks his power and his resources permit him to prevail over other weaker, less wealthy, less determined adversaries," an embittered Dopp said at one point during the court fight.

Charming, witty, always polite, Jay hid his rougher side from most people. "He had this very gentle, very quiet voice," says one friend. "They all speak so softly. It's the Pritzker whisper. Jay used to say, 'If you raise your voice, it shows you're out of control. Let the other guy get out of control.' Once, I heard Jay on the speakerphone with a guy who was screaming at him, 'You asshole. You *destroyed* me.' And Jay said—very quietly—'I'm sorry you feel that way.'"

Over the years, the Pritzkers have donated more than $500 million to institutions and charities, not only in Chicago, but around the country.

On June 5, 2002, they gave, with more fanfare than usual, $30 million to the University of Chicago. The gift, for biomedical research, was in celebration of a milestone for the family: On June 5, 1902, a Russian immigrant named Nicholas Pritzker had founded a law firm in Chicago that would become, over the next one hundred years, the seat of the family's fortune and its business empire.

Nicholas was ten years old when he arrived in Chicago in 1881 with his parents, who had fled the Jewish ghetto near Kiev. As a boy, Nicholas helped to support his family, working as a newsboy and a tailor's assistant and shining shoes. He taught himself English by translating the *Chicago Tribune* into Russian, using first an English-German dictionary and then a German-Russian one. He studied pharmacy and became a druggist, and then, while supporting a wife and three sons, he got a law degree through DePaul University's evening program.

Eventually, Nicholas's three sons—Harry, Abram Nicholas, and Jack—also got law degrees and joined their father at the firm he had founded, Pritzker & Pritzker. It was Jay's father, Abram Nicholas, or "A.N.," who, after graduating from Harvard Law School, began to move the family into investing. During the Depression, he and his brother Jack laid the foundation of the family's wealth by buying up real estate and troubled companies at distressed prices.

"A.N. Oh God. What a piece of work," says a family friend. "He was almost bigger than life. Hysterical." Tough and blunt, "he'd just cut through it," says this friend. In his eighties, A.N. was racing around making deals, recalls another friend. "He was blind [by this time]," says this person, "and doing these deals that Jay then had to go behind his back and unwind because Jay couldn't bear to tell his father that he couldn't do business anymore. Jay treated his father with *such* respect."

A.N. introduced his three sons to the family business early on, bringing them to the office when they were little boys and quizzing them over dinner about math problems and financial issues. Jay finished high school when he was 14 and then went to Northwestern University, where he majored in accounting. He served as a naval flight instructor at an air station outside Chicago during World War II, attended Northwestern's law school, and then joined Pritzker & Pritzker. In 1953 he borrowed about $95,000 from his father's main banker, the First

National Bank of Chicago, and made his first acquisition, the Colson Company, then a run-down manufacturer of metal goods in Elyria, Ohio. He brought in his brother Robert to run it.

An engineer, Robert was the only third-generation Pritzker not to have gotten a law degree. Shy, unassuming, far quieter than Jay, he was adept at turning around troubled businesses. Colson was the first company in the Marmon Group, a holding company that Robert ran and that over time came to own all of the Pritzkers' manufacturing interests. Jay would buy the companies, and Robert would return them to fiscal health. Together, the brothers transformed Marmon into a $6 billion-a-year company, which prospered until 2001, when its earnings took a nosedive, dropping about 60 percent.

In early 2002, soon after his daughter Liesel hired attorneys to investigate his handling of her trusts, Robert was forced, after 48 years, out of his job as CEO of the Marmon Group by Tom, Penny, and Nick. Friends say that Robert's illness—he has Parkinson's disease—and his advancing age made the decision to let him go inevitable. But other family members were outraged by the dismissal, particularly because Robert himself was, according to one close friend, "devastated and very hurt." There was the feeling within the family that the new triumvirate had done something that was out-of-bounds. "Jay and Robert were *very* close," says one family friend. "If I *ever* said something that was even a little bit critical of Robert, Jay would say, 'He's my *brother.*' And that was the end of the conversation."

Asked, many years ago, what he would do if members of his family began to feud over their fortune, Jay said that "if we are going to have a problem, it's probably going to be a ne'er-do-well." No Pritzker, he said, "has a right to anything until he has made a contribution doing something and doing it well. He doesn't have to be in the family business. He can be a Yugoslavian poetry professor. But he had better be a good one." Much as Jay doted on his family, he also expected every one of them to achieve. "With Jay, you had to be the *best,*" says a friend. Says another,

"He was a warm, wonderful person, but he was also tough. His standards were very, very high." He adds, "Being number one was very important to Jay." When his youngest son, Danny, wanted to devote his life to music after college, Jay insisted that he go to law school. There were big arguments, recalls one friend, but Jay won. Other friends remember that Tom went to meetings at the office when he was just seven years old, and that they now wonder whether he did so because he was truly interested or merely because he wanted to please his father.

In 1972, around Christmastime, Jay's oldest child, Nancy, waited until her family left on a ski vacation and then went to the garage, got into Jay's car, placed a copy of David Halberstam's book *The Best and the Brightest* at her side, and turned on the engine. She was found later that day, dead at the age of 24. Her suicide was "the most horrendous tragedy of Jay's life," says a friend, adding that it was shortly after Nancy's death that he had his first heart attack. Nancy had suffered from depression, and it is believed that she had been diagnosed as bipolar. But the book she chose to leave beside her—a powerful indictment of America's involvement in Vietnam and of how destructive arrogant overachievers can be—weighed on Jay, says one friend. Was it a message for him? Had he been too tough on his beloved daughter? "He lived every second with guilt about Nancy, but he internalized it, and that created problems with his kids," says a friend. "After the suicide of Nancy," says another, "all the love and everything else was transferred to the next child, Tommy."

There are those who say that had Tom not gone into the family business he would now be, as one puts it, "meditating in Nepal." Serious and shy, much more contemplative than his father, Tom has long been interested in Buddhism. Although Jay was very proud of the articles Tom wrote for scholarly magazines about Asian art, the interest in Buddhism merely amused him. "I remember having lunch with Jay one day," a friend recalls. "And he said that Tom's kids' nanny had died and the children found a frog on the [family] farm and they thought it was her, reincarnated, and so Jay had to catch the frog for them. He thought it was very funny." Tom, one old friend believes, went into the family business largely because his father wanted him to.

"One if my earliest memories is of Tom with a clipboard," says a family friend. "Jay would talk, and Tom would write it down. It was Tom's training." Tom joined the family business in 1978, after he had gotten his law and business degrees, and for the next decade he was moved around the Pritzker empire from job to job, his performance closely watched over by Jay. In time, Tom came to win not only his father's trust but his admiration. Jay would boast that Tom's work on deals had brought millions into the Pritzkers' coffers—when he helped take Levitz Furniture public in 1993, for instance, and founded the biotech investment firm Bay City Capital, and got the family to invest $1 million in First Health, a company that today has a market capitalization of nearly $2.5 billion.

Jay brought his other two sons into the business as well, but with different results. Danny worked on a few deals, friends close to the family business say, but they did not go well, and eventually he left to start his own record company and a soul-rock band, Sonia Dada, ventures the family financed to the tune of $25 million. John rose quite high in the ranks of Hyatt, but although Jay hoped he would run the company one day, John wasn't interested in making a career of it. He, too, was given family money to found several companies, but, as with Danny's projects, sources say, John's investments—including those in a sporting goods store and an environmentally friendly train—did not yield much in the way of profits.

Jay tested everyone, says Mel Klein, "to see their abilities." "He gave the same opportunity to each family member," Klein says. "He *loved* his family." But Jay could be blunt, almost cruel, in his assessment of those who didn't excel at making money. "One day we were talking about this venture" in which John was involved, recalls a business partner of Jay's, "and he looked at me and said, 'There is a reason John isn't with us in Chicago, and it's a matter of [his] competency.'" Jay seemed not to understand how cutting this remark was or that it might hurt his son if it got back to him, because he said the same thing to a number of people.

In anointing Tom, Nick, and Penny, some friends say, Jay chose well. In the last few years, Nick has made millions by aggressively expanding the family's huge casino holdings around the world and cutting deals to build new Hyatt hotels. Possibly the toughest of the triumvirate, Penny has spearheaded the growth of the family's commercial real estate empire and created Classic Residence by Hyatt, a company that builds and manages high-end housing for the elderly. In a family that favored its sons, Penny had to beg her grandfather A.N. to allow her into the business. He rebuffed her entreaties more than once and, in the end, only agreed to let her work for the company as a secretary.

If not as wizardly at deal-making as Jay was, Tom, Nick, and Penny have held their own.

It was Penny who dealt with one of the Pritzkers' biggest public embarrassments—the collapse, in 2001, of Superior Bank. Purchased in 1988 by Jay and an old friend of his, the New York real estate developer Alvin Dworman, the savings bank got into trouble with regulators because of accounting problems with its huge portfolio of loans to low-quality borrowers. For months, the Pritzkers and Dworman fought over who should take the blame, until Penny, friends say, finally decided that the family would pay the entire $460 million fine levied by bank regulators. "It was right after 9/11," says an associate of Penny's, "and she called me and said, 'My family is *not* going to litigate with the federal government at a time like this.'"

It was one case where Tom, Nick, and Penny were more conciliatory than was Jay, who for years had fought with the Internal Revenue Service, which more than once charged the family with using its trusts and complicated offshore transactions to avoid paying taxes. The most famous court fight took place after A.N. died, in 1986, at the age of 90. Although he was a billionaire almost twice over, the family claimed that, at his death, A.N. had been worth only $25,000. His estate, they claimed, was too small to owe taxes.

At the heart of the Pritzkers' case were the trusts that the family is fighting over today. For years before A.N. died, he had been shifting the family's wealth into numerous trusts in the Caribbean. The IRS called the trusts sham and insisted that the Pritzkers owed the government $53.2 million in taxes. In 1994, however, the government settled with the family, which paid a mere $9.5 million plus interest. At the time, the IRS had been unable to discover exactly how much was in the trusts—the family had made sure they were protected from outside scrutiny. But what the Pritzkers did not foresee was how vulnerable the trusts would be if their family itself did not hold together.

Robert was unhappy in his second marriage, to Liesel's mother, Irene, and that, some friends say, made Jay unhappy as well. It was Jay, one friend says, who more than once arranged, when Robert was hospitalized for intestinal surgery in the late 1980s, for his brother to be unhooked from all the machines and taken to the Palmer House Hilton to see his girlfriend, Mayari Sargent, who is now Robert's wife. When asked about this, a spokesman for Robert said, "We simply do not comment on personal matters. We will not dignify this." But Irene's friends say it was this kind of behavior that made her very angry at the Pritzkers. "They treated her very badly," says someone who is close to Irene, who filed for divorce in 1989 after nine years of marriage. Robert and Irene were officially divorced in 1991, but they continued to fight bitterly over their children for years after that.

Liesel was seven when her parents divorced, Matthew nine, and, if the court records are any indication, the two children spent much of their childhood bearing the brunt of their parents' rage. In her filings, Irene accused Robert of being a bad father, whose conduct was "at times . . . injurious" to his children. She accused him of trying to buy the children's love—with a pet ferret for Liesel and a puppy for Matthew—and blamed Robert for Matthew's health problems. According to Irene's court filings, both children preferred their new stepfather, James Bagley, to Robert—so much so that they had begun to use Bagley's last name. Robert was such a poor father, Irene contended, that by the time Liesel was ten years old she no longer wanted to see him. "She has no relationship with Robert," Irene told the court in 1994, "nor does she desire one."

According to Robert's filings, his children had been turned against him by their mother and stepfather. Irene, he said, became enraged when Liesel and Matthew spoke about their father or tried to talk with him on the phone; in front of them, she referred to his girlfriend as a "bimbo" and a "slope"—Mayari is part Asian—comments a spokesman for Irene now denies she made. Irene, according to Robert, told her children their father, like all Pritzkers, was a bully. Robert also contended that James Bagley told Liesel that her father was a liar. He said much worse, Irene would later contend, in a filing during her 1997 divorce from Bagley. She charged that Bagley "detested" Robert. Bagley would refer to him as "a Jew pig" and a "manipulative Jew." (Bagley has denied these allegations.)

By the spring of 1994, Robert's anger at Irene appears to have boiled over. His attorneys threatened legal action if Liesel and Matthew's school did not stop using "Pritzker-Bagley" as their last name. And when he learned, from a newspaper article, that Liesel was to star in the 1995 Warner Bros. movie *A Little Princess* without his having been consulted, his lawyers challenged the movie studio. In the end, the children returned to using Pritzker as their name, Liesel was able to star in the movie, under the stage name "Liesel Matthews," and Robert won the right to see his daughter more often. In May of that year, ten-year-old Liesel attended Robert's wedding to Mayari, under a court order.

All of this might have been just another brutal divorce in which the children were used as pawns, except for what happened next. In October 1994, Tom Pritzker and the family's attorney Marshall Eisenberg, who were trustees of all the Pritzker trusts, gave up their control of Liesel's and Matthew's—to Robert. By the following March, Robert had completely emptied out two of his children's trusts. He had also, according to Liesel's lawsuit, reduced the value of several others by selling their assets to trusts held by their cousins for less than market value. In return, according to Liesel's suit, she and her brother were given promissory notes.

In the transaction that has sparked the most controversy, Robert took all the assets from two of Liesel's and Matthew's trusts—approximately $4.3 million apiece—and donated them to the Pritzker Foundation. Included in those assets were 52 shares held by each child in H Group Holding—the company that includes most of Hyatt. According to people familiar with the transaction, Liesel's shares were then valued at approximately $143,000—which sources close to the Pritzkers say had been their value when they were acquired by Liesel's trust. Shortly after the shares were donated, however, H Group bought them from the foundation for $94.2 million, more than six hundred times their stated value. Liesel's attorneys have suggested that the shares were worth even more than that. They contend that H Group got itself a very sweet deal, and that Liesel's shares—which she wants returned to her—could now be worth as much as $500 million.

Irene, friends say, had no idea of what Robert had done—out of anger, they say, at her. She began to suspect something was wrong toward the end of 2001, when Matthew heard his cousins talking about a family agreement to split up the Pritzker fortune, "and how he and Liesel were going to get shortchanged," says a source. Always on her guard with the Pritzkers, her friends say, Irene hired a law firm to investigate the situation. According to Pritzker friends, she would soon stumble onto the chance to take "her revenge" on the family she had come to loathe, something a spokesman for Irene denies, saying, "Liesel's lawsuit has nothing to do with Irene."

Although many of Jay Pritzker's friends say he died believing that his family was at peace and that his wishes would be followed, his closest friends say that is far from the truth. He was too embarrassed, "as a father," says one friend, to tell most people what was happening among his sons. There had been tension even before the 1995 meeting; upset that their brother would be running the business, Danny and John had told their father they wanted to "take their money out," says this friend. The larger allowances and payouts Jay offered in his June 1995 letter did not mollify them. Sometime after the meeting, they came back and, once again, told him they wanted out. To appease them, he gave Danny, John, and Gigi each $30 million. "They were squeezing Jay when he was sick," says another family friend, referring to Danny and John.

In 1997, Jay had a stroke, and Tom, Nick, and Penny took over the day-to-day running of the empire. After that, one friend says, Jay's life became miserable. He lost some of his memory. He would go into the bathroom, says one man, "and not be able to find his way out." He couldn't remember deals that he had done. But what upset him most was how angry his younger sons had become. "He was overwrought" about that, says a close friend. After his death, says this friend, the animosity among the sons erupted. "The bitterness was just terrible," the friend says. "It was sibling rivalry taken to the tenth power. It was horrible, just horrible." "You'd be in a room with them, and you could see the tension," says a friend of Tom's. His brothers resented it when Tom would not let them use the Falcon 900 jet; they complained that he blocked charitable donations they wanted to make. They felt that Tom was "arrogant," says a family friend, and they chafed at having to go to him if they needed money. As time went by, friends say, Tom's brothers and a number of the cousins felt they were being excluded from the family business. They also felt that Tom, Nick, and Penny were investing in their own deals, but ignoring those that they brought in.

By the summer of 2000, Danny and John had joined forces with Penny's brothers, Tony and J.B. The two, both of whom are investors, had come to feel as excluded and as concerned about the management of the family business, friends say, as John and Danny. Together, the four of them wrote a letter to Tom, Nick, and Penny, asking to have their concerns addressed. "It was a very conciliatory letter," says one friend. But the two sides hit an "impasse," says this friend, and shortly after that the four cousins hired a top Chicago litigator, who threatened legal action. Soon an entire room at Pritzker & Pritzker was filled with boxes of documents. Some say the dissenters were looking for a "smoking gun," a reason to justify breaking up the family's trusts. Others say they were genuinely shocked by what they found in the records—specifically, $480 million that they alleged Tom, Nick, and Penny had paid themselves without anyone's knowledge. They began to lobby the older cousins, and soon had all but Gigi on their side. "These people have more money than they need," says one person. "It wasn't that they wanted more. They became concerned about how Tom, Nick, and Penny were administering the family's money." "They portrayed it as fraud and thievery," says one friend of Jay's, who is among the many who were outraged by the allegations. The $480 million, Jay's business partners insist, was given to Tom, Nick, and Penny over the years by Jay himself. "They were allowed to coinvest in deals and to take pieces of equity in them," says Mel Klein, who was involved in several of those deals. If the cousins got less money, Klein and others say, it was because their deals didn't make nearly as much money as Tom's, Nick's, and Penny's did. Other friends say it wasn't the fact that Tom, Nick, and Penny got more money that upset the cousins, but the sheer magnitude of the amount involved. The cousins, friends say, found no evidence that Jay had authorized payments that even approached $480 million. "They did not feel that what was taken out was equitable or appropriately disclosed," says one friend. In their view, breaking up the empire was the only solution.

Tom did not have to bend to his cousins' and brothers' demands. That he did so, friends say, is a sign of how bad things were. As the trustee of nearly all of the family's trusts, Tom had almost unlimited power and could have overridden his brothers and cousins. But they were threatening to sue him and Nick and Penny, and the animosity was tearing the family apart. He feared what the publicity of a court fight would do to his family, and what the infighting would do to his elderly mother. "He was looking for peace at any cost," says one friend of Jay's. "He agonized over this."

The "peace" the cousins arrived at, near the end of 2001, was supposed to have remained a secret. Each of them signed a strict confidentiality pledge, promising never to reveal the contents of the agreement or the events that had led to it. And for almost a year no one outside the family knew of the plan they had decided on. Over the next ten years, while Tom, Nick, and Penny continued to run the businesses, the family would slowly liquidate many of the Pritzker holdings—by selling a number of companies, trading others among themselves, and taking some, possibly including Hyatt, partly public. They also agreed to take half of the Pritzker Foundation's $600 million in assets and give it to foundations that each cousin would establish.

What they didn't count on was that Irene and her daughter would challenge them. Matthew, who wants to maintain a relationship with his family, has so far opted not to sue, and is said to be in settlement talks with the family. But Liesel, whose hostility toward her father never abated, is angrier. "For her, it's a matter of principle," says a friend of Irene's. "The other day," a friend of Robert's recalls, "Robert said, and he didn't say it angrily, because Robert doesn't get angry, but he said, 'Here my daughter Liesel is suing me. She has $160 million in trusts. I don't have $160 million.' . . . This whole thing is so sad. I mean, Bob is really shaking badly from Parkinson's now. Even with the medication."

Why did Robert empty out his children's trusts? Today that remains a mystery. The family does not dispute the basic facts of Liesel's lawsuit. They argue, as Robert's longtime attorney Lowell Sachnoff explains, that "everything that Robert did was specifically authorized by the trusts and the family's generational plan, and [it is] legal." Their argument is the very one Jay used in 1995, when he laid out his vision of the family's future: The trusts were designed to benefit the family and its businesses, not individual members. To support those goals, the trustees had the power to do almost anything they wished with the trusts' assets. Around 1989, they say, Jay made a decision to move Liesel and Matthew down a generation because, as the products of Robert's late-in-life second marriage, they were so much younger than their cousins and needed less money, in his view. In a remarkable bit of legerdemain, Jay, in effect, made Liesel Robert's grandchild, not his daughter.

There is little doubt that Jay made this decision, and that he knew and approved of what Robert did with his children's trusts. But what is mystifying is why Tom and the family's lawyer resigned as trustees. If diminishing Liesel's and Matthew's trusts was part of a legitimate family policy, why didn't they help implement it instead or turning the job over to Robert? And why did they wait until 1994 to do it? The answers, and the heart of the mystery, lie in Robert's motive. Was he so angry at his children that he punished them by gutting their trust funds? Some friends of the family say they just don't know, but in a recent legal filing Robert's attorneys flatly deny that anger was a motive. One theory is that Jay was planning to reduce Liesel's and Matthew's trusts anyway, but let Robert do it as a means of venting his anger. Either way, if the Pritzkers do not settle with Liesel and Matthew before the case ends up in court, it could turn out to be one of the most riveting trust fights in recent legal history.

The Pritzkers contend that Liesel has misunderstood everything. "She regards this as her inheritance, and it is not," says a friend of the family. But that, then, would apply to her 11 cousins as well. The Pritzker fortune was not meant to be their inheritance, either. And yet, that is how they are treating it by breaking it up and grabbing pieces of it for themselves. That they would fight Liesel at all astonishes some people, but that they would cite the rules of the trusts and Jay's wishes in their case against her is considered even more outrageous. The minute they signed the family agreement, they overrode everything that Jay had wanted, and they overrode everything the trusts were established to do. The family argues that Liesel is very well taken care of—she has, they say, $160 million in trusts still in her name, although much of the money has been tied up in long-term loans to cousins' trusts. They say she isn't entitled to a $1.4 billion share of the fortune. Unlike themselves.

Sadly, friends say, the peace that Tom tried to buy with the family agreement never came. Even though John and Danny have said they realize the agreement is the best possible solution, they have also told people they wish they had never signed it. Along with some of their cousins, they continue to criticize the way Tom, Nick, and Penny are running the business. And they continue to voice suspicions about the $480 million paid to the trio. "They are just *wild* about it," says one man. "There is such bitterness." In some way, the agreement seems to have made things worse. Tom, a friend says, has grown "emotionally sick" over his failure to keep the family together and over what the feuding has done to his mother. Cindy Pritzker, says a friend of hers, has been devastated by the fighting in her family. In January, this friend says, she took several of her grandchildren to the Super Bowl, "trying to create bonds between them even though their parents are feuding. It's been very, very difficult for her. Some of her children have used their children as weapons."

Sometime after Jay died, a friend of his visited his grave at Memorial Park Cemetery. "There were all these drawings and cards from his grandchildren on the tombstone," this person recalls, "all these notes to 'Grandpa.'" When he was alive, "Jay had the power to keep everything together by the sheer force of his incredible personality," says a friend of Robert's. "But no one could replace him." For one hundred years, love and money defined the Pritzker family. Now, it seems, there is only money.

Did the booming American markets and economy obliterate the middle class or merely bring out some excess during a period of creativity? On two successive weeks, *The New York Times Magazine* cover
stories looked at opposing views on the boom effect. Here Paul Krugman sees the cup as half empty, describing a new Gilded Age of
inequality in which corporate leaders are modern robber barons.

Paul Krugman

For Richer

THE DISAPPEARING MIDDLE

WHEN I WAS A TEENAGER growing up on Long Island, one
of my favorite excursions was a trip to see the great Gilded Age mansions
of the North Shore. Those mansions weren't just pieces of architectural
history. They were monuments to a bygone social era, one in which the
rich could afford the armies of servants needed to maintain a house the
size of a European palace. By the time I saw them, of course, that era was
long past. Almost none of the Long Island mansions were still private
residences. Those that hadn't been turned into museums were occupied
by nursing homes or private schools.

For the America I grew up in—the America of the 1950s and
1960s—was a middle-class society, both in reality and in feel. The vast
income and wealth inequalities of the Gilded Age had disappeared. Yes,
of course, there was the poverty of the underclass—but the conventional
wisdom of the time viewed that as a social rather than an economic prob-

lem. Yes, of course, some wealthy businessmen and heirs to large fortunes lived far better than the average American. But they weren't rich
the way the robber barons who built the mansions had been rich, and
there weren't that many of them. The days when plutocrats were a force
to be reckoned with in American society, economically or politically,
seemed long past.

Daily experience confirmed the sense of a fairly equal society. The
economic disparities you were conscious of were quite muted. Highly educated professionals—middle managers, college teachers, even lawyers—
often claimed that they earned less than unionized blue-collar workers.
Those considered very well-off lived in split-levels, had a housecleaner
come in once a week, and took summer vacations in Europe. But they
sent their kids to public schools and drove themselves to work, just like
everyone else.

But that was long ago. The middle-class America of my youth was
another country.

We are now living in a new Gilded Age, as extravagant as the original. Mansions have made a comeback. Back in 1999 this magazine
profiled Thierry Despont, the "eminence of excess," an architect who spe-
cializes in designing houses for the superrich. His creations typically
range from 20,000 to 60,000 square feet; houses at the upper end of
his range are not much smaller than the White House. Needless to say,
the armies of servants are back, too. So are the yachts. Still, even J. P.
Morgan didn't have a Gulfstream.

As the story about Despont suggests, it's not fair to say that the fact
of widening inequality in America has gone unreported. Yet glimpses of
the lifestyles of the rich and tasteless don't necessarily add up in people's
minds to a clear picture of the tectonic shifts that have taken place in the
distribution of income and wealth in this country. My sense is that few
people are aware of just how much the gap between the very rich and
the rest has widened over a relatively short period of time. In fact, even
bringing up the subject exposes you to charges of "class warfare," the
"politics of envy," and so on. And very few people indeed are willing to
talk about the profound effects—economic, social, and political—of that
widening gap.

Yet you can't understand what's happening in America today without understanding the extent, causes, and consequences of the vast increase in inequality that has taken place over the last three decades, and in particular the astonishing concentration of income and wealth in just a few hands. To make sense of the current wave of corporate scandal, you need to understand how the man in the gray flannel suit has been replaced by the imperial CEO. The concentration of income at the top is a key reason that the United States, for all its economic achievements, has more poverty and lower life expectancy than any other major advanced nation. Above all, the growing concentration of wealth has reshaped our political system: It is at the root both of a general shift to the right and of an extreme polarization of our politics.

But before we get to all that, let's take a look at who gets what.

THE NEW GILDED AGE

The Securities and Exchange Commission hath no fury like a woman scorned. The messy divorce proceedings of Jack Welch, the legendary former CEO of General Electric, have had one unintended benefit: They have given us a peek at the perks of the corporate elite, which are normally hidden from public view. For it turns out that when Welch retired, he was granted for life the use of a Manhattan apartment (including food, wine, and laundry), access to corporate jets, and a variety of other in-kind benefits, worth at least $2 million a year. The perks were revealing: They illustrated the extent to which corporate leaders now expect to be treated like ancien régime royalty. In monetary terms, however, the perks must have meant little to Welch. In 2000, his last full year running GE, Welch was paid $123 million, mainly in stock and stock options.

Is it news that CEOs of large American corporations make a lot of money? Actually, it is. They were always well paid compared with the average worker, but there is simply no comparison between what executives got a generation ago and what they are paid today.

Over the past thirty years most people have seen only modest salary increases: The average annual salary in America, expressed in 1998 dollars (that is, adjusted for inflation), rose from $32,522 in 1970 to

$35,864 in 1999. That's about a 10 percent increase over 29 years—progress, but not much. Over the same period, however, according to *Fortune* magazine, the average real annual compensation of the top one hundred CEOs went from $1.3 million—39 times the pay of an average worker—to $37.5 million, more than one thousand times the pay of ordinary workers.

The explosion in CEO pay over the past thirty years is an amazing story in its own right, and an important one. But it is only the most spectacular indicator of a broader story, the reconcentration of income and wealth in the U.S. The rich have always been different from you and me, but they are far more different now than they were not long ago—indeed, they are as different now as they were when F. Scott Fitzgerald made his famous remark.

That's a controversial statement, though it shouldn't be. For at least the past 15 years it has been hard to deny the evidence for growing inequality in the United States. Census data clearly show a rising share of income going to the top 20 percent of families, and within that top 20 percent to the top 5 percent, with a declining share going to families in the middle. Nonetheless, denial of that evidence is a sizable, well-financed industry. Conservative think tanks have produced scores of studies that try to discredit the data, the methodology, and, not least, the motives of those who report the obvious. Studies that appear to refute claims of increasing inequality receive prominent endorsements on editorial pages and are eagerly cited by right-leaning government officials. Four years ago Alan Greenspan (why did anyone ever think that he was nonpartisan?) gave a keynote speech at the Federal Reserve's annual Jackson Hole conference that amounted to an attempt to deny that there has been any real increase in inequality in America.

The concerted effort to deny that inequality is increasing is itself a symptom of the growing influence of our emerging plutocracy (more on this later). So is the fierce defense of the backup position, that inequality doesn't matter—or maybe even that, to use Martha Stewart's signature phrase, it's a good thing. Meanwhile, politically motivated smoke screens aside, the reality of increasing inequality is not in doubt. In fact, the census data understate the case, because for technical reasons those data tend to undercount very high incomes—for example, it's unlikely that they reflect the explosion in CEO compensation. And other evidence makes it clear not only that inequality is increasing but that the action gets bigger the closer you get to the top. That is, it's not simply that the top 20 percent of families have had bigger percentage gains than families near the middle: The top 5 percent have done better than the next 15, the top 1 percent better than the next 4, and so on up to Bill Gates.

Studies that try to do a better job of tracking high incomes have found startling results. For example, a recent study by the nonpartisan Congressional Budget Office used income tax data and other sources to improve on the census estimates. The CBO study found that between 1979 and 1997, the after-tax incomes of the top 1 percent of families rose 157 percent, compared with only a 10 percent gain for families near the middle of the income distribution. Even more startling results come from a new study by Thomas Piketty, at the French research institute Cepremap, and Emmanuel Saez, who is now at the University of California at Berkeley. Using income tax data, Piketty and Saez have produced estimates of the incomes of the well-to-do, the rich, and the very rich back to 1913.

The first point you learn from these new estimates is that the middle-class America of my youth is best thought of not as the normal state of our society, but as an interregnum between Gilded Ages. America before 1930 was a society in which a small number of very rich people controlled a large share of the nation's wealth. We became a middle-class society only after the concentration of income at the top dropped sharply during the New Deal, and especially during World War II. The economic historians Claudia Goldin and Robert Margo have dubbed the narrowing of income gaps during those years the Great Compression. Incomes then stayed fairly equally distributed until the 1970s: The rapid rise in incomes during the first postwar generation was very evenly spread across the population.

Since the 1970s, however, income gaps have been rapidly widening. Piketty and Saez confirm what I suspected: By most measures we are, in fact, back to the days of *The Great Gatsby.* After thirty years in which the income shares of the top 10 percent of taxpayers, the top 1 percent, and so on were far below their levels in the 1920s, all are very nearly back where they were.

And the big winners are the very, very rich. One ploy often used to play down growing inequality is to rely on rather coarse statistical breakdowns—dividing the population into five "quintiles," each containing 20 percent of families, or at most 10 "deciles." Indeed, Greenspan's speech at Jackson Hole relied mainly on decile data. From there it's a short step to denying that we're really talking about the rich at all. For example, a conservative commentator might concede, grudgingly, that there has been some increase in the share of national income going to the top 10 percent of taxpayers, but then point out that anyone with an income over $81,000 is in that top 10 percent. So we're just talking about shifts within the middle class, right?

Wrong: The top 10 percent contains a lot of people whom we would still consider middle class, but they weren't the big winners. Most of the gains in the share of the top 10 percent of taxpayers over the past thirty years were actually gains to the top 1 percent, rather than the next 9 percent. In 1998 the top 1 percent started at $230,000. In turn, 60 percent of the gains of that top 1 percent went to the top 0.1 percent, those with incomes of more than $790,000. And almost half of those gains went to a mere thirteen thousand taxpayers, the top 0.01 percent, who had an income of at least $3.6 million and an average income of $17 million.

A stickler for detail might point out that the Piketty-Saez estimates end in 1998 and that the CBO numbers end a year earlier. Have the trends shown in the data reversed? Almost surely not. In fact, all indications are that the explosion of incomes at the top continued through 2000. Since then the plunge in stock prices must have put some crimp in high incomes—but census data show inequality continuing to increase in 2001, mainly because of the severe effects of the recession on the working poor and near poor. When the recession ends, we can be sure that we will find ourselves a society in which income inequality is even higher than it was in the late '90s.

So claims that we've entered a second Gilded Age aren't exaggerated. In America's middle-class era, the mansion-building, yacht-owning classes had pretty much disappeared. According to Piketty and Saez, in 1970 the top 0.01 percent of taxpayers had 0.7 percent of total income—that is, they earned "only" 70 times as much as the average, not enough to buy or maintain a megaresidence. But in 1998 the top 0.01

percent received more than 3 percent of all income. That meant that the thirteen thousand richest families in America had almost as much income as the twenty million poorest households; those thirteen thousand families had incomes three hundred times that of average families.

And let me repeat: This transformation has happened very quickly, and it is still going on. You might think that 1987, the year Tom Wolfe published his novel *The Bonfire of the Vanities* and Oliver Stone released his movie *Wall Street,* marked the high tide of America's new money culture. But in 1987 the top 0.01 percent earned only about 40 percent of what they do today, and top executives less than a fifth as much. The America of *Wall Street* and *The Bonfire of the Vanities* was positively egalitarian compared with the country we live in today.

UNDOING THE NEW DEAL

In the middle of the 1980s, as economists became aware that something important was happening to the distribution of income in America, they formulated three main hypotheses about its causes.

The "globalization" hypothesis tied America's changing income distribution to the growth of world trade, and especially the growing imports of manufactured goods from the third world. Its basic message was that blue-collar workers—the sort of people who in my youth often made as much money as college-educated middle managers—were losing ground in the face of competition from low-wage workers in Asia. A result was stagnation or decline in the wages of ordinary people, with a growing share of national income going to the highly educated.

A second hypothesis, "skill-biased technological change," situated the cause of growing inequality not in foreign trade but in domestic innovation. The torrid pace of progress in information technology, so the story went, had increased the demand for the highly skilled and educated. And so the income distribution increasingly favored brains rather than brawn.

Finally, the "superstar" hypothesis—named by the Chicago economist Sherwin Rosen—offered a variant on the technological story. It argued that modern technologies of communication often turn competition into a tournament in which the winner is richly rewarded, while the runners-up get far less. The classic example—which gives the theory its name—is the entertainment business. As Rosen pointed out, in bygone days there were hundreds of comedians making a modest living at live shows in the borscht belt and other places. Now they are mostly gone; what is left is a handful of superstar TV comedians.

The debates among these hypotheses—particularly the debate between those who attributed growing inequality to globalization and those who attributed it to technology—were many and bitter. I was a participant in those debates myself. But I won't dwell on them, because in the last few years there has been a growing sense among economists that none of these hypotheses work.

I don't mean to say that there was nothing to these stories. Yet as more evidence has accumulated, each of the hypotheses has seemed increasingly inadequate. Globalization can explain part of the relative decline in blue-collar wages, but it can't explain the 2,500 percent rise in CEO incomes. Technology may explain why the salary premium associated with a college education has risen, but it's hard to match up with the huge increase in inequality among the college-educated, with little progress for many but gigantic gains at the top. The superstar theory works for Jay Leno, but not for the thousands of people who have become awesomely rich without going on TV.

The Great Compression—the substantial reduction in inequality during the New Deal and the Second World War—also seems hard to understand in terms of the usual theories. During World War II Franklin Roosevelt used government control over wages to compress wage gaps. But if the middle-class society that emerged from the war was an artificial creation, why did it persist for another thirty years?

Some—by no means all—economists trying to understand growing inequality have begun to take seriously a hypothesis that would have been considered irredeemably fuzzy-minded not long ago. This view stresses the role of social norms in setting limits to inequality. According to this view, the New Deal had a more profound impact on American society than even its most ardent admirers have suggested: It imposed norms of relative equality in pay that persisted for more than thirty years, creating the broadly middle-class society we came to take for granted. But those norms began to unravel in the 1970s and have done so at an accelerating pace.

Exhibit A for this view is the story of executive compensation. In the 1960s, America's great corporations behaved more like socialist republics than like cutthroat capitalist enterprises, and top executives behaved more like public-spirited bureaucrats than like captains of industry. I'm not exaggerating. Consider the description of executive behavior offered by John Kenneth Galbraith in his 1967 book, *The New Industrial State:* "Management does not go out ruthlessly to reward itself—a sound management is expected to exercise restraint." Managerial self-dealing was a thing of the past: "With the power of decision goes opportunity for making money. . . . Were everyone to seek to do so . . . the corporation would be a chaos of competitive avarice. But these are not the sort of thing that a good company man does; a remarkably effective code bans such behavior. Group decision-making insures, moreover, that almost everyone's actions and even thoughts are known to others. This acts to enforce the code and, more than incidentally, a high standard of personal honesty as well."

Thirty-five years on, a cover article in *Fortune* is titled "You Bought. They Sold." "All over corporate America," reads the blurb, "top execs were cashing in stocks even as their companies were tanking. Who was left holding the bag? You." As I said, we've become a different country.

Let's leave actual malfeasance on one side for a moment, and ask how the relatively modest salaries of top executives thirty years ago became the gigantic pay packages of today. There are two main stories, both of which emphasize changing norms rather than pure economics. The more optimistic story draws an analogy between the explosion of CEO pay and the explosion of baseball salaries with the introduction of free agency. According to this story, highly paid CEOs really are worth it, because having the right man in that job makes a huge difference. The more pessimistic view—which I find more plausible—is that competition for talent is a minor factor. Yes, a great executive can make a big difference—but those huge pay packages have been going as often as not to executives whose performance is mediocre at best. They key reason executives are paid so much now is that they appoint the members of the corporate board that determines their compensation and control many of the perks that board members count on. So it's not the invisible hand of the market that leads to those monumental executive incomes; it's the invisible handshake in the boardroom.

But then why weren't executives paid lavishly thirty years ago? Again, it's a matter of corporate culture. For a generation after World War II, fear of outrage kept executive salaries in check. Now the outrage is gone. That is, the explosion of executive pay represents a social change rather than the purely economic forces of supply and demand. We should think of it not as a market trend like the rising value of waterfront property, but as something more like the sexual revolution of the 1960s—a relaxation of old strictures, a new permissiveness, but in this case the permissiveness is financial rather than sexual. Sure enough, John Kenneth Galbraith described the honest executive of 1967 as being one who "eschews the lovely, available and even naked woman by whom he is intimately surrounded." By the end of the 1990s, the executive motto might as well have been "If it feels good, do it."

How did this change in corporate culture happen? Economists and management theorists are only beginning to explore that question, but it's easy to suggest a few factors. One was the changing structure of financial markets. In his new book, *Searching for a Corporate Savior,* Rakesh Khurana of Harvard Business School suggests that during the 1980s and 1990s, "managerial capitalism"—the world of the man in the gray flannel suit—was replaced by "investor capitalism." Institutional investors weren't willing to let a CEO choose his own successor from inside the corporation; they wanted heroic leaders, often outsiders, and were willing to pay immense sums to get them. The subtitle of Khurana's book, by the way, is *The Irrational Quest for Charismatic CEOs.*

But fashionable management theorists didn't think it was irrational. Since the 1980s there has been ever more emphasis on the importance of "leadership"—meaning personal, charismatic leadership. When Lee Iacocca of Chrysler became a business celebrity in the early 1980s, he was practically alone: Khurana reports that in 1980 only one issue of *BusinessWeek* featured a CEO on its cover. By 1999 the number was up to 19. And once it was considered normal, even necessary, for a CEO to be famous, it also became easier to make him rich.

Economists also did their bit to legitimize previously unthinkable levels of executive pay. During the 1980s and 1990s a torrent of academic papers—popularized in business magazines and incorporated into consultants' recommendations—argued that Gordon Gekko was right: Greed is good; greed works. In order to get the best performance out of executives, these papers argued, it was necessary to align their interests with those of stockholders. And the way to do that was with large grants of stock or stock options.

It's hard to escape the suspicion that these new intellectual justifications for soaring executive pay were as much effect as cause. I'm not suggesting that management theorists and economists were personally corrupt. It would have been a subtle, unconscious process: The ideas that were taken up by business schools, that led to nice speaking and consulting fees, tended to be the ones that ratified an existing trend, and thereby gave it legitimacy.

What economists like Piketty and Saez are now suggesting is that the story of executive compensation is representative of a broader story. Much more than economists and free-market advocates like to imagine, wages—particularly at the top—are determined by social norms. What happened during the 1930s and 1940s was that new norms of equality were established, largely through the political process. What happened in the 1980s and 1990s was that those norms unraveled, replaced by an ethos of "anything goes." And a result was an explosion of income at the top of the scale.

THE PRICE OF INEQUALITY

It was one of those revealing moments. Responding to an e-mail message from a Canadian viewer, Robert Novak of *Crossfire* delivered a little speech: "Marg, like most Canadians, you're ill-informed and wrong. The U.S. has the longest standard of living—longest life expectancy of any country in the world, including Canada. That's the truth."

But it was Novak who had his facts wrong. Canadians can expect to live about two years longer than Americans. In fact, life expectancy in the U.S. is well below that in Canada, Japan, and every major nation in

Western Europe. On average, we can expect lives a bit shorter than those of Greeks, a bit longer than those of Portuguese. Male life expectancy is lower in the U.S. than it is in Costa Rica.

Still, you can understand why Novak assumed that we were number one. After all, we really are the richest major nation, with real GDP per capita about 20 percent higher than Canada's. And it has been an article of faith in this country that a rising tide lifts all boats. Doesn't our high and rising national wealth translate into a high standard of living—including good medical care—for all Americans?

Well, no. Although America has higher per capita income than other advanced countries, it turns out that that's mainly because our rich are much richer. And here's a radical thought: If the rich get more, that leaves less for everyone else.

That statement—which is simply a matter of arithmetic—is guaranteed to bring accusations of "class warfare." If the accuser gets more specific, he'll probably offer two reasons that it's foolish to make a fuss over the high incomes of a few people at the top of the income distribution. First, he'll tell you that what the elite get may look like a lot of money, but it's still a small share of the total—that is, when all is said and done the rich aren't getting that big a piece of the pie. Second, he'll tell you that trying to do anything to reduce incomes at the top will hurt, not help, people further down the distribution, because attempts to redistribute income damage incentives.

These arguments for lack of concern are plausible. And they were entirely correct, once upon a time—namely, back when we had a middle-class society. But there's a lot less truth to them now.

First, the share of the rich in total income is no longer trivial. These days 1 percent of families receive about 16 percent of total pretax income, and have about 14 percent of after-tax income. That share has roughly doubled over the past thirty years, and is now about as large as the share of the bottom 40 percent of the population. That's a big shift of income to the top; as a matter of pure arithmetic, it must mean that the incomes of less-well-off families grew considerably more slowly than average income. And they did. Adjusting for inflation, average family income—total income divided by the number of families—grew 28 percent from 1979 to 1997. But median family income—the income of a family in the middle of the distribution, a better indicator of how typical American families are doing—grew only 10 percent. And the incomes of the bottom fifth of families actually fell slightly.

Let me belabor this point for a bit. We pride ourselves, with considerable justification, on our record of economic growth. But over the last few decades it's remarkable how little of that growth has trickled down to ordinary families. Median family income has risen only about 0.5 percent per year—and as far as we can tell from somewhat unreliable data, just about all of that increase was due to wives working longer hours, with little or no gain in real wages. Furthermore, numbers about income don't reflect the growing riskiness of life for ordinary workers. In the days when General Motors was known in-house as Generous Motors, many workers felt that they had considerable job security—the company wouldn't fire them except in extremis. Many had contracts that guaranteed health insurance, even if they were laid off; they had pension benefits that did not depend on the stock market. Now mass firings from long-established companies are commonplace; losing your job means losing your insurance; and as millions of people have been learning, a 401(k) plan is no guarantee of a comfortable retirement.

Still, many people will say that while the U.S. economic system may generate a lot of inequality, it also generates much higher incomes than any alternative, so that everyone is better off. That was the moral *BusinessWeek* tried to convey in its recent special issue with "25 Ideas for a Changing World." One of those ideas was "the rich get richer, and that's O.K." High incomes at the top, the conventional wisdom declares, are the result of a free-market system that provides huge incentives for performance. And the system delivers that performance, which means that wealth at the top doesn't come at the expense of the rest of us.

A skeptic might point out that the explosion in executive compensation seems at best loosely related to actual performance. Jack Welch was one of the ten highest-paid executives in the United States in 2000, and you could argue that he earned it. But did Dennis Kozlowski of Tyco, or Gerald Levin of Time Warner, who were also in the top ten? A skeptic might also point out that even during the economic boom of the late 1990s, U.S. productivity growth was no better than it was during the great postwar expansion, which corresponds to the era when America was truly middle-class and CEOs were modestly paid technocrats.

But can we produce any direct evidence about the effects of inequality? We can't rerun our own history and ask what would have happened if the social norms of middle-class America had continued to limit incomes at the top, and if government policy had leaned against rising inequality instead of reinforcing it, which is what actually happened. But we can compare ourselves with other advanced countries. And the results are somewhat surprising.

Many Americans assume that because we are the richest country in the world, with real GDP per capita higher than that of other major advanced countries, Americans must be better off across the board—that it's not just our rich who are richer than their counterparts abroad, but that the typical American family is much better off than the typical family elsewhere, and that even our poor are well-off by foreign standards.

But it's not true. Let me use the example of Sweden, that great conservative bête noire.

A few months ago the conservative cyberpundit Glenn Reynolds made a splash when he pointed out that Sweden's GDP per capita is roughly comparable with that of Mississippi—see, those foolish believers in the welfare state have impoverished themselves! Presumably he assumed that this means that the typical Swede is as poor as the typical resident of Mississippi, and therefore much worse off than the typical American.

But life expectancy in Sweden is about three years higher than that of the U.S. Infant mortality is half the U.S. level, and less than a third the rate in Mississippi. Functional illiteracy is much less common than in the U.S.

How is this possible? One answer is that GDP per capita is in some ways a misleading measure. Swedes take longer vacations than Americans, so they work fewer hours per year. That's a choice, not a failure of economic performance. Real GDP per hours worked is 16 percent lower than in the United States, which makes Swedish productivity about the same as Canada's.

But the main point is that though Sweden may have lower average income than the United States, that's mainly because our rich are so much richer. The median Swedish family has a standard of living roughly comparable with that of the median U.S. family: Wages are if anything higher in Sweden, and a higher tax burden is offset by public provision of health care and generally better public services. And as you move further down the income distribution, Swedish living standards are way ahead of those in the U.S. Swedish families with children that are at the 10th percentile—poorer than 90 percent of the population— have incomes 60 percent higher than their U.S. counterparts. And very few people in Sweden experience the deep poverty that is all too common in the United States. One measure: In 1994 only 6 percent of Swedes lived on less than $11 per day, compared with 14 percent in the U.S.

The moral of this comparison is that even if you think that America's high levels of inequality are the price of our high level of national income, it's not at all clear that this price is worth paying. The reason conservatives engage in bouts of Sweden-bashing is that they want to convince us that there is no trade-off between economic efficiency and equity—that if you try to take from the rich and give to the poor, you actually make everyone worse off. But the comparison between the U.S. and other advanced countries doesn't support this conclusion at all. Yes, we are the richest major nation. But because so much of our national income is concentrated in relatively few hands, large numbers of Americans are worse off economically than their counterparts in other advanced countries.

And we might even offer a challenge from the other side: Inequality in the United States has arguably reached levels where it is counterproductive. That is, you can make a case that our society would be richer if its richest members didn't get quite so much.

I could make this argument on historical grounds. The most impressive economic growth in U.S. history coincided with the middle-class interregnum, the post–World War II generation, when incomes were most evenly distributed. But let's focus on a specific case, the extraordinary pay packages of today's top executives. Are these good for the economy?

Until recently it was almost unchallenged conventional wisdom that, whatever else you might say, the new imperial CEOs had delivered results that dwarfed the expense of their compensation. But now that the stock bubble has burst, it has become increasingly clear that there was a price to those big pay packages, after all. In fact, the price paid by shareholders and society at large may have been many times larger than the amount actually paid to the executives.

It's easy to get boggled by the details of corporate scandal—insider loans, stock options, special-purpose entities, mark-to-market, round-tripping. But there's a simple reason that the details are so complicated. All of these schemes were designed to benefit corporate insiders—to inflate the pay of the CEO and his inner circle. That is, they were all about the "chaos of competitive avarice" that, according to John Kenneth Galbraith, had been ruled out in the corporation of the 1960s. But while all restraint has vanished within the American corporation, the outside world—including stockholders—is still prudish, and open looting by executives is still not acceptable. So the looting has to be camouflaged, taking place through complicated schemes that can be rationalized to outsiders as clever corporate strategies.

Economists who study crime tell us that crime is inefficient—that is, the costs of crime to the economy are much larger than the amount stolen. Crime, and the fear of crime, divert resources away from productive uses: Criminals spend their time stealing rather than producing, and potential victims spend time and money trying to protect their property. Also, the things people do to avoid becoming victims—like avoiding dangerous districts—have a cost even if they succeed in averting an actual crime.

The same holds true of corporate malfeasance, whether or not it actually involves breaking the law. Executives who devote their time to creating innovative ways to divert shareholder money into their own pockets probably aren't running the real business very well (think Enron, WorldCom, Tyco, Global Crossing, Adelphia . . .). Investments chosen because they create the illusion of profitability while insiders cash in their stock options are a waste of scarce resources. And if the supply of funds from lenders and shareholders dries up because of a lack of trust, the economy as a whole suffers. Just ask Indonesia.

The argument for a system in which some people get very rich has always been that the lure of wealth provides powerful incentives. But the question is, incentives to do what? As we learn more about what has actually been going on in corporate America, it's becoming less and less clear whether those incentives have actually made executives work on behalf of the rest of us.

INEQUALITY AND POLITICS

In September the Senate debated a proposed measure that would impose a onetime capital gains tax on Americans who renounce their citizenship in order to avoid paying U.S. taxes. Senator Phil Gramm was not pleased, declaring that the proposal was "right out of Nazi Germany." Pretty strong language, but no stronger than the metaphor Daniel Mitchell of the Heritage Foundation used, in an op-ed article in *The Washington Times,* to describe a bill designed to prevent corporations from rechartering abroad for tax purposes: Mitchell described this legislation as the "Dred Scott tax bill," referring to the infamous 1857 Supreme Court ruling that required free states to return escaped slaves.

Twenty years ago, would a prominent senator have likened those who want wealthy people to pay taxes to Nazis? Would a member of a think tank with close ties to the administration have drawn a parallel between corporate taxation and slavery? I don't think so. The remarks by Gramm and Mitchell, while stronger than usual, were indicators of two huge changes in American politics. One is the growing polarization of our politics—our politicians are less and less inclined to offer even the appearance of moderation. The other is the growing tendency of policy and policy makers to cater to the interests of the wealthy. And I mean the wealthy, not the merely well-off: Only someone with a net worth of at least several million dollars is likely to find it worthwhile to become a tax exile.

You don't need a political scientist to tell you that modern American politics is bitterly polarized. But wasn't it always thus? No, it wasn't. From World War II until the 1970s—the same era during which income inequality was historically low—political partisanship was much more muted than it is today. That's not just a subjective assessment. My

Princeton political science colleagues Nolan McCarty and Howard Rosenthal, together with Keith Poole at the University of Houston, have done a statistical analysis showing that the voting behavior of a congressman is much better predicted by his party affiliation today than it was 25 years ago. In fact, the division between the parties is sharper now than it has been since the 1920s.

What are the parties divided about? The answer is simple: economics. McCarty, Rosenthal, and Poole write that "voting in Congress is highly ideological—one-dimensional left/right, liberal versus conservative." It may sound simplistic to describe Democrats as the party that wants to tax the rich and help the poor, and Republicans as the party that wants to keep taxes and social spending as low as possible. And during the era of middle-class America that would indeed have been simplistic: Politics wasn't defined by economic issues. But that was a different country; as McCarty, Rosenthal, and Poole put it, "If income and wealth are distributed in a fairly equitable way, little is to be gained for politicians to organize politics around nonexistent conflicts." Now the conflicts are real, and our politics is organized around them. In other words, the growing inequality of our incomes probably lies behind the growing divisiveness of our politics.

But the politics of rich and poor hasn't played out the way you might think. Since the incomes of America's wealthy have soared while ordinary families have seen at best small gains, you might have expected politicians to seek votes by proposing to soak the rich. In fact, however, the polarization of politics has occurred because the Republicans have moved to the right, not because the Democrats have moved to the left. And actual economic policy has moved steadily in favor of the wealthy. The major tax cuts of the past 25 years, the Reagan cuts in the 1980s and the recent Bush cuts, were both heavily tilted toward the very well-off. (Despite obfuscations, it remains true that more than half the Bush tax cut will eventually go to the top 1 percent of families.) The major tax increase over that period, the increase in payroll taxes in the 1980s, fell most heavily on working-class families.

The most remarkable example of how politics has shifted in favor of the wealthy—an example that helps us understand why economic policy has reinforced, not countered, the movement toward greater inequality—

is the drive to repeal the estate tax. The estate tax is, overwhelmingly, a tax on the wealthy. In 1999, only the top 2 percent of estates paid any tax at all, and half the estate tax was paid by only 3,300 estates, 0.16 percent of the total, with a minimum value of $5 million and an average value of $17 million. A quarter of the tax was paid by just 467 estates worth more than $20 million. Tales of family farms and businesses broken up to pay the estate tax are basically rural legends; hardly any real examples have been found, despite diligent searching.

You might have thought that a tax that falls on so few people yet yields a significant amount of revenue would be politically popular; you certainly wouldn't expect widespread opposition. Moreover, there has long been an argument that the estate tax promotes democratic values, precisely because it limits the ability of the wealthy to form dynasties. So why has there been a powerful political drive to repeal the estate tax, and why was such a repeal a centerpiece of the Bush tax cut?

There is an economic argument for repealing the estate tax, but it's hard to believe that many people take it seriously. More significant for members of Congress, surely, is the question of who would benefit from repeal: While those who will actually benefit from estate tax repeal are few in number, they have a lot of money and control even more (corporate CEOs can now count on leaving taxable estates behind). That is, they are the sort of people who command the attention of politicians in search of campaign funds.

But it's not just about campaign contributions: Much of the general public has been convinced that the estate tax is a bad thing. If you try talking about the tax to a group of moderately prosperous retirees, you get some interesting reactions. They refer to it as the "death tax"; many of them believe that their estates will face punitive taxation, even though most of them will pay little or nothing; they are convinced that small businesses and family farms bear the brunt of the tax.

These misconceptions don't arise by accident. They have, instead, been deliberately promoted. For example, a Heritage Foundation document titled "Time to Repeal Federal Death Taxes: The Nightmare of the American Dream" emphasizes stories that rarely, if ever, happen in real life: "Small-business owners, particularly minority owners, suffer anxious moments wondering whether the business they hope to hand down to their children will be destroyed by the death tax bill. . . . Women whose children are grown struggle to find ways to reenter the work force without upsetting the family's estate tax avoidance plan." And who finances the Heritage Foundation? Why, foundations created by wealthy families, of course.

The point is that it is no accident that strongly conservative views, views that militate against taxes on the rich, have spread even as the rich get richer compared with the rest of us: In addition to directly buying influence, money can be used to shape public perceptions. The liberal group People for the American Way's report on how conservative foundations have deployed vast sums to support think tanks, friendly media, and other institutions that promote right-wing causes is titled "Buying a Movement."

Not to put too fine a point on it: As the rich get richer, they can buy a lot of things besides goods and services. Money buys political influence; used cleverly, it also buys intellectual influence. A result is that growing income disparities in the United States, far from leading to demands to soak the rich, have been accompanied by a growing movement to let them keep more of their earnings and to pass their wealth on to their children.

This obviously raises the possibility of a self-reinforcing process. As the gap between the rich and the rest of the population grows, economic policy increasingly caters to the interests of the elite, while public services for the population at large—above all, public education—are starved of resources. As policy increasingly favors the interests of the rich and neglects the interests of the general population, income disparities grow even wider.

PLUTOCRACY?

In 1924, the mansions of Long Island's North Shore were still in their full glory, as was the political power of the class that owned them. When Governor Al Smith of New York proposed building a system of parks on Long Island, the mansion owners were bitterly opposed. One baron— Horace Havemeyer, the "sultan of sugar"—warned that North Shore towns would be "overrun with rabble from the city." "Rabble?" Smith said. "That's me you're talking about." In the end New Yorkers got their parks, but it was close: The interests of a few hundred wealthy families nearly prevailed over those of New York City's middle class.

America in the 1920s wasn't a feudal society. But it was a nation in which vast privilege—often inherited privilege—stood in contrast to vast misery. It was also a nation in which the government, more often than not, served the interests of the privileged and ignored the aspirations of ordinary people.

Those days are past—or are they? Income inequality in America has now returned to the levels of the 1920s. Inherited wealth doesn't yet play a big part in our society, but given time—and the repeal of the estate tax—we will grow ourselves a hereditary elite just as set apart from the concerns of ordinary Americans as old Horace Havemeyer. And the new elite, like the old, will have enormous political power.

Kevin Phillips concludes his book *Wealth and Democracy* with a grim warning. "Either democracy must be renewed, with politics brought back to life, or wealth is likely to cement a new and less democratic regime—plutocracy by some other name." It's a pretty extreme line, but we live in extreme times. Even if the forms of democracy remain, they may become meaningless. It's all too easy to see how we may become a country in which the big rewards are reserved for people with the right connections; in which ordinary people see little hope of advancement; in which political involvement seems pointless, because in the end the interests of the elite always get served.

Am I being too pessimistic? Even my liberal friends tell me not to worry, that our system has great resilience, that the center will hold. I hope they're right, but they may be looking in the rearview mirror. Our optimism about America, our belief that in the end our nation always finds its way, comes from the past—a past in which we were a middle-class society. But that was another country.

Presented in contrast to Paul Krugman's article a week earlier, this Michael Lewis piece in *The New York Times Magazine* notes that many companies of the boom were admirably egalitarian, sharing newfound riches with employees. In addition, staid giant companies were forced to become more efficient to compete with these upstarts. Scandal? In Lewis's view, it's an inevitable by-product of any boom.

Michael Lewis

In Defense of the Boom

WALL STREET DIDN'T DO IT

A FEW WEEKS AGO, on *Moneyline,* a guest who didn't fully understand just how much times have changed invoked some corporation's ability to beat Wall Street's forecasts for its quarterly earnings. Before you could say "market manipulation," the program's host, Lou Dobbs, said, "Do you really think anybody's paying attention to that silly expectation stuff anymore?" He dismissed forecasts as "the game of the late '90s." And he had a point. For many years, Wall Street analysts have lowballed their earnings estimates so that their corporate customers could announce to the press that they had "beaten" those estimates. This particular game was exposed beginning in the late 1990s by fledgling web sites, which routinely published more accurate earnings forecasts than the Wall Street pros. By the middle of 1998 the stock market began to trade off the Web estimates rather than the Street estimates—

which tells you how fully understood this quarterly forecast game had become even before the boom reached its turn-of-the-century heights.

But so long as the stock market rose, Lou Dobbs was happy to listen to Wall Street and corporate big shots blather on about how they had beaten their earnings forecasts. He didn't scorn them; like every other serious reporter, he treated them as useful informants (when he wasn't distracted by his bid to make his internet fortune in a doomed start-up called Space.com). And yet now, somehow, Lou Dobbs, like every other serious reporter, knows enough to raise his eyebrows and harshen his tone when anyone mentions earnings estimates. As wide-eyed as he was three years ago, he is narrow-eyed now. You can't put one over on Lou Dobbs!

And that, in a way, is the point. If you can't put one over on Lou Dobbs, whom can you put one over on?

The markets, having tasted skepticism, are beginning to overdose. The bust likes to think of itself as a radical departure from the boom, but it has in common with it one big thing: a mob mentality. When the markets were rising and everyone was getting rich, it was rare to hear a word against the system—or the people making lots of money from it. Now that the markets are falling and everyone is feeling poor, or, at any rate, less rich, it is rare to hear a word on behalf of either the system or the rich. The same herd instinct that fueled the boom fuels the bust. And the bust has created market distortions as bizarre—and maybe more harmful—as anything associated with the boom.

The recent wave of outrage about Wall Street's behavior began, you may recall, when New York State Attorney General Eliot Spitzer deployed an obscure state law to shoehorn out of Merrill Lynch every e-mail message Merrill employees had ever sent relating to the internet boom. It was easy to see why Spitzer chose Merrill Lynch as his target. He has political ambitions (he wants to be governor of New York, at least), and unlike Goldman Sachs or Morgan Stanley or one of the other big investment banks more central to the internet bubble, Merrill actually serviced lots of small customers. It's a firm that voters can relate to.

What I didn't understand was Spitzer's hunger for Merrill's old e-mail. If the New York attorney general wanted to prove that the firm's analysts had been wildly optimistic about the internet, and that their optimism helped the firm's investment bankers attract internet business, and that there was, therefore, a deep conflict of interest on Wall Street, all he needed was an internet search engine.

If you go back and read the public record, you can see clearly what people on Wall Street did between April 1995, when Netscape invented the internet Initial Public Offering, or IPO, and the spring of 2000, when internet stocks crashed. The story was never hidden, because Wall Street never tried to hide it. Indeed, you can pinpoint the very moment when Merrill Lynch signed on to the boom, and in what spirit they joined the party.

Until late in 1998, which was three years or so into the boom, Merrill and its brokers actually fought a rearguard action against internet stocks. The internet looked as if it would all but eliminate the commissions investors paid to buy and sell stocks and gut the already weakened core business of Merrill Lynch. The head of Merrill's stockbrokers, John Steffens, actually said that the internet was "a serious threat to Americans' financial lives." Partly as a result of this self-serving truculence, Merrill had lagged badly behind Goldman Sachs and Morgan Stanley and the other up-market firms in its ability to rake in fees from internet stock offerings. At the same time, Merrill Lynch was also—and this is the key point—becoming ridiculous to the nearly five million account holders who kept their money at Merrill Lynch. You couldn't be running ads on TV saying you were "bullish on America" and at the same time be telling your customers they should be ignoring or dumping the hottest sector the U.S. stock market had ever seen.

On December 16, 1998, the contradiction finally became too much for Merrill Lynch to bear. On that day, the share price of Amazon.com touched $242. Merrill Lynch's internet analyst, Jonathan Cohen, announced that the shares were worth at best $50 and that it was time to sell. Across town, Henry Blodget, a 32-year-old freelance-magazine-writer-turned-internet-analyst for an obscure, second-tier firm called CIBC Oppenheimer, was saying that Amazon's stock would reach $400 a share. Sure enough, Amazon promptly rose to a split-adjusted high of $678. Cohen was wrong, and Blodget was right, and Merrill Lynch was the laughingstock of the market. And so Merrill fired Cohen, hired Blodget, and, in effect, bought into Amazon.com at four hundred bucks a share.

It occurred to no one at the time that Merrill Lynch was conspiring to drive up internet stocks. They were simply giving their brokerage customers what they wanted. Internet stocks had been rising too fast for too long for Merrill Lynch to be saying anything other than that internet stocks would continue to rise. Merrill's investment bankers, theretofore incidental victims of their internet analyst's bearish views, became incidental beneficiaries of the firm's new bullishness. They were quite open about this. They were happy to tell reporters, on the record, precisely what Eliot Spitzer would later claim he had uncovered as he pored over old e-mail. For instance, on April 13, 1999, Scott Ryles, the head of Merrill's technology banking division, explained his new success to Bloomberg News. "It's difficult to take companies public when your analyst has a less-than-constructive view on some of the biggest companies out there," Ryles said. Having Blodget on board was great, he said, because Blodget "has been unabashedly bullish and has been proved right. . . . It's clear the internet stocks have been some of the best-performing stocks, and retail investors as well as institutional investors want that product."

The old e-mail was unnecessary to expose the absence of fire walls between bankers and analysts on Wall Street. Their overlapping interests were hidden in plain sight. Spitzer's investigation did not expose a clearer picture of the inner workings of Wall Street during the boom. What it did give investors, who had no problem at all with banker-analyst conflicts of interest as stocks soared, were villains to blame after stocks tanked. And Spitzer also used this e-mail to suggest to an angry investing public that he had discovered some previously unknown dark truth: *Henry Blodget hadn't believed a word he had said.*

But to anyone who had followed Henry Blodget in real time, this was obviously not quite right. Go back and read what Blodget said and when he said it. From the start of his astonishing Wall Street career, he had a very specific conviction about the future of the internet. He thought that internet companies would displace their real-world counterparts. He saw that businesses with high fixed costs were at extreme peril. He looked at Barnes & Noble, for instance, and saw that it would go out of business if an online competitor stole even 20 percent of its revenues.

Even back when he first expressed these views, in early 1997, they weren't earth-shatteringly original. All sorts of respectable people thought the internet would transform American commerce much faster than it ultimately did. And in the context of this sensational belief, Blodget behaved almost prudently. Many times he declined opportunities to pump stocks even higher than they were. Many times he cautioned investors against being too optimistic about e-commerce revenue forecasts. Many times he acknowledged that what he did for a living was largely guesswork. Around the time of his name-making, correct prediction that Amazon's stock would rise to $400 a share, a radio interviewer asked him what he thought of Merrill Lynch's more pessimistic view. "We are all looking into the future," he said. "We all have the same information, and we're just making different conclusions about what the future will hold." But what investor wanted to hear any of this? By the time Henry Blodget went to work for Merrill Lynch, the market was actually running ahead of Henry Blodget. By the end of the boom, he had gone from leading the market to trying to keep pace with it.

The most embarrassing thing about Henry Blodget was not that he was lying but that he was speaking his mind. He actually *believed* Amazon.com was a good long-term buy at $400 a share. He actually *believed* the internet would be an engine for corporate profits.

No matter. The supply of scandal on Wall Street always rises to meet the demand, and Spitzer found what he was looking for. From the tens of thousands of Merrill Lynch e-mail messages, he culled one of Henry Blodget's written toward the end of 2000, which, when released to the media, did the job he—Spitzer—needed it to do. In it Blodget responds to e-mail from a Merrill Lynch banker who wanted him to express greater optimism about some internet company. He writes:

> The more I read of these, the less willing I am to cut companies any slack, regardless of the predictable temper tantrums, threats and/or relationship damage that are likely to follow. If there is no new e-mail forthcoming from [Merrill manage-

ment] on how the instructions below should be applied to sensitive banking clients/situations, we are going to just start calling the stocks . . . like we see them, no matter what the ancillary business consequences are.

Out of context, during a crash, that sounds pretty damning. It sounds as if Henry Blodget never called a stock as he saw it. But in context, at the end of a boom that has made Henry Blodget a little god, who knows? It's hardly uncommon on Wall Street for analysts to play head games with their firms' bankers and brokers. To me, knowing Blodget's record, it sounds as if the young analyst is simply flexing his muscles. He's saying: If you mess with my turf, I'll mess with yours. It's hard to say. And that's the point: Motives in any company, let alone a Wall Street one, are far too messy to be honestly discerned from a handful of carefully selected e-mail messages. The notion that they're more revealing of Blodget's true feelings than the public record is risible.

The Spitzer investigation is a curious exercise. It doesn't clarify history so much as distort it. It portrays the financial losses of countless madly greedy, very knowledgeable speculators as a kind of theft by a handful of people who acted in bad faith. Just enough of the texture of the financial 1990s has been (conveniently) forgotten to allow for this new, bizarre interpretation of the boom. At any rate, to judge from both the newspapers and the court filings, a lot of people have come to believe this story, and it's not hard to see why. It pays. It pays Eliot Spitzer, who gets credit for cleaning up Wall Street—which neither he nor anyone else will ever do. (Just wait till the next boom.) It pays investors who lost money, along with their ambulance-chasing attorneys, who now have fresh ammo in their lawsuits against Merrill Lynch. And, oddly enough, it pays Merrill Lynch. By forcing Merrill Lynch to agree that its advice was corrupt, Eliot Spitzer helped the firm avoid saying something much more damning and much more true: that its advice on the direction of stock prices is useless. Always. By leading the firm to the conclusion that it had misled the American investor, Spitzer helped it to avoid the much more embarrassing conclusion that the American investor had misled Merrill Lynch.

The whole of the muckraking machinery is designed to facilitate this simple inversion: The culprits of the 1990s, reckless speculators, are being recast as the victims. What the various investigations appear to be doing is cleaning up the markets and making it safe for sober investors. What they are actually doing is warping the immediate past and preserving investors' dignity along with their capacity to behave madly with their money the next time the opportunity presents itself. The rewriters of the boom are able to do this as well as they have because, for both legal and political reasons, all sorts of people who might resist the distortions are discouraged from speaking out. Certainly no one on Wall Street can defend himself without the risk of incurring legal bills far greater than he already has. Certainly, no public figure of any sort is going to stand up and take the position that the rich guys who have gotten themselves exposed and pawed over by the New York attorney general should be left alone. And so the attorney general, in effect, has the stage to himself.

At this very moment, Merrill Lynch is behaving just as it behaved during the boom: scrambling to get out in front of the mob. It has coughed up the $100 million it was fined by Eliot Spitzer, has run huge ads apologizing to American investors for its behavior, has publicly humiliated Henry Blodget, and has said it will never again promote stocks it doesn't truly believe in. It's a pity Merrill didn't try a bit harder to defend itself. There is a lot to say, if not exactly on behalf of Wall Street, then at least on behalf of the recent boom Wall Street helped to fuel.

SILICON VALLEY WAS NOT A BUBBLE

The first good thing to say about the boom is what it did to the value system of the ordinary business schlep. It turned him from a person who complained about the company he worked for to a person who wondered, albeit for one brief moment, if maybe he didn't have his own better idea of how to do things. If he did, he went to Silicon Valley. What distinguished Silicon Valley from everyplace else on the planet was (a) it had lots of start-up capital and (b) the people who controlled that capital understood that, if you wanted to win big, you had to be willing to fail. Failure on Wall Street has always been construed as a crime. Failure in the valley was more honestly and bravely understood as the first cousin of success.

It's odd that their quest for justice has led the various regulators and prosecutors to big Wall Street firms. The striking fact about the boom, as it happened, was the insignificance of big Wall Street firms. The big Wall Street firms would never have had the nerve. The people who drove the stock market in the 1990s did not work on Wall Street. They worked as venture capitalists; they created companies. If in 1998 you told a venture capitalist that Henry Blodget—or any Wall Street analyst—would ultimately be held responsible for anything, he would have wondered what you had been smoking. You might as well blame the waiter for the size of the restaurant: The Wall Street people were the *help*. It might have been one of the most delightful aspects of the boom—the way it inverted the old financial status structure. All sorts of unlikely characters—seemingly half the population of India, for instance—now had a shot at fame and fortune.

Enron. WorldCom. Global Crossing. Adelphia Communications. Tyco. Bad things happened inside these places, no doubt about it, but these places were afterthoughts: The boom could have just as easily happened without them. The emblematic character of the boom was not Kenneth Lay or Bernie Ebbers or Dennis Kozlowski. The emblematic character was Jeff Bezos. Bezos was the original big-time internet entrepreneur. He famously quit his job on Wall Street, threw his chattels in his car, and drove across the country to Seattle, with a view to transforming the book business. He thought it would take him ten years. It took him three, in large part because a Silicon Valley venture capitalist named John Doerr made sure Bezos had the capital to do it.

Three years ago Bezos was a hero and Doerr was the most vocal, eloquent champion of the internet entrepreneur. By 1999 people in Silicon Valley actually wore campaign buttons that said "Gore and Doerr in 2004." Today Doerr has vanished from the public stage—"could not be reached for comment," they usually write, of a man who was just a few years ago impossible not to reach. Bezos has become something like an antihero, one of those internet hypesters who was given a lot more capital than he deserved to create an internet business that still—a full eight years later—has made only very small profits.

Many investors are trying to forget that they ever sank money into Amazon, and why. Various editors are trying to forget that they made Bezos their Person of the Year or their Most Influential Man of the internet. Anyone on Wall Street who plugged Amazon.com is now a defendant, alongside Bezos and Doerr, in lawsuits brought by small shareholders who lost money on Amazon stock. There's now even a stage play, off Broadway, called *21 Dog Years,* in which a former Amazon employee named Mike Daisey takes full advantage of other people's willingness to believe the stupidest clichés about the internet boom. "Daisey fears that he lost his soul when he was blinded by talk of stock options and strike prices and started to believe the myth of uncountable riches for all as soon as the options mature," reads an ad for the show. "He wonders if he, too, stopped being about something real." (It is convenient how people seem to discover the need to be "about something real" only after the money dries up.)

There are two things to say about all of this. More than two things, probably, but I'll control myself. The first is: Look what Jeff Bezos did. That a Princeton graduate with a bright future on Wall Street would quit his lucrative, prestigious, but socially pointless job to create a company—well, that was a kind of miracle. That his company would actually realize its original ambition: How could that happen? But it did. Nearly $2.5 billion worth of books a year are now sold over the internet, and some huge percentage of those are sold by Amazon. And even skeptics understand that those numbers are merely the beginning of a powerful trend. But who in 1996 had ever heard of Amazon.com? It was a silly name on a plaque of a small house in a bad neighborhood in Seattle. The very best a reasonable person might have hoped for in 1996 was that the oddly named Amazon.com would be acquired by Barnes & Noble and then ruined, to prevent Barnes & Noble from having to compete with it. Instead Amazon.com has lowered book prices, made it far easier for readers to buy books, and thus increased the chances that an author will make a living. Is that a bad thing? (Nobody suggests that Barnes & Noble is unsound. But whose future would you rather have, Barnes & Noble's or Amazon.com's? Whose name?)

The other thing to say about the excessive ambition of Amazon.com is: Was it so completely unreasonable for Jeff Bezos—or, for that matter, any other internet entrepreneur—to behave as he did? It's easy to say so in retrospect but, really, at the time, what should he have done differently? He expanded as fast as he could because (a) the market threw capital at him and (b) he believed, rightly, that if he didn't he would be swallowed up by the competition. The job of the entrepreneur isn't to act prudently, to err on the side of caution. It's to err on the side of reckless ambition. It is to take the risk that the market allows him to take. What distinguishes a robust market economy like ours from a less robust one like, say, France's, is that it encourages energetic, ambitious people to take a flier—and that they respond to that encouragement. It encourages nerve, and that is a beautiful thing. As the business writer George Anders puts it, "The personality that allows you to be Jeff Bezos in the first place does not have a shutoff valve." If it did, Amazon.com wouldn't exist.

On June 3, 2002, Merrill Lynch published its first new, improved research report about the internet. It was, as you might expect, designed to debunk all of the stuff Merrill Lynch was saying about the internet two years before. In addition to the usual disclaimers, this one came with a little box on the cover that said, "Investors should assume that Merrill Lynch is seeking or will seek investment banking or other business relationships with the companies in this report." The report, which promised to poke holes "in various internet myths," focused on the academic work of Dr. Andrew Odlyzko, formerly of AT&T Labs Research and currently the director of the Digital Technology Center at the University of Minnesota. It quoted, derisively, both *BusinessWeek* and the former chairman of the Federal Communications Commission, Reed Hundt, for saying that (in *BusinessWeek*'s words) "internet traffic is doubling every three months." The problem with all that was said and written about the internet, according to Dr. Odlyzko, was that "there wasn't any hard data behind it." The doubling of traffic every three months? "In every single instance that I tried to investigate, I always ended up with statements by people from WorldCom's UUNet unit. . . . I did not hear anybody else make authoritative statements that their traffic was growing at this rate. My management at AT&T would often talk about such growth rates, but they were always careful to say internet traffic, not our internet traffic."

The point was: All sorts of seemingly reliable sources were assuming that internet traffic was growing at a rate that amounted to 1,000 percent or more a year, when it was actually growing at somewhere between 70 and 150 percent a year. (It still is.) This is the assumption that underpinned Amazon's mad expansion, and, for that matter, the entire internet boom. Many internet businesses that failed would certainly have succeeded if more customers were online. Internet businesses that succeeded would have done better, more quickly. If internet usage had grown the way people were saying it was growing back in 1996, all that unused pipe laid by Global Crossing and WorldCom would look inadequate to meet the demand. If that many more people had come online that quickly, Amazon might indeed have put Barnes & Noble out of business in those first few years.

And so Dr. Odlyzko makes an interesting point. But in doing it he makes another, even more interesting one, albeit without meaning to, that helps to explain the exuberance of the late 1990s. That feeling of fantastic possibility everyone seemed to have by early 1997 wasn't just manufactured out of whole cloth. Between December 1994 and December 1996 internet traffic had grown at an unthinkably rapid rate. "During those two years," says Dr. Odlyzko, "the annual growth rate was about 1,000 percent per year, doubling about every 100 days. . . . That really was a period of manic growth." It wasn't until the end of 1997 that traffic-growth rates began to slow, and no one noticed.

In short, the financial climate the manic adoption of the internet had given rise to persisted for several years after the manic growth slowed. In retrospect, this is hardly surprising, as by 1997 all manner of social and financial interests had aligned themselves with the growth rates of the previous two years. And, really, what happened technologically in this country between 1994 and 1996 was a kind of miracle. At the time who could honestly foresee what was going to happen next? Everyone was guessing; and if even Alan Greenspan couldn't exactly figure out what was going on, you and I can be forgiven our lack of prescience. It wasn't a question of whether this technology was going to transform many aspects of American business. It was only a question of how quickly it was going to do it.

A year or so ago a reporter who covers Silicon Valley for *The Wall Street Journal* sat in on a new technology company's conference call. Back when success was fashionable, they used to do this a lot, to get the feel of the thing, to write a "color" piece that served as a kind of invitation to investors interested in the IPO. *The Journal*'s reporter had given the impression to the company's founders that she was sincerely interested in the company, but only on the condition that one of its investors, Jim Clark, the founder of Silicon Graphics, Netscape, and Healtheon/WebMD, join the discussion. (Disclosure: My book *The New New Thing* was about Clark.) The reporter was shrewd. Had she called Clark directly, he would have no doubt avoided her. Like everyone else in Silicon Valley, Clark seems to have figured out that the media were happy to hold everyone but themselves accountable for the internet frenzy, and so the best thing to do in these dark times is to hide in some well-stocked cellar. And sure enough, the minute Clark came on the line, *The Journal* reporter turned the conversation from the matter at hand into a grilling about Clark's behavior during the 1990s.

Of course, this very same journalist was, just a few years ago, a great fan of internet companies. Like every other newspaper, *The Journal* was once interested mainly in fantastic success and added its share of fuel to the internet boom. Now, like every other newspaper, *The Journal* is interested mainly in failure. Failure, even in Silicon Valley, is suddenly a form of corruption. And that's a pity. Because the other, earlier attitude actually produced some real, measurable returns.

THROWING OUT THE BOOM
WITH THE BATHWATER

If your measure of social progress is corporate profits, it is easy to take a dim view of the boom. It is more difficult to do so if you step back a bit and survey the bigger economic picture.

An obvious point about stock market downturns always seems to get lost right after one of them occurs. Stock market losses are not losses to society. They are transfers from one person to another. For instance, at the end of 1999, I sank a bunch of money into an internet company called Exodus Communications. I was a greedy fool to have done it, but I had been to a Merrill Lynch conference (them again!) that featured Exodus Communications, and the story Henry Blodget and a few other people told was so good that I figured that even if Exodus Communications didn't wind up being a big success, enough people would believe in the thing to drive the stock price even higher and allow me to get out with a quick profit. Everyone else was getting rich without working; why not me? I should have sensed that the moment I finally decided internet stocks were a buy is precisely when they became a sell. Instead, I jumped into Exodus Communications at $160 a share and watched it run up a few points—and then collapse.

What happened to my money? It didn't simply vanish. It was pocketed by the person who sold me the shares. The suspects, in order of likelihood: (a) some Exodus employee; (b) a well-connected mutual fund that got in early at the IPO price; or (c) a day trader who bought it at $150.

About the trillions that have been shaved off the stock market in the past two and a half years, the more general question is: From whom did it come and to whom did it go? A coming book, *In the Company of Owners,* written by the sociologist Joseph Blasi and the economist Douglas Kruse with the *BusinessWeek* reporter Aaron Bernstein, ingeniously answers this second question. The professors combed through the record of stock-option sales by ordinary employees of the one hundred biggest New Economy–type companies. And they found that, while the executives of these companies made off with great wads of cash, the ordinary employees, as a group, did far better. Through the boom, investors forked over $78 billion to the regular employees of one hundred start-ups. The grunts of the bankrupt Excite@Home, for instance, made off with an estimated $660 million before their company went under.

The astonishing thing, to the authors, was the egalitarian structure of boom companies. "No other industry," they write, "has ever attempted, much less achieved, the depth, breadth and extent of wealth-sharing found among these firms." Of course, the recriminations of the bust imply that the "wealth-sharing" was mainly a giant con game. But to anyone who thinks about it for even a moment, this obviously was not true. The people who worked for these companies, in the main, believed in what they were doing and proved it by holding on to many outstanding shares until the bitter end. Employees of Exodus Communications held some huge numbers of Exodus Communications shares at its moment of doom.

Back in 1984, an economist named Martin Weitzman wrote what should have been a world-changing book called *The Share Economy.* In it he described, as a kind of economic utopia, what would come to be the innovative corporate structure of the 1990s. Weitzman pointed out that recessions may be inevitable, but that their most tragic consequence, unemployment, doesn't have to be. The layoffs that came with recessions occurred because wages tended to be "sticky," i.e., companies couldn't persuade their workers to accept lower wages in bad times. Unable to trim payrolls, companies instead laid off workers.

In bad times, in effect, labor overpriced its services. The solution Weitzman proposed was breathtakingly simple: Make some part of what workers are paid a function of the company's fortunes. Give them stock instead of cash. In good times the stock would have more value and be the equivalent of a raise. In bad times the stock would lose value and be the equivalent of a pay cut.

For more than a decade Weitzman's idea was hailed as brilliant by his profession and went ignored by the wider world. Then, in spectacular fashion, it took hold. Suddenly a more rational structure—in which workers had a stake in their enterprise—gained popular acceptance. And now, just as suddenly, it is thought to be discredited. Why?

I don't imagine that stock market trauma is ever, in and of itself, a good thing for an economy. But this most recent one was not nearly so bad, economically or even morally, as advertised. The most forward-looking companies in America experimented with a corporate structure based on worker ownership. It made a lot more sense than the old-fashioned corporate structure. People like me who played craps with some hot stock received an expensive lesson about playing craps in the stock market. Our punishment was swift and just. It was the rewards of the boom that seemed, in retrospect, wacky and arbitrary.

But were they? Compare the boom, as many amateur historians now seem to want to do, to the early-seventeenth-century tulip craze in Holland. If speculators drive up the price of tulip bulbs to ridiculous heights, a result is a lot of rotting tulip bulbs. But if speculators drive up the price of tech stocks to ridiculous heights, a result is vast numbers of young people with technical training and a lust for entrepreneurship, a higher social status for the entrepreneur, and, uncoincidentally, many interesting business ideas that are at the moment ahead of their time but one day may well be right on it. A result is also, in this case, hundreds of thousands of miles of surplus optical fiber, which is a bit wasteful—we don't need it yet—but not a total waste: We will need it one day soon. Another result, finally, is a lot of formerly sleepy big companies that had the living hell scared out of them by upstarts—and scrambled to make themselves more efficient. Say what you will about the boom: It kept people on their toes.

The massive transfer of greenbacks into the engineering department of American society had some useful side effects. Or, if you want to argue that it hasn't, you have some explaining to do. You need to explain, for instance, the continuing rapid growth of a great many of the companies created during the boom. "From the end of 1999 to the end of 2001," write the authors of *In the Company of Owners,* employment in the top one hundred boom-era companies climbed 26 percent. That's 177,000 jobs. These companies have real customers and real sales, which have continued to grow after the high-tech bust and the demise of the dot-coms. As of July 2002, just eight of the one hundred have failed. Only three more beyond these experienced falling revenues. According to the authors, the rest are growing and have accounted for an increase of $59 billion in combined sales in the past three full years.

And what is to be made of the robust productivity numbers that began to roll in 1995 and continue to roll in to this day? "Productivity," which is the measure of output per worker hour, is by far the best measure of the health of the economy. It is the closest that economic statistics come to capturing the wealth of the nation. A coming paper written by Professor William Nordhaus of Yale, to be published by the Brookings Institution, shows that, beginning in 1995, there was a mysterious surge in worker productivity. Mysterious because ultimately no one can say precisely where it or any other surge in productivity comes from, or why. But ultimately, Nordhaus would argue, "it comes from technological change. People find better ways to do the same things."

What were the late 1990s all about if not about using new tools to find new, better ways to do the same things? Indeed one way of viewing this entire financial period is as an attempt by the market to pay people for innovation rather than for profits, on the assumption that innovation, in the long run, would lead inevitably to greater profits.

The disjuncture between corporate profits and economic productivity suggests a couple of intriguing questions. The first is: Are corporate profits overrated? Not long ago Professor Nordhaus (who is, I should say, more of a New Economy agnostic than an apologist) asked a similar question: Do industries with high rates of productivity growth also enjoy high rates of growth in corporate profits? No. Just the opposite. That is, the industries of the future, the fast-growing ones, the ones in which people are most rapidly becoming more productive, are among the least profitable. American economic life tends always to conform to the interests of investors, but that doesn't mean that it always should. The internet-telecom boom is one of many examples of an extremely useful technology bursting upon the scene that failed to make corporate profits. There are huge, immeasurable social and economic benefits to improving the speed and availability of information; and yet companies have had, to put it mildly, some trouble making money by speeding up information or making it more widely available.

But the same charge might be made against a lot of other new technologies, starting with, say, the airplane. Warren Buffett, who got himself badly singed by US Airways stock, is fond of introducing air travel as an example of a technology that has regularly failed to make investors a penny. But what's bad for Warren Buffett isn't bad for America. We're not better off economically without air travel. Investors are simply better off steering clear of companies that sell it. The sad truth, for investors, seems to be that most of the benefits of new technologies are passed right through to consumers free of charge. (Microsoft, thanks to its monopoly powers, is the main exception.)

For this reason, sane, cautious investors like Warren Buffett make a point of avoiding high-technology investments. For this reason, too, a sane, rational stock market channels less than the socially optimal amounts of capital into innovation. Good new technologies are a bit like good new roads: Their social benefits far exceed what any one person or company can get paid for creating them. Even the laissez-faire wing of the economics professions has long agreed that government might profitably subsidize innovation by, for instance, financing university engineering departments. Government has obviously done this, albeit in a haphazard fashion. Still, there remains a huge gap between the optimum investment in technical progress and the amount we usually invest to achieve it. In this respect, the late 1990s were an exception.

That suggests another interesting question. Not: Were the late 1990s a great disaster for the U.S. economy? But: As a social policy, might we try to re-create the late 1990s?

THE OLD OLD THING IS BACK

A few months ago there was a vivid illustration of the price we pay, not for the boom, but for the irrational reaction against it. It had to do with a money manager named Bill Gross. For the past thirty years Gross has run a very conservative bond fund in southern California called Pimco; more recently he has also written a monthly online investment column. The column is an outlet for Gross's literary ambition. His articles are nicely written and fun to read. They were also generally ignored, until recently. That changed when (a) Pimco, the closest place in the financial markets to that space beneath your mattress, swelled from $230 billion in assets to $301 billion and replaced Fidelity's Magellan Fund as the world's biggest mutual fund, and (b) Gross decided he wanted to write about the integrity of American commerce.

Casting about for material for his March column, his eye fell upon an item in the "Credit Markets" column buried in the back of Section 3 of *The Wall Street Journal*. A woman at GE Capital was quoted saying that GE had decided to sell $11 billion in bonds because "absolute yield levels are at historic lows . . . so we think now is the right time to be doing an offering like this." That struck Gross as an outrageous lie.

Now at this point in the story any ordinary person might wonder, "He got upset by *that*?" Yes, he did. "Historic lows?" Gross thundered in his column. Then he proceeded to talk bond talk. "Maybe three months and one hundred basis points ago, but not now, I'm afraid." He then went on to explain to his readers what GE was actually doing: shoring up its balance sheet on the sly. During the boom GE had taken advantage of low short-term interest rates and investor lassitude to borrow a lot of money short-term and less money long-term. It was like the owner of a house who had opted for the 30-day floating-rate instead of the 30-year fixed-rate mortgage: It was exposed to rising interest rates. At any moment, investors might change their minds about the company and cease to lend it money; if they weren't going to do it on their own, Gross was going to help them. "GE Capital," wrote Gross, "has been allowed to accumulate $50 billion of unbacked commercial paper"—short-term loans—"because of the lack of market discipline. By issuing $11 billion in debt, GE was sensing its vulnerability." Gross concluded by charging GE with dishonesty and saying that "Pimco will own no GE commercial paper in the foreseeable future."

A few hours after Gross hit "send" and posted his column, GE's stock began what would be a quick 10 percent drop, GE's financial officers were on the phone to Gross making hysterical sounds, and reporters on GE-owned CNBC were accusing Gross of talking down GE bonds so that he might snap them up cheaply for himself. By the time Gross finished explaining himself in late April, GE had lost a quarter of its market value, and the company was holding hastily thrown together conference calls to reassure investors. In the end, GE announced that it would restructure its operations. Gross had written his thousand words or so to slake his literary vanity and chosen, pretty much arbitrarily, GE for his material. He himself could not quite believe how much trouble he was able to cause. "My point was a general one about corporate honesty," he says, more than a little sheepishly, "and I wound up hitting GE. And I really didn't give a darn about GE."

It's hard not to take pleasure in the misfortune of others, especially when those others are rich and powerful. Who does not squeal with delight when he sees yet another article about Jack Welch's divorce? But still: This is absurd. The country's biggest company, sensing its balance sheet is out of whack, goes and tries to do something about it and, for its troubles, gets swatted around by a bond guy in need of material for his column.

At any rate, when a bond guy can terrorize GE, it isn't GE who suffers. Not really. Raise the cost of capital to GE, and GE can live with it. GE doesn't like it, but GE can live with it. The person who really suffers from terror in the financial markets is the person who needs capital and who is on the brink of not getting it. The capital markets are a game of crack the whip: The gentle curve experienced by the big guy at the front is felt by the little guy in the rear as a back-snapping hairpin turn. When GE can be terrorized by a single mutual fund is when the venture capitalists of Silicon Valley start giving back the $100 billion of capital to its original owners, rather than invest it in start-ups.

That's the odd thing about the present moment: It is widely understood as a populist uprising against business elites. It's closer to an elitist uprising against popular capitalism. It's a backlash against the excessive opportunity afforded the masses. (No more free capital!)

The big issue in capitalism is who gets capital, and on what terms. And when the little guy does not get capital, the big guy usually benefits. Look around. Who is winning the bust? The old guard. Corporate authority of the ancient, hoary kind, bond traders, leveraged-buyout firms, regulated utilities. There's no more talk of the need to break up Microsoft. Instead there's new talk about letting AT&T get back together again. Even the big Wall Street firms, beleaguered as they might seem, have probably actually improved their positions relative to online brokers.

THE VIRTUES OF VICE

There's plenty to criticize about American financial life, but the problems are less with rule-breaking than with the game itself. Even in the most fastidious of times it is boorishly single-minded. It elevates the desire to make money over other, nobler desires. It's more than a little nuts for a man who has a billion dollars to devote his life to making another billion, but that's what some of our most exalted citizens do, over and over again. That's who we are; that's how we seem to like to spend our time. Americans are incapable of hating the rich; certainly they will always prefer them to the poor. The boom and everything that went with it—the hype, the hope, the mad scramble for a piece of the action, the ever escalating definition of "rich," the grotesque ratcheting up of executive pay—is much closer to our hearts than the bust and everything that goes with it. People who view us from a distance understand this. That's why when they want to attack us, they blow up the World Trade Center and not the Securities and Exchange Commission. Why don't we understand this about ourselves?

It is deplorable that some executives fiddled their books and stole from their companies. But their behavior was, in the grand scheme of things, trivial. Less than trivial: expected. A boom without crooks is like a dog without fleas. It doesn't happen. Why is that? Why do periods of great prosperity always wind up being periods of great scandal? It's not that it happens occasionally. It happens every time. The railroad boom makes the internet boom look clean. The Wall Street boom of the 1980s, the conglomerate boom of the 1960s, when they came to an end, had their evil villains and were followed by regulatory zeal that appears to have had exactly zero effect the next time the stock market went up.

Is it possible that scandal is somehow an essential ingredient in capitalism? That a healthy free-market economy must tempt a certain number of people to behave corruptly, and that a certain number of these will do so? That the crooks are not a sign that something is rotten but that something is working more or less as it was meant to work? After all, a market economy is premised on a system of incentive designed to encourage an ignoble human trait: self-interest. Is it all that shocking that, when this system undergoes an exciting positive transformation, self-interest spins out of control?

Of course, it is good that the crooks are rounded up. We can all move on feeling as if justice was done, and perhaps the next time around fewer people will succumb to temptation. But in the meantime it's worth asking: How did the crooks get away with it in the first place? Where were the bold regulators and the fire-breathing journalists five years ago, when it actually would have been a little brave, possibly even a little useful, to inveigh against the excesses of the boom? Where in the stock market of five years ago was Eliot Spitzer? (Fully invested with Jim Cramer, who wrote the book about how to use the media to juice one's own portfolio.) Where was the press? Egging on the very people they now seek to humiliate. The very people who are now baying so loudly for blood were in the most cases creating the climate that rewarded corrupt practices.

Around the time the Enron scandal broke last October, there was a good example of just how effortlessly the celebration of the 1990s became the retribution of the 2000s. As gleefully reported by *Forbes* magazine, *Fortune* magazine was about to go to press with a cover article for its November 26 issue about the post-9/11 economy in which "the smartest people we know" were consulted. As it happened, one of those people was Kenneth Lay, the chairman and chief executive of Enron Corporation. The issue was laid out, with Lay's picture right there on the cover when the Enron scandal broke. You might think that would pose a big problem for *Fortune* magazine, but if it did, the magazine didn't show it. Using a nifty 1990s piece of photo-editing software, the editors were able to erase Ken Lay. *Fortune* published on schedule and, ignoring all the flattery it had lavished on Enron over the past few years, piled right onto the scandal. It took only a few months before two of *Fortune*'s writers had sold their Enron book for $1.4 million.

Good for them, I say. We all have to earn a living. But the next time some editor, or regulator, or politician seeking reelection, begins to shriek about the inequities of the boom, someone needs to turn to him and ask: Where were you when it was happening? And if the answer happens to be, "Making the boom work for me," the best thing you can do is forgive him for it. Really, it wasn't such a bad way to spend your time.

Infrastructure was easily sold to government and business as a costly but necessary investment in the future. But today 4,000 miles of unused fiber-optic cable litter Oregon's once-promising high-tech superhighway. Jeffrey Kosseff of *The Oregonian* presents tangible reasons why no one should ever be so gullible about tossing big money at an unproven dream.

Jeffrey Kosseff

Amid Telecom Ruins, a Fortune Is Buried

OREGON EXPERIENCED ONE of the most extravagant building booms in its history during the late '90s. But today the state has little to show for about $1 billion invested in what was billed at the time as essential infrastructure.

The money is buried—most of it along the Interstate 5 corridor—in the form of more than 140,000 miles of fiber-optic cable. At most, 5 percent of the fiber is being used. Forget dot-coms. The truly excessive overinvestment of the technology boom was in the internet's pipeline, the hair-thin strands of glass that snake across the state and nation, carrying pulses of light that translate into huge volumes of e-mail messages, web pages, and online video.

Dozens of companies invested billions in fiber-optic networks. As it turns out, one or two would have been more than sufficient to meet consumer demand.

Many lost in this race to build the Information Superhighway. Of the 33 companies that laid fiber in Portland, 14 have filed bankruptcy, and their investors are unlikely to ever earn any of their money back. Telecommunications stocks nationwide are worth about $1 trillion less than their peak valuation in early 2000. And thousands of Oregon telecom employees saw their high-paying jobs vanish.

"It was very much like the gold rush," said John Walker, an economic historian at Portland State University. "For any one of them, it makes sense to build the fiber. For all of them to build separate fiber, it doesn't."

The jobs and money are gone, but the high-tech fiber remains.

Ten long-distance fiber-optic routes, totaling more than 4,000 miles, run through the state, usually with two or more companies each stringing dozens of strands of fiber within the same piece of conduit, according to *The Oregonian*'s review of data from government agencies and telecom companies.

Even applying conservative estimates to costs of construction, the companies spent more than $570 million laying long-distance fiber cables across Oregon, and they shelled out at least $265 million more equipping the 5 percent of fiber that is used. Then they spent more than $170 million more digging up Portland streets to connect mainly downtown businesses.

If they need the remaining 95 percent of the fiber in the future, companies will have to spend tens of billions of dollars more to make it usable by placing lasers and amplifiers on the route.

It's the financial equivalent of building ten Fox Towers, one next to another, only to be surprised by a 95 percent vacancy rate.

"You feel everybody involved either knew or should have known the spectacular risks that were taken," said Reed Hundt, chairman of the Federal Communications Commission from 1993 to 1997 and now a senior adviser at the high-profile business consulting firm McKinsey & Co.

The fiber-optic building boom took place nationwide, but it was particularly frenzied in Oregon, the most direct path to run fiber between two high-tech meccas—Silicon Valley and Seattle. And telecom carriers also use Oregon to connect their U.S. networks to undersea cable from Asia.

The shakeout from these disastrous investments partially explains

Oregon's deep economic problems. Not only did the fiber carriers slash thousands of jobs in the state, but thousands more were cut at the area's numerous equipment makers such as Tektronix and now-defunct Oresis Communications.

Economic historians say that while the amount of money invested and lost in fiber is staggering, such reckless spending is not unprecedented. Canals, railroads, and telegraphs all sparked similar investment rushes in their technological infancy.

And the overindulgent spending did create a reward for consumers— at least those in metropolitan areas. The cost of transporting data has plunged, as the supply has far outpaced demand.

But two questions linger. How did it happen? And was the money wasted or will the fiber-optic lines eventually be used?

DEREGULATION OPENS DOOR

The door opened to the telecom boom in 1996. The federal government deregulated the telecom industry, making it possible for any new company to lay fiber across the nation and compete against the giants, such as AT&T and the Baby Bell local phone monopolies.

Like teenagers who throw wild parties when their parents go out of town for the weekend, telecom companies and their investors put on their dancing shoes as soon as the regulators went away.

"The only regulation was the free market," said David Leatherwood, who built Enron Broadband's portion of the $150 million FTV network, which runs through Oregon on its way to Boise, and now is president of Intelepoint, a Portland telecom consulting firm.

At the time, research firms—which often counted telecom companies as their top clients—predicted internet traffic would double every few months.

Stock analysts such as Jack Grubman, the former Salomon Smith Barney analyst, were bullish on telecom stocks while they were involved with the companies' business deals. (Congress and stock exchanges are now investigating Grubman for possible conflicts of interest.)

Some telecom companies, including now-bankrupt WorldCom, misled investors as to how much of their networks were being used.

Investors saw a brilliantly lit future. They poured billions of dollars into new and established companies. Level 3 Communications and Qwest Communications International, both of Colorado, emerged and built fiber along railroad tracks. The Williams Cos., a Tulsa, Oklahoma, energy conglomerate, strung cable along gas pipelines. And the established companies—AT&T, MCI-WorldCom, and Sprint—continued to expand.

"This was the most deregulated, competitive story we've ever seen literally since the railroads," Hundt said.

The fiber glut looks like ridiculous oversupply now. But the companies that buried all that cable weren't seen as foolhardy at the time. Quite the opposite. Wall Street rewarded them. In 1999 and 2000, shares of most companies with large fiber networks, such as Level 3 and Qwest, soared despite weak balance sheets and income statements.

The companies all rode the market on the belief that the internet would rapidly become not just another form of communication, but a way of life.

"The hope was all these e-commerce models would take over and there would be massive downloading of video and music on the consumer side," said Glen Macdonald, vice president of Adventis, a Connecticut telecom research firm. "Everyone would be buying everything online instead of going to stores to shop."

Even the government got into the act. The Bonneville Power Administration spent $50 million building a fiber network in Oregon, which it leases to telecom carriers and rural public utility districts. And the state of Oregon deregulated Qwest's profits in the state to help persuade the company to invest $120 million in the state, including $70 million worth of long-haul fiber and other network upgrades in rural areas.

DEMAND FALLS SHORT

According to Telegeography, a Washington, D.C., research firm, the long-haul networks that run through Oregon can carry 1,148 terabits of data per second—enough bandwidth to run about 15 always-on, high-speed internet connections for every person in the United States.

The demand for internet-supplied information has not proven that great. Although internet use has increased, it hasn't doubled every few months. And most of the use has occurred not with high-speed cable modems but with dial-up connections, which gobble up less bandwidth.

Adventis estimates that telecom companies nationwide spent $70 billion too much on long-haul networks.

Ironically, the success of telecom technology research has contributed to the glut.

A process called dense wavelength division multiplexing enables companies to cram more data onto a single fiber.

On fiber-optic lines, voice and data travel over lightwaves. Every time a carrier is able to add another color to the spectrum, it adds another channel, capable of handling the equivalent of thirty-two thousand calls at once. Some of AT&T's fibers carry traffic on 160 colors, spokesman Dave Johnson said.

So it's not surprising that, according to Telegeography, less than 2 percent of the state's long-haul fiber is lit, and the remainder is dark, waiting for companies to spend billions more equipping it with amplifiers and other technology that enables it to carry data. The companies that use the fiber and some other experts estimate slightly higher use—maybe 5 percent at most.

TODAY'S LOSS, TOMORROW'S GAIN?

Investors have a long history of investing in hot, unregulated technologies until there is a glut. And that history tells us that investors' losses may eventually become society's gain.

In the early nineteenth century, U.S. businesses built canals throughout the East to cut costs of delivering coal, said Mark Clark, associate professor of history at the Oregon Institute of Technology.

"If you wanted to build a canal, people were more than willing," he said. "They said, 'If canals were a good idea, let's keep building them.'"

Toward the end of the century, companies invested in yet another hot new form of transportation—trains, which Hundt said closely paralleled the fiber boom because of the huge number of builders and large investment.

And fiber's earliest ancestor, the telegraph, also spawned tremendous excess investment, said Walker, the Portland State professor. After a telegraph line between Washington, D.C., and Baltimore received attention, cities across the nation built lines, even though they were rarely used, he said.

In all three cases, the short-term result was lost money, consolidation, and economic pain.

The collapse of the canal industry rocked the economy, Clark said. Even state governments suffered from their canal investments.

"You got this craze, and they built too much," he said. "The shakeout led to one of the first major recessions."

Once the railroads were built, their owners couldn't make enough money to survive.

"More than half of all the railroad mileage in the 1870s was in bankruptcy," Hundt noted.

Many telegraph lines sat idle, because, as with fiber-optic lines, many companies built along the same route.

But under each of these disastrous investments was a bright spot.

Although many of the canals were never completed, some, such as the Erie, eased transportation for years to come. The remaining railroad giants bought up the assets of those that failed and became an economic force. Western Union amassed telegraph lines and became a long-standing, successful monopoly.

Despite the investor casualties of the free market, Walker thinks it's the only way for new technologies to develop.

"It is a part of how market systems work," Walker said. "When you have one of these discontinuous leaps in technology, you get one of these gold rush reactions. In some short-run sense it's wasteful, but doing things this way is better than central planning."

TREASURE AWAITS DISCOVERY

Benefits of the telecom boom have begun to show in the form of lower prices, but it's still unclear whether all the fiber will ever be used.

Bandwidth prices have plunged to where it costs 10 percent or 20 percent of what it once did to carry data. For businesses especially, that has resulted in huge savings.

The survivors, Hundt said, are buying up fiber assets at low prices, and they'll be ready to meet any demand for bandwidth for centuries to come.

"It's not a good story for investors," Hundt said, "but it's a great story for the rest of the economy."

Of course, it will require tens of billions of dollars more in investments to equip the fiber with lasers, amplifiers, and other gadgets that carry bursts of light along the narrow glass strands.

About 85 percent of the cost of building a fiber network comes from lighting it, said Kevin Dennehy, vice president of networks at Montana-based Touch America, which has fiber on the FTV route and is considering bankruptcy.

"We'll be doing additional lighting as business demand dictates," Dennehy said.

But in much of Oregon, it's difficult to take advantage of the long-haul fiber, because local connections are either unavailable or too expensive.

Outside of the Portland, Salem, and Eugene areas, it's rare to find much competition for local broadband connections, creating high monopoly pricing that reduces the number of services sold.

"In many communities, the connections aren't there," said John Irwin, chairman of the Oregon Telecommunications Coordinating Council, which has proposed legislation to increase broadband availability in rural parts of the state. "In other communities it's there, but it's so expensive that businesses and consumers can't afford it."

Another problem is that many homes and businesses don't have access to high-speed internet connections, because phone companies have not yet upgraded many of their local networks.

"You've got all these superhighways out there, but you've got dirt roads leading up to them," said Jere Retzer, executive director of Northwest Access Exchange, a consortium that connects university and corporate networks in Portland.

"There would have been good business models and potential for profitability if there were access out to the homes and small businesses."

As individual investors watched their shares tank, top executives of highly publicized U.S. business disasters were rewarded with billions of dollars from salary and the unloading of their shares. However, this trend didn't simply involve the Enrons, Global Crossings, and World-Coms, but took place again and again in many different industries and parts of the country. Chris O'Brien and Jack Davis of the *San Jose Mercury News* examined stock sales of insiders at tech firms in their Silicon Valley backyard to come up with a story guaranteed to make an investor's skin crawl.

Chris O'Brien and Jack Davis

Rich Man, Poor Company

RUNNING COMPANIES that became almost worthless didn't stop dozens of Silicon Valley insiders from pocketing billions of dollars by selling their stock during the tech boom and bust.

The *Mercury News* examined the stock sales record of insiders at forty companies in Silicon Valley that have lost virtually all their value since the stock market peaked in March 2000. The executives, board members, and venture capitalists at these companies walked off with $3.41 billion, while their companies' total market value plunged 99.8 percent to a mere $229.5 million at the end of September.

It represented a remarkable transfer of wealth from the pockets of thousands of anonymous investors—from day traders to pension funds—into the wallets of executives and directors who turned out to be winners even when their companies became some of Silicon Valley's biggest losers.

Coming at a time of public discontent with corporate ethics, the disconnect between the performance of these companies and the executives' fantastic rewards is symptomatic of the problems that have ignited calls to reform executive compensation and corporate governance.

"The people who bought the stock they sold are the victims here," said Charles Elson, director of the Center for Corporate Governance at the University of Delaware. "This money was taken from investors who didn't have the same information as these insiders and lost their money."

The *Mercury News* compiled a list of local companies whose stock price dropped at least 99.5 percent from March 2000, when the Nasdaq peaked, to September 30, 2002. Those companies were then ranked by the amount of stock sold by insiders—roughly three hundred—since the beginning of 1997.

This means the list leaves off some spectacular flameouts where executives weren't shy about selling stock. For instance, JDS Uniphase missed the cut, with a 97.1 percent drop, even though executives sold $1.17 billion in stock between May 1997 and November 2002, even as the optical components company was firing two-thirds of its employees. Also absent is software company Ariba, whose stock dropped 98.7 percent and where insiders sold $1.26 billion between October 1999 and November 2002.

The survey also excludes some of the valley's household names. Not included are John Chambers, who between August 1997 and February 2000 sold $296.2 million in Cisco stock; Larry Ellison, who in January 2001 sold $894.8 million in Oracle stock; and Scott McNealy, who from May 1997 to July 2002 sold $107.9 million in Sun Microsystems stock. These corporate giants generally are older and remain strong competitors even as their stock prices have tanked.

SUPPOSED GOOD BETS

The forty companies on the *Mercury News* list are primarily software, hardware, and telecommunications companies—the infrastructure providers that were supposed to be good bets rather than flighty dot-coms.

These companies are a seriously wounded bunch. While not true of every company, as a group, they have a variety of problems. Most had major restructurings that led to mass firings. Fifteen went bankrupt. Several more are running out of cash.

Almost half the companies face lawsuits from angry shareholders. Five of the top fifteen companies had to restate earnings, some from periods when insiders were selling stock. And a handful of the companies have been cited in investigations by Congress and the Securities and Exchange Commission into investment banks accused of manipulating IPOs.

Though option grants usually get the most attention, much of the stocks sold by insiders at these companies were shares they gained from being founders or early-stage venture investors prior to IPOs. Once their standard 180-day lockup periods ended, many of these insiders began selling their stock like there was no tomorrow.

For some of their companies, there isn't much of a tomorrow:

- John Little, founder and CEO of Portal Software, sold $127.5 million of stock in Portal, which is on the verge of being delisted by Nasdaq. Portal, which sells billing software, topped the *Mercury News* list with insiders selling $704 million in stock—more than its total revenue since the May 1999 IPO.

- David Peterschmidt, CEO of Inktomi, sold $90.5 million of stock at the number two company on the list. Inktomi, once a promising internet search engine company, in November sold off a major division to raise cash it needs to survive.

- K. B. Chandrasekhar, founder and former CEO of the former Exodus Communications, cashed out $135.1 million in stock at the web hosting company before it went bankrupt. Chandrasekhar is now founder and CEO of Jamcracker. Exodus was bought out of bankruptcy by Cable & Wireless, which recently announced more layoffs at the hosting division.

- Dennis Barsema, former CEO of Redback Networks, sold $138.4 million in stock before he left in July 2000 after two and a half years at the helm. Barsema later became CEO at Onetta, another networking start-up. He donated $20 million in stock to his alma mater, Northern Illinois University. Meanwhile, Redback announced another round of layoffs November 14 and says it may have to raise more financing to stay afloat.

- Jerry Shaw-Yau Chang, former CEO of Clarent, sold a measly $16.5 million, though insiders at his telecom company dumped $355.8 million. Mired in accounting irregularities, the company has restated financial statements for 2000 and part of 2001, and been unable to report earnings for most of 2002.

- Thomas Jermoluk, former CEO of At Home, sold $50.3 million before the cable broadband giant filed for bankruptcy. The company, known as Excite@Home, once boasted a market value of $13 billion before vaporizing following squabbles with its main shareholder and partner, AT&T. Jermoluk is now a venture partner at Kleiner Perkins Caufield & Byers.

Executives at every company contacted either did not return phone calls or declined to comment, in many cases citing pending litigation. The one exception was Frederick D. Lawrence, former CEO of Adaptive Broadband, who agreed—after speaking with his lawyer—to discuss executive compensation though not the specifics of his company.

He pointed out that executive pay plans are publicly available and that most investors never bother to read them. And when insiders sell stock, they must also publicly disclose the sales in filings to the SEC.

"People really work hard in these industries," Lawrence said. "They spend hours away from friends and family. Although that's not an excuse for any poor behavior."

NO SURPRISE

However, Nell Minow, editor of the Corporate Library, a research center that focuses on corporate governance, said the heavy insider stock sales are no surprise. Minow is a leading critic of allowing insiders to sell their stock because it creates the temptation to push the envelope on things like accounting.

"They sell the stock and then they restate the earnings," Minow said. "That brings it one step closer to being a Ponzi scheme."

The increasing use of stock and options to compensate executives over the past decade grew out of a broader shareholder value movement. The idea was to align the interests of executives with the stockholders who, in theory, are more important than employees or managers.

But the practice has come under fire from critics who say stock grants have forced executives to become too focused on short-term results and doing whatever it takes to boost the stock price. That in turn can lead to everything from laying off employees after a bad quarter to feeling pressure to bend or break accounting rules to make the numbers.

"Their decisions are distorted," said Neelam Jain, assistant professor at Jones Graduate School of Management at Rice University. "What the managers are trying to do is maximize their own profits and not the firm's profits."

Graef Crystal, a leading compensation expert in Las Vegas, believes the problem has been overblown. He points out that while many executives sold their stock, many of them could have sold far more, which they elected to keep and which eventually became worthless.

DID THEY KNOW?

"The fact that they left huge amounts of money on the table does not suggest they knew something was coming," Crystal said.

But the criticism of these insider stock sales continues to grow. That backlash increased in November, when the Conference Board released an annual survey of 2,841 companies in 14 industries that showed executive pay and perks continued to rise in 2001 even as the stock market and economy slumped.

At the same time executive compensation has exploded, bankruptcies have soared, and publicly traded companies are facing record numbers of shareholder lawsuits. According to the Securities Class Action Clearinghouse at Stanford Law School, the number of shareholder suits rose from 213 in 2000 to 488 in 2001—despite a law passed in 1996 by Congress to discourage such litigation.

While many companies dismiss such litigation as a nuisance, observers say many corporate insiders still underestimate the anger of investors who lost big sums during the boom and bust and are still feeling burned.

"This is not a victimless crime," said Charlie Cray, director of Citizen Works' Campaign for Corporate Reform. "The argument is that they're taking risks. But they're taking risks with other people's money.

"This is really a question of fairness."

There's good reason why corporate compensation committees give the green light to excessive pay and perks for CEOs. More than likely, the CEO has the committee members in his back pocket. Diana B. Henriques and Geraldine Fabrikant of *The New York Times* Business Day conducted a survey that confirms the worst fears of investors about who actually makes the call on executive compensation.

Diana B. Henriques and Geraldine Fabrikant

Deciding on Executive Pay

WHEN AMERICA'S BIGGEST COMPANIES decide how much to pay their top executives, most of them leave the decision to a group of their board members known as the compensation committee. In theory, members of this committee are independent enough of the company's executives to deny them raises or force them to take pay cuts when the company is faring poorly.

In practice, it can be a very different story. An examination of almost two thousand corporations finds that at hundreds of them, members of the compensation committee work for or do business with the company or its chief executive. In some cases, they even belong to the executive's family.

Legislation enacted this summer after a wave of costly corporate scandals is silent about the makeup of the compensation committee, although the new law set high standards of independence for another important boardroom committee, the audit committee, which oversees a company's financial controls and the auditing of its books.

Yet compensation committees are "definitely more clubby" than they should be, said Roger W. Raber, chief executive of the National Association of Corporate Directors, which thinks that only board members with no personal or business ties to the company should serve on its compensation committee. "They just don't have the rigor of oversight that we see with other committees, especially audit committees."

Mr. Raber added: "That, to me, is going to be the continuing crisis: looking at some of the pay practices, especially the severance packages. We have another storm to go through, and frankly, it's going to be ugly."

The study by *The New York Times* of almost two thousand of the largest American corporations, measured by their stock market value, shows that 420 of them, more than 20 percent, had compensation committees in 2001 with members who had business ties or other relationships with the chief executive or the company that could compromise their independence. Dozens of those members were company executives.

At more than seventy companies, even the chairman of the compensation committee had such ties, and in nine cases the chairman was actually an executive of the company.

These are just the connections that have been fully disclosed to investors.

That such ties are not always disclosed was illustrated yesterday, when Frank E. Walsh Jr., a former member of the compensation committee at Tyco International, pleaded guilty to charges of failing to report that Tyco had paid him a $20 million fee for his role in a company deal.

Potential conflicts of interest cropped up at some of the nation's best-known companies.

For example, at Clear Channel Communications, the nation's largest radio chain, only one of the five people on its compensation committee is free of potential conflicts. The committee has retained—indeed, sweetened—pay packages that guaranteed raises for the chairman, L. Lowry Mays, and his two sons, regardless of company performance. The sons have severance agreements that entitle them to 14 years of salary, bonuses, benefits, and stock options if they quit because the board fails to choose one of them to succeed their father as chief executive. Clear Channel said the committee met existing federal guidelines for independence.

At the Great Atlantic and Pacific Tea Company, which owns the Waldbaum's, Food Emporium, and A&P supermarket chains, only one of the three people on the compensation committee is independent. A second is the family lawyer for the 38-year-old chief executive, Christian W. E. Haub, and a third works for Mr. Haub's parents, the company's controlling shareholders. The committee has regularly approved raises and larger bonuses for Mr. Haub, despite the company's worsening business problems. The company said it was considering revising the committee's composition, but said the pay was appropriate.

And three of the eight people who set the final pay package for John F. Welch Jr. when he was chief executive of General Electric have done business, through their own companies, with GE. Their decision, which at first looked like a pay cut for Mr. Welch, actually gave him a 50 percent raise for the year. That raise substantially improved Mr. Welch's pension after he retired in early September 2001. The company declined to comment on the arrangement, although it has subsequently taken steps to increase the independence of its board.

These cases and others cited here are based on an analysis by *The New York Times* of a database compiled by the Corporate Library, an investor information service; on the most recently available corporate proxy statements, in most cases those filed for the 2001 fiscal year; and on interviews with compensation experts and securities lawyers. The database defines directors as independent unless they have family, business, or professional ties to the company or are owners or beneficiaries of some other entity that profits directly from the company's activities, like a law firm or major supplier.

A DECADE OF WARNINGS:
EVEN DEFINITIONS ARE UP FOR GRABS

Compensation committees are made up of company directors, but they may work with an outside consultant or the company's own personnel executives. Typically, their job is to evaluate the performance of senior management and decide on the top executives' pay. "Historically, it has been extremely rare that a board would ever countermand, or even question, what the compensation committee decided to do," said Paul R. Dorf, managing director of Compensation Resources, a consulting firm.

Experts concede that even committees with minor or nonexistent conflicts of interest can approve outsize pay for lackluster or even poor performance. John W. Snow, chosen by President Bush last week as Treasury secretary, was paid more than $50 million in his nearly 12 years as chairman of the railroad company CSX even as profits fell and its stock lagged the market.

"But it's one thing to say the CEO is overpaid; it's a step further to say, 'and his business partner is on the compensation committee,'" said Nell Minow, editor of the Corporate Library site.

Since at least the early 1990s, oversight groups like the National Association of Corporate Directors have called for fully independent compensation committees. "Achieving both the appearance and the reality of independence demands no less," the directors' group said in a 1992 report.

In the wake of recent scandals, both the New York Stock Exchange and the Nasdaq market have proposals before the Securities and Exchange Commission that would require independent compensation committees as part of their listing standards.

"But those are far from a done deal," said Holly J. Gregory, a corporate lawyer at the law firm of Weil, Gotshal & Manges. Both proposals are subject to SEC review and public comment, she said.

Moreover, the two proposals define independence differently, allowing some business ties so long as boards determine that they are not material. The proposals also exempt companies with a controlling shareholder, and would not go into effect for several years.

Right now, about all that market regulators require of compensation committees is that they explain their decisions in the annual proxy statement. But many of those reports, several securities lawyers said, are little more than boilerplate detailing a rationale that can be mystifying or contradictory.

Paul Hodgson, a senior research associate at the Corporate Library, pointed to the Carnival Corporation, the cruise ship operator. At Carnival, a compensation committee with three members—only one of whom has no ties to the company—approved a $40.5 million total pay package, including stock options, for the chief executive, Micky Arison, in 2001. The committee's proxy report notes that Mr. Arison himself actually recommends the size of his bonus and that there is "no specific relationship" between that bonus and company performance.

Tim Gallagher, a Carnival spokesman, said Mr. Arison's compensation was determined by a variety of factors, including the company's performance, its strategic position, and its success in weathering the slump in leisure travel after September 11.

One reason that cases like these persist is that mutual funds and other institutional investors have not used their power to demand strong, conflict-free compensation committees, said Bruce R. Ellig, the author of *The Complete Guide to Executive Compensation* (McGraw-Hill, 2001).

Institutional investors have to step up, Mr. Ellig added. "It's not the small shareholder who can stand up and say, 'Excuse me, Mr. Chairman, but I think you're overpaid.'"

SOME CASE STUDIES: QUESTIONABLE TIES AT 200 COMPANIES

More than two hundred large corporations—including some of the nation's best-known and most widely admired companies—have had compensation committees with members who have disclosed ties to the company or its chief executive.

When General Electric's compensation committee negotiated Mr. Welch's final preretirement pay package, its members included three men whose companies have done business with General Electric: Sam Nunn, the former senator and a partner in the law firm of King & Spalding, which has worked for the company; Roger Penske, who has an indirect stake in a trucking partnership engaged in a joint venture with the company; and Kenneth Langone, chief executive and controlling shareholder of Invemed Associates, which also has done business with the company.

General Electric's proxy statement for 2001 suggests that Mr. Welch had been given a pay cut: $16.1 million in salary and bonus, down from $16.7 million a year earlier.

But in fact the figure in the proxy represents just eight months of service by Mr. Welch, who retired in early September 2001. His annual rate of pay, therefore, was about $24 million—a 50 percent increase for the year. Over the previous five years, when the company's performance was much stronger, his annual raises never exceeded 33 percent.

Few would have considered 2001 a banner year for Mr. Welch. The company's stock fell sharply after the embarrassing collapse of its bid for Honeywell during the summer.

But a raise in 2001 was particularly beneficial to Mr. Welch because it increased his monthly pay, a crucial factor in determining the size of his pension, according to Graef Crystal, a compensation consultant. Specifically, his annual pension was based on how much he made in his top-earning 36 months of service over the previous ten years. Without the 2001 raise, his annual pension would have been about $7.5 million, rather than the $9 million he received, Mr. Crystal said.

Earlier this year, General Electric made changes to its board to increase its independence and changed the makeup of its compensation committee.

Clear Channel, based in San Antonio, is the nation's largest radio station chain and a major provider of live entertainment. The company was a coproducer of the Broadway hit *The Producers* and handled national tours for stars like Madonna and the Backstreet Boys. It owns television stations and billboard companies, and manages major sports figures, including Michael Jordan and Andre Agassi.

But since 1990, the company has been dogged by antitrust investigations and complaints from the music industry that its radio stations will not play music by artists who are not represented by the company's promotion unit.

But those uncertainties are not reflected in the company's pay policies, compensation experts say. Mr. Mays, the 66-year-old cofounder and chief executive, has two sons working at the company—and all three men are guaranteed raises and stock option grants each year, in addition to the unusual 14-year severance plan set up for the sons.

This arrangement was approved by a previous committee. But having inherited the agreement, "the new committee has not backed off; on the contrary, they have compounded the problem rather than addressing it," said Brian Foley, an independent compensation consultant. For example, he said, the committee has given the sons additional payments that added millions to the value of their severance packages.

Clear Channel said the compensation deals were set up to ensure continuity of management and stability of leadership.

Clear Channel's five-member compensation committee includes only one outsider with no company ties: John H. Williams, a retired senior vice president of First Union Securities.

The other members include Vernon E. Jordan Jr. and Alan D. Feld, whose Washington law firm, Akin, Gump, Strauss, Hauer & Feld, has collected legal fees from the company. Another member is B. J. McCombs, who was a cofounder of the company with Mr. Mays and whose children's trust funds, along with trusts for Mr. Mays's children, lease office space to Clear Channel.

A fourth member, Thomas O. Hicks, a partner in the investment firm Hicks, Muse, Tate & Furst, also has ties to the company. Pan American Sports Network, an affiliate of Hicks, Muse, purchased the television rights for the United States Open tennis tournament from a company later acquired by Clear Channel. When Pan American filed for bankruptcy protection in March, Clear Channel was left on the hook for payments that Pan American owed under the agreement.

And until August 2001, when he gave up his committee seat, the sixth member of Clear Channel's compensation committee was Lowry Mays himself.

A company spokeswoman said the board's lawyers had determined that Mr. Jordan and Mr. Feld qualified as independent under the new federal guidelines. Other committee assignments will be reviewed as new rules are adopted, she said.

The Great Atlantic and Pacific Tea Company's business has been in turmoil for years. In recent years, the company has closed stores, laid off workers, and eliminated its stock dividend. Last spring, it found it had been using unacceptable accounting for years and revised three previous years' results.

And in October, its president and chief operating officer, Elizabeth R. Culligan, left after less than a year in the job, dismaying Wall Street about the company's leadership. "We are concerned about management's ability to budget and execute on its business plan," complained Mark Husson, a industry analyst at Merrill Lynch.

Nevertheless, in 2001, Mr. Haub, the chief executive, received a cash salary and bonus totaling just under $1.2 million, a 53 percent raise over the previous year.

"I really did have to stop and wonder how he got paid a bonus for 2001," said Judith Fischer, managing director of Executive Compensation Advisory Services in Alexandria, Virginia. "It's very questionable."

Richard P. De Santa, vice president for corporate affairs at A&P, said the pay package reflected A&P's return to profitability in 2001.

Mr. Haub is the son of the controlling shareholders, and his mother, Helga, is a board member. The chairman of the compensation committee, John D. Barline, is a legal adviser to the Haub family. A second member, Rosemarie Baumeister, is an employee of the Haub family's interests in Germany, which do business with A&P.

Mr. De Santa said the board was considering changing the makeup of the committee, as part of a continuing effort to make the board more independent.

Many companies—like General Electric and Clear Channel—have provided outstanding returns to shareholders over the years despite potential conflicts on their compensation committees. And, while many directors with company ties would not comment publicly, several noted that those ties were fully disclosed, had been blessed by company lawyers, and were too insignificant to affect their judgment.

But although individual directors may feel they can serve faithfully despite such ties, a compensation committee with conflicts is often a signal that the board is not strong or independent enough, said Ms. Minow of the Corporate Library. "Particularly in this era when the investor community is very skeptical of boards of directors, it is really important that the boards be above suspicion."

POSSIBLE REMEDIES
AN UPHILL BATTLE FOR CHALLENGERS

Shareholders who try to challenge their chief executive's pay package in court or in the boardroom face an uphill fight, lawyers and shareholder activists say.

For one thing, it is hard to see problems coming, said Ed Durkin, director of corporate affairs for the United Brotherhood of Carpenters, whose pension funds have been demanding independent compensation committees at a number of companies for the last five years.

"The committee reports have no predictive value at all; some of it is not in the English language," Mr. Durkin said. As a result, he said, only experts can usually decipher the practical effect of various compensation policies on the chief executive or the shareholders.

And compensation committees are not required to disclose which experts they consulted to develop the chief executive's package. That makes it difficult to determine what other business ties, if any, the consultants have with the corporation or the chief executive, several securities lawyers noted. Compensation committees rarely hire a consultant not recommended by the chief executive, said Mr. Raber of the directors' group. "A lot of rubber-stamping goes on," he said.

The new listing standards proposed by the New York Stock Exchange and Nasdaq would require independent compensation committees, although each proposal has limiting features. Companies with a large controlling stockholder, like A&P, would be exempt under both plans, and the Nasdaq proposal permits one nonindependent committee member to serve for up to two years under "exceptional and limited circumstances."

The two plans define director independence a bit differently, lawyers noted, and it is not yet clear that they would ban some business ties that shareholders may find troubling.

Some companies that disclosed potential conflicts on their compensation committees in their most recent proxy statements have taken steps to increase their committees' independence. But business ties among outside directors serving on the committees remain fairly common, said Mr. Dorf, the compensation consultant. The New York Exchange and Nasdaq proposals "have yet to have an impact," he added.

In the past, litigation has not been a useful weapon for battling excessive executive pay, according to Michael Perino, visiting law professor at Columbia.

The courts—most significantly those in Delaware, where most large corporations are registered—have generally treated executive pay as a matter best left to the business judgment of the board, Professor Perino explained.

But some experts think that may be changing under the weight of the current scandals. "We're in a totally new environment now," said Amy Goodman, a corporate law expert at Gibson, Dunn & Crutcher in Washington. "You can't divorce executive compensation from what has happened as a result of all the scandals of the past year."

Steve Case and Jerry Levin created AOL Time Warner in a marriage of convenience that didn't turn out to be a match made in heaven. Johnnie L. Roberts of *Newsweek* magazine bares the egos, misconceptions, and incompatibilities of a combined media giant that soon suffered enormous financial losses. Stabilizing the America Online division and cleaning up business practices under investigation by the Securities and Exchange Commission have been high priorities of chairman and CEO Richard Parsons. To downplay its mega-merger mistake, AOL Time Warner changed its name to Time Warner and adopted the old ticker symbol TWX.

Johnnie L. Roberts

How It All Fell Apart

PERHAPS MONA LISA, with her uncertain smile, knew something at the time that nobody else did. In the fall of 1999, an upstart group with the lofty title of the Global Business Dialogue on Electronic Commerce had chosen the Louvre for its first conference. The setting certainly matched its ambitions—to set worldwide standards for cyberspace and electronic commerce. Among the conference heavyweights: Gerald Levin, the CEO of Time Warner, the world's largest media company, and Steve Case, chairman of America Online, the internet king. The two men wound up chatting about big ideas, the belief that companies should be values-driven, rather than mere slaves to profit targets. "We weren't talking about putting our companies together," at the Louvre, Levin would later note in a *Newsweek* interview. And despite the warm words, there was in fact unspoken tension between the two men. Earlier in 1999, Case had pushed regulators to force AT&T, Time Warner Cable, and the rest of the industry to carry AOL's broadband service over their data pipes. Case's hubris stunned them. "I don't trust him," Levin said about Case, according to someone who overheard him at the conference.

Just three months later, though, on January 10, 2000, Levin and Case were beaming before a mob scene of TV crews in Manhattan, making history with the announcement of their $350 billion blockbuster marriage. Combining AOL and Time Warner would create a behemoth that, they boasted, would touch the lives of people around the world an amazing 2.5 billion times each month through magazines, cable, and movies. AOL would be the turbocharged engine to bring Old Media into the "internet century" and deliver a dizzying 30 percent surge in profits on $40 billion in sales in the first year alone. "We've become a company of high-fives and hugs," Levin gushed. Ted Turner, the largest individual shareholder and vice chairman of the new company, said the deal felt like "the first time I made love some 42 years ago."

But this week, when AOL Time Warner holds a much-anticipated press conference, there won't be any backslapping. In fact, there won't be any Jerry Levin, who abruptly retired months ago. Case, the man who helped send his partner packing, will be there, though there likely will be a harsh spotlight on him. The man now running the show, Richard Parsons, will unveil a new AOL Time Warner strategy: to create a kind of "must-have AOL," in which consumers would pay extra for exclusive online offerings from Time Warner siblings. In effect, it turns the company's original model on its head, with Old Media reenergizing the New Economy division. The mantra from Parsons these days is to under-promise and overdeliver. After all, no one is in the mood to hear spin from a company that was never able to live up to its own hype. The combined company's stock, which peaked at $56.60 in May 2001, hit bottom in July 2002 at $8.70, and is now trading at about $16. That collapse has wiped out a stunning $280 *billion* in value for one of the market's most widely held stocks since the deal was announced. And its capitalization may take a further hit—the company faces its second investigation by the SEC and the Justice Department over its accounting.

The company's stock is so beaten down that, *Newsweek* has learned, several Wall Street buyout firms have explored making a bid for the company's assets, particularly its online operations. Among them, according to executives privy to the talks: Henry Kravis's Kohlberg Kravis

Roberts, the Blackstone Group, and JPMorgan Chase's deal-making czar, James Lee. The firms declined to comment.

There are easy explanations for AOL Time Warner's sudden fall. Who knew, when the deal was forged, that the dot-com era and booming economy were about to come to a wrenching end? And not even the gloomiest of forecasters could have predicted the attacks of September 11. Certainly, those were among the causes that sent the company into a tailspin. Yet the real problem with AOL Time Warner can be traced to its roots. A detailed reconstruction of the merger, based on interviews with dozens of key executives close to the deal, offers a clear picture of what went wrong: Case and Levin, and their companies, were never right for each other. While the popular strategy at the time of marrying New and Old Media may have made sense in the abstract, there were troubling signs from the very start that this marriage wouldn't work. The architects of the deal were incompatible, and their companies inevitably were, too. But they forced them together anyway, in an effort to secure their place in history.

Case and Levin's relationship, in fact, was far more contentious early on than many people believed. Barely a day and a half before their big announcement, *Newsweek* has learned, Case and Levin were locked in a fierce power struggle. Levin, who was to be CEO, was worried about ceding too much power to Case, the chairman-designate. Yet he knew that Case, whose company's soaring stock made the deal possible, couldn't be seen by investors as a figurehead. The showdown "went down to the wire," people involved in the matter say. Levin, they added, was even prepared to walk away from the deal at the last minute. But they struck a precarious solution, with Case to rule over public policy and technology matters, and Levin overseeing the core media and online businesses. For the TV cameras, though, the two executives painted a picture of harmony. "Jerry and I worked out very early our relative responsibilities," Case said at the press conference.

The companies' cultural differences also sprang up over a critical issue: the dazzling financial results AOL Time Warner promised to deliver. The companies clashed over these projections much earlier than previously believed. Joan Nicolais, who was Time Warner's chief contact with Wall Street analysts, fiercely opposed the aggressive projections of a quick 30 percent profit increase to win Wall Street's support, several colleagues say. She preferred to offer straight guidance to Wall Street. Nicolais criticized AOL's approach as "basically an elaborate spin machine," says one top executive. "She didn't think the numbers added up." Nicolais would eventually lose out to an AOL executive for the investor-relations post.

Why did Levin want this deal so badly? He won't say. "I'm yesterday's news," he told *Newsweek.* But there are clear signs of what he might have seen in AOL. He had always yearned to be on technology's leading edge. In 1975, as an executive at Time Inc.'s fledgling HBO division, he switched the network's signal from microwave to satellites, a pioneering move that transformed the business. Levin made other good tech calls, playing a crucial support role in the early development of DVD. Through the 1990s, he launched many costly efforts to become a central player in the digital age, including Time Inc.'s Pathfinder portal and a cable Information Superhighway. Levin was worried that Time Warner's culture would prevent him from operating on "internet time." AOL would help him get there.

Over the years Case had made fleeting appearances in Levin's life. They were both guests, for example, at the White House for a screening of *You've Got Mail,* a Warner Bros. movie that took its title from AOL's e-mail greeting. In Levin and Time Warner, Case saw what his company was missing: real assets, particularly a media company, with big, steady revenues and profits. Case was also increasingly worried that customers would dump his snail's-pace dial-up service for faster connections offered by the cable companies. His hot stock was burning a hole in his pocket.

Case and Levin deluded themselves early on with talk of a marriage of equals, even though AOL shareholders would own 55 percent of the stock. The truth became obvious when they announced their management structure in May 2000. As co-COO with Parsons, Bob Pittman, AOL's number two executive, managed to get the lion's share of the operations. AOL also swept out Time Warner executives from many senior staff positions. "That was basically the Case plan," says a Time Warner executive.

The AOL executives wasted little time behaving as if they were in charge. According to Time Warner officials, their AOL colleagues ridiculed

Parsons behind his back, often saying that he was history. The AOL crowd wasn't keen on Levin, either. They whispered that he often drifted off-message, and they considered him too lax with his underlings. Tensions also rose after a widely publicized incident in which AOL's Michael Kelly, who became AOL Time Warner's finance chief, addressed executives of both companies in a planning session. Recalling AOL's 1998 purchase of Netscape, he said, "We fired everyone. We will do that here," recalls an attendee.

AOL's arrogance was fueled largely by its lofty stock price. But in a troubling sign for the merger, the value of its shares started to fall to new lows with the bursting of the dot-com bubble. Even with its price dropping, though, Time Warner shareholders would still get enough AOL stock to make it worth their while. In June 2000, the shareholders of each company voted to approve the deal. The regulators' final blessing was still months away. AOL's declining stock price inevitably led to questions, even within the management ranks of Time Warner, about whether the deal should be finalized. According to two senior officials, discussions were held about whether to pay an enormous breakup fee of $5 billion and walk away from the deal. Some executives in the operating divisions of the company were in favor of aborting the transaction.

AOL executives tried to brush off doubts about the prospects of its business, particularly for online advertising. They argued that, as the industry leader, AOL would avoid the falloff in ads that its competitors were suffering. Besides, the combined company, with its broad mix of businesses and strong base of subscriptions, would be more immune to fluctuations in the ad market than other media giants. This was the mantra when the deal was finalized on January 11, 2001, with the blessing of the Federal Communications Commission. "AOL is in a totally different zone than a dot-com advertising vehicle," Levin said after the closing.

Financial results for the first full quarter of marriage, however, showed ominous signs. Advertising and e-commerce sales were both flat or down. The stock dropped almost 10 percent. Levin and Pittman tried to focus attention on a bump in subscriptions. "To me, this was proof positive that the merger is working," Levin said at the time. Added Pittman: "The story of this quarter is that our synergies are hitting, and they're hitting big." As some insiders saw it, Pittman and Levin seemed to be trying to one-up each other with bullish forecasts. Pittman appeared to be upstaging Levin, making little effort to douse rampant speculation that he was heir to the AOL Time Warner throne. Pittman popped up on the cover of *BusinessWeek* after the transaction closed. The headline: "Showtime—Bob Pittman's Job Is to Implement the Biggest Merger in History."

Pressures mounted as the stock fell after hitting its postmerger peak of around $60. The power of the bullish forecasts was waning. Then terrorists attacked on 9/11. Thirteen days later, using the attacks as an explanation, Levin finally stated what Joan Nicolais knew from the beginning, and what many observers had come to suspect. AOL Time Warner would fall well short of its projected $11 billion in cash flow— off by $1 billion, to be exact. It wouldn't be the last time it would back off from its much-ballyhooed projections. Its credibility on Wall Street sank.

Levin seemed to change after 9/11, publicly resetting his priorities, with shareholders falling down the list. He told a gathering of investors that he intended to spend heavily on the "public trust," notwithstanding the impact on profits. "I'm the CEO, and this is what I'm going to do," he reportedly said. "I don't care what anyone else says." Levin and Case were apparently on a collision course. Levin was intent on acquiring AT&T's sprawling cable empire, a transaction that would have spread Time Warner Cable across about a quarter of the nation. It was the way he went about it, however, that led to a confrontation with Case and a crisis in the boardroom, according to senior officials. Levin simply pursued the transaction without consulting the board, according to these sources. "Steve made it an issue that he hadn't liked Jerry's approach" and that he wouldn't tolerate it, says one person close to the situation. On December 5, 2001, Levin abruptly resigned. Their relationship had come full circle. Levin didn't trust Case from the start because of his tough stance on a cable issue. And now a new disagreement over cable was the final straw. As a parting victory for Levin, he helped get Parsons elevated as his successor over Pittman, the presumed heir.

The company rattled off bad news like a jackhammer. In April of 2002, it announced a massive $54 billion write-down, reflecting the company's deterioration since the merger. It was forced to pay an extraordinary $7 billion to purchase Bertelsmann's interest in AOL Europe, an obligation that came with the merger. Debt ballooned to $28 billion. In July, *The Washington Post* turned up alleged accounting improprieties at AOL during the months before the merger was completed. The article suggested that the funny accounting was done to prop up AOL's earnings to support the completion of the deal. Within days, the SEC and the Department of Justice launched investigations (still under way), sending AOL Time Warner shares to a low of $8.70. Pittman quit a few days later in the midst of the turmoil.

Perhaps no single shareholder has more right to be angry than AOL Time Warner's vice chairman, Ted Turner, whose stake in the combined company, once worth $7.2 billion, has plunged to about $2 billion. During a recent breakfast meeting with Parsons at the crowded Rainbow Room in Rockefeller Center, Turner, in a booming voice heard around the room, was calling Levin names that are unprintable here.

This week, only a couple blocks from the site of the original engagement almost three years ago, Parsons and a new lineup of top executives (notably, all from the Time Warner side of the family, except for Case) will announce a new set of vows for AOL. It's hard to say whether they'll pay off. After all, others have tried to charge for online media content, but consumers have been reluctant to start paying for things they've gotten for free. Parsons isn't making any huge promises. He just wants to start delivering results. The point, of course, is to focus everyone's attention on the company's potential and its future, rather than the soap opera of its relationship up to now.

More Starbucks coffee shops are just what we need, right? Stanley Holmes of *BusinessWeek* magazine believes that, with the U.S. market becoming saturated, Starbucks has no choice but to aggressively expand its overseas stores. In doing so, it faces image problems, staffing pressures, and international challenges on the way to becoming truly global. Drake Bennett, Kate Carlisle, and Chester Dawson also contributed.

Stanley Holmes, Drake Bennett, Kate Carlisle, and Chester Dawson

Planet Starbucks

THE STARBUCKS COFFEE SHOP on Sixth Avenue and Pine Street in downtown Seattle sits serene and orderly, as unremarkable as any other in the chain bought 15 years ago by entrepreneur Howard Schultz. A little less than three years ago, however, the quiet storefront made front pages around the world. During the World Trade Organization talks in November 1999, protesters flooded Seattle's streets, and among their targets was Starbucks, a symbol, to them, of free-market capitalism run amok, another multinational out to blanket the earth. Amid the crowds of protesters and riot police were black-masked anarchists who trashed the store, leaving its windows smashed and its tasteful green-and-white decor smelling of tear gas instead of espresso. Says an angry Schultz: "It's hurtful. I think people are ill-informed. It's very difficult to protest against a can of Coke, a bottle of Pepsi, or a can of Folgers. Starbucks is both this ubiquitous brand and a place where you can go and break a window. You can't break a can of Coke."

The store was quickly repaired, and the protesters have scattered to other cities. Yet cup by cup, Starbucks really is caffeinating the world, its green-and-white emblem beckoning to consumers on three continents. In 1999, Starbucks Corp. had 281 stores abroad. Today, it has about 1,200—and it's still in the early stages of a plan to colonize the globe. If the protesters were wrong in their tactics, they weren't wrong about Starbucks' ambitions. They were just early.

The story of how Schultz & Co. transformed a pedestrian commodity into an upscale consumer accessory has a fairy-tale quality. Starbucks has grown from 17 coffee shops in Seattle 15 years ago to 5,689 outlets in 28 countries. Sales have climbed an average of 20 percent annually since the company went public ten years ago, to $2.6 billion in 2001, while profits bounded ahead an average of 30 percent per year, hitting $181.2 million last year. And the momentum continues. In the first three quarters of fiscal year 2002, sales climbed 24 percent, year to year, to $2.4 billion, while profits, excluding onetime charges and capital gains, rose 25 percent, to $159.5 million.

Moreover, the Starbucks name and image connect with millions of consumers around the globe. It was one of the fastest-growing brands in a *BusinessWeek* survey of the top one hundred global brands published August 5. At a time when one corporate star after another has crashed to earth, brought down by revelations of earnings misstatements, executive greed, or worse, Starbucks hasn't faltered. The company confidently predicts up to 25 percent annual sales and earnings growth in 2002. On Wall Street, Starbucks is the last great growth story. Its stock, including four splits, has soared more than 2,200 percent over the past decade, surpassing Wal-Mart, General Electric, PepsiCo, Coca-Cola, Microsoft, and IBM in total return. Now at $21, it is hovering near its all-time high of $23 in July, before the overall market drop.

And after a slowdown last fall and winter, when consumers seemed to draw inward after September 11, Starbucks is rocketing ahead once again. Sales in stores open at least 13 months grew by 6 percent in the 43 weeks through July 28, and the company predicts monthly same-store sales gains as high as 7 percent through the end of this fiscal year. That's below the 9 percent growth rate in 2000, but investors seem encouraged. "We're going to see a lot more growth," says Jerome A.

Castellini, president of Chicago-based CastleArk Management, which controls about 300,000 Starbucks shares. "The stock is on a run."

But how long can that run last? Already, Schultz's team is hard-pressed to grind out new profits in a home market that is quickly becoming saturated. Amazingly, with 4,247 stores scattered across the U.S. and Canada, there are still eight states in the U.S. with no Starbucks stores. Frappuccino-free cities include Butte, Montana, and Fargo, North Dakota. But big cities, affluent suburbs, and shopping malls are full to the brim. In coffee-crazed Seattle, there is a Starbucks outlet for every 9,400 people, and the company considers that the upper limit of coffee-shop saturation. In Manhattan's 24 square miles, Starbucks has 124 cafés, with four more on the way this year. That's one for every 12,000 people—meaning that there could be room for even more stores. Given such concentration, it is likely to take annual same-store sales increases of 10 percent or more if the company is going to match its historic overall sales growth. That, as they might say at Starbucks, is a tall order to fill.

Indeed, the crowding of so many stores so close together has become a national joke, eliciting quips such as this headline in *The Onion,* a satirical publication: "A New Starbucks Opens in Rest-room of Existing Starbucks." And even the company admits that while its practice of blanketing an area with stores helps achieve market dominance, it can cut sales at existing outlets. "We probably self-cannibalize our stores at a rate of 30 percent a year," Schultz says. Adds Lehman Brothers Inc. analyst Mitchell Speiser: "Starbucks is at a defining point in its growth. It's reaching a level that makes it harder and harder to grow, just due to the law of large numbers."

To duplicate the staggering returns of its first decade, Starbucks has no choice but to export its concept aggressively. Indeed, some analysts give Starbucks only two years at most before it saturates the U.S. market. The chain now operates 1,200 international outlets, from Beijing to Bristol. That leaves plenty of room to grow. Indeed, about 400 of its planned 1,200 new stores this year will be built overseas, representing a 35 percent increase in its foreign base. Starbucks expects to double the number of its stores worldwide, to 10,000 in three years. During the past 12 months, the chain has opened stores in Vienna, Zurich, Madrid,

Berlin, and even in far-off Jakarta. Athens comes next. And within the next year, Starbucks plans to move into Mexico and Puerto Rico. But global expansion poses huge risks for Starbucks. For one thing, it makes less money on each overseas store because most of them are operated with local partners. While that makes it easier to start up on foreign turf, it reduces the company's share of the profits to only 20 percent to 50 percent.

Moreover, Starbucks must cope with some predictable challenges of becoming a mature company in the U.S. After riding the wave of successful baby boomers through the '90s, the company faces an ominously hostile reception from its future consumers, the twenty- or thirtysomethings of Generation X. Not only are the activists among them turned off by the power and image of the well-known brand, but many others say that Starbucks' latte-sipping sophisticates and piped-in Kenny G music are a real turnoff. They don't feel wanted in a place that sells designer coffee at $3 a cup.

Even the thirst of loyalists for high-priced coffee can't be taken for granted. Starbucks' growth over the past decade coincided with a remarkable surge in the economy. Consumer spending has continued strong in the downturn, but if that changes, those $3 lattes might be an easy place for people on a budget to cut back. Starbucks executives insist that won't happen, pointing out that even in the weeks following the terrorist attacks, same-store comparisons stayed positive while those of other retailers skidded.

Starbucks also faces slumping morale and employee burnout among its store managers and its once-cheery army of *baristas*. Stock options for part-timers in the restaurant business was a Starbucks innovation that once commanded awe and respect from its employees. But now, though employees are still paid better than comparable workers elsewhere— about $7 per hour—many regard the job as just another fast-food gig. Dissatisfaction over odd hours and low pay is affecting the quality of the normally sterling service and even the coffee itself, say some customers and employees. Frustrated store managers among the company's roughly 470 California stores sued Starbucks in 2001 for allegedly refusing to pay legally mandated overtime. Starbucks settled the suit for $18 million this past April, shaving $0.03 per share off an otherwise strong second quarter. However, the heart of the complaint—feeling overworked and underappreciated—doesn't seem to be going away.

To be sure, Starbucks has a lot going for it as it confronts the challenge of maintaining its growth. Nearly free of debt, it fuels expansion with internal cash flow. And Starbucks can maintain a tight grip on its image because stores are company-owned: There are no franchisees to get sloppy about running things. By relying on mystique and word-of-mouth, whether here or overseas, the company saves a bundle on marketing costs. Starbucks spends just $30 million annually on advertising, or roughly 1 percent of revenues, usually just for new flavors of coffee drinks in the summer and product launches, such as its new in-store web service. Most consumer companies its size shell out upwards of $300 million per year. Moreover, unlike a McDonald's or a Gap Inc., two other retailers that rapidly grew in the U.S., Starbucks has no nationwide competitor.

Starbucks also has a well-seasoned management team. Schultz, 49, stepped down as chief executive in 2000 to become chairman and chief global strategist. Orin Smith, 60, the company's numbers-cruncher, is now CEO and in charge of day-to-day operations. The head of North American operations is Howard Behar, 57, a retailing expert who returned last September, two years after retiring. The management trio is known as H_2O, for Howard, Howard, and Orin.

Schultz remains the heart and soul of the operation. Raised in a Brooklyn public-housing project, he found his way to Starbucks, a tiny chain of Seattle coffee shops, as a marketing executive in the early '80s. The name came about when the original owners looked to Seattle history for inspiration and chose the moniker of an old mining camp: Starbo. Further refinement led to Starbucks, after the first mate in *Moby-Dick,* which they felt evoked the seafaring romance of the early coffee traders (hence the mermaid logo). Schultz got the idea for the modern Starbucks format while visiting a Milan coffee bar. He bought out his bosses in 1987 and began expanding. Today, Schultz has a net worth of about $700 million, including $400 million of company stock.

Starbucks has come light-years from those humble beginnings, but Schultz and his team still think there's room to grow in the U.S.—even in communities where the chain already has dozens of stores. Clustering stores increases total revenue and market share, Smith argues, even when individual stores poach on each other's sales. The strategy works, he says, because of Starbucks' size. It is large enough to absorb losses at existing stores as new ones open up, and soon overall sales grow beyond what they would have with just one store. Meanwhile, it's cheaper to deliver to and manage stores located close together. And by clustering, Starbucks can quickly dominate a local market.

The company is still capable of designing and opening a store in 16 weeks or less and recouping the initial investment in three years. The stores may be oases of tranquillity, but management's expansion tactics are something else. Take what critics call its "predatory real estate" strategy—paying more than market-rate rents to keep competitors out of a location. David C. Schomer, owner of Espresso Vivace in Seattle's hip Capitol Hill neighborhood, says Starbucks approached his landlord and offered to pay nearly double the rate to put a coffee shop in the same building. The landlord stuck with Schomer, who says: "It's a little disconcerting to know that someone is willing to pay twice the going rate." Another time, Starbucks and Tully's Coffee Corp., a Seattle-based coffee chain, were competing for a space in the city. Starbucks got the lease but vacated the premises before the term was up. Still, rather than let Tully's get the space, Starbucks decided to pay the rent on the empty store so its competitor could not move in. Schultz makes no apologies for the hardball tactics. "The real estate business in America is a very, very tough game," he says. "It's not for the faint of heart."

Still, the company's strategy could backfire. Not only will neighborhood activists and local businesses increasingly resent the tactics, but customers could also grow annoyed over having fewer choices. Moreover, analysts contend that Starbucks can maintain about 15 percent square-footage growth in the U.S.—equivalent to 550 new stores—for only about two more years. After that, it will have to depend on overseas growth to maintain annual 20 percent revenue growth.

Starbucks was hoping to make up much of that growth with more sales of food and other noncoffee items, but has stumbled somewhat. In the late '90s, Schultz thought that offering $8 sandwiches, desserts, and CDs in his stores and selling packaged coffee in supermarkets would significantly boost sales. The specialty business now accounts for about

16 percent of sales, but growth has been less than expected. A healthy 19 percent this year, it's still far below the 38 percent growth rate of fiscal 2000. That suggests that while coffee can command high prices in a slump, food—at least at Starbucks—cannot. One of Behar's most important goals is to improve that record. For instance, the company now has a test program of serving hot breakfasts in twenty Seattle stores and may move to expand supermarket sales of whole beans.

What's more important for the bottom line, though, is that Starbucks has proven to be highly innovative in the way it sells its main course: coffee. In 800 locations it has installed automatic espresso machines to speed up service. And in November, it began offering prepaid Starbucks cards, priced from $5 to $500, which clerks swipe through a reader to deduct a sale. That, says the company, cuts transaction times in half. Starbucks has sold $70 million of the cards.

In early August, Starbucks launched Starbucks Express, its boldest experiment yet, which blends java, web technology, and faster service. At about 60 stores in the Denver area, customers can preorder and prepay for beverages and pastries via phone or on the Starbucks Express web site. They just make the call or click the mouse before arriving at the store, and their beverage will be waiting—with their name printed on the cup. The company will decide in January on a national launch.

And Starbucks is bent on even more fundamental store changes. On August 21, it announced expansion of a high-speed wireless internet service to about 1,200 Starbucks locations in North America and Europe. Partners in the project—which Starbucks calls the world's largest Wi-Fi network—include Mobile International, a wireless subsidiary of Deutsche Telekom, and Hewlett-Packard. Customers sit in a store and check e-mail, surf the web, or download multimedia presentations without looking for connections or tripping over cords. They start with 24 hours of free wireless broadband before choosing from a variety of monthly subscription plans.

Starbucks executives hope such innovations will help surmount their toughest challenge in the home market: attracting the next generation of customers. Younger coffee drinkers already feel uncomfortable in the stores. The company knows that because it once had a group of twentysomethings hypnotized for a market study. When their defenses were down, out came the bad news. "They either can't afford to buy coffee at Starbucks, or the only peers they see are those working behind the counter," says Mark Barden, who conducted the research for the Hal Riney & Partners ad agency (now part of Publicis Worldwide) in San Francisco. One of the recurring themes the hypnosis brought out was a sense that "people like me aren't welcome here except to serve the yuppies," he says. Then there are those who just find the whole Starbucks scene a bit pretentious. Katie Kelleher, 22, a Chicago paralegal, is put off by Starbucks' Italian terminology of *grande* and *venti* for coffee sizes. She goes to Dunkin' Donuts, saying: "Small, medium, and large is fine for me."

As it expands, Starbucks faces another big risk: that of becoming a far less special place for its employees. For a company modeled around enthusiastic service, that could have dire consequences for both image and sales. During its growth spurt of the mid- to late-1990s, Starbucks had the lowest employee turnover rate of any restaurant or fast-food company, largely thanks to its then unheard-of policy of giving health insurance and modest stock options to part-timers making barely more than minimum wage.

Such perks are no longer enough to keep all the workers happy. Starbucks' pay doesn't come close to matching the workload it requires, complain some staff. Says Carrie Shay, a former store manager in West Hollywood, California: "If I were making a decent living, I'd still be there." Shay, one of the plaintiffs in the suit against the company, says she earned $32,000 a year to run a store with 10 to 15 part-time employees. She hired employees, managed their schedules, and monitored the store's weekly profit-and-loss statement. But she was also expected to put in significant time behind the counter and had to sign an affidavit pledging to work up to 20 hours of overtime a week without extra pay—a requirement the company has dropped since the settlement. Smith says that Starbucks offers better pay, benefits, and training than comparable companies, while it encourages promotions from within.

For sure, employee discontent is far from the image Starbucks wants to project of relaxed workers cheerfully making cappuccinos. But perhaps it is inevitable. The business model calls for lots of low-wage workers. And the more people who are hired as Starbucks expands, the less they are apt to feel connected to the original mission of high service—bantering with customers and treating them like family. Robert J. Thompson, a professor of popular culture at Syracuse University, says of Starbucks: "It's turning out to be one of the great twenty-first-century American success stories—complete with all the ambiguities."

Overseas, though, the whole Starbucks package seems new and, to many young people, still very cool. In Vienna, where Starbucks had a gala opening for its first Austrian store last December, Helmut Spudich, a business editor for the paper *Der Standard,* predicted that Starbucks would attract a younger crowd than the established cafés. "The coffeehouses in Vienna are nice, but they are old. Starbucks is considered hip," he says.

But if Starbucks can count on its youth appeal to win a welcome in new markets, such enthusiasm cannot be counted on indefinitely. In Japan, the company beat even its own bullish expectations, growing to 368 stores after opening its first in Tokyo in 1996. Affluent young Japanese women like Anna Kato, a 22-year-old Toyota Motor Corp. worker, loved the place. "I don't care if it costs more, as long as it tastes sweet," she says, sitting in the world's busiest Starbucks, in Tokyo's Shibuya district. Yet same-store sales growth has fallen in the past ten months in Japan, Starbucks' top foreign market, as rivals offer similar fare. Add to that the depressed economy, and Starbucks Japan seems to be losing steam. Although it forecasts a 30 percent gain in net profit, to $8 million, for the year started in April, on record sales of $516 million, same-store sales are down 14 percent for the year ended in June. Meanwhile in England, Starbucks' second-biggest overseas market, with 310 stores, imitators are popping up left and right to steal market share.

Entering other big markets may be tougher yet. The French seem to be ready for Starbucks' sweeter taste, says Philippe Bloch, cofounder of Columbus Café, a Starbucks-like chain. But he wonders if the company can profitably cope with France's arcane regulations and generous labor benefits. And in Italy, the epicenter of European coffee culture, the notion that the locals will abandon their own 200,000 coffee bars en masse for Starbucks strikes many as ludicrous. For one, Italian coffee bars prosper by serving food as well as coffee, an area where Starbucks still struggles. Also, Italian coffee is cheaper than U.S. java and, say Italian purists, much better. Americans pay about $1.50 for an espresso. In northern Italy, the price is 67¢; in the south, just 55¢. Schultz insists that Starbucks will eventually come to Italy. It'll have a lot to prove when it does. Carlo Petrini, founder of the antiglobalization movement Slow Food, sniffs that Starbucks' "substances served in styrofoam" won't cut it. The cups are paper, of course. But the skepticism is real.

As Starbucks spreads out, Schultz will have to be increasingly sensitive to those cultural challenges. In December, for instance, he flew to Israel to meet with Foreign Secretary Shimon Peres and other Israeli officials to discuss the Middle East crisis. He won't divulge the nature of his discussions. But subsequently, at a Seattle synagogue, Schultz let the Palestinians have it. With Starbucks outlets already in Kuwait, Lebanon, Oman, Qatar, and Saudi Arabia, he created a mild uproar among Palestinian supporters. Schultz quickly backpedaled, saying that his words were taken out of context and asserting that he is "propeace" for both sides.

There are plenty more minefields ahead. So far, the Seattle coffee company has compiled an envious record of growth. But the giddy buzz of that initial expansion is wearing off. Now, Starbucks is waking up to the *grande* challenges faced by any corporation bent on becoming a global powerhouse.

Google. Can't live with it, can't live without it. The immense popularity of the Google search engine has made it a dominant force to be
reckoned with. This article by Stefanie Olsen in CNET News.com
considers whether its power is threatening the web's independence
or it is simply reaping the benefits of being very good at what it does.

Stefanie Olsen

The Google Gods

PATRICK AHERN HAS WITNESSED the power of Google—
and the difficulties of trying to do business without it.

Data Recovery Group, where he is president, would typically come
up around the fourth listing on Google's popular search engine last year.
Then in January, when Google removed the company from its listings
without explanation, Data Recovery saw a 30 percent drop in business.

"When you're number four that plays well; when you fall off, you
tend to lose phone traffic. And if you don't have the right relationship
with Google to find out what you could have done wrong, you're out of
luck," Ahern said, noting that this can have a dangerous domino effect.
"If you're not ranked in Google, Yahoo! won't list you. It's incestuous."

In the dot-com shakeout, Google has not only survived but reigns
supreme. Web surfers have flocked to the service, effectively voting it
the best search engine around. So powerful has Google become that
many companies view it as the web itself: If you're not listed on its
indexes, they say, you might as well not exist. And if you don't advertise

on Google or otherwise curry favor, critics add, you may never find out what it takes to get a prominent listing.

Pragmatists in the industry even say its dominance in web search gives Google a new responsibility to maintain fair access to as many sites as possible, leading some to suggest that it be regulated as a quasi-public agency. Last week, for example, an Oklahoma marketing firm filed suit against Google in federal court charging that Google unfairly began listing the company lower in search results.

"So many people are dependent on Google's free editorial traffic that it's like food out of their mouths to lose ranking," said Danny Sullivan, who runs Searchenginewatch.com. "Search engines are not in the business of supporting people's companies. But if they are going to provide editorial, they need to provide support. These are some of the issues they face."

Only a few years ago, when traffic was more evenly distributed among search services, web sites clamored to get free listings from familiar names such as Lycos and AltaVista. But the dot-com collapse led portals and search engines to sell sponsored links and license editorial results from a third party—a market that Google, based in Mountain View, California, has come to dominate since its founding in 1998.

Leading portals and internet service providers such as Yahoo!, America Online, and Earthlink have turned to Google to power their searches because of its simple, straightforward style and consistency for serving up germane results. Such companies typically mix Google's results with listings of their own to maintain some autonomy and uniqueness on the web. It is these deals that have catapulted Google ahead of competitors and sent web site operators scrambling for prominent listings in its search results.

"It's not like we've put all our eggs in one basket—it's just that there is no other basket," said Greg Boser, president of web marketing consultancy WebGuerrilla, which helps companies improve their visibility in search engines.

In many ways, this is no exaggeration. Google averages about 15 million visitor hours each month, compared with Yahoo! search at 6 million hours, according to Sullivan. Search hours are calculated by factoring the number of site visitors by the average number of minutes each spends at the site.

Yahoo! recently renewed its partnership with Google for an unspecified term, a deal some doubted would happen because of the search darling's growing threat. Yahoo! has even given Google more editorial voice and played down its own directory results. Search engine experts say that in comparison tests, a search on Google and on Yahoo! varies little for popular terms like Britney Spears or NFL.

Google software engineer Matt Cutts said that the search engine business is healthier and more competitive than ever, with many niche providers and international forces. "What we worry about is providing the best results to users; we don't worry about market share," he said. "That will all work itself out."

Exactly how the system works itself out, however, is what worries people in the industry. Boser and others are concerned that paid advertisers get crucial advice that maximizes their editorial listings.

"As you're spending money with them as an advertiser, that spending does not buy you position; that spending buys you advice on how to *get* position—a by-product of the advertising sport," said Data Recovery's Ahern, a client of WebGuerrilla.

Ahern learned that the term "data recovery" was a valuable commodity in paid search, worth as much as $10 per click. As a result, he was forced to spend several thousand dollars a month on pay-per-click advertising on Google and rival Overture to compensate for losing up to 85 percent of his traffic earlier this year. Ahern no longer buys Google ads because his top position has been restored, but it has been an expensive process.

The depth of concern about the search industry's practices was made clear at a conference earlier this year, where participants stressed the need for policies to protect web sites dependent on the engines.

Among the proposals were calls for fair and consistent spam-reporting policies in which Google and others reply to all complaints, not just those from advertisers. Also suggested were standards for a formal review system that helped sites understand why they're not listed and thereby give them information necessary to improve their chances.

Craig Silverstein, Google's chief technology officer, denies that advertisers get preferential treatment in its editorial listings. On the issue of information about changes in rankings, he said it is impractical to provide support for everyone, considering that the company indexes nearly 2.1 billion pages. But Google is examining its system, well aware that growing criticism could damage its credibility with the public at large.

In an effort to beat Google at its own game, some marketers have adopted guerrilla tactics that try to manipulate search rankings. This has led to a proliferation of "link farms"—elaborate linking schemes designed to manipulate one of Google's only publicized algorithms, PageRank, which factors a site's popularity based on the number of web pages that link to that site.

Many industry executives speculate that Google changed its search algorithm in September to combat link farms, which caused a shift in listings and a lower number of documents served up for any given query. The changes have thrown webmasters into a frenzy, as shown in thousands of messages on industry sites such as SearchEngineForums.

Daniel Brandt, who publishes the watchdog site Google-watch.org, complains that PageRank is the equivalent of a popularity contest that favors major, established web sites. "We don't know which comes first—whether Google is reflecting popularity or if it's creating popularity," he said.

Silverstein asserts that Google does not provide preferential treatment to advertisers in text results or target smaller sites for delisting. Google alters its algorithms all the time to improve search quality, he said, and sites might have seen changes recently because of a "fresh crawl" that updates up to three million documents more regularly.

As for tactics such as spam and link farms, Google says those just make accurate searches more difficult for surfers. That, in turn, could affect Google's credibility at a time when trust is more important to the company than ever.

"There's a constant battle between abusive technologies and providing relevant search results," Silverstein said. "When you use something as a tool and you don't have control over it, that's an issue, an issue of trust. You need to be able to trust us that we are acting in the best interests of our user."

Others dismiss much of the complaint about Google as conspiracy theory, saying it should not be required to baby-sit sites that have simply fallen victim to the internet's evolution.

"Google is a great scapegoat when people get mad. But it's about protecting relevancy," said Jessie Stricchiola, president of Alchemist Media, which helps companies improve traffic to their web sites. "The cannibalization of search results has the potential to become problematic, because you have one chance with ten distribution channels. But that's the nature of how the web is evolving—that's not Google's fault."

Make no mistake about it: America's largest retailer doesn't want
unions. This article by Karen Olsson in *Mother Jones* magazine takes us
inside Wal-Mart for a look at organizing efforts by some of its associates seeking improved wages and benefits. It also depicts the company's anti-union response that is dispatched to stores where labor
organizing appears to be a threat. Meanwhile, battles in the courtroom
between unions and the company continue.

Karen Olsson

Up Against Wal-Mart

JENNIFER MCLAUGHLIN IS 22, has a baby, drives a truck,
wears wide-leg jeans and spiky plastic chokers, dyes her hair dark red,
and works at Wal-Mart. The store in Paris, Texas—Wal-Mart Supercenter #148—is just down the road from the modest apartment complex
where McLaughlin lives with her boyfriend and her one-year-old son;
five days a week she drives to the store, puts on a blue vest with "How
May I Help You?" emblazoned across the back, and clocks in. Some days
she works in the Garden Center and some days in the toy department.
The pace is frenetic, even by the normally fast-paced standards of retailing; often, it seems, there simply aren't enough people around to get the
job done. On a given shift McLaughlin might man a register, hop on a
mechanical lift to retrieve something from a high shelf, catch fish from a
tank, run over to another department to help locate an item, restock the
shelves, dust off the bike racks, or field questions about potting soil and
lawn mowers. "It's stressful," she says. "They push you to the limit. They

just want to see how much they can get away with without having to hire someone else."

Then there's the matter of her pay. After three years with the company, McLaughlin earns only $16,800 a year. "And I'm considered high-paid," she says. "The way they pay you, you cannot make it by yourself without having a second job or someone to help you, unless you've been there for twenty years or you're a manager." Because health insurance on the Wal-Mart plan would deduct up to $85 from her biweekly paycheck of $550, she goes without, and relies on Medicaid to cover her son, Gage.

Complaints about understaffing and low pay are not uncommon among retail workers—but Wal-Mart is no mere peddler of saucepans and boom boxes. The company is the world's largest retailer, with $220 billion in sales, and the nation's largest private employer, with 3,372 stores and more than one million hourly workers. Its annual revenues account for 2 percent of America's entire domestic product. Even as the economy has slowed, the company has continued to metastasize, with plans to add 800,000 more jobs worldwide by 2007.

Given its staggering size and rapid expansion, Wal-Mart increasingly sets the standard for wages and benefits throughout the U.S. economy. "Americans can't live on a Wal-Mart paycheck," says Greg Denier, communications director for the United Food and Commercial Workers International Union (UFCW). "Yet it's the dominant employer, and what they pay will be the future of working America." The average hourly worker at Wal-Mart earns barely $18,000 a year at a company that pocketed $6.6 billion in profits last year. Forty percent of employees opt not to receive coverage under the company's medical plan, which costs up to $2,844 a year, plus a deductible. As Jennifer McLaughlin puts it, "They're on top of the Fortune 500, and I can't get health insurance for my kid."

Angered by the disparity between profits and wages, thousands of former and current employees like McLaughlin have started to fight the company on a variety of fronts. Workers in 27 states are suing Wal-Mart for violating wage-and-hour laws; in the first of the cases to go to trial, an Oregon jury found the company guilty in December 2002 of systematically forcing employees to work overtime without pay. The retailer also faces a sex-discrimination lawsuit that accuses it of wrongly denying promotions and equal pay to 700,000 women. And across the country, workers have launched a massive drive to organize a union at Wal-Mart, demanding better wages and working conditions. Employees at more than 100 stores in 25 states—including Supercenter #148 in Paris—are currently trying to unionize the company, and in July the UFCW launched an organizing blitz in the Midwest, hoping to mobilize nearly 120,000 workers in Michigan, Kentucky, Ohio, and Indiana.

Wal-Mart has responded to the union drive by trying to stop workers from organizing—sometimes in violation of federal labor law. In ten separate cases, the National Labor Relations Board has ruled that Wal-Mart repeatedly broke the law by interrogating workers, confiscating union literature, and firing union supporters. At the first sign of organizing in a store, Wal-Mart dispatches a team of union busters from its headquarters in Bentonville, Arkansas, sometimes setting up surveillance cameras to monitor workers. "In my 35 years in labor relations, I've never seen a company that will go to the lengths that Wal-Mart goes to, to avoid a union," says Martin Levitt, a management consultant who helped the company develop its anti-union tactics before writing a book called *Confessions of a Union Buster*. "They have zero tolerance."

The retaliation can be extreme. In February 2000, the meat-cutting department at a Wal-Mart in Jacksonville, Texas, voted to join the UFCW—the only Wal-Mart in the nation where workers successfully organized a union. Two weeks after the vote, the company announced it was eliminating its meat-cutting departments in all of its stores nationwide. It also fired four workers who voted for the union. "They held a meeting and said there was nothing we could do," recalls Dotty Jones, a former meat cutter in Jacksonville. "No matter which way the election went, they would hold it up in court until we were old and gray."

If you've seen one Wal-Mart, you've seen the Paris store, more or less: a gray cinder-block warehouse of a building, with a red stripe across the front, flags on the roof, WAL★MART spelled in large capitals in the center, and the company credos ("We Sell for Less" and "Everyday Low

Prices") to the left and the right. Inside, the cavernous store is bathed in a dim fluorescent light that makes the white walls and linoleum look dingy, and on a Friday shortly before Christmas, the merchandise is everywhere: not only in bins and on shelves, but in boxes waiting to be unloaded, or just stationed in some odd corner, like the pine gun cabinets ($169.87) lined up by the rest rooms. Television monitors advertise thermometers and compact discs, Christmas carols play over the audio system, and yet there's a kind of silence to the place, a suspension of ordinary life, as shoppers in their trances drift through the store and fill carts with tubs of popcorn, a microwave, a chess set, dog biscuits. Here Protestant thrift and consumer wants are reconciled, for the moment anyway, in carts brimming with bargains.

Wal-Mart's success story was scripted by its founder, Sam Walton, whose genius was not so much for innovation as for picking which of his competitors' innovations to copy in his own stores. In 1945, Walton bought a franchise variety store in Newport, Arkansas. The most successful retailers, he noticed, were chains like Sears and A&P, which distributed goods to stores most efficiently, lowered prices to generate a larger volume of sales, and in the process generated a lot of cash to finance further expansion. These, in turn, would serve as basic principles of Walton's business. As he explains in his autobiography, *Sam Walton, Made in America,* he drove long distances to buy ladies' panties at lower prices, recognizing that selling more pairs at four for a dollar would bring greater profits than selling fewer pairs at three for a dollar. The women of northeastern Arkansas were soon awash in underwear, and a discounter was born. Walton opened his first Wal-Mart Discount City in 1962 and gradually expanded out from his Arkansas base. By 1970 Wal-Mart owned 32 outlets; by 1980 there were 276; by 1990, 1,528 in 29 states.

The company grew, in no small part, by dint of its legendary frugality—a habit that started with Sam Walton himself, who drove an old pickup truck and shared hotel rooms on company trips and insisted on keeping the headquarters in Arkansas as plain as possible. Payroll, of course, tends to be a rather larger expense than hotel rooms, and Walton kept that as low as he could, too. He paid his first clerks 50 to 60 cents an hour—substantially below minimum wage at the time—by taking questionable advantage of a small-business exemption to the Fair Labor Standards Act. In 1970, Walton fended off an organizing push by the Retail Clerks Union in two small Missouri towns by hiring a professional union buster, John Tate, to lecture workers on the negative aspects of unions. On Tate's advice, he also took steps to win his workers over, encouraging them to air concerns with managers and implementing a profit-sharing plan.

A few years later, Wal-Mart hired a consulting firm named Alpha Associates to develop a "union avoidance program." Martin Levitt, the consultant who worked on the program, says that Wal-Mart does "whatever it takes to wear people down and destroy their spirit." Each manager, he says, is taught to take union organizing personally: "Anyone supporting a union is slapping that supervisor in the face." The company also encouraged employees to believe in the good intentions of "Mr. Sam," who peppered his autobiography with tributes to his "associates": "If you want to take care of the customers you have to make sure you're taking care of the people in the stores."

Yet many Wal-Mart workers allege that the company Walton left behind when he died in 1992 is anything but a benevolent caretaker. "We're underpaid, and I'm worried about my retirement," says an overnight stocker in Minnesota who asked not to be identified. "I imagine I'll be working until I'm ninety." Her daughter works as a stocker, too, but after nine years she doesn't make enough to support her children. "She's had to go down to the food bank, and I've sent stuff over for them," her mother says. "They just can't do it." On the job, she adds, workers are forced to scramble to make up for understaffing. "We're short—we have a skimpy crew at night. We've got pallets stacked over our heads, and we can't get caught up with all of it."

A quick look around at the store in Paris makes clear what an employee is up against: thousands of items (90,000 in a typical Wal-Mart) that customers are constantly removing from the shelves and not putting back, or putting back in the wrong place, or dropping on the floor—the store a kind of Augean stable, with a corps of blue-vested Herculeses trying to keep things clean. (When I mention this to Jennifer McLaughlin, she tells me that's why no one likes to work the 2 a.m. to 11 a.m. shift, because "all it is, is putting stuff back.") To get the job done, according to the dozens of employee lawsuits filed against the company, Wal-Mart routinely forces employees to work overtime without pay. In the Oregon wage-and-hour case, a former personnel manager named Carolyn Thiebes testified that supervisors, pressured by company headquarters to keep payroll low, regularly deleted hours from time records and reprimanded employees who claimed overtime. In 2000, Wal-Mart settled similar lawsuits involving 67,000 workers in New Mexico and Colorado, reportedly paying more than $50 million.

Wal-Mart blames unpaid overtime on individual department managers, insisting that such practices violate company policy. "We rely on our associates," says spokesman Bill Wertz. "It makes no business sense whatsoever to mistreat them." But Russell Lloyd, an attorney representing Wal-Mart employees in Texas, says the company "has a pattern throughout all stores of treating their workers the same way." Corporate headquarters collects reams of data on every store and every employee, he says, and uses sales figures to calculate how many hours of labor it wants to allot to each store. Store managers are then required to schedule fewer hours than the number allotted, and their performance is monitored in daily reports back to Bentonville. To meet the goals, supervisors pressure employees to work extra hours without pay.

"I was asked to work off the clock, sometimes by the store manager, sometimes by the assistant manager," says Liberty Morales Serna, a former employee in Houston. "They would know you'd clocked out already, and they'd say, 'Do me a favor. I don't have anyone coming in—could you stay here?' It would be like four or five hours. They were understaffed, and they expected you to work these hours."

When Judy Danneman, a widow raising three children, went to work as an hourly department manager in West Palm Beach, Florida, she quickly realized that she would have to climb the management ladder in order to survive—because, as she puts it, "my kids had this bad habit of eating." The only way to do that, she says, was to work off the clock: "Working unpaid overtime equaled saving your job." When she finally became an assistant manager, Danneman knew she had to enforce the same policy: "I knew for my department managers to get their work done, they had to work off the clock. It was an unwritten rule. The majority of them were single mothers raising children, or else married women with children. It was sad, and it was totally demanding and very draining and very stressful."

In fact, more than two-thirds of all Wal-Mart employees are women—yet women make up less than 10 percent of top store managers. Back when she was first lady of Arkansas, Hillary Clinton became the first woman appointed to the Wal-Mart board, and tried to get the company to hire more women managers, but that effort apparently went the way of national health insurance. Wal-Mart today has the same percentage of women in management that the average company had in 1975.

Attorneys representing workers contend that Wal-Mart is too tightly controlled from headquarters in Arkansas to claim ignorance of what's happening in its stores. "In Bentonville they control the air conditioning, the music, and the freezer temperature for each store," says Brad Seligman, a lawyer with the Impact Fund, a nonprofit legal organization in Berkeley. "Most companies divide stores into regions, and then you have a home office of senior management. At Wal-Mart, the regional managers are based in Bentonville; they're on the road Sunday to Wednesday, and then back meeting with management Thursday to Saturday. They're the ones who make the fundamental employee decisions—and the home office knows exactly what they are doing."

The company insists it adequately trains and promotes female managers. But in 2001, a Wal-Mart executive conducted an internal study that showed the company pays female store managers less than men in the same position. "Their focus at Wal-Mart has always relentlessly been on the bottom line and on cost cutting," says Seligman. "Virtually every other consideration is secondary—or third or fourth or fifth."

To protect the bottom line Wal-Mart is as aggressive at fighting off unions as it is at cutting costs. Employees approached by coworkers about joining a union are "scared to even talk," says Ricky Braswell, a "greeter" at the store in Paris. "They're afraid they'll lose their jobs."

In Paris, it was Jennifer McLaughlin's boyfriend, 21-year-old Eric Jackson, who first started talking about a union. Raised by a mother who works in a factory, Jackson always assumed he would find a job after high school rather than go on to college. But the few factory jobs in Paris are highly sought after, so Jackson wound up at Wal-Mart, which employs 350 people out of a local workforce of only 22,000. "People ain't got no other place to go," he says. "There's no other jobs to be had."

Jackson started as an evening cashier earning $5.75 an hour, and it wasn't long before he was regularly asked to perform the duties of a customer service manager, supervising the other cashiers and scheduling their breaks. He asked for a promotion, but three months later he was still doing the extra work for no extra pay. "I took it because I wanted more money, but I never got the raise," Jackson says. "They knew they could do it to me." He fought for the promotion and eventually won, but by then he had already contacted a local union office about organizing the store.

"When Eric first suggested it, I looked at him like he was on crack," says McLaughlin. "I said, 'You can't take down a company like Wal-Mart with a union.'" Nevertheless, Jackson arranged for a UFCW organizer to come to Paris and meet with a small group of workers one June afternoon at the Pizza Inn. But the company soon caught wind of the organizing effort. As one worker left an early meeting of union supporters, he spotted a Wal-Mart manager in the parking lot. From then on, workers seen as pro-union were watched closely by management.

"By the time we had our first meeting, they were holding their first anti-union meeting," says McLaughlin. The response came straight from the company's union-avoidance playbook: Troops from the Bentonville "People Division" were flown in, and employees were required to attend hour-long meetings, where they were shown anti-labor videos and warned about unions. "They tend to treat you like you're simple, and they use real bad scare tactics," says McLaughlin. Those who supported the union, she says, were told, "Some people just don't belong at Wal-Mart."

McLaughlin isn't shy about speaking her mind, and in the meeting she confronted one of the men from the People Division. "Let me tell you, I used to have epilepsy," she told him. "My dad was in a union, and we had health insurance, and I got better. I don't have health insurance. If my child got epilepsy, what would I do? Doesn't a union help you to get company-paid insurance?" The man, she recalls, became flustered.

"Jennifer, I don't have an answer about that," he said. "I'll have to get back with you."

The meetings were just the beginning. "The videos and group meetings are the surface cosmetics," says Levitt, the former consultant. "Where Wal-Mart beats the union is through a one-on-one process implemented from Bentonville. They carefully instruct management to individually work over each employee who might be a union sympathizer." In Paris, Eric Jackson was called into a back room by five managers and made to watch an anti-union video and participate in a role-playing exercise. "I was supposed to be a manager, and one of them was the associate who came to me with a question about a union," says Jackson. "So I quoted the video. I said, 'We do not believe we need a union at Wal-Mart,' and they were like, 'Good, good!' and then I said, 'We're not anti-union—we're pro-associate,' just like I'm supposed to say."

Before the onslaught by the company, says McLaughlin, she talked to more than 70 workers at the Paris store who were prepared to sign cards calling for a vote on union representation, but that number quickly dwindled. Those who'd signed cards felt they were being watched. "All of a sudden the cameras start going up," says Chris Bills, who works in the receiving area. "Now there's three in receiving. This one manager took up smoking so he could sit with us on our breaks." Other hourly employees learned for the first time that they were actually counted as managers. "They said we were considered management, so we shouldn't get involved with the union stuff," says Dianne Smallwood, a former customer service manager who worked at the store seven years. Employees opposed to the union were given "pro-associate" buttons to wear, while managers amended the dress code to exclude T-shirts with any kind of writing on them, apparently to prevent workers from wearing union shirts.

Wal-Mart declined to let *Mother Jones* interview store managers or representatives from the People Division in Bentonville, but says it sends out people from corporate headquarters "to answer questions associates may have and to make sure that all store personnel are aware of their legal requirements and meet those requirements exactly." But the company has also made clear that keeping its stores union-free is as much a part of Wal-Mart culture as door greeters and blue aprons. "Union representation may work well for others," says Cynthia Illick, a company spokeswoman. "However, it is not a fit for Wal-Mart."

With the company so determined to ward off unions, the prospects of employees in towns like Paris, Texas, winning significant improvements in wages and working conditions seems awfully slim. "It's a long process," Jennifer McLaughlin concedes. "I wish it could be done in the next year, but people come and go, and for every one union card you get signed, two other ones who signed cards have gotten fired or left. It's real frustrating, and a lot of times I don't want to do it no more. But I'm not going to give up until I end up leaving the store."

In the end, the success of the organizing drives may depend on labor's ability to mobilize more than just store employees. "We'll never bring Wal-Mart to the table store by store," says Bernie Hesse, an organizer for UFCW Local 789 in Minneapolis. "I can get all the cards signed I want, and they'll still crush us. They'll close the frigging store, I'm convinced. We've got to do it in conjunction with the community." That means going to small businesses and religious leaders and local officials, he says, and convincing them that it's in their interest to stand up to Wal-Mart. "As a community we've got to say, 'All right, if you want to come here and do business, here's what you've got to do—you've got to pay a living wage, you've got to provide affordable health insurance.'"

Putting together such a broad initiative can be "like pulling teeth," Hesse says, but the stakes are high. If employees succeed in improving wages and working conditions at the country's largest employer, they could effectively set a new benchmark for service-sector jobs throughout the economy. Some 27 million Americans currently make $8.70 an hour or less—and by the end of the decade, Hesse notes, nearly 2 million people worldwide will work at Wal-Mart.

"These are the jobs our kids are going to have," he says.

Each year $45 billion is spent on computers in public and private class-rooms. Julie Landry, writing in *Red Herring*, came to the conclusion that the tech companies benefit, not the students. The magazine *Red Herring* closed in 2003, a victim of the dot-com fallout, but it earned a rep-utation for this type of thought-provoking coverage of all things tech.

Julie Landry

Is Our Children Learning?

IN A WELL-APPOINTED CLASSROOM in New York City, a pair of sixth graders at Mott Hall School are doing what corpo-rate executives the world over are doing—creating PowerPoint presen-tations. For the students, the purpose is to learn about the human liver. They are copying and pasting information from medical web sites and selecting the right background colors and clip art. But after spending 20 minutes just designing the introduction page, the students still can't answer the most basic question: What does the liver do? "I don't know; we were supposed to do the gallbladder," answers a shy Latino girl with pigtails. They are learning how to use PowerPoint, but they have no idea what the content means.

Similar situations are playing out in private and public schools across the United States. Students are learning not just PowerPoint, but Excel and a host of other applications. They are doing so on the latest and greatest PCs and the sleekest laptops. One private Catholic school in New York City even has wireless connections throughout its classrooms and hallways. Yet, after hundreds of exhaustive studies, there remains no conclusive proof that technology in the classroom actually helps to teach students. In fact, in some cases it hinders learning. And even if there is a benefit, the amount of money and resources being expended to put technology into the classroom does not match the current or expected benefit.

Since 1990, school districts and states have spent more than $40 billion on computers, software, and network connectivity for schools. At least 50 cents of every dollar spent on educational supplies goes to technology. Meanwhile, at least 35 states are facing budget shortfalls for 2003, and any cuts to education are likely to hit arts programs or facilities improvements long before technology. "Getting money for technology is not a problem around here—they'd probably cut the electricity before they'd cut that," says one teacher at Marymount School, a private Catholic institution for girls on New York's Upper East Side.

The major computer hardware and software manufacturers are not only feeding this insatiable desire for technology, they are the cause of the hunger in the first place. Selling into the $350 billion education market, the tech titans get anywhere from 5 percent (Oracle and Texas Instruments) to 26 percent (Apple Computer) of their total revenue. They count on this market to add to the bottom line, even though they may be selling the twenty-first-century equivalent of snake oil.

OLD-SCHOOL IDEAS

Technology's claim to revolutionize learning isn't new. "Books will soon be obsolete in the schools," wrote Thomas Edison in 1913, just after he had invented the Kinetophone, one of the earliest devices to synchronize sound and a projected image. "It is possible to teach every branch of human knowledge through the motion picture. Our school system will be completely changed in the next ten years."

Nearly a hundred years later, technology companies are promising the same sweeping changes. While everyone agrees that there's a place for technology in schools (it makes record-keeping more efficient, helps teachers analyze student learning trends, and is good for all sorts of back-office administrative functions), educational software and hardware companies have long boasted that their products are the answer to shrinking budgets and overcrowded classrooms. The right technology, they argue, can help educate the 53 million students in public and private schools in the United States. With technology, students can easily learn to read and write and do arithmetic. Without it, the companies say, students will fall behind, their analytical skills becoming as dusty and antiquated as a blackboard.

Nearly every tech company selling into the education market has commissioned independent studies that find, not surprisingly, that technology has a positive effect on education. Microsoft claims the use of laptops improves critical-thinking skills and "time spent on task." Apple has found that "students, especially those with few advantages in life, learn basic skills—reading, writing, and arithmetic—better and faster if they have a chance to practice those skills using technology." Texas Instruments says that "handheld graphing technology can be an important factor in helping students develop a better understanding of mathematical concepts, score higher on performance measures, and raise the level of their problem-solving skills." Even former junk bond king Michael Milken is pushing educational technology, through his foundation and a company called Knowledge Universe, which he cofounded with Oracle CEO Larry Ellison and media mogul Rupert Murdoch.

In closely controlled, short-term research studies, the tech companies' claims can be proven. The studies, however, tend to be tightly choreographed—monitoring everything from the time spent on a computer to what skills are practiced and what type of students are practicing them. But real classrooms aren't tightly controlled. They are a hodgepodge of different software and hardware, not to mention students. As such, it's hard to distinguish the influence of technology from that of enthusiastic teachers and supportive administrators.

A West Virginia study found that fifth-grade students who had access to computers for six years gained an average of 14 points on an 800-point basic-skills test. Researchers concluded that about 11 percent of those 14 points, a mere 1.5 points, were attributable to technology tools, which cost $7 million per year. Researchers also noted that the state spent $430 million to renovate school buildings and increase teacher salaries; they acknowledged these factors might have had an effect on teacher and student motivation. And, in fact, at places like the SEED (Schools for Educational Evolution and Development) School in Washington, D.C., a four-year-old charter boarding school, students show off their brand-new dorms with far more pride than the computers they use in classrooms and labs.

In the last comprehensive study of its kind, a 1998 research project by the Educational Testing Service (ETS), a private testing organization that produces the Scholastic Aptitude Test and others, found that school computer use was associated with increasing math scores for eighth graders by one-third of a grade level. However, researchers cautioned, "the appearance of higher test scores in students who use technology more frequently may be due to the technology, or it may be due to the fact that such students come from more affluent families, and so are better academically prepared in the first place."

In some cases, introducing technology into the classroom may actually have a detrimental effect. In her controversial book *Failure to Connect: How Computers Affect Our Children's Minds for Better and Worse* (Simon & Schuster, 1998), former principal Jane Healy argues that computers should be used sparingly in schools. She finds that heavy visual emphasis could be harmful to early childhood development because pictures require less effort to process than text. She also cites the instant feedback of computer applications as a possible factor in children's increasing inattentiveness. Ms. Healy warns, "Some of the 'habits of mind' fostered by this software are dangerous. . . . Attention is guided by noise, motion and color, not by the child's brain."

THE EDUCATION PRECEDENT

In a nod to the questionability of technology as an effective teaching tool, the Bush administration says it plans to adjust its policy on education and technology. As part of a new law that takes effect in fall 2002, the U.S. Department of Education will launch a five-year, $15 million project to study the effects of technology on education. Though the study is slated to kick off in fall 2002, the structure and depth of the study is still being decided—typical of the "build it first, think about it later" government mentality. The new law, called No Child Left Behind, also requires that 25 percent of technology funding be allocated for training teachers to use the new tools. Prior to the law, federal policy tended to have a single mission: outfitting schools with technology and getting them connected to the internet. For instance, the E-Rate program, introduced by the U.S. Federal Communications Commission in 1996, has been funneling about $2 billion each year to schools and libraries in low-income communities for discounted internet connectivity.

"What you have seen with No Child Left Behind is a real shift away from just providing increased access, which is still an important priority, toward making sure that teachers and administrators know how to use it effectively," says John Bailey, head of the Office of Educational Technology at the Department of Education.

Technology companies, in fact, are more than happy to step in and guide teachers in how to use their software. Some firms offer free training as an incentive for schools to buy their products. Gateway, through its corporate giving program, and the WorldCom Foundation both provide free internet training to thousands of schools, and Intel's Teach to the Future program has set aside $100 million to show 400,000 teachers how to integrate technology into their teaching.

Training teachers to use technology, however, doesn't turn technology into a better teacher. As the ETS study points out, "Apparent higher achievement levels of students with teachers who are computer-proficient may be due to this proficiency, or it may be due to these same teachers having more teaching experience and knowledge of their subject matter."

The new federal law also places an emphasis on testing and uses test scores to determine the allocation of federal funds. Naturally, technology companies are angling to make sure their products support the new federal emphasis. Nearly every new offering—from traditional education publishers like Scholastic to start-ups like educational-software maker Lightspan—comes packaged with claims of raising test scores. In the short term, such a sales pitch may persuade superintendents to buy, but in the longer term, the basic question of whether technology is an effective teaching tool is still not answered, and further, it's unknown if standardized tests themselves adequately measure learning. "Test scores are pretty brutal proxies for success in the workforce," says Roy Pea, a professor of education at Stanford University. "What kids need to know and be able to do is changing as the world changes."

THE OAKLAND GRADERS

California's Oakland Unified School District has been trying to save its troubled schools for years. The majority of the district's middle schools rank in the lowest 10 percent in California on statewide Academic Performance Index tests, and its high school graduation rate for the 2000–2001 school year was just 40 percent, compared with about 80 percent statewide. Oakland's students, urban and predominantly African-American and Asian, are exactly the type of students technology is supposed to help, and it does. Numerous studies have indicated that technology does have the power to engage students who aren't interested in books or lectures, and that engagement sometimes results in better grades and test scores. As a result, Oakland is looking to programs like online teacher collaboration to give students living in the poorer areas of the city the same advantages as students in wealthier areas.

"In this district, technology is probably the only way, because we haven't been able to provide a consistent quality of instruction across the schools," says Derek Mitchell, director of technology and student achievement for the Oakland school district. "We're confident about technology's ability to provide our students with opportunities and resources they couldn't get otherwise."

Educational software companies agree. "We've got 72 percent of children that aren't reading at grade level by third grade and that still aren't by ninth grade," says Andrew Morrison, founder and CEO of Cognitive Concepts, a literacy training firm in Evanston, Illinois. "If you can [get them up to grade level] for $1,000 a class and it's proven to work, I don't see how you could afford not to. Shy of hiring more teachers and putting them one-on-one with the kids, it's hard to have the same effect without the technology."

Start-ups like Carnegie Learning, which makes math tutoring software, say that when technology has a sound basis in learning research, it can make just as much of an impact as an attentive teacher. Carnegie Learning says that its software, which uses techniques based on ten years of cognitive research at Carnegie Mellon University, has helped boost test scores by as much as 30 percent by adapting its lessons as the student progresses through each question.

Yet, students who are engaged are not necessarily learning to think. It often takes an expectant look or an encouraging smile from a teacher or tutor to motivate students—something they'll never get from a computer, no matter how advanced. That's why it may be more effective in the long run to train and hire additional teachers, although that is clearly more expensive. The authors of the West Virginia study determined that reducing average class size from 21 to 15 would cost $636 per student—$191 million in salaries alone for 5,739 additional teachers—while adding computers would cost only about $86 per student. It's also difficult to imagine how some states justify their emphasis on technology when many schools struggle to build enough space to house all their students, often resorting to trailers in the parking lot as ad hoc classrooms.

Schools need more substantial proof that their investment in technology has made learning better—not just cheaper or faster. They should take computer and software sellers' claims with a sizable grain (boulder?) of salt. Tech companies aren't likely to change their tune; they're raking in money from the education market. Schools should also consider whether the modest gains achieved with expensive technology are worth the sacrifice in funding to other programs. After all, the only skills the Oakland students are sure to learn is how to surf the web better and design PowerPoint presentations.

The stock ratings of star Wall Street analysts turned from gospel to blasphemy when the New York State Attorney General's Office investigated hyped recommendations and close ties to investment banking. John Cassidy in *The New Yorker* starts at the beginning of the investigation and follows a dramatic and damaging trail of internal company e-mail messages and memos that led to a historic $1.4 billion settlement with ten top investment firms.

John Cassidy

The Investigation: How Eliot Spitzer Humbled Wall Street

TOWARD THE END OF 2000, Eric Dinallo, the head of the investor-protection bureau in the New York State Attorney General's office, was talking with his father, Greg Dinallo, a novelist, about the stock market. Investors had already lost billions of dollars, and Greg, who had written episodes of *Quincy, M.E.* and *The Six Million Dollar Man* before turning to thrillers, was complaining about Wall Street analysts who kept "buy" recommendations on technology and internet stocks even though so many of them were plummeting. "When analysts recommend these stocks, what is their interest in it?" he asked. Eric, an athletic 39-year-old, with short, spiked gray hair, thought this was a good question. The investor-protection bureau existed to protect the interests of ordinary investors. Traditionally, it had targeted individual fraudsters and "boiler rooms" that pumped up penny stocks, but there was no reason it couldn't investigate big Wall Street firms. On January 12, 2001, Dinallo sent a memorandum to his boss, Eliot Spitzer, listing his department's priorities in the coming year. At the top of the list he wrote,

"Investigation of abuses by investment advisors." The next entry was "Investigation of investment banking firm analysts."

Dinallo had joined the Attorney General's office at the start of 1999, shortly after Spitzer, a Democrat, defeated the Republican incumbent, Dennis Vacco, in a bitter contest that was resolved only after a recount. Previously, Dinallo had worked in the Manhattan District Attorney's office, where he took part in the successful prosecution of senior executives from A. R. Baron, a crooked brokerage firm. It was, perhaps, surprising for an ambitious young prosecutor to leave the Manhattan DA's office for the Attorney General's investor-protection bureau, but Dinallo knew that Spitzer, the son of a wealthy real estate developer, had grand ambitions for himself and his office.

Spitzer was 39 when he defeated Vacco, on a Clintonian platform of cleaning up the environment, controlling the spread of guns, and supporting the death penalty. During Spitzer's first two years in office, he had sued power-plant operators in Ohio and elsewhere, for sending air pollution to New York; General Electric, for failing to clean up the Hudson River; and several leading gun manufacturers, for selling unsafe products. Spitzer liked to bait conservative audiences by telling them that his activist agenda was an outgrowth of "federalism," the right-wing legal movement that advocated the use of state courts, rather than federal courts, to resolve many big issues. At the start of 2001, Spitzer was looking for some bold new initiatives, and he approved Dinallo's idea of taking a closer look at stock analysts.

During the 1990s, an unprecedented number of Americans had entrusted their money to the stock market, and some had ended up losing heavily. Many Wall Street firms had used the promise of supposedly independent research to draw the public into the market. Some firms even set up mutual funds exclusively devoted to technology and internet stocks, which they promoted with the aid of their star analysts.

As a young prosecutor without close political ties to the financial industry, Spitzer was well placed to launch a populist crusade. "Most people on the Street knew that the issue of analysts and investors was a festering sore," Spitzer said recently. "People had talked about it, but nobody had ever done anything." If there is one thing Spitzer dislikes, it is inaction. Ever since boyhood, he has been competitive and hyperactive. In conversation, he perches his long, angular body on a chair and leans forward, fixing his bright, blue-gray eyes on his interlocutor, as if awaiting the starter's pistol. Although sometimes accused of being a publicity hound, he could hardly be described as a media pretty boy. His chin is prodigious; his teeth are imperfect; his nose is impressive; his brow is furrowed; his hair is receding; and his ears are like jug handles. But he fairly radiates energy and ambition.

Initially, Spitzer had no idea where the analyst inquiry might lead. "It was just one of many investigations," he recalled. "There was no premonition that this was a more important case. It was like everything else. You say, 'Let's see where it takes us.'"

As the top legal official in New York state, Eliot Spitzer heads a sprawling bureaucracy that employs more than 1,800 people in offices ranging from Buffalo to Hauppauge. His headquarters takes up 11 floors at 120 Broadway, a grand old office building between Cedar Street and Pine Street which once served as the headquarters of the Equitable Life Assurance Society. The investor-protection bureau, on the twenty-third floor, is one of seven bureaus in the public-advocacy division.

With Spitzer's approval, Dinallo hired Bruce Topman, a 60-year-old Wall Street attorney, to lead the analyst investigation. During a long career as a litigator, Topman, a slight, dapper fellow who wears French cuffs and suspenders to the office, had defended dozens of firms against the government. Now that his children had left college, he didn't need to earn as much money, and he decided to do something public-spirited. When he arrived at 120 Broadway, he was struck by the disparity of resources between the public and private sectors. Big Wall Street firms have hundreds of lawyers. The investor-protection bureau employed just ten, and Topman was assigned two of them: Gary Connor, a 55-year-old office veteran, and Patricia Cheng, a 34-year-old expert in information retrieval. Fortunately for Topman, they were determined investigators. "It turned out to be a good combination," Connor said. "Bruce had experience of litigating securities cases. Pat is a computer wizard. And I had experience with the Martin Act."

The Martin Act is an obscure but powerful New York statute that dates back to 1921. Under its auspices, the Attorney General can bring civil or criminal charges against any person or business involved in a fraudulent purchase or sale of securities anywhere within the state. Since the vast majority of stock and bond sales go through Wall Street, the Martin Act gives New York's Attorney General oversight power over much of the country's financial industry. During the 1970s, one of Spitzer's predecessors, Louis Lefkowitz, used the Martin Act to attack corruption on Wall Street, but in the ensuing years most people on the Street had forgotten that the legislation even existed.

Topman and his colleagues initially focused on a legal complaint that had been filed with the New York Stock Exchange in March 2001. Debases Kanjilal, a 46-year-old pediatrician living in Jackson Heights, Queens, claimed to have lost half a million dollars by following the investment advice of Henry Blodget, a well-known internet analyst at Merrill Lynch. Kanjilal had bought stock in a company called InfoSpace at $122 and held on to it even as it dropped below $10. According to his lawyer, Jacob Zamansky, Kanjilal had wanted to sell several times, but a Merrill Lynch broker dissuaded him, citing bullish research reports by Blodget. Zamansky claimed that Blodget had recommended InfoSpace's stock only because the firm was planning to purchase another company, Go2Net, which was one of Merrill Lynch's investment banking clients.

In April 2001, Topman sent a lengthy subpoena to Merrill Lynch, asking for internal documents relating to internet initial public offerings, internet stock recommendations, and the compensation of internet stock analysts. A couple of months later, he issued a second subpoena, this one asking for information about Merrill's relationship with GoTo.com (no relation to Go2Net), an internet-search company that Blodget had recently downgraded. *The Wall Street Journal* reported that the downgrade came just hours after GoTo.com chose Credit Suisse First Boston instead of Merrill Lynch to manage an upcoming stock offering. Merrill Lynch denied that the two events were linked, but Topman and Dinallo agreed that the timing was suspicious.

Henry Blodget, whose fair, Waspish features had become familiar to CNBC viewers during the stock market boom, represented a new breed of stock analyst. As recently as the 1980s, most people on Wall Street regarded research as a backwater, a view that was reflected in the layout of big investment banks. Analysts generally sat on a floor of their own, well away from the firm's big money-makers: the traders, who place bets on the direction of market movements; and the investment bankers, who manage stock and bond issues for corporations, as well as advising them on mergers and acquisitions. Physical isolation was just one of the "Chinese walls" that were supposed to separate analysts from other parts of the firm. Internally, the analysts were ranked somewhere between the retail brokers, who buy and sell stocks on behalf of ordinary investors, and the cafeteria staff.

As the 1990s progressed, this picture changed dramatically. Longstanding restrictions on the financial industry were relaxed, allowing firms of all kinds to join together. Union Bank of Switzerland acquired PaineWebber; Salomon merged with Smith Barney, which was owned by Travelers Group, which then merged with Citicorp. These deals, and many more like them, blurred the traditional line between retail brokerages, such as Merrill Lynch and Dean Witter, which catered principally to the investing public, and investment banks, like Morgan Stanley and Goldman Sachs, which dealt primarily with corporations. The new all-purpose financial supermarkets that resulted from the merger wave, such as Citigroup, JPMorgan Chase, and Morgan Stanley Dean Witter, were, in the words of Paul Volcker, a former chairman of the Federal Reserve Board, "bundles of conflicts of interests."

These conflicts were particularly evident in the burgeoning technology sector, where countless cash-strapped companies were looking to raise money and the big Wall Street banks were competing for the business of underwriting their IPOs. In this febrile environment, many leading analysts were taking on roles that had traditionally been reserved for investment bankers, such as helping companies to go public and marketing their stock to investors. For example, when Priceline.com went public in March 1999, Richard Braddock, its chief executive, said that the company chose Morgan Stanley Dean Witter to manage its IPO mainly because the firm employed Mary Meeker, a top-ranked internet analyst. The month after Priceline.com's stock started trading on the Nasdaq, Meeker issued a positive recommendation, which she retained until March 2002, when the stock had fallen almost 97 percent from its peak value of $162.

Meeker's career demonstrated how the once lowly analyst had been transformed into what people on Wall Street call a "rainmaker"—a generator of lucrative deals. (For every $100 million that a company raises in an IPO, it pays the investment banks that organize the offering $7 million in commissions.) Blodget, who is 36 years old, emerged as Meeker's main rival, but despite a privileged background his rise to Wall Street fortune was an unlikely one. He grew up on the Upper East Side, where he attended St. Bernard's School. He went to Phillips Exeter Academy, in New Hampshire, and then to Yale, where he majored in history. After graduating in 1988, he taught English for a year in Japan and then wrote a book about his experience, but he was unable to find a publisher. Like many aspiring journalists, he took a series of junior editorial jobs, including one as a fact checker at the National Audubon Society, which let him go after a couple of months, and another as a proofreader at *Harper's*. A person who knew him well at that time describes him as a quiet, withdrawn young man, who was increasingly disillusioned by his failure to make a living as a writer.

In 1994, Blodget took an entry-level position at Prudential Securities, a big retail brokerage. According to some accounts, his father got him the job. Two years later, he joined Oppenheimer & Company, a small brokerage firm, where he went on to become a research analyst covering internet stocks. In December 1998, Blodget staged the publicity coup that made his career, by placing a price target of $400 on Amazon.com, which was then trading at about $240, a level that many analysts considered ludicrously overvalued. One of the doubters was Merrill Lynch's internet analyst, Jonathan Cohen, who reckoned that Amazon's stock was worth just $50. Blodget's timing was better. Within a month, Amazon's stock had surpassed his target, and he was being hailed as an oracle of the New Economy. Early in 1999, Cohen announced his resignation from Merrill Lynch. Blodget took his job.

Under securities laws, the word "document" means all communications in paper and electronic form, including written notes, memos, e-mails, and attachments. Since 2001, the Securities and Exchange Commission, Wall Street's primary overseer, has required firms to save all their e-mails for at least three years, in case regulators want to inspect them. In the early summer of 2001, Merrill Lynch's compliance department started turning over boxes of documents to Spitzer's office. Whenever a new batch came in, Clayton Donnelley, a soft-voiced paralegal, scanned and numbered each document to maintain a permanent record. By the end of the Merrill Lynch investigation, he would be up to 99,439.

Some of the first documents to catch the investigators' attention were e-mails that had originated in the hundreds of brokerage offices that Merrill Lynch maintains across the country. The firm is famous for its "thundering herd" of brokers, who, in advising their clients, rely, in part, on the advice of their colleagues in the research department. When the stock market slumped in 2000 and 2001, these brokers felt the public's anger, some of which they passed on to Blodget.

On June 15, 2000, Scott Jones, a broker based in Austin, Texas, e-mailed Blodget to complain about his coverage of InfoSpace, the company at the center of the investor lawsuit, whose stock was plummeting. "Why do we continue to talk so positively about this stock?" Jones demanded. "I very rarely hear of other analysts talking this stock up. Maybe we should reevaluate our stance. I am really concerned for our clients."

On July 10, 2000, Michael DeVito, a Merrill Lynch broker in Greenwich, Connecticut, wrote to Blodget, "From your recent reports, it seems that InfoSpace is your favorite stock. Should we worry that the chairman has sold over 1MM shares before their quarterly earnings? Are we planning a secondary for the stock? Any input would be appreciated. As FCs"—financial counselors—"we rely on your guidance."

Blodget's own e-mails showed that he, too, had concerns. In a message he sent to a colleague in the research department in June 2000, he admitted that he had "enormous skepticism" about InfoSpace. Yet the following month, a day after Go2Net hired Merrill Lynch to represent it in a possible sale of the company to InfoSpace, he issued a research bulletin reiterating his buy ratings on InfoSpace's stock and declaring, "We continue to believe that InfoSpace has the best technology platform for wireless internet."

Blodget's support didn't prevent InfoSpace's stock from falling further. In October 2000, a Merrill Lynch broker in Louisville named Jeff Sexton asked Blodget about a wire story that said InfoSpace's annual report contained handwritten parts. "Before joining Merrill Lynch, I was a securities lawyer for seven years," Sexton wrote. "Shame on me for not doing the due diligence that I and other FCs assume you and other analysts are doing, but a handwritten annual report for a company that you have a buy rating on with a target of $100 is disconcerting to me to say the least." Blodget forwarded this e-mail to one of his subalterns, Virginia Syer, with a note that said, "I am so tired of getting these things. Can we please reset this stupid price target and rip this piece of junk off whatever list it's on. If you have to downgrade it, downgrade it." But, in fact, Blodget didn't downgrade InfoSpace until December 11, 2000—after its purchase of Go2Net had been completed, and after its stock had fallen below $15.

The InfoSpace e-mails provided Bruce Topman and his colleagues with some encouragement. Topman believed that all successful investigations developed what he termed an "entry point," in the form of a cooperative witness, a revealing document, or a recorded conversation. Dinallo also subscribed to the entry-point theory. When he was at the District Attorney's office, he had often used wiretaps as his point of entry, but he viewed e-mails as potentially an even better form of evidence. "E-mails are more direct," he explained. "They are casual, but intimate. People tend to say what they mean without much consideration or artifice. It is like a water-cooler conversation caught on the record. Plus, the context is right there—the back-and-forth, the attachments, everything."

Fortunately for Spitzer's investigators, Blodget and his colleagues turned out to have been frequent and candid online correspondents, partly because they got along so well. "My sense is that people who worked with Henry liked him enormously," one official said. "They liked working with him, and they were loyal to him. From our point of view, that brought a lot of benefits, because it meant there was a fierce exchange of views. People said what they really meant. It was that open channel of communication that gave us a window into what Henry did."

GoTo.com, the subject of Topman's second subpoena, was a California-based company that pioneered the practice of charging firms to be included in its search engine results. At the peak of the market, this appeared to be a clever idea, but following the Nasdaq crash of April 2000, GoTo.com found itself running out of cash and unable to issue more stock. In September 2000, it hired Merrill Lynch to help it raise money from European investors. At that point, Blodget didn't have any rating on GoTo.com's stock, but Thomas Mazzucco, an investment banker in Merrill Lynch's Palo Alto office, promised GoTo.com that this would change, and Blodget told one of his colleagues, Kirsten Campbell, to start researching the company. Campbell spoke with the firm's executives and ran some numbers through her computer. GoTo.com was still making heavy losses, and internet advertising was in a slump. Not surprisingly, Campbell concluded that GoTo.com didn't deserve a positive recommendation.

Merrill Lynch's stock-rating system was based on a five-point scale: 1—buy; 2—accumulate; 3—neutral; 4—reduce; 5—sell. Each covered stock was ascribed a short-term and a long-term rating. For example, a rating of 2–1 meant short-term accumulate and long-term buy. In November 2000, Blodget suggested initiating coverage of GoTo.com with a rating of 2–2, but Campbell exploded. "Who are we trying to please by doing a 2–2," she wrote in an e-mail. "I don't want to be a whore for f-ing mgmt. If 2–2 means that we are putting half of Merrill retail into this stock because they are out accumulating it then I don't think that's the right thing to do. We are losing people money and I don't like it. John and Mary Smith are losing their retirement because we don't want Todd"—Todd Tappin, GoTo.com's chief financial officer—"to be mad at us."

The internal discussions about GoTo.com continued for several months. At the start of 2001, with the firm's stock trading in the single figures, Campbell proposed initiating coverage at 3–2, but the prospect of a neutral rating pleased neither GoTo.com nor Merrill Lynch's investment bankers. Eventually, a compromise was reached. On January 11, 2001, Blodget initiated coverage with a 3–1 rating: short-term neutral and long-term buy. In an accompanying research report he noted the continued weakness in the online advertising market but added, "We believe that GoTo will be a survivor." Later in the day, a fund manager at American Express e-mailed Blodget to ask, "What's so interesting about GoTo except banking fees????" Blodget replied, "Nothin."

A few months later, Blodget upgraded GoTo.com to 2–1, citing a stronger than expected first quarter. He also helped to organize a series of meetings between the company's senior executives and institutional investors. Hardly by coincidence, GoTo.com was planning another stock issue, and Merrill Lynch was vying with Credit Suisse First Boston to manage the offering. On May 25, 2001, GoTo.com informed Merrill it was leaning toward Credit Suisse. Later that day, Edward McCabe, another of Blodget's research colleagues, sent him an e-mail saying he had prepared a downgrade for GoTo.com's stock, because of "valuation" concerns. (During the previous month, the stock price had doubled.) Blodget's reply consisted of three words: "beautiful fuk em." Two weeks later, on the same day that GoTo.com officially hired Credit Suisse as the lead underwriter of its upcoming stock issue, Blodget downgraded GoTo.com from 2–1 to 3–1.

When Bruce Topman saw the "fuk em" e-mail, he knew he had found his entry point. From then on, he believed there was a good chance he could make a case against Blodget and Merrill Lynch for failing to disclose the analyst's conflicts of interest.

During the first week of August 2001, Topman, Connor, and Cheng interviewed Blodget for five days in a conference room at 120 Broadway. Beyond confirming that he hadn't issued a single "reduce" or "sell" rating during his time at Merrill Lynch, the analyst gave little away. He pointed out that he had always described internet stocks as high-risk investments, and that he had advised investors to keep only a small percentage of their wealth in them. When Topman asked how he decided which stocks to cover, he conceded that he took into account whether Merrill Lynch had an investment banking relationship with the company, but denied that that was the only factor.

At this stage, Blodget seemed unruffled by the Attorney General's investigation. A few days before his first interview, he e-mailed Campbell, who had also been called to testify about her role in covering

GoTo.com. "Based on what I know, there's nothing to be concerned about," he wrote, adding that he considered it "hugely ironic" that they were being investigated over a stock that they had rated neutral: "If ever there was a better example of independent, high-quality research, I don't know what it is." Blodget also tried to reassure Campbell about a recent decision by Merrill Lynch to settle the InfoSpace lawsuit brought by Debases Kanjilal, which had surprised many people on Wall Street. Blodget insisted to Campbell that, contrary to media reports, Kanjilal received only about 5 percent of what he was asking for. "The decision to settle was still mystifying to me, given that we haven't done anything wrong, but it is what it is," he went on. "Much of this blame game is to be expected, now that the bubble has burst, but it is still frustrating and annoying, especially given the effort we put into detailing the risks in these stocks."

It is unclear whether Blodget believed what he wrote to Campbell. (He refused to be interviewed for this article.) Although he did warn that internet stocks were risky, he also luxuriated in his role as their champion. In March 1999, for example, he published a lengthy report entitled "Overview of Our Investment Philosophy," in which he freely conceded that most internet stocks were "absurdly expensive" on traditional grounds, and that most internet companies would not survive. Nonetheless, he declared, "the real risk is not losing some money—it is missing a much bigger upside."

Blodget was calm and polite during the depositions, but his overall attitude was glib, and this infuriated Spitzer's staff. The investigators had found his e-mails self-deprecating and funny. Their author came across as the wry aspiring writer he once was, rather than the self-important Wall Street multimillionaire he had turned into. But, during the interviews, the investigators started to view him as just another evasive defendant. "Given the e-mails, I expected him to be more candid," one official said. "But he clamped down, and that upset us. That didn't help at all."

The events of September 11, 2001, brought the Blodget case to a virtual standstill. Merrill Lynch was forced to evacuate its offices in the World

Financial Center, and the flow of documents to 120 Broadway was interrupted. Spitzer, meanwhile, got involved in coordinating the many charitable efforts that sprang up after the attack, and the analyst investigation didn't get back on track until November.

By then, Blodget's life had changed. In October, he married his longtime girlfriend. A few weeks later, he announced his resignation from Merrill Lynch. "It just seemed like a good time to pursue the next thing," he told the *Times,* adding that he was planning to write a book about the internet-stock bubble and its dénouement. The resignation had little impact on the investigation. Blodget was still tied to Merrill Lynch through an agreement that covered his legal bills; Dinallo and Topman still had to persuade their boss that they had a case worth pursuing.

As an experienced prosecutor, Spitzer knew what it took to build a strong case. From 1986 to 1992, he was an Assistant District Attorney in the Manhattan DA's office, where he led an investigation into the Gambino crime family's role in the garment industry. To win the trust of people in the business, Spitzer set up a garment factory on the Lower East Side and operated it for several months while collecting wiretaps and other incriminating evidence.

Once he became Attorney General, Spitzer demanded that his investigators display a similar level of diligence and initiative. When he read the evidence relating to InfoSpace and GoTo.com, he doubted that it was strong enough to support a high-profile case against a defendant as well financed and as determined as Merrill Lynch. Some of the e-mails were damning, but none of them amounted to incontrovertible evidence of systemic wrongdoing. Spitzer also thought that the case was too narrow. From the beginning, he had viewed the analyst investigation in a broad context. Although he was outraged by Blodget's behavior, he saw it as symptomatic of the conflicts of interests that had arisen throughout the financial industry, not just at Merrill Lynch. "I kept coming back to the fundamentals: What is it that I'm trying to do here?" he explained recently. "And what I'm trying to accomplish is insuring that when Joe Smith in Utica goes to see his broker and is told, 'Our analyst thinks you should buy this stock,' then Joe Smith is getting advice that is honestly believed."

Spitzer likes to think of himself as a defender of ordinary people. His grandparents were Jewish immigrants who lived in a fourth-floor walkup on East Fifth Street. His father, Bernard Spitzer, who is now 78, went to City College and then to Columbia, where he studied engineering. After working in the real estate industry for some years, he set up his own firm, Spitzer Engineering, which now operates more than a dozen upscale Manhattan apartment houses (including the Fifth Avenue building where Spitzer lives with his wife, Silda Wall, and three daughters). By the 1970s, Bernard Spitzer had moved his family—Eliot is the youngest of three children—to a big house in Riverdale, but he often reminded them of their obligations to the less fortunate. At dinner, he would talk to them about serious issues of the day, such as the Vietnam War, which he opposed, and George McGovern's presidential candidacy, which he supported.

After Horace Mann, Spitzer went to Princeton, where he majored in public policy at the Woodrow Wilson School and served as president of the student government. Princeton at the start of the 1980s was hardly a hotbed of political activism. Candidates for office included a "Jihad Party," made up of hard-partying frat boys who wore towels and face masks. "It wasn't an office that I recall many people fighting for," one of Spitzer's fellow students said. "Even without Jihad, the slate would have been pretty thin."

Despite his extracurricular activities, Spitzer was a diligent student. During a course in microeconomics, the insight that markets don't always work efficiently, and that governments sometimes have to step in and impose remedies, made a big impression on him. He remembered it years later when he was investigating the garment industry. Rather than try the Gambinos on extortion charges, which would have been tricky to prove and would, in any case, have left their trucking monopoly intact, he filed an antitrust suit, charging the mobsters with stifling potential competition. In return for avoiding jail, the Gambinos paid a $12 million fine and promised to stay out of the trucking business.

As Attorney General, Spitzer continued to use the courts strategically. In suing General Electric for failing to clean up the Hudson River, he helped break a political and legal logjam that had kept the issue unresolved for years. "Even though we lost the case initially, it was incredibly effective at spurring the Environmental Protection Agency to action," Michele Hirshman, Spitzer's deputy, recalls. Spitzer applied the same type of thinking to the analyst investigation. Ultimately, he was less interested in indicting culpable individuals, such as Blodget, than in changing the way Wall Street operated. But for this strategy to be successful he needed to demonstrate that the conflicts of interest he had uncovered were pervasive. In February 2002, he told Dinallo and Topman to broaden their focus from InfoSpace and GoTo.com to include all of Blodget's stock ratings. The investigators issued another subpoena to Merrill Lynch, demanding all of the internet group's e-mails, on any subject, dating back to 1997.

In less than a month, thirty boxes of documents, containing tens of thousands of fresh e-mails, arrived at 120 Broadway. Dinallo added two more lawyers to the investigative team and started reading intensely himself, often staying at the office until after midnight. "No grass grows under Eliot's feet," he explained. "He wanted to either settle the case or file an action. We wanted to make sure we had looked at every single document. There was some tension there."

It didn't take long for the investigators to find more embarrassing material. On October 10, 2000, Eve Glatt, an assistant in the Merrill Lynch research department, sent Blodget a news story that said 24/7 Media, an online advertising company, was having problems with its technology. "Don't know if you saw this," Glatt wrote, "nothing revolutionary—but it probably confirms what you and Virg"—Virginia Syer—"have talked about for some time." Blodget, who rated 24/7 Media's stock as 2–2, or accumulate-accumulate, e-mailed back, "That it's a pos, yes?" Glatt seemed confused by this acronym, so Blodget sent her a clarification: "pos = piece of shit." To which Glatt replied, "Exactly my point. Do you have a cheat sheet for your abbreviations? (I think I need one.)" Blodget then sent Glatt a message that read:

lol = laugh out loud
gt = great

pos = piece of shit
nfw =
pls = puleeeeez
imho = in my humble opinion

Glatt wrote back to express her gratitude: "I even understand nfw. Thanks."

Most of the exchanges weren't this entertaining, but some, such as one concerning LifeMinders, an online company that delivered lifestyle advice, were almost as damaging. "LFMN at $4," Blodget wrote to Glatt on December 4, 2000. "I can't believe what a POS that thing is. Shame on me/us for giving them any benefit of doubt." "Yeah, hard to believe," Glatt replied. "SO glad we don't have a 1–1, not that a 2–1 is all that much better."

It turned out that "pos" wasn't the only epithet that Blodget and his colleagues had applied to their stock picks. Among the other phrases they used were "dog," "piece of junk," and "powder keg." Every couple of days, Dinallo would take another bunch of e-mails upstairs to the twenty-fifth floor, where Spitzer and Dieter Snell, one of his closest advisers, would inspect them. Snell, a tall, fair 47-year-old from New Jersey, led the team of federal prosecutors that convicted Ramzi Yousef of plotting to blow up airliners over the Pacific. He and Spitzer told Dinallo to press on. Although the new e-mails were revealing, they didn't necessarily demonstrate that Blodget and his colleagues had been in cahoots with Merrill Lynch's investment bankers—the central charge that needed proving. In order to buttress this argument, the investigators focused on Blodget's dealings with Internet Capital Group, a financial firm that Merrill Lynch had taken public in August 1999.

ICG, as it was commonly referred to, invested money in other internet companies and helped them to prepare for IPOs. Its stock hit $212 in December 1999, but in the following ten months it fell to less than $15. Despite this precipitate slide, Blodget maintained the same rating: 2–1—accumulate-buy. On October 4, 2000, Blodget wrote to Sofia Ghachem, a colleague in the research department, and noted that they had failed to highlight how risky ICG was. "Part of the reason we didn't highlight it is b/c we wanted to protect icg's banking business," Ghachem replied. "But anyway, none of this is relevant—the whole sector has corrected now." The following day, Blodget e-mailed another member of the research group, and said he thought ICG's stock was "going to 5," but still he didn't downgrade it.

A few days after his exchange with Ghachem, Jack M. Watkins Jr., a Merrill Lynch broker in Winter Haven, Florida, e-mailed Blodget to say, "Henry, I feel like I need some help with what I should tell my clients regarding ICGE. I have never been hit like this and some of my clients are getting pretty upset." Blodget wrote back, "Jack, No hopeful news to relate, I'm afraid. This has been a disaster, and I'm sorry we all have been in front of it. There are no 'operations' here to fall back on, so there really is no 'floor' to the stock." Yet Blodget didn't downgrade ICG for another month, and even then he dropped it just one notch, to 2–2.

Such modest moves did little to pacify brokers who were now being besieged by furious customers. On November 30, 2000, a broker from Grand Rapids, Michigan, complained to Andrew Melnick, the head of the research department, "I have had it with the analysts' postmortem downgrades or upgrades, this kind of hindsight my 13-year-old daughter can do us for free. Why in the hell are we paying these guys multi-million salaries for this kind of work?" Melnick forwarded the e-mail to the research analysts, and Blodget copied it to three investment bankers, with an angry note that indicated he was tired of being criticized for pandering: "The more I read of these, the less willing I am to cut companies any slack, regardless of the predictable temper-tantrums, threats, and/or relationship damage that are likely to follow."

The internal row about ICG followed an earlier argument, over Blodget's intention to downgrade another internet company, called Aether Systems. In his note, Blodget asked the investment bankers to speak with Melnick, among others, about resolving such disputes. If he didn't get some new guidance on how to deal with "sensitive banking clients/situations," he added, his group was "going to just start calling the stocks (stocks, not companies), including AETH, like we see them, no matter what the ancillary business consequences are."

When Dinallo saw Blodget's declaration, he was elated. Unlike some of the previously discovered e-mails, this one wasn't jocular, and it hadn't been written in haste. It stated clearly, and in Blodget's own words, that he had been shaping his stock ratings to reflect Merrill Lynch's investment banking interests. Dinallo thought it was the best piece of evidence he had seen in his career.

By late March 2002, Spitzer and his senior colleagues were finally convinced that they had enough evidence to sue Merrill Lynch under the Martin Act. In the twelve months from December 1999 to November 2000, Blodget's team, according to its own calculations, had helped to produce $115 million in investment banking revenues for Merrill Lynch. Some of that money was returned to Blodget in the form of salary increases and bonuses. In 1999, his first year at Merrill, he earned about $3 million. The following year, his compensation was raised to $5 million. In 2001, despite the continued slump in the market, he earned $12 million in salary and bonus, and he also reportedly received a severance payment of about $2 million.

Spitzer informed Merrill Lynch that it was facing a serious legal problem, but the firm's attitude remained defiant. It had retained as outside counsel Skadden, Arps, Slate, Meagher & Flom, one of the biggest law firms in the country, and Robert Morvillo, a leading criminal defense attorney. During a presentation in Spitzer's office, the lawyers argued that Blodget's e-mails were being taken out of context, and that he had done no wrong. The denials were so dogmatic that Spitzer began to wonder whether Merrill Lynch's senior executives really knew what was in the Blodget e-mails. "The reason I wondered is that, frankly, it took a while for them to respond," Spitzer now says. "I would have expected them to have had a faster response, and they didn't."

In the first week of April, Merrill Lynch finally asked Spitzer what it would take to stop the investigation and settle the case. He said that the firm would have to pay a fine and introduce reforms to ensure the independence of its research analysts. Merrill Lynch signaled that it might be willing to accept these terms, but only on the condition that the Attorney General's office agree to seal the evidence it had collected. Spitzer refused to consider such a move. He believed it was essential to publish the evidence, so that individual investors could use it to seek restitution through the courts. He told Merrill Lynch that it had two choices: Either the Blodget e-mails would become public as part of a settlement agreement that showed the firm in a reasonably positive light, or they would become public as part of a lawsuit.

What type of lawsuit was yet to be determined. The most serious option was a criminal indictment, but Spitzer was reluctant to go that far. In the late 1980s, an ambitious young federal prosecutor named Rudolph Giuliani indicted Drexel Burnham Lambert on racketeering charges, and the firm went bankrupt when lenders refused to extend it more credit. More recently, Arthur Andersen went under after it was indicted on criminal charges relating to its accounting at Enron. Spitzer thought that the Justice Department's decision to bring criminal charges against Andersen had been a mistake. He didn't want to put Merrill Lynch out of business for actions he believed had been common on Wall Street. "The problems were structural," he says. "Everybody had permitted analysts to become appendages of the investment banking system. It didn't seem reasonable to drop the criminal axe on Merrill Lynch because of this. It did make sense to say to them, 'You've got to change the way you do business in a pretty fundamental way.'"

The alternative to a criminal indictment was some sort of civil suit. Gary Connor suggested filing an action under Section 354 of the Martin Act, which empowers the Attorney General to launch a public investigation of a company, with public hearings, and public disclosure of documents. Spitzer liked Connor's idea. He told Dinallo and Topman to prepare a lawsuit in case the settlement talks broke down.

On Friday, April 5, 2002, Dinallo spent most of the day at New York–Presbyterian Hospital, where his wife was having their second child. Every couple of hours, he called to check in with Bruce Topman, who was working on the lawsuit with Connor and Cheng. Upstairs on the twenty-fifth floor, a group of lawyers from Merrill Lynch was gathered around a conference table in Spitzer's office, a big, L-shaped room that is decorated in blue. On one wall there is a drawing of a young Spitzer making a presentation in court; on another, a photograph of an older Spitzer meeting Bill Clinton.

The meeting wasn't going well. Spitzer, who was accompanied by Snell and another of his senior aides, Beth Golden, wanted Merrill Lynch to acknowledge that it had misled investors and make a public apology, but the firm's lawyers kept repeating that Blodget's e-mails were being misinterpreted. Spitzer felt his temper rising. In what context, he wondered, was it justifiable for an analyst to describe one of his recommended stocks as a "piece of shit"? Spitzer suspected that some people on the Merrill Lynch side still doubted his willingness to go to court against such a big firm. After several hours of futile exchange, one of the lawyers said to him, "Merrill Lynch has a lot of powerful friends." Spitzer was furious at what he took as an implied threat. "Nobody is going to talk to me that way and expect to get a result," he snapped. "I've tried for weeks to negotiate with you guys in good faith. That's not going to be what I respond to."

After the meeting broke up without agreement, Spitzer decided to act. On the morning of Monday, April 8, Dinallo and Connor walked over to the State Supreme Court, at 60 Centre Street, to request a hearing under the Martin Act. The ex parte judge, Justice Martin Schoenfeld, kept them waiting all morning in his clerk's office. When he was finally ready, Schoenfeld read through a 38-page complaint, which had been completed only the night before. It detailed some of Blodget's e-mails and alleged that Merrill Lynch's stock ratings "were tarnished by an undisclosed conflict of interest: The research analysts were acting as quasi-investment bankers for the companies at issue." Shortly after noon, the judge signed the order that Dinallo had requested. He instructed Merrill Lynch to hand over more documents to the Attorney General and to state clearly in its stock circulars whether it had an investment banking relationship with the company concerned.

Having obtained the order he wanted, Spitzer issued a press release in which he claimed that he had discovered "a shocking betrayal of trust by one of Wall Street's most trusted names," and said the revelation of wrongdoing at Merrill Lynch "must be a catalyst for reform throughout the entire industry." The message in these words and actions was clear: Spitzer had declared war on Wall Street.

————

The court order, and the media frenzy it engendered, came as a shock to Merrill Lynch. That very morning, Rudolph Giuliani, who had set up a consulting firm after leaving City Hall, had spoken to Spitzer on Merrill's behalf, reminding him that the company had stayed in New York after September 11, and asking him to proceed with caution. Spitzer didn't tell Giuliani that Dinallo and Connor were already in court.

When Merrill Lynch's lawyers heard about the court order, their first reaction was to ask Spitzer whether Merrill's asset management division, which runs dozens of mutual funds, would have to shut down. (Under the Investment Company Act of 1940, any financial firm that is subject to a court order can be barred from doing certain types of business.) Spitzer, who hadn't anticipated this development, called Stephen Cutler, the head of the SEC's enforcement division. It was the first time that Cutler had been informed of the lawsuit by Spitzer, and he told him that the court order would disrupt large parts of Merrill Lynch's business. Spitzer dispatched Dinallo back to Centre Street, where, in response to a request from Merrill Lynch's lawyers, Judge Schoenfeld agreed to stay his order while the two sides resumed settlement discussions.

Publicly, the firm continued to insist that the Blodget e-mails had been taken out of context. Whatever merits this argument had from a legal perspective, it proved economically unsustainable. Within a week, Merrill Lynch's stock market valuation had fallen by more than $5 billion. The firm's chief executive, David Komansky, and its president, E. Stanley O'Neal, decided that they had no alternative but to settle the case on Spitzer's terms. Komansky satisfied one of Spitzer's demands by publicly apologizing for the Blodget e-mails, saying that they "fall far short of our professional standards, and some are inconsistent with our policies."

Nonetheless, when talks resumed in Spitzer's office, Merrill Lynch representatives complained bitterly about being singled out from their peers, many of which employed analysts who had been just as involved in investment banking as Blodget. "Where is the horizontal equity in this?" they demanded. "Why us first?" Spitzer had some sympathy for this line of reasoning, he later conceded, but he didn't express it. Instead, he said, "Horizontal equity is a good thing. I believe in it. But I never found it terribly persuasive when I was prosecuting street crime and a guy said, 'Look, you missed the guy over there who did the same thing.'"

Spitzer did assure Merrill Lynch that he intended to deal with its rivals later. He wanted a settlement with Merrill Lynch that he could also impose on the rest of Wall Street. Initially, he asked for a complete separation of stock research and investment banking. Merrill Lynch didn't think this was practical, but it agreed to a series of reforms. From now on, its analysts would be paid only for providing services intended to benefit investors, and investment banking would play no role in their compensation. The firm would set up an internal committee to review its stock ratings for objectivity and integrity, and its compliance department would oversee any contacts between analysts and investment bankers.

The other big issue was the size of the fine that Merrill Lynch would have to pay. Having made almost $600 million in after-tax profits during the first quarter of 2002, the firm could hardly plead poverty. Spitzer settled on a figure of $100 million. "It was a real number," he said. "It got their attention. It didn't bankrupt them, but it forced them to wake up. But the money to me was never the most important part. The most important part was the set of reforms that they had to adopt."

On Monday, May 21, 2002, Spitzer announced that the two sides had reached an agreement. "By adopting the reforms embodied in the settlement, Merrill Lynch is setting a new standard for the rest of the industry to follow," he declared. Accompanying this statement was a clear threat to the rest of Wall Street. Spitzer's investigation had attracted the attention of prosecutors in other big states, such as California and New Jersey, who were now preparing to launch their own investigations of firms other than Merrill Lynch. Spitzer vowed to cooperate with these states, and with the national regulators, and to be "as aggressive as possible" in pushing for industry-wide reforms.

Spitzer's assault on Merrill Lynch shocked the industry's official regulators almost as much as it shocked Wall Street. Faced with an aggressive local prosecutor muscling his way into their terrain, the SEC, the New

York Stock Exchange (NYSE), and the National Association for Securities Dealers (NASD) quickly launched a joint investigation into Wall Street research practices, along with the North American Securities Administrators Association (NASAA), which represents the fifty states.

Publicly, Spitzer welcomed this cooperative effort. Given his meager investigative resources, he knew he couldn't investigate all of Wall Street. The regulators divvied up the top dozen firms. At the national level, the SEC, the NYSE, and the NASD took several firms each to examine. At the local level, New York and California each took two firms, and eight other states—Alabama, Arizona, Illinois, Massachusetts, New Jersey, Texas, Washington, and Utah—took one each. By the beginning of June, every big firm on Wall Street was being scrutinized by two sets of investigators. Goldman Sachs, for example, was dealing with the NYSE and the Utah securities commissioner; Credit Suisse First Boston was answering to the NASD and the Secretary of the Commonwealth of Massachusetts. Privately, Spitzer referred to the enlarged investigation as "a multiheaded hydra monster" and worried about the potential chaos he had wrought. But he also believed that Wall Street had brought its fate upon itself by using its money and influence in Washington to block effective regulation and reform.

As the progenitor of the analyst investigation, New York could choose the firms it wanted to investigate. It selected Morgan Stanley Dean Witter, which employed Mary Meeker, and Salomon Smith Barney, which employed Jack Grubman, a leading analyst in the telecommunications sector. Dinallo kept intact the team that had humbled Merrill Lynch—Bruce Topman, Gary Connor, and Patricia Cheng—and gave it responsibility for scrutinizing Salomon Smith Barney. Dinallo's deputy, Roger Waldman, took charge of examining Morgan Stanley. Before the investigations were completed, the two firms would each produce more than two hundred thousand documents—twice as many as Merrill Lynch had handed over.

On the surface, at least, Mary Meeker and Jack Grubman had much in common. Meeker was one of the best-known figures in the online world, a friend of Amazon's Jeff Bezos, AOL's Steve Case, and eBay's Meg Whitman. Grubman, although less well known, was equally influential in the telecommunications industry, where he advised WorldCom,

Global Crossing, Qwest, and many other upstart firms. In the past, both Meeker and Grubman had openly admitted that they helped to raise money for many of the companies they covered. "What used to be a conflict is now a synergy," Grubman famously told *BusinessWeek* in 2000.

Despite the apparent similarities between Meeker and Grubman, the two investigations quickly headed in different directions. Meeker's e-mails generally avoided criticizing companies that she was recommending to investors, even when their financial results failed to match her previous predictions, which was often. "How is it possible that Mary Meeker's e-mails don't have the same crap in them as these other guys' e-mails?" one investigator said. "She was more experienced? She was more careful? She's a woman? What is it? I don't know. Maybe she was a true believer. Maybe she absolutely never had a doubt, even though she turned out to be wrong." To build a legal case, the investigators needed some evidence that Meeker had deliberately misled investors or omitted relevant information from her reports, but they couldn't find any. "You could call it a negligence case, by the way," the investigator said. "But it's not the same two-facedness you see elsewhere."

Topman's team, on the other hand, had another serious case on its hands. The NASD, which is basically a self-governing Wall Street club, had already deposed Grubman as part of an ongoing investigation into his relationship with Winstar Communications, a wireless internet provider that went bankrupt in April 2001. The NASD's investigators were experienced professionals, and the damaging evidence that they had collected was quickly made available to Spitzer's investigators.

Jack Grubman is an imposing 49-year-old with receding black hair and thick eyebrows that hang heavily over his dark eyes. He was born in 1954 in Oxford Circle, a working-class neighborhood of Philadelphia. His father, Izzy, was a construction worker and an amateur boxer, who, according to some accounts, could tear a phone book in half. Grubman also boxed as a youngster, but it was his facile brain rather than his fists that distinguished him. After attending Northeast High School, where he was a member of the debate team, he majored in mathematics at Boston University. Afterward, he claimed to have graduated from MIT, but *BusinessWeek* exposed that untruth when it profiled him in 2000. "At some point, I probably felt insecure, and it perpetuated itself," he said on admitting the deception.

After leaving BU in 1975, Grubman got a master's degree in math at Columbia. In 1977, he took a job as a quantitative researcher at AT&T, which was then the monopoly supplier of phone service to the entire country. Grubman spent eight years at AT&T, during which time the Justice Department split the company into eight local telephone operators, the Baby Bells, and a national long-distance service that retained the AT&T name. Grubman balked at AT&T's entrenched bureaucracy, and in 1985 he shifted to Wall Street, becoming a telecommunications analyst at PaineWebber. He made his reputation by arguing that deregulation would allow smaller, nimbler companies to usurp the position of his former employer—an analysis that proved correct. In 1994, he moved to Salomon, where his disdain for AT&T only increased.

Between 1996 and 2001, Salomon Smith Barney issued $190 billion worth of stocks and bonds for 81 telecom firms, many of which were building their own networks. The stock market boom facilitated this remarkable exercise in raising capital, but Grubman orchestrated it. Through close personal links to people like Bernie Ebbers, the chairman of WorldCom; Philip Anschutz, the founder of Qwest; and Gary Winnick, the founder of Global Crossing, he helped to generate more than a billion dollars in investment banking fees for Salomon Smith Barney. In return, he earned an average of $20 million a year, which made him the highest-paid stock analyst ever.

Grubman's problems began in April 2000, when the Nasdaq crashed. Many of his favorite companies were losing money, and they needed to raise more just to stay in business, which was now increasingly difficult. Still, Grubman continued to defend their long-term prospects, arguing that the coming switch to "broadband" communications would greatly increase the demand for network capacity. In reality, demand was falling sharply as the economy slipped into a recession. In the first half of 2002, a number of firms linked to Grubman went bankrupt, including XO Communications, Global Crossing, and Metromedia Fiber Network.

When Spitzer's investigators started going through the documents from Salomon Smith Barney, they discovered that Grubman had been even more unpopular with his firm's retail brokers than Blodget had been at Merrill Lynch. Like Merrill, Salomon Smith Barney employed tens of thousands of people nationwide, many of them notable figures in their local communities. "Grubman is an absolute disgrace to our firm as an 'analyst,'" one broker wrote in 2000. "Maybe as a 'banker' he makes the firm a lot of money, but on the retail side the damage he has caused us is a disgrace! I hope many clients sue!" "Grubman is an investment bank whore!" another broker wrote in the same year. "When is the firm going to stop pimping him?" By 2001, the brokers were even angrier. "In my 16 years in the retail brokerage business, NEVER have I received such misguided, horrific recommendations from an analyst," one of them commented. "Some of his calls may, perhaps, put us in positions where we have to defend ourselves legally. Why does management and our research department continually defend his advice."

Salomon Smith Barney supposedly maintained extensive Chinese walls to protect the integrity of its analysts, but other documents handed over to Spitzer indicated that many of the firm's senior executives knew the brokers' skepticism was justified. Early in 2001, John Hoffmann, the head of global equity research management, gave an internal presentation in which he pointed out that of the almost 1,200 stock ratings that Salomon Smith Barney had outstanding on January 29, 2001, just one was an "underperform," and none at all were "sell." (Like Merrill Lynch, Salomon Smith Barney used a five-point grading system, but its wording was slightly different: 1 meant buy; 2—outperform; 3—neutral; 4—underperform; 5—sell.) Jay Mandelbaum, the head of Salomon Smith Barney's brokerage arm, was so disgusted by the firm's analysts that he threatened to cut off his division's contribution to the research budget.

The Grubman investigation was quickly overtaken by outside events. In late June 2002, WorldCom, the nation's second-largest long-distance company, said it had uncovered a multibillion-dollar accounting fraud, and Grubman was called to testify on Capitol Hill. He insisted that he had believed in the companies he covered, and said he was sorry that investors were suffering losses. His apology received less coverage than the revelation of his salary and an admission that he had been so close to WorldCom that he had attended several of the firm's board meetings. In late July, WorldCom filed for bankruptcy, and Grubman's reputation was further tarnished.

Spitzer was monitoring these developments closely. Every morning when Dinallo got to work, there was a message from his boss asking for an update on the investigation. To make a case against Salomon Smith Barney, the Attorney General's office needed to show that Grubman, despite his public protestations, hadn't really believed in his upbeat reports. At least some of his e-mails suggested that this had been the case, Dinallo informed Spitzer.

In April 2001, when Winstar had filed for bankruptcy protection, Frank Yeary, a Salomon Smith Barney investment banker, recommended to Grubman that he reassess the risk facing other telecommunications companies. "Agreed," Grubman replied. "Also to be blunt we in research have to downgrade stocks lest our retail force . . . end up having buy-rated stocks that go under." But these words did not lead to action. For several months, Grubman failed to downgrade any of the companies that he covered. He explained why in a subsequent e-mail to another colleague: "Most of our banking clients are going to zero and you know I wanted to downgrade them months ago but got huge pushback from banking."

In August 2002, while the investigators were searching for more evidence, Grubman quit his job, claiming that the controversy surrounding him had made it impossible for him to continue. Under the terms of a severance agreement, Salomon Smith Barney paid him more than $30 million and agreed to continue paying his legal bills. These were about to increase substantially, as Spitzer's investigators turned their attention to one of Grubman's most notorious stock recommendations.

In November 1999, Grubman had shocked the rest of Wall Street by upgrading AT&T, a company he had criticized for years, from neutral to buy. He tried to justify his volte-face by saying that the phone giant's purchase of a big cable company, Telecommunications Inc., had transformed its prospects, but this explanation was greeted with skepticism. At the time of the upgrade, AT&T was preparing to spin off its cellular division in a stock offering that was expected to be one of the biggest yet. The investment banks that were hired to manage the issue stood to make tens of millions of dollars each in fees. As long as Grubman remained critical of AT&T, Salomon Smith Barney was unlikely to be one of them. Shortly after the upgrade, AT&T selected Salomon Smith Barney to comanage the stock issue, along with Goldman Sachs and Merrill Lynch. The offering took place in April 2000, and Salomon Smith Barney pocketed more than $40 million. Six months later, Grubman downgraded AT&T, changing his rating back to "neutral."

Timing wasn't the only interesting angle of the AT&T story: Sanford Weill, the chairman of Citigroup, Salomon Smith Barney's parent company, was a member of AT&T's board; and Michael Armstrong, AT&T's chairman, was a member of Citigroup's board. At the time of the upgrade, some people on Wall Street had speculated that Weill might have played some role in it. This had never been confirmed, but Dinallo and Spitzer thought it was worth pursuing. On July 19, 2002, the Attorney General's office sent a subpoena to AT&T demanding any documents it had relating to its decision to hire Salomon Smith Barney to comanage the wireless stock offer.

In investigating Weill, Spitzer was targeting the most successful financier of his generation, a man who was the chairman of Carnegie Hall and had an entire medical college named after him and his wife, at Cornell University. Weill was born into an immigrant family in Bensonhurst seventy years ago. During a long career, he had created two big firms: Shearson Loeb Rhoades, which he sold to American Express in 1981; and Travelers Group, which he merged with Citicorp in 1998. He was known as an intimidating boss, whose tirades sometimes reduced his underlings to tears, but, unlike some of his colleagues, he had been quick to realize the threat that Spitzer's investigation represented. The day after Merrill Lynch reached a settlement with the Attorney General, Weill sent Spitzer a letter saying that Salomon Smith Barney would adopt the same rules Merrill had agreed to, and would do more if its rivals agreed to do the same. Over the summer, Citigroup introduced further reforms, but the revelations about Grubman and WorldCom continued to hit its stock price.

The week after Labor Day, Weill tried to regain the initiative. He shunted aside Michael Carpenter, Salomon Smith Barney's chief executive, and replaced him with one of his closest aides, Charles Prince, Citigroup's general counsel. A few days after being appointed, Prince went to see Spitzer and said he wanted to reach a settlement with the government as soon as possible. "My mandate is to try and get this cleaned up and done," he said.

News of the AT&T investigation confirmed the opinion of many on Wall Street and in Washington that Spitzer was a deranged publicity hog willing to go to any lengths to further his own political ambitions. This was an overstatement, but Spitzer had by now developed a comprehensive critique of the financial industry, which some people in his office jokingly referred to as "Spitzer's Grand Unified Field Theory." In speeches and in interviews, he declared that the entire stock market boom had degenerated into a conspiracy to enrich the insiders—analysts, investment bankers, and senior corporate executives—at the expense of ordinary investors.

This version of events was exaggerated, but it did contain some truth. During the boom years, Wall Street banks had often granted the executives of companies they did business with generous allocations of stock in "hot" IPOs, which could be sold to other investors at a premium—a practice known as "spinning." Between June 1996 and August 2000, for example, Salomon Smith Barney gave WorldCom's Bernie Ebbers stock in 21 IPOs, which netted him profits of more than $11.5 million. Qwest's Philip Anschutz received stock in 57 IPOs and pocketed almost $5 million.

To Spitzer, "spinning" represented nothing less than commercial bribery. On September 30, 2002, his office sued Ebbers, Anschutz, and three other executives who had been close to Grubman: Stephen Garofalo, the chairman of Metromedia Fiber Network; Clark McLeod, the founder of McLeodUSA; and Joseph Nacchio, the former chief executive of Qwest. The complaint accused the defendants of "fraudulent practices"— namely, the failure to disclose their IPO allocations—and demanded that they give back more than $28 million in profits.

Ebbers's lawyer dismissed the suit as a publicity stunt, but the prospect of Spitzer taking people to court for what was a common practice unnerved many businesspeople. "If you can turn this"—spinning—"into a case of commercial bribery, then you can make anything into commercial bribery," one senior Wall Street figure fumed. Some of Spitzer's fellow regulators also reacted angrily to the CEO lawsuit, because, once again, Spitzer hadn't informed them in advance of going to court. "Before we file a civil suit, we would talk about it at great lengths with other agencies to make sure it wouldn't impede a criminal investigation," one SEC official explained. "Eliot didn't tell any other agency what he was doing."

Although the national and local regulators were supposed to be cooperating, relations between Spitzer and Harvey Pitt, the chairman of the SEC, had been deteriorating since earlier in the summer, when Spitzer had publicly accused the SEC market regulators of being "asleep at the switch" during the recent wave of corporate accounting scandals. The difference between Spitzer and Pitt was primarily one of philosophy. As a lawyer who had worked for the financial industry for thirty years, representing everybody from Ivan Boesky to Merrill Lynch, Pitt believed that the only effective form of regulation was self-regulation. Since arriving at the SEC the previous summer, he had been pushing the NYSE and the NASD to strengthen their rule books to prevent the sort of abuses that Spitzer was investigating. At the start of May 2002, the SEC approved a new set of guidelines for analysts proposed by the NYSE and the NASD, which contained many of the sanctions that Spitzer had been calling for. "Harvey Pitt didn't give speeches," Lori Richards, the head of the SEC's compliance inspections department, said recently. "He did something better. He changed the rules." (Pitt resigned as chairman in November 2002.) To Richards, and to others at the SEC, Spitzer's role has been exaggerated. "From my point of view, he did not discover the conflicts of interest on Wall Street," Richards said. "He discovered the results—the e-mails. The e-mails were colorful, and they attracted public attention."

By coincidence, the day after Spitzer filed the CEO lawsuit he was due to have dinner with Pitt, Dick Grasso, the chairman of the NYSE, and Robert Glauber, the chairman of the NASD. Grasso, a bullet-headed 56-year-old, had arranged the dinner in the hope of reaching a resolution to the analyst investigation. In September alone, the Dow had fallen by more than 10 percent. Grasso didn't believe that Spitzer's activities were solely responsible for the market's troubles—uncertainty about terrorism and a possible war against Iraq were also important factors—but he couldn't see how it could recover without an end to the investigation.

The dinner took place at Tiro a Segno, an Italian club on MacDougal Street. After some initial pleasantries, Pitt said that he wanted the SEC to work with the other agencies to arrive at a far-reaching agreement with Wall Street. Spitzer echoed Pitt's sentiments. Despite his public clashes with the SEC chairman, he knew that the only way to get comprehensive reform was for all the regulators to join together. As a state prosecutor, he had neither the authority nor the expertise to impose changes on the entire financial industry.

A couple of weeks later, on Columbus Day, the regulators met again, this time in Washington, at the Georgetown Club, where they reached an outline agreement on the sort of settlement they wanted to arrive at. As the dinner was breaking up, the SEC's Stephen Cutler drew Spitzer and Dinallo aside to tell them some news. Over the weekend, one of Salomon Smith Barney's lawyers had called him to say that the firm had discovered a new batch of Grubman e-mails, some of which were potentially damaging.

The call to Cutler marked the culmination of a long-running dispute about the pace at which Salomon Smith Barney was producing e-mails. Back in April 2002, when investigators from the NASD had been deposing Grubman as part of the Winstar investigation, Barry Goldsmith, the head of enforcement at the NASD, had noticed that Grubman was a heavy e-mail user, often writing from his BlackBerry handheld computer. Goldsmith asked Salomon Smith Barney to recheck its electronic files for Grubman's messages, and, sure enough, a lot of them had been missed. More e-mails were turned over during the summer, but not enough to satisfy the investigators. In August, Cutler told the firm that if it wanted to reach a settlement it would first have to deliver more documents, so that the investigations could be completed.

On the morning of October 15, 2002, the new e-mails started arriving at 120 Broadway. Included among them was a long series of messages that Grubman had sent from his BlackBerry to Carol Cutler, an analyst for the Government of Singapore Investment Corporation, a money-management firm that had invested heavily in telecommunications stocks recommended by Salomon Smith Barney. (Carol Cutler is no relation to Stephen Cutler.) Grubman, who is married with twins, and Cutler, who is single, appeared to be on intimate terms. Their e-mails covered a period of several months, but the investigators focused on an exchange that took place over a single weekend: Saturday, January 13, and Sunday, January 14, 2001.

At 11:18 a.m. on Saturday, Cutler asked Grubman whether he had read about her fellow Midwesterner Ronald Reagan missing his own ninetieth birthday party because of illness. "Ronald Reagan is one of my clan, and I feel him leaving," Cutler wrote. "I so wish I could of had the opportunity to meet him." During the rest of the day, the two chattered back and forth, interspersing gossip about work with explicit sexual banter and queries about each other's personal history. "I don't like to focus on the past, but if it is a tale to be told then I'll tell it," Grubman wrote at 3:15 p.m. "I'm actually proud of my path—and it was much more difficult than what most people have to contend with and I've turned out pretty cool."

"I'd say so," Cutler replied.

At 5:18 p.m., Grubman brought up his AT&T upgrade of November 1999, boasting, "Everyone thinks I upgraded T"—AT&T—"to get lead for AWE"—AT&T Wireless. "Nope. I used Sandy to get my kids in 92nd St. Y pre-school (which is harder than Harvard) and Sandy needed Armstrong's vote on our board to nuke Reed in showdown. Once coast was clear for both of us (i.e., Sandy clear victor and my kids confirmed) I went back to my normal negative on T. Armstrong never knew that we both (Sandy and I) played him like a fiddle."

To anybody familiar with the upper echelons of New York society and the internal politics of Citigroup, Grubman's casually written e-mail was potentially explosive. The 92nd Street Y preschool is a highly selective nursery school on the Upper East Side which caters to about 175 toddlers, whose parents pay between twelve and fifteen thousand dollars a year for a curriculum that emphasizes Jewish rituals and culture. "Reed" referred to John Reed, Citigroup's former cochairman, who resigned in February 2000, after the board voted to make Weill the sole leader of the firm. When the e-mail was sent, Michael Armstrong was the chairman of AT&T and a director of Citigroup. The e-mail clearly alleged that Weill had asked Grubman to upgrade AT&T in order to gain Armstrong's support in a boardroom battle with Reed, and that, in return, Weill had helped to get Grubman's children into an exclusive preschool.

If Cutler realized the import of this allegation, she didn't let it show. "Good for you!" she wrote back to Grubman at 5:51 p.m. "Very good school so good for kids. I never knew real reason for sure. But I felt like there was pressure." Then, at the end of her e-mail, Cutler returned to personal issues: "What's your daughter's name?" It took Grubman a while to reply to this message, and when he did he also mixed business with family matters. "I knew it would cause grief," he wrote at 7:11 p.m. "The biggest thing that pissed me off is that T did exactly as I knew they would for precisely the reasons I thought. Her name is Elizabeth (btw: aren't you interested in my son's name?)."

"David Benjamin," Cutler replied at 7:33 p.m. "David was your mother's name—Mildred Davis. She died in 1992. Benjamin is your middle name. All correct? Does she have a middle name and do you call her by her full name Elizabeth." A few minutes later, Cutler sent Grubman another note: "Btw, what did you mean that T did exactly as you knew they would for precisely the reasons you thought?" Grubman answered Cutler's questions sequentially. "OK smartie, Mils is Lizzie's middle name," he wrote at 7:44 p.m. At 7:50 p.m., he added, "That the stock would collapse because the core business would fall apart."

On Sunday, the exchange of e-mails continued, with Cutler wondering why Grubman hadn't told her the reasons for the AT&T upgrade before and assuring him that he could trust her. "I will never judge you Jack," she wrote. "And if there is any shadow of a doubt about that, let it go." "No, we just never discussed," Grubman replied. "I always viewed T as a business deal between me and Sandy."

Spitzer ordered his investigators to determine the veracity of Grubman's claims as quickly as possible, and during the ensuing weeks he pestered

Dinallo constantly. "Eric and everyone downstairs were living it eigh-teen hours a day and doing most of the work," he recalls. "I was living it five hours a day, because I also had the rest of the office to think about."

The first issue that needed resolving was why Salomon Smith Bar-ney had taken so long to turn over the new e-mails. Concealing evidence is a criminal offense. Robert McCaw and Lewis Liman, two senior part-ners at Wilmer, Cutler & Pickering, were acting as the bank's outside counsel. They insisted that a technological problem had caused the delay. Some of Spitzer's investigators reacted skeptically to this story, but their boss eventually accepted it.

After reading Grubman's e-mails, Bruce Topman discovered a two-page memo that the analyst had sent to Weill on November 5, 1999, a couple of weeks before he issued his upgrade. Entitled "Re: AT&T and the 92nd Street Y," it began with Grubman informing Weill that he had had a "good meeting" with Michael Armstrong the previous day and that he was planning to meet other AT&T executives the following week. "On another matter," Grubman continued, "as I alluded to you the other day, we are going through the ridiculous but necessary process of pre-school applications in Manhattan. For someone who grew up in a household with a father making $8,000 a year and for someone who attended public schools, I do find this process a bit strange, but there are no bounds for what you do for your children." After noting that he had attached a list of the 92nd Street Y's directors to his note, Grubman went on, "If you feel comfortable and know some of those board mem-bers well enough, I would greatly appreciate it if you could ask them to use any influence they feel comfortable in using to help us as well."

Officials at the 92nd Street Y confirmed to the investigators that Grubman's son and daughter started attending the nursery school in September 2000. One of the Y's directors, Joan Tisch, said that Weill, who was a longtime friend, had approached her about Grubman's chil-dren and had indicated that Citigroup would be willing to make a dona-tion to the Y, which turned out to be a million dollars, payable in five annual installments. Armed with this evidence, Spitzer's team confronted the two principals.

On Wednesday, October 30, 2002, Dinallo, Snell, Topman, and Golden deposed Grubman in a conference room on the twenty-third floor of 120 Broadway. He confirmed that Weill had asked him to reexamine AT&T and that he had requested Weill's help in getting his children into preschool, but he denied that the two things were connected. When asked about his claim that Weill had wanted the AT&T upgrade in order to help him "nuke" Reed, he said he had made it up to impress Carol Cutler.

Two weeks later, Hirshman, Snell, and Topman interviewed Weill at his lawyer's midtown office. He claimed that he had asked Grubman to take another look at AT&T because he believed, as a director of the company and a longtime admirer of its chairman, Armstrong, that it was transforming itself for the better. He insisted that he hadn't told Grubman what to write and that he had expected the analyst to reach his own conclusions. The interview lasted all day, with a short break for lunch. Weill also confirmed that he had helped to get Grubman's children into the preschool, but he said it was simply a favor for a valued employee.

On November 13, 2002, the same day that Weill was interviewed by Spitzer's team, Charles Gasparino, a reporter at *The Wall Street Journal* who had been covering the investigation since the beginning, revealed the existence of Grubman's messages to Carol Cutler and quoted from part of the AT&T e-mail, citing as his source "a person who has reviewed it." The following day, the 92nd Street Y saga was everywhere, including the front page of the *Times,* where it ran under the headline "Wall St. and the Nursery School: A New York Story." Weill issued a public statement denying that he had told Grubman what to write. He and his colleagues were furious that any part of Grubman's e-mails had been leaked, especially since he had already repudiated some of them.

Many people on Wall Street assumed that Spitzer's office had leaked the material in order to exert more leverage on Salomon Smith Barney and Citigroup. "It was really very calculated," a senior executive at another firm said. "It put a lot of pressure on Citi. They held Sandy to ransom." But Spitzer, for his part, emphatically denies that he or any of his staff was the source of the story. "None of that came from us—not a single piece of it," he insists. "Charlie Gasparino is a good reporter, aggressive, has good sources. He started calling us a couple of days before the article came out and said, 'I've got this stuff.' We called over to Citigroup and said to them, 'Look, somebody is leaking all or part of this. It's going to be a problem.'"

Even if Spitzer didn't leak Grubman's e-mails to Carol Cutler, he certainly used the media on other occasions, especially during the settlement negotiations with the Wall Street firms, which began in late October. In one meeting at the New York Stock Exchange, Ted Levine, general counsel for UBS PaineWebber, confronted Spitzer. "You really can't do this," Levine said. "We can't have everything we say reported in the media." Spitzer angrily denied he was the source of the stories, and accused the firms of leaking—a charge that didn't impress many of the Wall Street executives present. "That very day, there was an article in the *Journal* about conversations between Eliot Spitzer and Stephen Cutler, which people on the Street weren't party to," one of them said. "There is no way it could have been leaked by the Street."

One Wall Street executive says he has never seen anything like the media manipulation that took place during the analyst probe. "Nothing compares to this," he said. "Leaking documents, leaking testimony, leaking the intentions of the regulators. Everything was leaking." Spitzer's courting of reporters also irked some of his fellow regulators, particularly those at the SEC and the NASD, which have a reputation for carrying out investigations discreetly. Spitzer, on the other hand, saw media management as a legitimate and effective tool to build momentum for reform. Unlike the national regulators, who have to deal with Wall Street on an ongoing basis, he saw himself as an independent outsider, whose role was to uncover abuses and remedy them in any way he could. If that involved making some powerful people uncomfortable, he was willing to do that.

By the end of November, the regulators and the Wall Street firms had agreed on the broad outlines of a settlement, but there were many detailed issues left to resolve concerning the roles that analysts could play. Cutler, who had taken the lead in the discussions with the banks, drew up a lengthy "touchpoints" document, which barred analysts from taking part in IPO pitches and investor road shows but allowed them to vet potential stock offerings and to talk to investment bankers under the supervision of their firm's compliance department.

Spitzer, who had originally called for a complete separation of analysts and investment bankers, showed himself more willing to compromise than many people on Wall Street had anticipated. He also backed off a suggestion that the investment banks be forced to finance a new independent-research consortium; and he agreed to an alternative proposal, under which Wall Street would provide investors with independent research from existing sources, such as Value Line and Standard & Poor's. The one thing Spitzer insisted on was a ban on spinning. Even when some of his fellow regulators argued that such a move would amount to criminalizing CEOs, Spitzer refused to drop this demand.

As the investigations across the country intensified, some people on Wall Street started to see that dealing with Spitzer was preferable to dealing with other state regulators. Demetrios Boutris, the corporations commissioner of California, was calling for a minimum fine of $100 million for each investment bank, regardless of what it had done. William Galvin, the Secretary of the Commonwealth of Massachusetts, had released damaging internal e-mails from Credit Suisse First Boston and recommended a criminal prosecution of the firm. "What brought people to the table was the fear that this could go out of control," said a Wall Street executive who was involved in the settlement negotiations. "There was no way of controlling what the states might do. It was a populist issue. Don't forget, the investment banking industry was being assaulted by the Attorney General of the state where it is based. If you couldn't get a sympathetic hearing with Spitzer, what the hell were you going to get in Idaho?"

Meanwhile, Spitzer's patience had almost run out with the endless rounds of negotiations. "It's a mess," he confided just before Thanksgiving. "We had a meeting the other day, just the government side, and there must have been 45 or 50 people in the room. I am firmly of the view that if you put more than three people in a room nothing happens." Spitzer was also aware that allowing the investigation to drag on for too long would be politically dangerous. On November 21, the *Daily News,* an important publication for a New York Democrat, ran an editorial calling for Spitzer's activities to be curbed. Earlier in the month, the

News had endorsed Spitzer in a successful reelection bid, but now it spotted "disturbing signs that in his zeal to reform Wall Street, Spitzer has crossed the line between responsible leadership and—dare we say it?—abuse of prosecutorial power."

Spitzer was keen to allay such concerns, but before he could call a truce he had to decide what to do about Grubman and Weill. The case against Grubman was straightforward: His own e-mails demonstrated that he had upgraded AT&T for ulterior motives. The evidence against Weill was more circumstantial. After more than a month of digging, the investigators still hadn't turned up anything to suggest that he hadn't believed in AT&T's prospects when he asked Grubman to reconsider his opinion. Some people in Spitzer's office believed the allegation in Grubman's e-mail that Weill wanted AT&T's stock upgraded to win Armstrong's support, but they could hardly force Grubman to retract his sworn testimony disowning it.

In the first week of December, Spitzer and his senior colleagues reached a tentative decision not to take any legal action against Weill. (The NASD, which carried out its own investigation, reached the same conclusion a couple of weeks later.) "The issue was very simple," Spitzer explained. "Was there a knowing effort to pressure an analyst to issue a false report? As a prosecutor, if you can prove that case you bring that case. If you can't prove that case you don't bring it. There was a back-and-forth between Sandy Weill and Jack Grubman, but nowhere will you find evidence that Sandy Weill didn't believe this was a good stock that should be bought. He was on the board. He believed in it. If he believed in it, then one might not like the fact that an analyst felt pressure from him, but there was no violation. We are bound by the evidence."

Spitzer was determined to get an agreement between Wall Street and the regulators by Christmas, even if it was only an agreement in principle. On Tuesday, December 17, he decided that the settlement talks had gone on long enough. While attending an event at the Kennedy Library, in Cambridge, he called his deputy, Michele Hirshman, and said, "I think we need to have a meeting tomorrow where we call people in and tell them this is it." The following morning, Spitzer called Dick Grasso and Stephen Cutler to tell them that he planned to issue an ultimatum. Cutler thought Spitzer's gambit was unnecessary, but Spitzer wasn't to be dissuaded. At lunchtime, representatives from five banks gathered in his office to hear him declare, "Either we close this today and get an agreement or the negotiating effort is over and we'll go back to doing what we do best, which is making cases."

Within 48 hours, ten of Wall Street's biggest banks had agreed to the regulators' terms, which included a series of reforms designed to ensure the independence of research analysts, a ban on issuing IPO stocks to corporate executives, and fines totaling $1.4 billion. Spitzer had thought only five firms would agree to settle: Credit Suisse First Boston, Goldman Sachs, Merrill Lynch, Morgan Stanley, and Salomon Smith Barney. But five more signed on: Bear Stearns, Deutsche Bank, JPMorgan Chase, Lehman Brothers, and UBS. In the end, there were no major holdouts. As confirmation faxes from the banks arrived at the Attorney General's office, one of Spitzer's deputies marveled at his negotiating strategy. "He's pulled a Spitzer," he said to himself. "He's rammed through an agreement when everybody else was sitting around worrying about details that were not really important."

On Friday, December 20, Dick Grasso stepped up to a podium in the gilded boardroom of the NYSE and hailed what he called a "historic occasion"—the unveiling of a settlement that would "restore public confidence in the finest system of enterprise that the world has ever known." Stephen Cutler then outlined the agreement in more modest language, saying it contained "significant reforms that will serve investors for years to come."

Spitzer was dressed in his usual outfit: a dark suit, a starched shirt, and a striped tie—the very picture of Brooks Brothers antichic. He thanked each member of his investigative team, down to Clayton Donnelley, who had numbered and indexed all the e-mails, and hailed their work in uncovering conflicts of interest on Wall Street. Eric Dinallo, who was standing next to Spitzer, felt regret that the biggest case of his career was coming to an end. Bruce Topman, who was sitting nearby, had no mixed feelings. Giving up private practice and working for the government had been the right decision, he thought.

After the speeches, reporters asked questions, surprising Spitzer and his colleagues with their skeptical tone. Why was this an agreement in principle rather than a final agreement? And why didn't it contain any admission of wrongdoing on the part of the Wall Street firms? "How can you restore public confidence without any admission of wrongdoing or individual indictments?" a reporter from the *Los Angeles Times* inquired.

Three and a half months later, there is still no final settlement, although one is supposed to be finalized in April. Moreover, there haven't been any criminal indictments brought against individual transgressors—an omission that led one media pundit to accuse Spitzer of "premature capitulation." Grubman has agreed to be banned from the securities industry and to pay a fine of $15 million—less than half the severance payment he received. Blodget may have to pay a similar fine, but the only Wall Street executive facing the possibility of jail time is Frank Quattrone, an investment banker at Credit Suisse First Boston, who is accused of encouraging his colleagues to destroy evidence.

Sitting in his office recently, Spitzer appealed to history in defense of his actions. "Every now and again, I sit here and say, 'Where were we a year ago?'" he said. "We were in a world where nobody accepted the fundamental premise of our argument—that Wall Street's business model was rotten. We needed to persuade the policy makers and the investment banks that the fundamental notion we were articulating was right. We've done that. At the margins, there will always be these disagreements on whether we have done enough on the individuals. That's fine. You get used to that."

The reforms that resulted from Spitzer's crusade are hardly revolutionary, but even his critics concede they were necessary. "I think the actual settlement and the changes it brought were good for the industry," one senior Wall Street executive said. "But I can make the argument that it should have been done by regulation, as opposed to enforcement."

Of course, it was the very failure of the national regulators that prompted Spitzer to get involved in the first place. Like Ferdinand Pecora, the counsel to the Senate Banking & Currency Committee who exposed Wall Street's double-dealing before and after the Great Crash of 1929, Spitzer uncovered behavior that big financial firms would have preferred to keep concealed. When the settlement is finally completed, he will release more of the e-mails he has collected, and not just from Merrill Lynch and Salomon Smith Barney. "These folks were earning $20 million a year," he said. "And in many cases they were betraying the public's trust."

Some impoverished investors are already using the evidence that Spitzer uncovered to get a portion of their money back. In February, Merrill Lynch agreed to pay several hundred thousand dollars to a couple in Ohio who bought internet stocks on its advice. Jacob Zamansky, the lawyer who sued Merrill Lynch on behalf of Debases Kanjilal two years ago, also organized this suit. "This case demonstrates what is going to happen when all the other e-mails are released," Zamansky said from his downtown office. "Lawyers like me will be able to use the evidence to extract restitution for investors. The major Wall Street firms will be fighting a war of attrition with their customers for the next five years."

With the analyst investigation almost over, Spitzer's officials are now examining other parts of the financial industry, including hedge funds that use their vast purchasing power to influence stock prices, and finance companies that lend to the poor, sometimes at extortionate rates of interest. Regardless of how these investigations go, many people in the Democratic Party think that Spitzer will run for governor in 2006, when George Pataki is unlikely to seek reelection. Spitzer admits he is considering that possibility, and, if he does, Henry Blodget and Jack Grubman are sure to figure prominently in his campaign. "Given where we've come in the past year, and how aggressive we've been, and, frankly, the risks I took personally doing this, not only do I feel no remorse but I feel I can stand up and say, 'Fellas, judge me based on what we have done,'" he said. "I've lost friends for being too tough. I've lost friends for not being tough enough. So be it."

Some securities analysts never feared uttering the dreaded word "sell." Loch Adamson, writing in *Worth* magazine, looks at the role of research and specifically at Prudential Securities, which jettisoned investment banking to encourage analyst independence. Prudential Securities subsequently merged with Wachovia Securities in mid-2003 to form a new firm bearing the latter's name that is 62 percent owned by Wachovia Corp. and 38 percent owned by Prudential Financial Inc.

Loch Adamson

Inside the Rock

PRUDENTIAL SECURITIES senior analyst Nick Heymann hates surprises, especially when they concern companies that he covers. Last winter, sensing trouble at Tyco, the 46-year-old research veteran called three former Tyco employees to find out what they knew about the intricacies of the Bermuda-based conglomerate's balance sheet. Within hours, Heymann received a mysterious phone call from someone he thought was a bona fide investor with close ties to the company. The man directed him to yet another Tyco source, who, he promised, could help resolve some of Heymann's questions. "I thought the guy was doing me a favor," the tall, slightly tousled-looking analyst recalls, leaning back in his chair and smiling ruefully. "So I picked up the phone and called the number, and after two or three minutes explaining who I was and what I was doing—you know, all gassed up—this guy goes, 'You don't have to tell me a single thing, or anybody else, if you ever want to see your wife and kids again.'" It wasn't the first time that Heymann, one of the wild men of Wall Street (ignore the elegant suit; he defies decorum when he opens his mouth), has had his life threatened for making negative comments about what he derisively calls "a cult stock." But the frequency, ferocity, and sophistication of the threats that Heymann has received in the past year have surprised even him.

Prudential Securities' research has been a lightning rod ever since the brokerage firm disbanded its investment banking division in December 2000 and started encouraging its equity analysts to make tough, uncompromising investment calls. Death threats are just one extreme; Prudential analysts have also won accolades from investors for their independence and candor. "Prudential's people are really trying to figure out what's going on," says Robert Smith, portfolio manager of the $4 billion T. Rowe Price Growth Stock Fund. Smith especially likes the work of senior food analyst John McMillin, senior retailing analyst Wayne Hood, and, of course, Heymann, whose voice was a lonely clarion call for caution when he launched coverage of Tyco in January 2002 with a hold rating because of his concerns about its accounting. At the time, Tyco was trading at nearly $55 a share, and every other analyst on the Street had rated it a buy or a strong buy. So why not issue a sell? Heymann, who didn't have any hard proof that the company was lying, wanted to bring investors around to his way of thinking without causing a full-on panic. "Sometimes you don't have to yell 'Fire!' from the back of the theater to let people know they're in danger," he says. "We just thought we'd yell 'Movie over' and hopefully get more people out of the stock with less damage." Investors who heeded Heymann's warning were thankful as the stock plunged to less than $10 a share by July on charges of fraudulent accounting.

Many of the Prudential analysts' most-lauded calls in the past two years have been timely, if not almost prescient, sells. In July 2001, financial services analyst Bradley Ball put a sell rating on Providian Financial at $59 a share because he didn't like the look of its credit losses and weak earnings quality; Providian ultimately dropped to $2 a share. In October 2001, energy analyst Carol Coale was the very first on Wall Street to downgrade Enron from a buy to a sell when she realized that she had been deceived by management (the stock was trading at around $20 a share at the time). Wayne Hood slapped a sell on discount retailer Kmart at $5.46 a share in early January 2002, discouraging investors from buying when he suspected that a bankruptcy filing was imminent. Prudential's changing status is most clearly reflected by *Institutional Investor* magazine's All-America Research Team, which is selected through nominations and votes from leading buy-side investors. In the 2001 team, Prudential ranked number ten in the weighted listing of firms (which gives extra credit to analysts who place higher in their sectors); in the latest ranking, released in October 2002, it rose to number eight.

Heymann and his colleagues, however, are no longer free to talk to the press about the companies that they cover after a startling decision by Prudential Securities in late November to ban its analysts from giving interviews. The media responded with all the petulance and vindictiveness of third graders (playground rules are very much in effect here, and no one likes being spurned). To be fair, Prudential is far from alone. More and more Wall Street firms are making it difficult for reporters to access their analysts, largely because they want to stay off the regulatory radar screen and avoid possible litigation from investors who act—wisely or unwisely—on their investment recommendations.

Prudential's decision, the firm insists, had little to do with regulatory oversight or class-action lawsuits. "It was driven by the idea that the client comes first and that the product we offer is valuable," explains research director Steve Buell, a soft-spoken man whose outer calm belies a fierce intellect (he holds a doctorate in neurobiology). Prudential is now in the awkward position of having to safeguard its research for investors, who pay for it, from reporters, who don't. Analysts sometimes receive as many as one hundred calls a day from journalists, but giving interviews eats into their schedules just as surely as investment banking once did. The decision to cordon off its analysts had been under discussion since summer 2002, around the time that Prudential agreed to give *Worth* unfettered access to its analysts at One New York Plaza so we could explore the transformation of the firm's research team. Two months and more than twenty interviews later, it is clear that the group is more important than ever to Prudential—the very future of its business depends on research. It is also clear that this may be the last time a journalist is allowed such a long and hard look inside the Rock.

Prudential's transformation has been largely overshadowed by the black cloud of animosity and distrust currently engulfing Wall Street.

Although touting questionable stocks simply for financial gain has been illegal since the Securities Exchange Act was ratified in 1934, New York attorney general Eliot Spitzer seems intent on pushing through new, more stringent rules. (Enforcing an existing rule isn't nearly as sexy as writing a new one, and despite his professions of political modesty, Spitzer will almost certainly try to cash in his popularity chips at the polls.) For its part, Wall Street is edging toward self-correction. Citigroup has separated its investment banking from its research division—without doing away with either. CEO Sandy Weill, in an act of singular savvy, hired Sallie Krawcheck, the 37-year-old former CEO of Sanford Bernstein—one of the most respected investment research firms in the industry—to run Citigroup's newly independent stock analysis and brokerage unit. Krawcheck, a former analyst with a stellar reputation, now has the unenviable task of restoring some credibility to Salomon Smith Barney, where telecom analyst Jack Grubman's flip-flopping coverage of AT&T and WorldCom made it appear that he was obeying some mandate other than his own intelligence.

The bigger question, of course, is whether independent research will survive in any form at the largest institutional level, or whether the very nature of its own support structure now dooms it to failure. Prudential's model relies on commissions from brokerage activities and asset management fees to support its research department. Sales and trading revenue suffered during the recent bear market, however, making it more difficult to fund research at a time when Prudential needs its analysts to help pull the entire division out of the abyss. "At this point, it's hard to say whether Prudential's strategy will be viable or not," says Vanessa Wilson, an analyst who covers Prudential for Deutsche Bank. "It's not as though Prudential started with a research department and then built sales and trading around it, like Sanford Bernstein did. They had a full-service investment bank, and they took it apart. There's really no going back."

Prudential's new strategy is a throwback to an earlier era, when sell-side research was provided to brokerage clients as a service rather than as a product. Those were the days of fixed commissions on stock transactions, and Wall Street firms could charge hefty brokerage fees large enough to cover analysts' salaries. The advent of negotiable commissions in the mid-1970s transformed the underlying cost structure of the business. As trading departments were no longer capable of supporting firms' research efforts on their own, investment banking was asked to pick up the slack. By the late 1990s, Wall Street research had lost any semblance of independence. The poster child for this inherent conflict of interest was Salomon Smith Barney's Grubman, who leveraged his research not only to help win investment banking business for his firm but also to get his kids into an exclusive preschool. Even analysts with the purest of motives were affected, because until very recently, investment bankers at most major brokerage houses contributed directly to their performance reviews. "Human nature is such that some analysts inevitably watered down their comments," says Prudential brokerage analyst David Trone, who has been in the unusual position of being both observer and participant. "The weaker ones let it bias their ratings."

At Prudential, investment banking pressures were arguably never very great. "To be honest, we weren't a major force in serving corporate issuers in the first place," says John Strangfeld, vice chairman of parent Prudential Financial and the chief architect of the new plan. Strangfeld was handpicked by Prudential Financial chairman and CEO Art Ryan to rethink the troubled Prudential Securities business in fall 2000. Unlike his predecessor, Hardwick Simmons (now chairman of Nasdaq), who tried unsuccessfully to push staid Pru toward the forefront of the investment banking business, Strangfeld felt no particular compulsion to follow the model set by the Street. Having spent 23 years working his way up the ranks of Prudential Financial's money management operation, Strangfeld remained loyal to institutional investors, not corporate issuers. "I think it's easier, as a new person coming in, to suggest a fresh approach," he says. "We saw a sustainably different opportunity, and pragmatically speaking it was more compatible with our areas of strength." Strangfeld did not limit the reorganization to investment banking. He also jettisoned the corporate bond underwriting team. By the end of 2000, he had laid off some 600 employees from both departments.

Strangfeld also revamped Prudential's investment ratings system.

Since May 2001, Prudential analysts have had just three labels at their disposal: buy, sell, and hold. An analyst can apply a sell to any stock expected to decline in value 15 percent or more in the next 12 to 18 months; a buy must offer the same potential to increase over that period. Analysts are also required to assign an industry-relative rating to their entire sector—market outperform, perform, or underperform—to give investors a simple macroeconomic view of an entire industry. Prudential analysts have embraced their newfound freedoms. "We're actually doing research," Heymann says, "as opposed to screwing around trying to tell somebody why lime green is going to be next spring's color and why they ought to buy a whole wardrobe of lime-green suits before they go out of style." Prudential's sells, as a percentage of its total coverage, approached 7 percent during the collapse of the internet bubble. That may not sound like a lot, but it was more than three times the number of sells that any other top Wall Street firm was posting at the time.

The new investor-oriented strategy stands in stark contrast to the Prudential of the early 1990s, when a scandal rocked the firm and threatened to put it out of business. In 1993, several states accused Prudential of defrauding thousands of investors in the sale of limited partnerships. Prudential agreed to a multimillion-dollar settlement, and by the time successive claims were filed and restitution was made, the total exceeded $1.5 billion. Angry investors have long memories, and the limited-partnership scandal is an institutional black mark that haunts the firm to this day. "It's no secret that Prudential had its problems," says Ed Yardeni, who worked as Prudential's chief economist in the 1980s before leaving to join C. J. Lawrence, which was later acquired by Deutsche Bank (where he reinvented himself as an investment strategist). Yardeni returned to Pru as chief investment strategist in April 2002, not least because he approved of the department's newfound sense of mission. "There's nothing like adversity to refocus business strategy," he says dryly.

Part of Prudential's recent strength lies in its willingness to look beyond Wall Street when trying to find new talent. Rather than hiring graduates straight out of business school, Pru has taken to recruiting industry experts—individuals with years of experience, well-developed Rolodexes, and a thorough understanding of the more arcane technical aspects of their industries—and training them to work as analysts. Most firms do the opposite. "A great analyst has to have a huge repertoire of skill sets," research director Buell says. "You need to be compulsive, anal, numbers-oriented, a pocket-protected geek, and you need to be a marketer—to be able to tone up and slim down your conversation depending on your audience." Among the company's 52 senior analysts, 89 associate analysts, and nine emerging analysts (who are currently preparing to launch coverage), there are two MBAs, two Ph.D.'s, a former Navy SEAL, two attorneys, a biomechanical engineer, several software developers, and former executives from General Motors, Chevron, and Lucent. Prudential's analysts are paid in line with Wall Street averages: According to a survey compiled by research group McLagan Partners, a typical *Institutional Investor*–ranked analyst had a base salary of $200,000 in 2001; total compensation, including bonus, was about $2.8 million. An unranked analyst received, on average, a $150,000 base salary and $860,000 in total compensation. Compare those figures with the princely sums paid to top-tier analysts whose firms did investment banking during the boom years: Salomon Smith Barney's Grubman reportedly made more than $15 million a year.

Prudential's strategy has found new converts within the brokerage community. Since streamlining its core business, Prudential has lost just one senior analyst to a competitor. By contrast, it has added several analysts, including enfant terrible Mike Mayo and his banking-research team from Credit Suisse First Boston. Mayo had earned a reputation at CSFB for making controversial calls, including posting sell ratings on some of the banks he covered, an almost unheard-of affront to those companies. After Mayo was let go in the wake of CSFB's merger with Donaldson, Lufkin & Jenrette—an effective rebuke for his unwillingness to toe the corporate line—he and his entire crew decamped to Prudential. "Our coming here had everything to do with the change [in strategy]," says brokerage analyst David Trone, who was Mayo's partner at CSFB and is now one of Pru's rising stars. "Our whole team had other options, but we chose to come here because we knew we'd have the freedom to work independently." More recently, Mayo was in the news again in early September when he became the first analyst in three years to downgrade Citigroup to a sell.

One of the dirty little secrets of Wall Street research is that it's not uncommon for companies or investors to try to intimidate analysts to keep them quiet or to prevent them from making negative comments. In an industry in which analysts must compete fiercely to distinguish their research from the crowd's, the possibility of getting shunned by a company's executives—not being able to schedule meetings with senior management or being intentionally excluded from question-and-answer sessions during conference calls—is a major concern. It's something of a catch-22: Analysts may ultimately risk their own access to a company by posting sell ratings, but investors appreciate their candor (never mind that it comes at a cost). "Even Sanford Bernstein analysts have been much more hesitant [than Prudential's] to use the sell side of recommendations," says Crit Thomas, director of growth equity investments for the Armada Funds group. "It's been very refreshing to see a firm as big as Prudential put a stake in the ground."

Prudential doesn't stop there. The firm has been working hard to fuse its fundamental analysis with sophisticated quantitative measures as a means of cross-checking the 544 companies that it covers. Two screens in particular help analysts identify when executives have been fiddling with the books. The first, called the earnings-torpedo screen, tries to determine whether a company has become more aggressive in booking revenue and profits. It looks for instances in which a company's receivables rise relative to sales and cash flow drops—an indication that actual earnings are softening—or for a change in the way management reports revenue (such as booking revenue on the basis of verbal orders instead of received purchase orders). The second screen measures cash flow. Companies doing business with less creditworthy clients, for example, may be able to boost earnings in the short term by using accounting accruals (whereby income is booked even though payment may not have been received yet). In the long term, companies that use more conservative accounting practices—and whose earnings streams are fueled by hard cash, not by an overextension of paper credit—are less likely to have negative earnings surprises; their stocks tend to perform better.

Although no investment system is fail-safe (not even Pru's earnings-torpedo test works if the balance-sheet numbers have been doctored), the double vetting has helped Prudential create a select list of 20 to 25 companies that it uses to build its model portfolios. Every stock on the committee's A-list must be "twice blessed," says chief quantitative strategist Ed Keon Jr. "Historically, some firms on the Street have used select lists to highlight some of their investment banking clients. We're just trying to find the best names we can." The list, which is reviewed and reapproved by Prudential's Investment Policy Committee every Monday afternoon, represents a fusion of the analysts' best choices, the quantitative team's top picks, and the strategic weightings assigned to different industry sectors according to Prudential's macroeconomic strategy. As of early December 2002, it included such familiar, consumer-oriented names as Anheuser-Busch; Bed, Bath & Beyond; Home Depot; Kellogg; and Procter & Gamble. There were also a few surprises: publisher Gannett and energy companies ConocoPhillips and Equitable Resources.

Despite layoffs, the weak economy, and declining consumer confidence, Prudential doesn't expect Americans to put away their wallets anytime soon. Real incomes are up, and the combination of soaring real estate prices and forty-year-low mortgage rates have allowed many homeowners to take equity out of their homes and boost their disposable income. Going back to 1960, Pru's chief quantitative strategist Keon found that during the 55 quarters in which incomes rose and confidence dropped, consumer spending actually rose nine times out of ten. He and his team took the analysis even further by looking at quarters in which confidence and income dropped simultaneously. "You'd think that under those circumstances Americans would curtail their spending," he says. "But that happened only half the time." Nor was the drop in spending commensurate with the loss in confidence: In three separate instances when consumer confidence dropped by about a third, spending fell by just 1 or 2 percent.

Not surprisingly, going into 2003, Prudential has overweighted consumer-related stocks. Retailing analyst Wayne Hood expects consumer spending to continue to benefit from "a laundry list of catalysts," including modest growth in real income, stable initial claims for unemployment, reduced interest rates, and the prospect of further tax cuts by the Republican Party. His favorite retailer is the stylish and seemingly ubiquitous Target. Consumer spending can also be traced in unusual ways through the food group, where senior analyst John McMillin, a 17-year veteran of Pru, keeps close tabs on a fast-changing lineup of companies. McMillin has witnessed 12 major takeovers of food companies in the past two years. "The game now is to try to pick the acquiring company that has made the best deal," he says. McMillin sees two companies executing particularly well: Unilever and Nestlé.

Prudential's real strength lies in finding opportunities where others fear to tread. Take the brokerage industry, where analyst Trone thinks that investors, spooked by the Spitzer investigation and negative headlines, have overreacted. "The market has discounted tens of billions of dollars [in legal settlements] for these firms," Trone says. "I've looked at everything—losses in court, settlements, expenses to pay lawyers, negative press, customer attrition, administrative costs to implement all of these various new regulations—and there is simply no way that these firms are going to incur that kind of [financial] impact."

American investors have been badly burned by the stock market, and it remains to be seen when, exactly, their confidence will begin to return. No one at Prudential—not even the firm's vocal and opinionated investment strategist Ed Yardeni—is willing to forecast that. "This is by far the most challenging market environment I've ever seen," says Yardeni, who began his career on Wall Street in the 1970s. Although he is increasingly concerned about the possibility of deflation, Yardeni has spent much of fall 2002 opining about what he calls the liquidity bubble—the $2.7 trillion in Americans' savings deposits sitting on the sidelines. Yardeni actually suspects that by lowering the Fed funds rate 50 basis points, to 1.25 percent, in November, Federal Reserve Board chairman Alan Greenspan may have been stealthily trying to burst the liquidity bubble. After the latest rate cut, investors simply can't expect to make money in savings deposits; they must begin to reconsider stocks if they intend to increase their assets. Yardeni also believes that investors can no longer assume that they'll be able to time the market; they need to focus on getting individual stocks right. One way of screening is to compare the dividends that a stock pays to the current interest rates on savings accounts. "Dividends may sound like an old-fashioned concept,"

Yardeni says, "but companies that pay dividends, and have been growing dividends, should definitely be in investors' portfolios."

Most investors are concerned about the very real threat of war with
Iraq. In fact, one of the greatest challenges facing Prudential's analysts is
trying to determine how a potential conflict would impact their companies, and for that they've turned to Chuck Gabriel, who heads Prudential's 11-person research group in Washington, D.C.

Since January 2002, when he got his hands on the new defense budget numbers, Gabriel has been convinced that President Bush is intent
on pursuing Saddam Hussein. "They'd added $50 billion to the bud-
get—and it was front-loaded for readiness, not for weapons," he says.
"We knew we were looking at a wartime budget." Despite the president's militaristic swagger, though, Gabriel doesn't think defense stocks
will necessarily be a good place to invest. The defense budget has
exploded in recent years, and the buildup is far more mature than most
investors realize. "We're about to lock in the fifth consecutive year of
an uptick in defense spending that began in October 1998," Gabriel
explains. "During the past 50 years—throughout the Cold War—there
has never been a period when we've had more than five years in a row of
increases." Gabriel thinks that defense spending will grow again in
2004, for a record sixth year, but that 2003 will likely be the peak year
in terms of the size of the increase.

The greatest peril to Prudential comes not from the distant threat of
war in Iraq but from a very real business threat right here at home. No
one at Prudential—not even research director Buell—was willing to
talk about the possibility, but rumors were flying this fall about a proposed joint venture with Wachovia. The deal would have combined Prudential Securities' platoon of 5,500 financial advisers with Wachovia's
8,100 brokers to form an army large enough to rival Merrill Lynch's. The
talks with Wachovia broke down within weeks, however, and have not
resumed. For the time being, parent Prudential Financial seems unwill-
ing to relinquish any control of Prudential Securities. That could change
if an appropriate buyer materializes. Although Prudential vice chairman
John Strangfeld continues to assure all comers that he is committed to
safeguarding the research team's independence, the research department

itself could still figure into a package deal. Prudential may never go back to its integrated investment banking model, but its objective research strategy could easily be subsumed by another company with no such scruples.

Few of Prudential's competitors would mourn its loss, nor would the companies covered by Prudential miss its sell ratings. Only those analysts who have risked their reputations, their professional access, and their own safety would likely mourn the passing of their newfound freedoms. But analysts (particularly those who work inside the Rock) are a hardy, resourceful lot, and the vast majority of them would likely find new jobs on Wall Street. The only people who would ultimately lose if Prudential's grand research experiment failed would be investors. The crisis on Wall Street may yet work in Prudential's favor if enough investors come to realize that objective research is not a given but a godsend—and that it pays to know who is providing it.

Government regulation often doesn't go according to plan. The Securities and Exchange Commission's Regulation Fair Disclosure was enacted in the summer of 2000 to bar U.S. companies from selective disclosure of important nonpublic information by company executives to favored market pros. However, Bob Drummond of *Bloomberg Markets* found that it's certainly not working as planned, with individual investors losing out due to its ineffectiveness.

Bob Drummond

Unfair Disclosure

ON FRIDAY, NOVEMBER 1, 2002, Veritas Software Corp. said in a news release that its chief executive, Gary Bloom, would be a keynote speaker the next Monday, November 4, at a Goldman Sachs Group Inc. software conference. As dictated by Regulation Fair Disclosure—the U.S. Securities and Exchange Commission's two-and-a-half-year-old rule that forbids companies from selectively releasing news to favored investors—the company's release said Bloom's presentation would be carried live on the world wide web so all investors could hear his views at the same time.

On that same Friday, three days before Bloom was to hold the webcast, he spoke on a private conference call to a group of investors who'd been invited by Citigroup Inc.'s Salomon Smith Barney. "CEO Gary Bloom's message was that Veritas has a road map to innovate, sell, and deliver the future of storage by taking storage software technology into new markets," Salomon analysts Stephen Mahedy and Clint Vaughan wrote in a report dated November 4.

At 1 p.m. on Friday, the time Salomon had set for Bloom's nonpublic conference call, Veritas shares were up 3¢ to $15.28. After the call started, the stock jumped 5.5 percent for the day, closing at $16.09. Shares of Veritas, which is based in Mountain View, California, and which commands about half of the global market for data backup software, rose again on Monday. By the time Bloom's publicly available Goldman webcast started at 3:30 p.m., Veritas stock had surged 17 percent—to $17.81—from the time of Friday's nonpublic chat with Salomon clients.

"Veritas has been a one-trick pony for a long time," says Steve Kenniston, an analyst at market research firm Enterprise Storage Group, who listened in on the private conference call. He says participants on that call welcomed Bloom's strategy of seeking new markets. "They needed something different," Kenniston says.

Veritas spokeswoman Marlena Fernandez says the company didn't violate fair disclosure rules. "We manage our conversations in accordance with Reg FD and are confident our comments are consistent with previously communicated guidance," she says. Salomon analysts Mahedy and Vaughan didn't return calls.

Such abrupt stock price movements—taking place after private conferences between corporate executives, major investors, and securities analysts—prompted the SEC in 2000 to enact Regulation Fair Disclosure, known on Wall Street as Reg FD. The rule requires that public U.S. companies tell all investors when they release nonpublic information that's important enough to affect trading decisions. The law says public release of so-called material information to a select group must take place simultaneously in the case of an intentional disclosure and promptly in the case of an unintentional disclosure. Arthur Levitt, SEC chairman from 1993 to 2001, pushed for the rule after declaring that companies had cheated smaller funds and individual investors by keeping them in the dark while Wall Street insiders bought and sold shares based on the information they got at private briefings. (Levitt is now a director of Bloomberg LP, the parent of Bloomberg News.)

Reg FD or no Reg FD, not much has changed, according to an analysis of hundreds of reports to clients written by securities analysts since the rule took effect in October 2000. The events surrounding the

Veritas webcast are not unusual. Analysts and their firms' biggest investment clients still get privileged access to top executives—and stocks
still soar or dive during or after such talks. The analysts' reports surveyed
include those from Lehman Brothers Holdings Inc., Merrill Lynch &
Co., Morgan Stanley, and Salomon.

Almost every working day, the analyst reports show, CEOs and chief
financial officers from two or three public companies congregate with
analysts and investors in private lunches, closed-door meetings, or
unpublicized conference calls. "People just don't believe there's been any
change," says Jacob Zamansky, a New York securities lawyer. "Public
investors believe there's a rigged game. On disclosure, there's a lot of
talk and no action going on."

The week of December 8 illustrates how analysts and investors routinely meet privately with company executives. During that week, brokerage analysts sent reports to clients about private meetings with
executives from twenty companies, including Dell Computer Corp.,
Gap Inc., Lucent Technologies Inc., and United Parcel Service Inc.
CheckFree Corp., an electronic-bill-payment company, invited analysts
and investors to a December 12 meeting with CEO Peter Kight and
other executives at its Norcross, Georgia, headquarters. The meeting
was not carried by a webcast or conference call. Spokesman David
Fontaine says no significant news was discussed. CheckFree shares—up
2.8 percent at the meeting's scheduled 11:30 a.m. start—fell 4 percent
by the close of trading. "Without substantial revenue growth or a clear
indication of margin improvement, we cannot justify buying the shares
at current levels," Friedman, Billings, Ramsey Group Inc. analyst
Christopher Penny wrote to clients on December 13, reporting that the
meeting had given little assurance of significantly higher sales or lower
costs. Penny downgraded CheckFree to underperform from outperform.
The shares fell an additional 7.4 percent that day.

Reg FD applies to publicly traded companies; it puts no restrictions
or penalties on brokers or investors. Still, the five-page regulation is an
amendment to SEC insider-trading rules, adding possible penalties for
those who give out private information as well as recipients who trade
on it.

Reg FD doesn't forbid company executives from speaking to

investors privately—as long as they don't selectively reveal so-called material corporate news. For violations, the SEC can file civil or administrative complaints seeking to fine executives as much as $100,000 and companies as much as $500,000. Companies may satisfy their public disclosure requirements by revealing important developments either in news releases and filings with the SEC or through open and publicized conference calls and webcasts.

Besides risking violations of Reg FD, company executives take risks in closed-door communications because if stocks move, they must ask shareholders to trust that they followed the rules. Such acts of faith may be scarce after the scandals involving such companies as Enron Corp. and WorldCom Inc., says former SEC Commissioner Ed Fleischman. "It is clearly dangerous," says Fleischman, a lawyer at Linklaters in New York, who was an SEC commissioner from 1986 to 1992. "If you trip over the threshold of materiality, you're in trouble." There's also the danger that, if a company's stock moves for unknown or unrelated reasons about the time of a private discussion, executives may have to face investor questions or government investigations, he says.

The SEC so far has taken Reg FD enforcement actions against three companies. In a case announced November 25, Siebel Systems Inc., the world's largest customer service software company, agreed to pay $250,000 to settle an SEC complaint alleging that CEO Tom Siebel had given an optimistic talk to investors at a Goldman Sachs conference on November 5, 2001, based on nonpublic information about the company's sales prospects. The stock rose 20 percent that day to $20.81. Siebel Systems settled without admitting or denying wrongdoing.

On the same day, the SEC announced an action alleging that Raytheon Co.'s then CFO Franklyn Caine had called analysts in February and March 2001 to say quarterly earnings estimates were too high. The agency also filed a complaint saying that Secure Computing Corp. CEO John McNulty had told institutional investors in March 2002 that one of the largest computer networking companies, which wasn't identified by the agency, had agreed to include Secure Computing's software with its products. Company shares leaped 15 percent over two days by the time Secure Computing issued a news release the day after the CEO's private talk. Raytheon, Caine, Secure Computing, and McNulty settled with the SEC by agreeing to tougher-than-normal penalties for any future violations. They paid no monetary penalty and neither admitted nor denied wrongdoing.

The five-member SEC was split on how tough to be in these cases. Democrat Roel Campos dissented from SEC orders against Raytheon and Secure Computing because neither had imposed any penalty. Republicans Cynthia Glassman and Paul Atkins dissented from the Siebel Systems action because it had imposed a monetary penalty. "It took a while to bring the first cases, but we did take action," says Glassman. "I think it's a message to companies that we do intend to enforce Reg FD."

The SEC also issued a report criticizing Motorola Inc. The agency says an executive improperly called analysts to guide their earnings estimates. It didn't file a case against Motorola—the world's number two maker of mobile phones, after Nokia Oyj—because the company had sought counsel from its lawyers, the agency said.

Fund managers say they continue to meet privately with company executives. "We get plenty of opportunities to speak with CEOs and CFOs," says Brian Salerno, a manager of the $400 million Munder Future Technology Fund. "I don't think there's been much change in that." While companies don't provide specific earnings numbers in these sessions, the discussions give important context, Salerno says. "After Reg FD, I still get to talk with CEOs and CFOs about strategy and competition and hiring and firing decisions—things that tell you how the business is going," he says.

Money managers from smaller firms, along with investors who aren't invited to closed-door discussions, still are left scratching their heads when stocks jump and gyrate for no apparent reason, says Chad Horning, a fund manager at Goshen, Indiana–based MMA Praxis Mutual Funds, which manages about $400 million of equities. "We never had the access before Reg FD, and we don't now either," he says. "It was supposed to get better." MMA Praxis managers don't often get invited to discussions with executives or top analysts, Horning says. "It's often the assistant whom we talk to," he says. "We certainly are treated with a lower level of service than someone five times our size."

Even multibillion-dollar-fund managers can't be everywhere, and they often see stocks move without explanation, says Jay Tracey, who was chief investment officer at Berger Financial Group LLC until its $6 billion of funds were folded into Janus Capital Group Inc.'s funds in January. "More than once a day, I get the feeling there are people out there who know more about things than I do," says Tracey.

SEC spokeswoman Christi Harlan declined requests for comment about agency enforcement of the rule. At a February 5 Senate Banking Committee confirmation hearing, new SEC Chairman William Donaldson backed away from a previous statement—made when he was chairman of health insurer Aetna Inc.—that Reg FD was "crazy" because, he said, it cut off the flow of information that markets need. "I'm totally for the intention of the law, but at that time, there were some unintended consequences that were having just the reverse effect, shutting down information flow," Donaldson told senators, saying he would not seek to change the rule. He was confirmed as chairman by the Senate on February 13.

SEC Commissioner Harvey Goldschmid, a Democrat who was Reg FD's primary author when he was the agency's general counsel, says companies ignore Reg FD at their own peril. "Some in the business community may have begun to lose sight of the need for very strict compliance with the regulation," Goldschmid says. "The SEC will be rigorous in bringing enforcement actions to provide accountability, deterrence, and fair markets." He says he believes that small investors have been getting better information since Reg FD was enacted. "Anecdotally, it appears there is far less selective disclosure now than there was before FD," he says.

Former SEC Chairman Levitt says the agency has to send a clear message to companies by acting on more cases. "I wish there were more," he says.

Most companies try to stay within Reg FD's guidelines, and some have investor relations professionals monitor private meetings and brief executives on what can be discussed, says Cherie Rice, vice president of investor relations at Waste Management Inc. "I don't know anybody who takes it lightly," says Rice, whose Houston company is the biggest waste hauler in the U.S. The key, she says, is that executives should avoid important disclosures when they speak privately with analysts or share-holders. "We don't believe Reg FD's intent was for companies to never meet or talk to investors other than on a conference call or webcast," Rice says.

Investors will always try to get close to executives in the know, says Tracey, the former Berger manager. "Nothing in Reg FD says you can't quiz managers and get answers about their long-term plans or objectives," he says. "This is what we do," says Phil Ruedi, an analyst at mutual fund company T. Rowe Price Group Inc. "We invest in companies, and some people put a premium on this: Do you like management, the way they conduct themselves?"

Big money managers trade through several brokers so they can see more analyst reports of private meetings with company executives, Munder's Salerno says. "I probably get a hundred Wall Street reports a day—e-mailed to me from every brokerage under the sun," he says. Executive access is important enough that money managers select brokerages to handle hundreds of millions of dollars' worth of stock trades based on their connections with CEOs, says Jeff Huffman, who manages about $600 million at FleetBoston Financial Corp.'s Crabbe Huson Group in Portland, Oregon. "We have told brokers that's one of the things that will determine how we evaluate them against their peers: whether you can bring us into contact with company management," Huffman says. "We'll compensate brokers for that with our commission dollars." Private talks with executives give money managers a sense of the competence of company management, he says.

Face-to-face meetings are sometimes even more important to executives, particularly at smaller or newer companies, says Tara Spiess, investor relations director at Genta Inc., a Berkeley Heights, New Jersey, biotechnology company with $504 million in market value. "For a company that doesn't have much capital and has trouble getting in to see the right people, the banking relationship is essential; they can open the door to funds and to the big investors," Spiess says.

Executives of the biggest Wall Street firms participate in private sessions, analyst reports show. Goldman Sachs CEO Henry Paulson and CFO David Viniar met with Salomon analyst Guy Moszkowski, according to the analyst's November 10 report. The following day, Viniar had breakfast with Lehman Brothers analyst Mark Constant, says a note to Constant's clients. Lehman's co–chief operating officer Bradley Jack met with Morgan Stanley analyst Henry McVey, according to a December 5 report. The same analyst reported on November 4 about talks with Merrill Lynch's then president and now CEO Stanley O'Neal. Goldman Sachs spokesman Peter Rose says the firm's executives don't talk about material nonpublic information in private sessions. Officials from Lehman and Merrill declined to comment.

On November 21, Scientific-Atlanta Inc. vice president of investor relations Tom Robey met with analysts in New York, including a midday talk with Salomon telecommunications equipment analyst Daryl Armstrong, Robey says. Armstrong, who declined to comment, wrote to clients that he and Robey had discussed weak European demand and ways the maker of cable television set-top boxes could expand sales to homes with more than one television. Scientific-Atlanta stock jumped 13 percent that day and a total of almost 20 percent on November 21 and 22. That was the stock's biggest two-day rise in more than eight months and more than twice the 8 percent gain of the Standard & Poor's 500 Telecommunications Equipment Index during that period. The company didn't issue any public statements.

"I'm paid to talk to investors and analysts—all day every day—with the proviso that I don't talk about nonpublic information," Robey says. The executive says he and other company officials carefully stick to a set of facts that have already been made public. He says he doesn't know why shares jumped last November. "I'm 100 percent confident that I didn't slip," says Robey. He says he and other executives speak with analysts to answer questions about competition and general industry trends. "If I knew why the stock went up and down, I'd be a richer man," he says.

Genta CEO Raymond Warrell and other executives spoke with investor clients of UBS Warburg LLC on April 4, 2002, says Genta's Spiess. Investors asked about rumors that Genta had added in a study more patients than planned, possibly delaying approval progress for Genasense, a treatment designed to make chemotherapy more effective, she says. Warrell said the study had been expanded, adding that Genta hadn't changed its Genasense timetable, Spiess says. Genta shares plunged 17 percent that day to $13.20—the biggest drop among 276 members of the Russell 2000 Health Care Index. Trading volume was 3.4 times the daily average for the previous month.

The company arranged a publicly available conference call with Warrell before the markets opened on April 5. "Being that it was not webcast and the stock took a hit because of this supposed time line increase, we decided to have the call," Spiess says. "You have to be very aware of what you're saying. If not, you'd better be prepared to write very quickly and get a press release out." On June 3, Genta announced it would delay seeking approval for Genasense while it expanded clinical trials. The stock that day plummeted 22 percent to $7.19.

Former SEC Chairman Levitt began speaking out in 1998 against selective disclosure. "As far as I'm concerned, that's cheating, and it's a stain upon our market," he said in a November 1998 interview with Bloomberg News. The rule was proposed in December 1999, prompting opposition from A.G. Edwards Inc., Lehman, Merrill, and other securities firms. Those firms said the restrictions would keep companies from giving investors information they need. Criticism by those firms was buried in an avalanche of more than 6,100 letters, most of which were from small investors supporting the rule, according to SEC records. The measure was approved 3-to-1 on August 10, 2000, with Laura Unger, the commission's only Republican, voting no. After Reg FD got enacted, Unger said the rule didn't adequately describe what kind of information was covered and might ensnare innocent executives. "We don't intend to enforce the rule before we make clear what the rule is," Unger said in April 2001, after becoming the agency's acting chairwoman.

Under Reg FD, the SEC tells companies that if an executive trips up and gives important nonpublic news to analysts and investors, then the executive's company must promptly release the information publicly. It can issue a press release or file a public form, called an 8-K, with the SEC. The SEC has released informal guidance that a public disclosure isn't prompt if it comes more than 24 hours after the executive spoke to a select group. While after-the-fact disclosure may help demonstrate good faith to SEC investigators, it doesn't necessarily get a company off the hook, says Richard Rowe, a Washington lawyer and former SEC corporation finance director. And if stocks react before public disclosure, that can signify the importance of information, he says. "The movement of the stock itself is certainly evidence supporting materiality," Rowe says.

After stock trading closed on November 21, Flowserve Corp., the largest maker of pumps for oil and chemical companies, filed a form 8-K with the SEC. "During a conversation this week with securities analysts, Flowserve Corp. reaffirmed its full-year 2002 estimated earnings per share," the Irving, Texas, company said in the filing. The filing reached the public after Flowserve shares bounced up 5.5 percent on November 21. A day earlier, Wachovia Securities analyst Wendy Caplan issued a report saying institutional investors had met that week with Flowserve CEO Scott Greer and CFO Renee Hornbaker.

Michael Conley, Flowserve's investor relations director, says executives said no more than they had earlier. The identical earnings guidance may have been given more credibility when repeated late in a reporting period, he says. "Laying out an earnings number early in the quarter, perceptions may be different than later in the quarter, when you presumably know more," Conley says. He says the company filed the 8-K in an effort to meet the spirit of Reg FD.

Sealed Air Corp., which makes Bubble Wrap and other packaging materials, released information to Salomon clients and Morgan Stanley investors on December 16 before realizing how they would react, says investor relations director Philip Cook. CEO William Hickey and other executives of Sealed Air told investors they didn't expect that a $900 million settlement of asbestos liability lawsuits would have an effect on forecasts the company would earn $2.40–$2.45 per share in 2003. The news came as a relief to investors worried about a bigger earnings hit, Morgan Stanley analyst Edings Thibault concluded. "In tough markets, there tends to be an expectation of bad news," says Thibault, who accompanied clients to meet with the executives. "Sometimes no news is good news."

Sealed Air stock was up almost 5 percent by 12:07 p.m. on December 16, when Salomon analyst George Staphos put out an urgent "flash note" to brokerage clients about the comments. Sealed Air executives, seeing investor reaction, decided to then tell the public, says Cook. The company put out a press release at 12:24 p.m. By day's end, Sealed Air's shares had gained 10 percent. "As those meetings went on, we realized investors were unclear about the settlement," Cook says. "Because of Reg FD, we moved quickly to get that guidance out there."

Closed-door sessions are inherently dangerous because company officials can't predict how their audiences will react, says Fleischman, the former SEC commissioner. For example, at a private dinner in Phoenix with Waste Management executives on September 23—the night before the company was to hold a live public webcast—some money managers and analysts reacted less to what they heard than what they didn't hear, says T. Rowe Price's Ruedi. "They got hurt because they didn't provide any guidance," says Ruedi, whose mutual funds owned 10.1 million Waste Management shares as of September 30. The next day, Waste Management shares fell 4.7 percent, their biggest one-day drop in more than two months. About one-quarter of the decline happened before the public webcast began at 11 a.m. New York time. "It's a catch-22," says Waste Management spokeswoman Sarah Simpson. "You want people who cover your company to know what's happening in the industry, but it can be dangerous to talk to them."

To make the rule work as it should, the SEC needs to get tough on Reg FD violators, says University of Colorado accounting professor Phil Shane, who conducted one of the earliest academic studies about Reg FD. "Because the regulation wasn't enforced for so long, it looked like it didn't have any teeth," he says.

Until the SEC rigorously enforces Reg FD, small fund managers and individual investors are likely to remain where they were before the rule was enacted: last in line to get the news.

McKinsey is the world's most prestigious and expensive consulting firm. Does it merit such distinction? The dismal performance of clients such as Kmart, Swissair, Global Crossing and, last but not least, Enron casts doubt on its expertise. John A. Byrne in *Business Week* chronicles the high-risk nature of some of its recommended business models, as well as what he sees as eroding culture and values.

John A. Byrne

Inside McKinsey

SHORTLY AFTER ENRON CORP. tumbled into bankruptcy in December 2001, McKinsey & Co. managing partner Rajat Gupta was worried. It wasn't only because former Enron CEO Jeffrey K. Skilling was once a McKinsey & Co. partner and loyal alum. Or that his firm had advised the giant energy trader for nearly 18 years on basic strategy, even sitting in on boardroom presentations to Enron's directors. Or even that many of the underlying principles of Enron's transformation, including its "asset-light" strategy, its "loose-tight" culture, and the securitization of debt, were eagerly promoted by McKinsey consultants.

Gupta was worried about something much more immediate: Had McKinsey crossed a legal line that would drag it into the unfolding morass? In a stunning exercise for the world's whitest of white-shoe management consultants, Gupta dispatched his chief legal counsel to McKinsey's offices in Houston to review the firm's work at Enron. The mission was to find any evidence linking McKinsey to the massive fraud behind Enron's business model.

The lawyer came back with good news: There were no shredded documents, à la Arthur Andersen LLP, and, more important, says Gupta, there was nothing in the files to show that McKinsey ever helped Enron engineer its controversial off-balance-sheet financing or its financial reporting strategy. "In all the work we did with Enron," maintains Gupta, "we did not do anything that is related to financial structuring or disclosure or any of the issues that got them into trouble. We stand by all the work we did. Beyond that, we can only empathize with the trouble they are going through. It's a sad thing to see."

Still, outsiders marvel that the secretive partnership has not been drawn into the debacle, given its extensive involvement at Enron. "I'm surprised that they haven't been subpoenaed as a witness, at least," says Wayne E. Cooper, CEO of Kennedy Information, a research and publishing firm that keeps tabs on consultants. "There was so much smoke coming out of the Andersen smoking gun that all the firefighters went after that one. McKinsey was lucky. They dodged a bullet."

The bad news, however, is that Enron, which was paying McKinsey as much as $10 million in annual fees, is just one of an unusual number of embarrassing client failures for the elite consulting firm. Besides Enron, there's Swissair, Kmart, and Global Crossing—all McKinsey clients that have filed for bankruptcy in relatively short order. And those are just the biggest. McKinsey also finds itself improbably lining up with other creditors to collect unpaid fees from recently bankrupt companies that soared during the late '90s only to crash later. Battery maker Exide Technologies and NorthPoint Communications Group Inc., an upstart telecom provider, are two such examples.

All of which raises uncomfortable questions about the world's most prestigious—and enigmatic—consulting firm. Did McKinsey's partners get caught up in the euphoria of the late '90s and suffer lapses of judgment? And if so, what does that say about the quality of its expensive advice? Did it stray from its core values? What accountability does it— or any consulting firm—have for the ideas and concepts it launches into a company?

After all, McKinsey was a key architect of the strategic thinking that made Enron a Wall Street darling. In books, articles, and essays, its partners regularly stamped their imprimatur on many of Enron's strategies and practices, helping to position the energy giant as a corporate innovator worthy of emulation. The firm may not be the subject of any investigations, but its close involvement with Enron raises the question of whether McKinsey, like some other professional firms, ignored warning flags in order to keep an important account.

The breakdowns of such visible clients could not have come at a more trying time. Instead of celebrating the end of his third and final three-year term as managing director, Gupta, 53, finds his firm roiled by a rare and potentially disruptive downturn in its business. Like most other consulting firms, McKinsey rode the e-business wave to record revenues—and record partner payouts—in 2000. When the boom turned to bust, the firm was stuck with far too many consultants and not nearly enough assignments. The utilization rate, or billable time, of its consultants has fallen to its lowest level in more than 32 years: just 52 percent versus the heady 64 percent level during the dot-com boom.

That's not to say that McKinsey has lost its standing. The firm remains the high priest of high-level consulting, with the most formidable intellectual firepower, the classiest client portfolio, and the greatest global reach of any adviser to management in the world. Most of the firm's top clients pay $10 million a year and up in fees, while McKinsey's largest client—which it declines to name—doled out $60 million for its advice last year. McKinsey serves 147 of the world's 200 largest corporations, including 80 of the top 120 financial services firms, 9 of the 11 largest chemical companies, and 15 of the 22 biggest health care and pharmaceutical concerns.

McKinsey partners learn early on to protect and cultivate their client relationships. The firm says that it has served more than 400 active clients for 15 years or longer. It may be the priciest of the management consultants, but longtime clients say it gives top service. "McKinsey will bring its most senior people in to discuss the things they would do if they were in our shoes," says Klaus Kleinfeld, CEO of Siemens Corp., a long-standing client. "You have lunch. You have dinner. And then projects evolve. Very often, competitive bidding doesn't happen."

Gupta shows little concern over the meltdown of high-profile clients. "In these turbulent times, with our serving more than half the

Fortune 500 companies, there are bound to be some clients that get into trouble," he says matter-of-factly. "We wouldn't have as many ongoing client situations if we didn't do good-quality work." And to be fair, McKinsey was hardly the only consultant to tie up with some high-flying upstarts in the '90s that later crashed.

When he became McKinsey's managing partner in 1994, Gupta's challenge was clear: He had to keep up McKinsey's growth while ensuring that size would not destroy the ethos of the close-knit partnership or undermine the firm's guiding principles. McKinseyites refer to these precepts, laid down by the firm's early leader, Marvin Bower, with near-religious conviction. Among the high-minded goals: Hire the best people and urge them to always put the client first—ahead of the interests of the firm.

In Gupta's early days as managing partner, some colleagues argued for keeping McKinsey small, to safeguard its culture and quality. Gupta was of another mind: He aggressively expanded abroad, opening up far-flung branches throughout Asia and Eastern Europe. In all, he expanded McKinsey's network to 84 worldwide locations from 58, boosted the consulting staff to 7,700 from 2,900, and lifted revenues to $3.4 billion from $1.2 billion in 1993. Meanwhile, the number of partners grew from 427 to 891. "It's a less personal place than it used to be," says Nancy Killefer, a senior partner in Washington, D.C. "In the old days, you knew everybody. That's not possible anymore."

Some observers believe the changes in McKinsey's culture went even deeper. Quietly, some current and former McKinsey consultants say the firm strayed from some of the ingrained values that have long guided it. Through the dot-com boom, for example, McKinsey allowed its focus on building agenda-shaping relationships with top management at leading companies to slip, as the firm took on some distinctly down-market clients and projects. Increasingly, McKinsey began advising upstarts and divisional managers at less prestigious companies.

Worse, some argue, there was a noticeable tilt toward bringing in revenue at the expense of developing knowledge—a claim McKinsey vehemently disputes. "In [an earlier] era, the whole place had this tremendous focus on ideas," recalls a former McKinsey consultant. "I think knowledge has taken a backseat to revenue generation. The more revenues you create, the more your compensation and standing in the firm increases."

Gupta downplays any shift in priorities. "The pendulum does swing a little bit. I'd say that client development in the last year or two is more in the forefront, simply because that is the biggest need right now," he says, using McKinsey-speak for bringing in new business.

Perhaps the most visible example of this shift, say observers, was the rise of Ron Hulme, an affable, low-key senior partner and a leader of its energy practice, who managed the Enron account from McKinsey's Houston offices. Like many of the firm's consultants, Hulme penned essays extolling the virtues of Enron. As McKinsey's annual billings climbed higher and higher at Enron—at one recent point exceeding $10 million—Hulme commanded greater influence in the firm, helping to lead partner conferences and key initiatives. Some insiders even considered him a potential successor to Gupta, though that's now an unlikely prospect, given Enron's collapse. "Despite his young age, he had tremendously high standing and power that derived from the Enron relationship," says a former McKinseyite. Hulme declined to comment.

Hulme did not initiate McKinsey's Enron business. Like many of the deepest and most lucrative corporate relationships, it began with one consultant who instantly impressed a client with his brilliance and insights. Jeffrey Skilling, then McKinsey's partner in charge of the worldwide energy practice, began advising Enron in the late '80s, but the relationship was cemented when he joined Enron in 1990 with the mandate to create a new way of doing business. Skilling, who once said he felt as if he were "doing God's work" at McKinsey, had proposed that Enron create a portfolio of fixed-price purchase and supply contracts that would supposedly eliminate supply risks and minimize the price fluctuations of the spot market for trading natural gas.

After joining Enron, Skilling repeatedly turned to McKinsey teams for analytical help and advice. "They infiltrated Enron with Jeff, and he was just the tip of the iceberg," says a former McKinsey consultant who worked at Enron. "There were all sorts of McKinsey people who went in over the years. They were so happy they had Enron locked up."

Indeed, several other prominent McKinsey consultants migrated to

Enron as employees, including partner Doug Woodham, who left the firm in 1994 for a four-year stint as vice president at Enron Capital & Trade Resources, where he led a team that developed an electric power and natural gas hedge fund. As Enron work became more financially driven, McKinsey teams there increasingly drew on partners with expertise in trading, risk management, and investment banking. At any given time, McKinsey had as many as twenty consultants at the energy company, several stationed in Enron's offices.

By and large, most of McKinsey's assignments at Enron were tactical or technical in nature: doing the prep work for entering new markets, formulating strategy for new products and services, and deciding whether Enron should acquire or partner with another company to gain access to a pipeline. But McKinsey also helped Enron formulate its now-discredited broadband strategy, in which it built a high-speed fiber network to support the trading of communications capacity. Among other things, McKinsey, over about six months, helped to gauge the size and growth of the market. And, like Enron and many others, it didn't see the telecom meltdown coming. McKinsey also helped to set up the finance subsidiary that Enron later portrayed as its growth engine, and also assisted the firm with its commodity risk management operations.

A former Enron senior executive says McKinsey consultants wielded influence throughout the organization. "They were all over the place," he says. "They were sitting with us every step of the way. They thought, 'This thing could be big, and we want credit for it.'" The extent of its work there and its access to senior management exposed the firm to much of Enron's inner workings. Over the years, McKinsey partners Hulme and Suzanne Nimocks had numerous one-on-one discussions with Skilling, according to former Enron executives.

Richard N. Foster, a senior partner, even became an adviser to Enron's board, attending a half-dozen board meetings in the 12 months up until October 2001. Foster was frequently asked to step out of those meetings while the partners conferred with company lawyers over confidential matters. Competitors privately gloat that the title of Foster's most recent book, *Creative Destruction,* aptly captures what went wrong at Enron. Embarrassingly, the book, published in April 2001, is filled with glowing references to Enron. "Dick Foster was very happy to see practice that enforced his theories of creative destruction at Enron," says a partner at another consulting firm. "McKinsey seems to have partners who develop academic theories and then run clinical trials on their clients." Foster declined to comment.

Some insiders offer a less benign interpretation of what went wrong at Enron. They don't claim McKinsey did anything illegal but do suggest it might have turned a blind eye to signs of trouble to preserve a lucrative relationship. "The problem for McKinsey with Enron isn't Andersen-type issues," says the former McKinsey consultant who worked at Enron. "Rather, it's 'Could they have seen the organization malfunctioning and spoken up?' The answer is yes. When you have a megaclient, 'This is what the client should hear' is twisted into, 'This is what is going to let us stay at the boardroom level.'"

Gupta won't be drawn into a detailed conversation on Enron. "Our view is not so much to have a public point of view here," he says. "I won't specifically talk about our work at Enron. We're constantly assessing whether we served everybody in the right way. I think we have."

Perhaps so. But many of the intellectual underpinnings of Enron's transformation from pipeline company to trading colossus can be traced directly to McKinsey thinking. Senior partner Lowell Bryan, one of the most influential of the firm's big thinkers today, has written extensively on securitized credit—the process of converting loans or receivables into securities. As far back as 1987, just after McKinsey began consulting for Enron, Bryan was writing that "securitization's potential . . . is great because it removes capital and balance sheets as constraints on growth." It was Bryan, too, who has written and spoken extensively on how capital-intensive companies such as Enron can generate greater value by finding ways to run low-asset businesses—what Skilling referred to as his "asset-light" strategy. Bryan was brought into Enron to convey these ideas to the company's top 100 executives. But he insists his ideas are not to blame. "I never said anything about fraud, accounting, or any of those issues."

If McKinsey has been humbled by the Enron experience, it certainly doesn't show it. When New York headquarters asked all consultants who favorably mentioned Enron in articles whether they wanted their citations taken off McKinsey's web site, not a single consultant said yes.

So all of the nearly thirty separate references to Enron in McKinsey-authored articles remain on the site.

As things began to unravel at Enron, some other important clients were also going off the rails. At Kmart, McKinsey produced work supporting the retailer's decision to sell more groceries in a bid to get shoppers to visit stores. It also was instrumental in creating BlueLight.com, which was intended to be spun off in an initial public offering but never made it to market.

McKinsey began consulting for the retailer in 1994. In the ensuing years, Kmart's competitive position steadily eroded. "That is a long enough time for a firm to know if its advice has impact," says an ex-McKinsey consultant. "But senior partners need to show revenue growth, so they are willing to continue to work with clients even if they feel there is no light at the end of the tunnel." McKinsey ended its relationship in 2000 after disagreeing with new CEO Charles Conaway, who pursued a disastrous price war against Wal-Mart. Still, McKinsey's involvement through the mid- to late 1990s, when Kmart swiftly and steadily lost ground to Wal-Mart, did not serve either client or consultant well.

At Swissair Group, McKinsey advised a major shift in strategy that led the once highly regarded airline to spend nearly $2 billion buying stakes in many small and troubled European airlines. The idea was for Swissair to expand into aviation services, providing everything from maintenance to food for other airlines as a way to increase revenues and profits. The strategy backfired, causing massive losses and a bankruptcy filing last October. McKinsey maintains it can't be held responsible for the outcome because it wasn't involved in the implementation of the strategy. At Global Crossing Ltd., McKinsey says its work was limited to only three projects, two of which involved information-technology outsourcing, so it cannot be blamed for the telecom provider's implosion.

The internet boom posed an especially difficult challenge for McKinsey. The blanket assumption was that the rules of the game were changing, and many McKinseyites saw their former MBA classmates emerge overnight as multimillion-dollar entrepreneurial celebrities. Inside the firm, Gupta was faced with all kinds of new pressures: whether McKinsey should start a venture capital fund, or go public itself, or start its own dot-com ventures as offshoots of the firm's consulting business; whether to accept equity instead of cash for an assignment with a start-up. The partnership declined to sell shares, as Goldman Sachs had done, but in other important ways it veered from the course it had long followed.

One of the most noticeable changes was a drift away from its long-standing policy of not linking its fees to client performance. Bower believed alternative fee arrangements could tempt consultants to focus on the wrong things. During the past 18 months, McKinsey has been structuring dozens of deals with blue-chip companies that call for the payment of an assignment-ending bonus if a client is satisfied with the results. In the past three years, it also began accepting payment in stock from approximately 150 upstart companies, though McKinsey points out that this is a small percentage of its 12,000 engagements in that time. Gupta says the change allowed the firm to serve smaller, innovative companies that didn't have the cash to pay McKinsey's standard fees of $275,000 to $350,000 a month. The equity was then sunk into a blind trust and liquidated as soon as possible into a profit pool for its partners. In another case, that of Spain's Telefónica, it added a clause in its contract giving it a cash kicker based on the rising stock price of an internet offshoot McKinsey was advising. The firm collected a $6.8 million bonus.

Yet even these concessions to the bonanza mentality during the boom's height didn't prevent defections. Many McKinsey consultants left for dot-com start-ups with names like Pet Quarters, Cyber Dialogue, Virtual Communities, and CarsDirect.com, many of which are now relegated to the junk heap of irrational exuberance. Across the firm, attrition rose only slightly during the boom, to over 22 percent a year in 1999 and 2000 from more typical levels of 18 percent. But some of the best people left, and some offices were hit hard by the exodus. In San Francisco, where McKinsey employs 150 professionals, a full third of the staff departed for other opportunities in 1999. "There was a whole group of people in the bubble who lost their way," says Larry Mendonca, the McKinsey partner who manages the San Francisco office. "They were trying to get their share of the bubble."

McKinsey got its share, of course. In its quest for revenue growth, it pursued a whole new class of clientele. Demand for consulting soared from both start-ups and large corporate clients, many of which had grown fearful that they were falling behind the internet curve. During the peak two years of the dot-com boom, McKinsey alone did more than one thousand e-commerce assignments, even as partners internally debated the true impact of the net on clients. "I was in the room saying, 'You're smoking dope here on this dot-com stuff,'" recalls Roger Kline, a long-time McKinsey partner who oversees the financial services practice.

But the firm even set up "accelerators," or facilities, to help entre-preneurs launch new dot-coms with direct McKinsey help. "Maybe we should have been a little more circumspect than we were," concedes Gupta. "But I don't think we made any big errors or excesses."

Not surprisingly, some of McKinsey's dot-com clients fared little better than Pets.com Inc. EB2B Commerce Inc., which engaged Mc-Kinsey in early 2000 to help it develop a strategy after a merger, was recently warned by Nasdaq that its stock could be delisted. The com-pany's shares have plummeted to 15¢ from $190 when McKinsey started working with it. Another high-tech client, Applied Digital Solutions Inc., which McKinsey helped in exchange for equity, is in the midst of a meltdown, with first-quarter losses of $17 million. Applied Digital's auditors resigned the account in May after an accounting dis-pute with the company, which describes itself as a developer of "life-enhancing personal safeguard technologies." Shares of Applied Digital now trade for 57¢.

To be sure, McKinsey's core blue-chip clients, which range from General Motors Corp. to Johnson & Johnson, remain the firm's true bread and butter—partly because only those big companies can afford its fees. "McKinsey is expensive," says Ralph Larsen, former CEO of J&J. "But what they provide is a fresh look at our thinking and a certain detachment. We use them carefully for selected projects, things of great significance, and they have been valuable to us."

In managing the firm through the boom and the bust, Gupta now finds himself caught in a classic supply-demand squeeze, the sort of management dilemma for which a client would turn to McKinsey for advice: He hired too many people just as demand began to plummet. In an average year, McKinsey will offer consulting jobs to 3,100 MBAs and professionals in the expectation of getting roughly 2,000 acceptances. In 2000, however, more than 2,700 people accepted offers to join the firm. They apparently knew what McKinsey didn't yet get: The boom was over. By the following year, with the bubble clearly burst, the firm's attrition rate fell to only 5 percent. Suddenly, just as demand for business started falling off, McKinsey had too many consultants on the payroll, with fewer leaving for other opportunities. "We honored every offer and didn't push people out," says Gupta, "and we had no professional layoffs other than our traditional up-or-out stuff."

As McKinsey begins its months-long process early next year to elect a new managing partner, the firm will likely toast Gupta as the man who led the firm to new growth records in new markets around the world. "In every generation, there are issues that come up that define the firm," he says. "We've had our share in the last decade. But I feel very proud of where we've come out." The question for his successor is whether he expanded the firm at the cost of the culture and values that made McKinsey tower above its peers.

The game plan of Alliance Capital Management, the largest publicly traded money manager, is to aggressively buy stocks as their prices slip, then sell them as the prices rise. That basic logic delivered solid returns and contributed to its prominence within the industry. However, doggedly sticking to that philosophy in recent times resulted in billions of dollars in losses from the stock of embattled companies that included Enron, WorldCom, Qwest, and Tyco International. Edward Robinson of *Bloomberg Markets* carefully follows Alliance on this slippery slope.

Edward Robinson

Alliance Capital's Bad Bets

WHEN ENRON CORP. fired Chief Financial Officer Andrew Fastow last October 24 for allegedly hiding huge losses in off-balance-sheet partnerships, a sense of alarm gripped Trent Webster, a portfolio manager at the Florida State Board of Administration. The Sunshine State's investment arm was sitting on 5.5 million Enron shares in an account run by one of its money managers, New York–based Alliance Capital Management LP. Enron's stock had plunged 62 percent since August 14, when CEO Jeffrey Skilling abruptly resigned for "personal reasons."

Webster called Daniel Nordby, a senior vice president in Alliance's Minneapolis office, and asked him why the firm continued to buy so many Enron shares. "Dan stated that they had made a research mistake," Webster wrote in an internal memorandum to Susan Schueren, chief of the domestic equities unit at the Florida board. "Dan acknowledged Alliance's mistake, saying that Alliance had stepped on a land mine."

Instead of fleeing the Enron minefield, Alliance Vice Chairman

Alfred Harrison, head of the firm's Large Capitalization Growth Team and the Florida account's lead manager, bought more than two million additional shares over the next three weeks, according to the pension fund's trading records. By the time Enron declared bankruptcy on December 2, the Florida board—which has $126 billion in assets and manages the pensions for 800,000 state workers and retirees—had watched $282 million vaporize.

Alliance, which had begun buying Enron stock for the Florida fund at $79 a share on November 6, 2000, sold its entire 7.6-million-share stake for 28¢ a share on November 30, 2001. "It was the grossest kind of speculation," says Thomas Herndon, the board's executive director until his retirement on June 28. "What in the world motivated them to do this in the face of such clear and present danger?"

Alliance is the eighth-largest fund management firm in the world, with $412 billion in assets. The firm has 2,440 institutional clients and manages pension plans for government workers and employees of such companies as Ford Motor Co. and Pfizer Inc. Alliance also manages university endowments and 330 mutual funds in the U.S. and elsewhere.

Alliance followed its Enron investments with a series of bad bets on other headline-making companies. After a buying spree that began in the first quarter, the firm is the largest institutional stakeholder in WorldCom Inc., which overstated earnings since 1999 by $7.18 billion and declared bankruptcy on July 20. Alliance is also the biggest holder of Qwest Communications International Inc., which disclosed on July 28 that it had incorrectly booked about $1.16 billion in revenue from 1999 to 2001.

The fund manager is the largest shareholder in Dynegy Inc., a Houston-based energy trader under investigation by the U.S. Securities and Exchange Commission over whether it inflated revenue through sham natural gas trades. In addition, Alliance is the number one investor in Tyco International Ltd., a Bermuda-based manufacturer the SEC is investigating for possible misuse of company funds by former CEO Dennis Kozlowski.

Taken together, this quartet of companies—Dynegy, Tyco, Qwest, and WorldCom—lost $160.2 billion in market capitalization from December 31, 2001, to August 12, a drop of more than 85 percent.

Alliance's investments in WorldCom and Qwest had combined paper losses of $1.4 billion. Its long-held positions in Tyco and Dynegy together dropped about $6 billion in value since December 31, according to Bloomberg data.

Alliance's flagship mutual fund, the $12 billion Alliance Premier Growth Fund, lost $744 million on Enron, according to an internal Alliance record furnished to the Florida pension fund. "This is a firm that is willing to make substantial commitments to a specific stock," says Geoffrey Bobroff, a former SEC enforcement official and president of Bobroff Consulting Inc., a firm in East Greenwich, Rhode Island, that advises asset managers on the marketing and pricing of mutual funds. "It's a strategy that has paid them handsome dividends in the past, but now it has bit them on the ass."

Alliance, through spokesman John Meyers, declined to make any of its executives available for interviews—including Harrison, Nordby, chairman and CEO Bruce Calvert, and president John Carifa. Bloomberg News pieced together the story of Alliance's Florida investments with the help of memos, letters, notes from meetings, and e-mails exchanged between executives of Alliance and the Florida board—and obtained under Florida's Open Records Act.

Founded in 1962, Alliance has long championed its own brand of growth investing, which Harrison's group defines as buying stocks of companies with market values of at least $5 billion that have produced earnings growth rates of 12–15 percent. Alliance prospered during the bull market; its assets under management swelled to $454 billion in 2000 from $146 billion in 1995. "They thrived in that environment," says Burton Greenwald, president of B. J. Greenwald & Associates, a Philadelphia-based asset management consulting firm. "Pure growth plays fueled Alliance's own growth."

As the dean of Alliance's growth school, Harrison, 64, developed its chief investing strategy, dubbed the "V-factor methodology." Under it, he aggressively buys stocks as they slip in price—the left side of the V—and sells as they rise—the right side. "Our approach is the antithesis of momentum investing," he wrote in an article sent to clients in September 2001.

Over the past year, Alliance has come to epitomize the bear market's hard lessons—just as it typified the boom's rewards. Harrison became so wedded to his V method of making big contrarian bets that he did not heed the numerous red alerts that flashed on Enron, says Donald Nast, associate professor of finance at Florida State University and a member of the Investment Advisory Council, a panel that helps the Florida pension fund set investment policy. "He was a very aggressive money manager, and he was trying to hit a home run," says Nast.

Alliance's losing streak has stunned officials in pension funds. "Today, we see that regulators are failing, the boards of directors are failing, and the accountants are failing," says Michael Musuraca, a trustee of the New York City Employees' Retirement System, a $35 billion pension fund that serves more than 350,000 city workers and retirees. "And if, in fact, asset managers are also beginning to fail, where does that leave people to go? Alliance Capital has a great reputation; it is a giant in the industry. This really does make you say, Where do I turn next?"

The rough patch has also rattled investors in Alliance itself. "Enron? WorldCom? Qwest? Who is minding the ship here?" asks Michael Abrams, senior portfolio manager at Cincinnati Financial Corp. and the firm's largest public stockholder, with 1.8 million shares. "They need to quit placing such huge bets, or else there has to be a change at the top," says Abrams. "They need to reevaluate their decision-making process."

Alliance's stock was down 36 percent this year as of August 9 compared with a 9 percent decline in the New York Stock Exchange Financials Index, which comprises 848 fund management firms, banks, and other financial companies. Of Alliance's main rivals, only Stillwell Financial Inc., parent of Janus Capital Management LLC, did worse, with a 53 percent drop.

Richard Jenrette founded Alliance four decades ago as the money management department of Donaldson, Lufkin & Jenrette Inc., the investment bank now owned by Credit Suisse Group. In 1985, Equitable Life Assurance Society acquired Alliance as part of its purchase of DLJ. Paris-based Axa SA, Europe's second-biggest insurer, took a 49 percent stake in Equitable in 1992 and increased that stake to 60 percent in 1994, gaining control of Alliance.

———

Axa now controls 53 percent of Alliance's operating limited partnership, Alliance Capital Management LP, and the public owns 30 percent of that partnership through a holding company called Alliance Capital Management Holding LP, which is traded on the New York Stock Exchange. About 16 percent of equity in the operating partnership is helped by employees of Sanford C. Bernstein & Co., the research and asset management firm that Alliance acquired in 2000 for $3.5 billion. Henri de Castries, Axa's CEO, and six of his deputies sit on Alliance's 17-member board of directors.

David Williams, a former oil industry analyst who served as Alliance's CEO from 1977–99, infused the firm with a culture that prized independence and encouraged money managers to develop their own investing styles—within a larger framework. In the large-cap group, for example, the portfolio managers assemble a weekly list of their favorite stocks, called the Favored 25. The money managers in the group must select at least 65 percent of their portfolios from the Favored 25, yet the mix is up to them. The remainder of the portfolio can be culled from the Alliance 100, a larger list of favored stocks.

"Williams decided not to force portfolio managers into a harness, and he gave them more latitude than they would find in other organizations," says Richard Ennis, a principal of Ennis, Knupp & Associates, a Chicago-based consulting firm that helps institutional investors select money managers. "Most fund management firms have taken a different route, setting up their investment process in such a way that clients all get much the same portfolio," he says. Williams, who's 69 and now runs a private equity firm with his wife, Reba, declined to comment.

Some of Alliance's institutional clients are bailing out. In April, Connecticut state treasurer Denise Nappier fired Alliance, which was managing $135 million of the state's pension fund. "She had concerns about staff turnover and poor performance over a number of quarters," says Bernard Kavaler, a spokesman in the treasurer's office. In June, the Ohio Police and Fire Pension Fund, which manages $8.7 billion for 55,000 police officers and firefighters, terminated Alliance's stewardship of $90 million in its domestic equities portfolio even though its Cleveland-based money managers had beaten their benchmark, the Russell 1000 Index, by 6.5 percentage points since they were hired in June 2000.

"After the Enron/Florida situation, our board lost confidence in Alliance," says William Estabrook, the fund's executive director. In the second quarter, institutional investors withdrew $2.5 billion in capital from Alliance, according to the company's second-quarter earnings statement.

The retail side of the shop is also hurting. Sales of Alliance's 330 mutual funds, which are offered by brokers to investors, have plummeted this year, with investors withdrawing $462 million in assets from the fund family through May 31, according to Financial Research Corp., a Boston-based consulting firm. Out of 568 fund groups, only 17 have done worse. In 2000, Alliance was the seventeenth-best-selling fund group, attracting $2.3 billion in new assets. In June, the withdrawal rate accelerated, with investors redeeming $576 million from Alliance's mutual funds.

"You don't want to toss your Alliance funds, but you do want to take a good look at them and make sure they are still employing the strategy you hired them for," says Daniel Culloton, a senior analyst at Morningstar Inc., a Chicago-based mutual fund research and ratings firm.

In the second quarter, Alliance's pretax earnings fell 16.5 percent, to $170 million, from the same period in 2001. Alliance's retail business contributed 52 percent of the firm's $2.9 billion in revenue last year, with institutional clients accounting for 24 percent. Both pieces of the business have grown at a rapid pace. Retail revenues have increased at a compound annual growth rate of 26 percent since 1997, and institutional revenues have expanded at a 22 percent rate. Revenue at Alliance's private client group, which manages money for wealthy individuals, grew to $407 million in 2001 from $105 million in 1999 with the acquisition of Sanford C. Bernstein.

Some of Alliance's customers remain unharmed by its woes. Oscar Peters, general manager of the $6.8 billion Los Angeles City Employees' Retirement System, says its Alliance-managed domestic equities account notched a 6.3 percent return from March 31, 1998, to March 31, 2002, besting its benchmark, the Russell 1000 Growth Index, by 5.4 percentage points. Jack Koltes, a portfolio manager in Harrison's group, did not follow his boss's lead on Enron. He made retailer Kohl's Corp. and Pfizer the two biggest holdings in the L.A. account as of December 1, 2001, according to Peters.

Mark Constant, an analyst at Lehman Brothers Holdings Inc., says Alliance's positions in Enron and WorldCom do not threaten the firm's long-term health because the losses are small compared with the firm's $412 billion in assets under management. Eight analysts who follow Alliance, including Constant, rate it a buy, while two rate it a hold and none rate it a sell, according to Bloomberg data. By comparison, T. Rowe Price Group Inc., a Baltimore-based mutual fund giant with $149 billion in assets under management, has six buy calls, eight hold calls and one sell call.

Constant says Alliance was bound to take a hit this year. With $75 billion invested in large-cap growth stocks, Alliance has wide exposure to the Standard & Poor's 500 Index, which plunged 21 percent for the year as of August 9. Constant says that Alliance's fund managers, just like other investors, have been victimized by fraudulent accounting practices at Enron, WorldCom, and other companies. "They are portrayed as big dummies, but they were buying cash flow streams that looked attractive, and, in retrospect, they weren't what they thought, because they had been lied to," says Constant.

Coleman Stipanovich, interim executive director at Florida's investment board, says that Alliance's bad run cannot be blamed solely on corporate wrongdoing. He says its method of picking and investing in stocks has gone awry. "There's something broken there," says Stipanovich.

Alliance's decisions on WorldCom, Qwest, Dynegy, and Tyco also indicate that the firm's investment approach may be out of sync with the goals of investors in a bear market, says Bobroff, the fund consultant. "As more investors close in on retirement, money managers need to take a less aggressive view, and you would think Alliance would be inclined to be more conservative and less aggressive, but that has not been their stand," he says.

No money manager at Alliance has attracted more attention from investors than Al Harrison. "He has a legendary aura to him," says Robert Kloss, comanager of the ING Financial Services Fund in Scottsdale, Arizona, which owns 200,000 Alliance shares. A native of Manchester, England, who used to spend afternoons with his father at the horse races, Harrison joined Alliance as a portfolio manager in 1978 in its Minneapolis office.

Harrison's V-factor methodology aims to find—and exploit—temporary dips in share prices. Unlike value-oriented investors, who seek out stocks with low price-earnings ratios, Harrison may buy a stock with a high P/E if he believes in the company's earnings outlook, according to Alliance sales literature. In the third quarter of 1997, for example, he bought Dell Computer Corp. stock as it skidded 30 percent in price, even though it had an average P/E multiple of 39 in that period compared with 24 at rival PC maker Gateway Inc.

Harrison's Alliance Premier Growth Fund, with holdings in companies such as Dell, Tyco, and Home Depot Inc., delivered a return of 234 percent from 1993 to 1999—compared with 136 percent at the rival Janus Fund and 78 percent at the T. Rowe Price Growth Stock Fund, according to Bloomberg data. "He's the Warren Buffett of growth stocks," says Lehman's Constant.

Alliance could make contrarian investments because of the quality of its research, Harrison told clients. Williams, former president of the New York Society of Security Analysts, made research gospel at the firm, says fund consultant Greenwald. Alliance employs more than 320 analysts and has the clout to summon CEOs to its offices to explain their businesses, according to a 1999 marketing presentation. The Sanford C. Bernstein acquisition in 2000 strengthened Alliance's research prowess with a franchise that provides analysis untainted by an investment banking agenda, Greenwald says.

"It is critically important to understand that Alliance Capital is a research-driven organization," CEO Calvert, a former analyst himself, testified to a subcommittee of the U.S. Senate's Commerce Committee in a May 16 hearing looking into the impact of the Enron collapse on state pension funds.

In the summer of 2000, Harrison's V approach started misfiring. In the Florida account, he bet that slumping tech stocks like Cisco Systems Inc., Nortel Networks Corp., and Yahoo! Inc. would rebound, according to the board's records. They didn't, and for the 2000–2001 fiscal year ended on June 30, Harrison's account recorded a minus 31 percent return, the poorest performance among the board's 17 active domestic equities managers. The Florida board placed Alliance on a watch list; Harrison's team now had to discuss its stock picks with the board monthly, not quarterly.

Harrison remained committed to the V, according to the September 2001 article sent to clients. On November 6, 2000, he began applying the method to his new favorite stock: Enron. Over the next 11 months, Harrison added Enron shares to Florida's account as they slid from $78 toward the $30–$40 range. He also purchased Enron shares for the Premier Growth fund, two corporate pension funds, and two other public pension funds, according to Alliance trading records. He told the board he met often with former Chairman Kenneth Lay and former CEO Jeffrey Skilling to discuss the business, according to memorandums of his meetings with the Florida pension fund's staff. Then, on October 24, finding CFO Fastow's termination a "positive," Harrison bought 302,500 more shares at $16.30 each for the board's portfolio.

By October 30, the board staff was so worried that in a conference call with Harrison, they asked him point-blank whether he understood how Enron made money. "Al responded that the earnings do look a little 'black boxy,'" according to notes that Benjamin Latham, director of research in the domestic equities unit, took during the meeting. In another meeting, on December 11 in the board's offices in Tallahassee, Harrison said he'd personally received assurance from Lay that the company's core business—its energy trading unit—was sound. "There was nothing about Ken Lay that gave the impression he was doing anything nefarious," Harrison told the board, according to the meeting record. "Al believes 98 percent of managers are truthful, and there was nothing wrong with [Enron's] earnings forecasts for this year or next," Latham's notes say.

The Florida board argues that under its investment contract with Alliance, Harrison and his team were obligated to base stock picks on their own analysis, not on faith in the veracity of a company's statements or its CEO's soothing assurances. In a breach-of-contract lawsuit against Alliance filed on May 2 in state court in Tallahassee, the board's lawyers state, "The [board] retained Alliance not to follow the herd mentality on

Wall Street but instead to capitalize on Alliance's claimed research excellence that, according to Alliance, had long been the cornerstone of its efforts to provide superior performance for its clients."

In a motion to dismiss the Florida board's suit filed June 10, Alliance's lawyers at Clifford Chance Rogers & Wells LLP argue that their client is being blamed for wrongdoing it did not commit. "The vast majority of the complaint's allegations do not relate to conduct attributable to Alliance Capital but rather to actions taken by Enron and its management," the motion says.

Alliance insists it did its homework. "The decision to invest in Enron was based on extensive research by the Alliance Capital research and portfolio management team into Enron's business, its growth prospects, and the company's fundamentals in relation to the price of its shares," Calvert told the Senate on May 16.

The board has yet to see that research. Herndon, the board's former executive director, says that in a face-to-face meeting with Calvert in April, he asked the CEO to produce the Enron analysis. "I told him that if they have a good story to tell us, then tell us," Herndon says. "We're going to get it anyhow when we issue subpoenas." Calvert refused, says Herndon.

The only research that Alliance has provided for its former client is a series of reports written by Sanford C. Bernstein analysts Duane Grubert and David Wideman last autumn. On November 1, the day after the SEC opened a formal investigation of Enron, Sanford C. Bernstein sent a report to clients entitled "Enron: Reports of Death Greatly Exaggerated, the Numbers Work, Outperform." It characterized the revelations of Enron's financial engineering as "negative spin" that would be overcome. By that time, Enron's stock had fallen to $11.99 from $42.93 on August 14, a 72 percent drop. Stipanovich scoffs at the report: "That dog was shot, buried, and a funeral had been held, and they were still telling us to own it."

On November 9, Dynegy proposed to buy Enron for about $23 billion in stock and assumed debt. Shortly after, Harrison met with Lay and Dynegy CEO Chuck Watson in New York to review the deal, according to Florida board notes on the meeting between its staff and Harrison on December 11. Harrison bought another 1.2 million Enron shares over the next two weeks. Alliance's stake in Dynegy stood at 10.7 percent of the company. The deal fell apart on November 28, Harrison's V was no match for Enron's financial earthquakes. On November 30, he sold the board's 7.5 million shares at 28¢ apiece to Lehman Brothers without informing Hendron or his staff, says Hendron.

The move outraged board officials. Donald Nast, the Investment Advisory Council member, says he was appalled that Harrison had not let the board decide how to dispose of its own shares. At 4:23 on the afternoon of November 28, Harrison sent an e-mail to Ken Menke, deputy chief of the domestic equities unit, that said: "I clearly have been wrong on the stock for not selling on the way down. We are obviously continuing to assess the situation." There was no mention of a pending stock sale. "To not indicate that [Harrison] was seriously considering selling this stock is almost to me outright dishonesty," Nast said in a council meeting on March 8, according to a transcript.

In the December 11 meeting with the board, Harrison said he had erred. "He apologized for not discussing it [the sale of Enron stock] with the SBA [state board of administration]," say the meeting notes. Two days later, the board terminated its 17-year relationship with Harrison and Alliance. In its lawsuit, the Florida board alleges that Alliance's actions were so negligent that it should recompense the board's losses and pay punitive damages.

The fallout was swift. In December, the Economic Crimes Division of the Florida attorney general's office began investigating whether Alliance and Enron had violated the state's civil racketeering and securities fraud laws. As part of the probe, investigators are examining whether Harrison had agreed to prop up Enron's stock at the behest of Frank Savage, a fellow Alliance director who also sat on Enron's board, according to Mary Leontakianakos, chief of the economic crimes unit. Savage was a member of Enron's finance committee and voted to approve off-balance-sheet investment partnerships run by ex-CFO Fastow that contributed to Enron's collapse, according to minutes of the committee meetings.

Savage, head of Savage Holdings Inc., a private equity firm, is also on the board of Bloomberg LP, the parent of Bloomberg News. W. Neil Eggleston, Savage's attorney, says his client did not communicate with Harrison about Enron or take part in any scheme to prop up Enron's stock. On December 11, Harrison told the Florida board staff that he did not know Savage was on Enron's board until two weeks prior, according to the board's notes of the meeting. In his Senate testimony in May, Harrison said he did not discuss Enron with Savage.

In January 2002, a group of labor union officials—including representatives of the AFL–CIO, the Service Employees International Union, and the New York City Employees' Retirement System—summoned Calvert to the New York group's Brooklyn headquarters to ask him what had gone wrong in Florida. According to union officials who attended, Calvert said he didn't want to be too apologetic given Alliance's overall performance in Florida; Harrison had produced a 1,500 percent total return for the fund's account. "These things happen," Calvert said, according to a union official at the meeting.

Sean O'Ryan, a senior official at the United Association of Journeymen and Apprentices of the Plumbing, Pipefitting, Sprinkler Fitting Industry of the United States and Canada, erupted on the speakerphone. "Do I hear you saying you are not apologetic?" O'Ryan shouted. "Worker savings have been lost here, and I am just appalled that anyone could not have the sense of outrage we have." Calvert's face turned red, and he threw his eyeglasses down on the table in front of him, say the union officials. The meeting concluded shortly afterward.

Then WorldCom blew up. The stock had become a favorite of Sanford C. Bernstein's value managers in the second half of 2001 as its price fell to $12.18 on September 17 from $22.34 on January 18. "We continue to focus on finding opportunities created by the telecom and technology bust," wrote Alliance chief investment officer Lewis Sanders in an article sent to clients in October 2001.

After the SEC opened on March 12 an investigation into WorldCom's accounting practices and company loans to executives, Alliance value managers in April and May bought 112 million shares, spending at least $139 million on the gamble, based on the stock's low of $1.24 in that period. This came after the firm had already purchased 102 million shares in the first quarter—at a cost of at least $623 million, based on the stock's low of $6.11 during that time, according to Bloomberg data.

On April 30, WorldCom ousted Chairman and CEO Bernard Ebbers following the disclosure he'd borrowed $408 million from the company at a 2.3 percent-per-year interest rate to guarantee personal margin loans.

On June 25, the Clinton, Mississippi–based telecommunications company disclosed that it had wrongly booked $3.8 billion in expenses for 2001 and the first quarter of 2002 as capital expenditures, a maneuver the SEC—in a complaint filed against the company the next day—called a fraudulent scheme to inflate earnings. On August 8, WorldCom announced that it had been overstating earnings an additional $3.3 billion beginning in 1999.

In a statement released on June 26, Alliance said that Sanford C. Bernstein's value-oriented money managers had made the WorldCom investments for institutional clients and that the stakes were less than 1 percent of a typical account. "Alliance Capital, on behalf of its clients, is a significant stockholder in WorldCom but believes the apparent fraud engaged in by WorldCom will not have a material adverse effect on Alliance Capital's results of operations or financial condition," the statement said.

On July 10, Alliance received another blow when Qwest disclosed that the U.S. Attorney's Office in Denver had opened a criminal investigation into its accounting practices. In the first quarter, Alliance added 117.4 million Qwest shares to its position; it holds an 8.1 percent stake in the company. The next-largest stockholder, Fidelity Investments, bought 17 million shares in the same period.

Michael Abrams, the fund manager at Cincinnati Financial, wonders whether Alliance's experiences with Enron, WorldCom, and Qwest will force Axa to assert more control over its subsidiary. Alliance has become a crucial factor in Axa's bottom line: In 2001, it contributed about 79 percent of Axa's earnings in asset management and 23 percent of its total earnings before goodwill. "Axa declines to comment on whether we are evaluating our relationship with Alliance Capital," says Chris Dufraux, a spokesman at Axa in Paris.

The Florida board's Enron fiasco raises a critical issue for pension funds: How much control should funds assert over their money managers? At the March 8 meeting of Florida's Investment Advisory Council, member Gil Hernandez asked Tom Herndon why the board had not sold Enron stock like other fund managers had, including the Alliance team that managed a New York State Common Retirement Fund's equities account and had sold its Enron shares in midsummer. "It would have been better off for the staff to say, 'Hey guys, instead of buying this stuff, this is the time to sell it to some other sucker,'" said Hernandez, according to a transcript.

Herndon replied that the fund was not prepared to substitute its judgment for that of its asset managers. "We don't have access to the research; we don't have access to the companies; we don't have the resources that these organizations have," he said. "So we are very cautious about second-guessing the managers."

In his final meeting with the Florida board's staff, on December 11, Harrison was asked what impact his Enron play would have on his career. He replied that he would persevere. "On his tombstone, he'd like it to read, 'He weathered the storms,'" the notes of the meeting say.

While the Enron hurricane has passed, leaving its wreckage behind, Alliance clients still face a series of squalls. Their names: WorldCom, Qwest, Tyco, and Dynegy.

Hedge funds could be our next financial bubble, some experts warn. The funds rake in hundreds of billions of dollars, but few people know about them or how they operate. *Fortune* magazine's Andy Serwer enters the secretive world that was once available only to the very rich, but is now expanding to include the accounts of pension funds and individual investors as well. New York attorney general Eliot Spitzer has made hedge funds more visible, but not in a positive way. Without admitting or denying wrongdoing, hedge fund Canary Capital Partners LLC in fall 2003 paid $40 million to settle civil charges from Spitzer that it arranged with several prominent mutual fund companies to improperly trade their fund shares.

Andy Serwer

Where the Money's Really Made

ACROSS THIS QUIET, snowy field, through the trees and over the fence, lurks a Wall Street monster. The locale is Westport, Connecticut, about a mile inland from Long Island Sound across I-95. The beast within those stark walls is Pequot Capital, a superpowerful $7 billion hedge fund that along with a dozen or so other mega-hedge funds— many sprinkled among towns nearby—is rocking mainstream Wall Street to its core. Here in Fairfield County, the richest county in the richest state in the richest country in the world, vast fortunes are being created, and rules of finance are being rewritten.

Don't for a minute think that this doesn't apply to you. The hedge fund boom has sweeping implications not just for Wall Street traders and a few thousand well-heeled investors, but increasingly for every American businessperson, investor, and retiree.

You know the $7 trillion–plus of stock market value that has evaporated over the past three miserable years? Well, guess what: The money didn't simply disappear. Some folks, often short-sellers at hedge funds, profited mightily from the decline. Nothing wrong with that. A hedge fund is supposed to make money in markets bull and bear. Some of the best did exactly that, first riding the bucking-bronco bull of the 1990s and then shorting the market on its steep, treacherous descent. By some guesstimates, hedge funds have outperformed the S&P 500 as well as the average equity mutual fund by substantial margins over the past five years. One hedge fund monitor says the group has beaten the S&P by an astounding 7 percentage points per year on average since 1998.

Such tantalizing performances have made even cynical investors salivate. Today, with stocks so weak and bond yields so low, hedge funds are Wall Street's last great game, it seems. Even so, the major players are people you've never heard of, who work for firms that few people know, who run billions of dollars in the utmost secrecy. At a time most of Wall Street is under fire (or getting fired), the top hedge fund managers have become its stealth power brokers, celebrities of a clandestine, moneyed world.

We'll meet some of these people in a minute, but first a few disclaimers. Contrary to what you might expect, this story will *not* tell you that the $675 billion hedge fund bubble is about to burst, though it might. You will also not hear from us that hedge funds—even the most aggressively short-selling kind—have become dangerous to the functioning of markets or that they unfairly "gang up" on worthwhile companies (a complaint that appears often enough in the press). You won't even get a blanket warning to stay away from these barely regulated entities, lest you lose your homestead. The industry is too sprawling, too complex, too multifaceted to support any such claims . . . at least on the basis of the evidence out there so far.

What you will get, rather, is a peek inside this strange, cloistered realm—a place where everybody who's anybody hails from the same colleges, earns their spurs at the same Wall Street firms (Goldman Sachs and Morgan Stanley, naturally), congregates in the same insular circles, and hobnobs at the same charity dinners. Members of the true hedge fund elite are so publicity-shy that few agreed to an on-the-record interview, and fewer still to pose for a photo. When we called the only photographer with stock photos of Ken Griffin, the 34-year-old manager of the $8 billion Citadel Investment Group in Chicago, Griffin quickly made arrangements with the photographer to buy the film. Likewise, we were unable to get a single recent picture of Steven Cohen of SAC Capital, one of the biggest and most controversial power brokers on Wall Street. Still, what we have discovered about these players and other major hedgers is likely to surprise you. And you can be sure of one thing: They don't want you to know about any of it.

More than any other sector of the economy, Wall Street is a place where trends are carried to excess: The Nifty Fifty bull market of the 1960s. The LBO–junk bond boom of the 1980s. The great period of irrational exuberance for technology stocks that ended so calamitously. Says Warren Buffett: "Hedge funds have become the latest Holy Grail."

The hundreds of billions of dollars that have poured into hedge funds in recent years have come in large part from the rich. For decades—going back to fabled investor Ben Graham's partnership in the 1920s and even earlier—hedge funds have marketed themselves to so-called accredited investors. Today that generally means people with $1 million or more in investable assets or an annual income north of $200,000, according to Tremont Advisers. The presumption is that such individuals are financially sophisticated enough to take care of themselves.

These days, though, funds that make investments in hedge funds are peddling themselves to less accredited investors as well—dentists, school principals, and the like—for minimum stakes as low as $25,000. What's more, a huge group of shareholders may be in hedge funds and not even know it: America's retirees. The state of California's $133 billion CalPERS fund, for instance, has plunked $550 million into hedge funds, including $50 million into Andor Capital of Stamford, Connecticut. The $21 billion Pennsylvania State Employees' Retirement System, or PennSERS, made an even bigger bet, recently investing some $2.5 billion, or roughly 12 percent of its assets, into hedge funds. (A spokesman says the investment is in funds of funds.)

The motivation is no mystery: Pension funds are looking to goose their feeble returns with a little of hedge funds' magic sauce. The basic ingredient of this sauce is hardly exotic. It's hedging—making one investment to protect against downside risk in another investment. That's what the first hedge funds did and what many still do today. (Many also use leverage or borrow to enhance their returns.) An example would be to buy Pepsi and short Coke, or buy Merck and short an index of drug stocks. Or go long on the dollar and short the pound. "It really is the best way to invest," says legendary hedge fund manager Julian Robertson. "You buy the ten best stocks in the world and short the ten worst, and you should do pretty well, unless something goes wrong."

Many funds today, however, do no hedging at all. In fact, the term "hedge fund" is a catchall that applies to thousands and thousands of investment funds of all strategies. As my colleague Carol Loomis wrote in a seminal *Fortune* article in 1970, a hedge fund can be *any* limited partnership that's constructed "in such a way as to give the general partners—the mangers of the fund—a share of the profits earned on the limited partners' money."

And what a share it is. In exchange for the lure of outsized returns, many funds impose an arrangement known as "one and twenty." It means that the manager's take is 1 percent of the fund's assets and 20 percent of profits. So the aforementioned Chicago star Ken Griffin could make $215 million in 2001, according to *Institutional Investor* magazine—though, to be fair, his fund was up an eye-popping 20 percent in a down market.

Buffett, who many years ago managed a hedge fund himself before running Berkshire Hathaway, is quick to point out that the term "hedge fund" is "nothing but a name." Nor is there anything inherently glamorous or mystical about it. "A fund is only as good as the person who runs it," he says. Buffett is right, of course. But the mounds of cash help explain why hedge funds are suddenly upsetting Wall Street's apple cart. The old-fashioned elite down at Wall and Broad accuse hedgies of sucking up capital, muscling trading desks with outsized commissions, and luring away the best traders, analysts, and money managers with promises of $100 million paydays. The most successful hedge fund managers—a few are now billionaires—are far wealthier than the CEOs of Wall Street's biggest firms.

Everything seductive and controversial about hedge funds can be summed up in three little letters: SAC. That's the $4 billion fund run by Steven Cohen, which has generated spectacular returns over the past decade. About half that kitty is said to be Cohen's personal wealth. Cherubic, balding, and about 5-foot-7, Cohen—or Stevie to his compadres—somewhat resembles the character George Costanza of *Seinfeld*. He is also said to be self-deprecating and a great dad. But Cohen, who started his career at the brokerage Gruntal & Co. (see "The Shabby Side of the Street" in the fortune.com archive), is also one of the world's most aggressive traders. He is security-conscious and secretive, and declined numerous requests for an interview. Getting anyone to speak about him on the record is next to impossible as well. One recent afternoon I called a former SACer named Scott Lederman, who sounded positively skittish. "I'd love to help you, but I can't," he said. "I've signed a confidentiality agreement. I just can't answer your questions."

Though Cohen, like many other big-league players, operates out of southwestern Connecticut, he is considered something of an outlier because of his controversial trading strategies. He is a practitioner of what he has termed "information arbitrage." As best we can tell, that means trading in part on the thousands of bits and pieces of information that flash across Wall Street trading desks every day. Trouble is, many in the business say that in the pursuit of that information, SAC employs tactics to gain a competitive advantage. How so? Cohen's firm is said to generate as much as 1 percent of the average trading volume of the NYSE every day and therefore produces mammoth commissions for investment banks. For that, sources say, SAC traders expect the best information possible from the banks, including what is known on Wall Street as the first call. If a salesperson, for instance, has a large block of stock for sale, he may be strongly urged to offer it to SAC before any of its rivals. (Cohen declined to comment.) "Does Steve expect the first call?" asks a close associate. "Absolutely. And he would scream and yell if he didn't get it. I don't know of anything illegal going on. There aren't a lot of rules."

Actually that's not quite right. There are rules. In fact, the Securities and Exchange Commission is investigating whether one of SAC's employees, Michael Zimmerman, received insider information about a possible downgrade of Amazon.com from his wife, Lehman Brothers analyst Holly Becker.

Cohen's no-holds-barred style ruffles not only big institutional traders (who get beaten on trades) but also others in his industry. Says a manager of a large, successful hedge fund: "If I see on a résumé that the person worked at SAC, I won't even interview them." Cohen's defenders say that kind of talk is envy. Last year SAC was up some 11 percent, while the market declined 22 percent. Unlike most other fund managers, Cohen passes on expenses to his limited partners—between 2 percent and 3 percent of assets—and takes a whopping 25 percent to 50 percent of the profits for himself. (SAC is closed to new investors.)

There are perhaps a dozen and a half funds in this universe of nearly six thousand investment partnerships that have more than fifty employees, says Phil Duff, former number two man at Julian Robertson's Tiger fund and onetime CFO of Morgan Stanley. "The ones with a billion-plus—they are in the big leagues," says Duff, who has since cofounded a hedge fund operation called FrontPoint.

Ah, yes, the big leagues. That's the very top of the hedge fund pecking order, where a score or so of managers have amassed fortunes of hundreds of millions and in some cases billions. Mostly unknown to even the nation's top CEOs, publicity-allergic men like Moore Capital's Louis Bacon, Tudor Group's Paul Tudor Jones, and Stanley Druckenmiller of Duquesne Capital, as well as up-and-comers including Griffin and Steve Mandel lord over $5 billion and $10 billion pools of capital. In the business they are known as the legends.

Many of the legends worked at or have connections to Robertson's Tiger fund, which was a star performer before it closed in March 2000, a value fund victim of the tech-stock boom. The grandee's charity of choice is the Robin Hood Foundation, founded by Paul Jones, which, yes, takes from the rich and gives to New York City's poor.

Even hedge funds with squeaky-clean reputations are notoriously secretive. No interviews. No pictures. No disclosure to anyone other than limited partners. Some of that is to protect trading positions. Some of it borders on the ludicrous. "My client called up this hedge fund he had a big chunk of money in to ask generally about its positions," says a fund-of-funds manager, "and they basically told him, 'None of your business.' And it was his money!" While that particular anecdote may sound indefensible, the recent kidnapping in Greenwich, Connecticut, of hedge fund manager Eddie Lampert has helped reinforce the group's craving for privacy. In case you haven't heard, Eddie Lampert, 40, one of the most successful hedge managers and according to some estimates worth some $800 million, recently spent nearly 30 hours handcuffed and bound with duct tape in a cheap hotel bathtub before he was freed. (The kidnappers were caught.)

For most hedge fund managers, building a business is a monumental and thankless task, involving dozens of dog-and-pony shows and endless hand-holding. For a tiny minority, those who can put together a stunning track record, it's a breeze. Such was the case with wunderkind Ken Griffin of Chicago's Citadel. Griffin grew up in Boca Raton and began trading out of his dorm room at Harvard in 1987. He was discovered by Frank Meyer of Glenwood Capital, a Chicago fund-of-funds operator, who bankrolled Griffin's first fund. Griffin started out trading convertible bonds but has since expanded into arbitrage and other investments.

Citadel is also a stealth operator, though it is one of the few hedge funds to have a web site. But not long ago the fund's name popped up in a very public spat, which surely made Griffin uncomfortable. It was March 2002, just days before Hewlett-Packard shareholders were set to vote on whether to approve the company's acquisition of Compaq. As you may remember, HP board member Walter Hewlett was bitterly against the deal, while CEO Carly Fiorina lobbied furiously for it. Two days before the vote, someone passed on a voice mail from Fiorina to HP's CFO, Bob Wayman, to the *San Jose Mercury News*, which included this tidbit about lining up support for the deal. Fiorina said, "We're getting information from some of our arbs—you may remember the guys at Citadel who have been very helpful." The implication being that arbitrageurs at Citadel were telling Fiorina how shareholders were going to cast their votes. Citadel later acknowledged its arbitrage fund held shares of HP stock but denied that anything improper was going on. Still, apparently it's not a bad thing to have friends in Chi-town.

Griffin has said that he has a strategy that works in all markets. So far it seems to. His funds were up some 11 percent last year. "Some people are good at one thing," says Meyer. "Ken is very good at all parts of this business." Says another associate: "This is a guy who prides himself on researching subjects thoroughly. Whether it's building his business or looking to buy million-dollar paintings, Ken really studies." Besides Chicago, Citadel now has offices in San Francisco, Tokyo, London, and, you guessed it, Greenwich, Connecticut. In fact Griffin is deeply enmeshed in the Connecticut "matrix," befriending fellow hedgie Paul Jones and ponying up big bucks to the Robin Hood Foundation. After dating several bombshells, Griffin is now engaged to Ann Dias, who recently shared office space with Julian Robertson.

One of the most vexing issues for Griffin, and indeed for all hedge fund moguls, is sustainability. The simple fact is that giant hedge funds have a way of blowing up. It can be the kind of atomic blast that Long-Term Capital created in 1998—which forced the Fed to intervene to prevent a market meltdown—or the more prosaic closing of Robertson's famed Tiger fund in 2000. Running one of those Goliaths is like being the head of the old Soviet Union. You're on top for a while, but often it ends badly.

Could it be that Louis Bacon is worrying about just that? At the top of his game and in the prime of his life at 46 years of age, the strikingly handsome Bacon runs Moore Capital, which with some $8 billion under management is one of the biggest hedge funds in the world. Bacon is fabulously wealthy and owns remarkable real estate properties in the U.S. and England. But he has a problem. Even though Moore Capital has racked up spectacular gains over much of its 14-year history, Bacon is reporting to his limited partners that his fund—and their capital—was down 4 percent last year. "Louis doesn't want to become the next Julian Robertson," says a source. That would be deeply painful for Bacon, who is incidentally Robertson's stepnephew.

Why is it that big funds implode? Simple burnout is one factor; running billions of dollars every day is grueling. Lack of flexibility is another: sticking to a strategy that worked in a bull market but doesn't in a bear market. The fickleness of hedge fund investors plays a big role too. Unlike Joe and Jane Mainstreet in a mutual fund, investors in hedge funds, who after all pay huge fees, are quick to yank their money out of a losing fund. Those redemptions may require the fund to sell some of its positions, and if that selling is done at a loss, it further depresses results, which creates a snowball.

Another issue is compensation for the manager when a hedge fund drops. If a fund is down 10 percent in year one—say from $1 billion to $900 million—the hedgie doesn't get his 20 percent cut. The following year the fund must climb more than 11 percent just to get back to even, with the hedge fund manager getting no cut of that gain. If a fund drops two years in a row, many managers simply opt to close up shop and start afresh from zero with a new fund rather than try to pull up the old fund from deep in the hole.

Size itself works against these giant hedge funds. Everybody understands the difficulty that the manager of a big mutual fund like Fidelity Magellan has finding enough big ideas to move a multibillion-dollar fund. But for many giant hedge funds, that problem is exacerbated by the fact that they short stocks, which mean they have to find shares to borrow. Shorting these days "is really, really hard," says a prominent hedge fund manager. "There are so many more hedge funds out there doing it, the supply of available shares is tight."

Looming above all those problems is the issue of managing. Most hedge fund managers are infatuated with investing and much less interested in running a business. As such, the hedgie is like any other entrepreneur. "A hedge fund business may grow great guns at first, but if it is successful the manager needs to delegate and maybe do some outsourcing," says David "Tiger" Williams, who runs a trading operation that serves some of the funds. Plus, a growing hedge fund will need systems, and a CFO, and back-office people, and compliance, and risk management. Some hedgies see the need for this, some don't. "When I am looking at a hedge fund to invest in, yes, I look at the track record, but I also look at the infrastructure," says Glenwood's Meyer. "The track record is looking backward. The systems in place help look forward."

No one is more aware of those facts than Paul Tudor Jones, 48, who heads up the $7 billion Tudor Group in Greenwich. Jones, who declined to speak to *Fortune*, has been in the game of hedge fund management for twenty years and is said to be fixated on maintaining a lasting business model. Instead of controlling all trading personally, the Memphis-born former cotton trader has farmed out some money management to top-end semiautonomous partners within Tudor. He has invested heavily in his office, and even though he is a true old-school macro investor (buying and selling all sorts of financial instruments all over the globe), he likes to view his fund as a sustainable company. Who knows? He might make it work.

Will the hedge fund business keep growing willy-nilly? Should you pour your money into hedge funds? Will hedge funds save the world? The answer to all those questions is almost certainly no. In fact, you probably could have asked the same questions thirty years ago and gotten the same answer. Harking back to that 1970 *Fortune* story, you get the feeling that for all the recent mania of late, there really is a *plus ça change* to this world of hedge funds. In that piece Carol Loomis wrote of some hedge funds having a very tough go of it, including Fairfield Partners. One of the men running Fairfield was Barton Biggs, who would leave the hedge fund business in 1973 and accept what turned out to be a very lucrative deal to join Morgan Stanley.

Biggs built Morgan Stanley's asset management business over the next several decades and also became one of the Street's leading investment strategists. Along the way he became well known for his pointed weekly research commentary on the markets. (Also along the way his niece, Fiona, married hedgie Stan Druckenmiller.) Biggs has been known as a sharp-eyed observer, quick to steer clients clear of manias. A year ago Biggs warned of a "hedge fund bubble" that was sweeping across Wall Street. That apparently was then, and this is now. In January, Biggs, 70, announced that he was leaving Morgan Stanley after nearly three decades at the firm. Was Biggs, now a very wealthy man, departing full-time to Lyford Cay? Actually no, he is leaving to start a hedge fund. It's called Traxis, if you ever get the call.

The Washington Consensus, a U.S. belief in free trade, privatization, and tax reform, is a fundamental policy of the Bush administration. William Finnegan, writing in *Harper's Magazine*, argues that its results have been mixed when applied to other nations. He also critiques the IMF and World Bank and asks whether our own free trade measures up to what we demand of other countries.

William Finnegan

The Economics of Empire

IN EARLY MARCH, President Bush, on the verge of declaring war on Iraq, was asked at a press conference why he thought "so many people around the world take a different view of the threat that Saddam Hussein poses than you and your allies." Mr. Bush replied, "I've seen all kinds of protests since I've been the president. I remember the protests against trade. There was a lot of people who didn't feel like free trade was good for the world. I completely disagree. I think free trade is good for both wealthy and impoverished nations. That didn't change my opinion about trade."

Mr. Bush's "opinion about trade" tends to pop up in unlikely places. Shortly after September 11, 2001, he declared, "The terrorists attacked the World Trade Center, and we will defeat them by expanding and encouraging world trade." This was an odd conflation, and *The New York Times*, reporting his words, felt obliged to flag the president's confusion with a delicate addendum—"seeming to imply that trade was among the concerns of terrorists who brought down the towers." The United

States trade representative, Robert B. Zoellick, was less delicate when he suggested in a speech around the same time that opponents of corporate-led globalization might have "intellectual connections with" the terrorists. The September 11 attacks were perpetrated, of course, by a genocidal death cult, not by unusually determined proponents of economic democracy.

But what the Bush administration is signaling in these muddled formulations (and in many less muddled statements—and, for that matter, in many major policy initiatives) is its transcendent commitment to a set of fixed ideas about international trade, finance, politics, and economic development. These ideas form a dogma—George Soros calls it "market fundamentalism"—that, as dogmas do, purports to explain everything, to fold every event into itself.

Sometimes known as the Washington Consensus,* other times simply as "free trade," this gospel has been the main American ideological export since anti-Communism (to which it is related) lost strategic relevance. It is promulgated directly through U.S. foreign policy and indirectly through multilateral institutions such as the World Bank, the International Monetary Fund, and the World Trade Organization. Its core tenets are deregulation, privatization, "openness" (to foreign investment, to imports), unrestricted movement of capital, and lower taxes. Presented with special force to developing countries as a formula for economic management, it is also, in its fullness, a theory of how the world should be run, under American supervision. Attacking America is, therefore, attacking the theory, and attacking the theory is attacking America.

The possibility that the Marines and high-altitude bombers might need to be involved in spreading the good news about free trade does not, in context, seem far-fetched. Consider "The National Security Strategy of the United States," issued by the White House in September

---

*The term was coined in 1989 by John Williamson, of the Institute for International Economics, to describe the conventional wisdom at the U.S. Treasury Department, the World Bank, and the International Monetary Fund on policy reforms that would aid development in Latin America. Williamson later expressed dismay at the "populist definition," as he called it, of the term that had taken hold in public debate, where the Washington Consensus became synonymous with market fundamentalism, globally applied.

2002. Presidents are required to submit a security strategy periodically to Congress, but the Bush edition received an unusual amount of attention because of its unprecedented assertion of an American right to strike U.S. enemies preemptively, as well as its vow to maintain American military supremacy over all rivals indefinitely. Just as notable, however, in another way, was the repeated, incongruous insertion of fundamentalist free-trade precepts. The Strategy claims to have discovered "a single sustainable model for national success"—the Washington Consensus. There is, in its authors' view, simply no other way. History has validated this messianic vision, and the American role in leading the world to its realization on this earth. "We will actively work to bring the hope of democracy, development, free markets, and free trade to every corner of the world," the Strategy avows. It even provides a list of policy particulars, such as "lower marginal tax rates" and "pro-growth legal and regulatory policies" (read: weaker environmental and labor laws), that it believes every country should adopt.

National security strategy outlines are written by committee, are full of boilerplate, and cannot be expected to withstand close literary inspection. Still, the Bush strategy's attempt to articulate a worldview is worth quoting in full: "The concept of 'free trade' arose as a moral principle even before it became a pillar of economics. If you can make something that others value, you should be able to sell it to them. If others make something that you value, you should be able to buy it. This is real freedom, the freedom for a person—or a nation—to make a living." This formulation makes vulgar Marxism look subtle and humane. The only "real freedom" is commercial freedom. Free speech, a free press, religious freedom, political freedom—all these are secondary at best. There is a lockstep logic here, an airbrushed history, that suggest a closed intellectual system—the capitalist equivalent, perhaps, of Maoism or Wahhabism.

But beyond the triumphalist theory—and capitalism obviously has much to be triumphal about—there is the practice. The Washington Consensus has been around long enough now that results are in from many countries, including from some of the most diligent followers of its policy prescriptions. These results are less than encouraging. Argentina, for instance, did everything it was told to do by Washington throughout the 1990s—privatization, deregulation, trade liberalization, tax reform—and found itself a much-touted example of the virtues of *neoliberalismo* until shortly before its collapse in 2001. Today, Argentina is suffering through the worst economic crisis in its history. Yet even major failures seem not to shake the faith of the true believers in the Bush administration, who include the president. Like other fundamentalisms, market fundamentalism seems impervious to argument or inconvenient facts. Inside the muscular church of laissez-faire, broadbrush ideas—all of them estimable in the abstract—get rolled together into a mesmerizing, internally coherent mantra.

But vulgarity and obtuseness should not be mistaken for sincerity. Not only is the case for President Bush's "opinion" that "free trade is good for both wealthy and impoverished nations" empirically feeble; there is plenty of evidence that rich countries, starting with the United States, have no intention of playing by the trade rules and strictures they foist on poorer, weaker countries as "a single sustainable model." We practice free trade selectively, which is to say not at all, and, when it suits our commercial purposes, we actively prevent poor countries from exploiting their few advantages on the world market. While President Bush extols a simple, sweeping, unexceptionable creed at every opportunity, however inappropriate, his administration, guided by figures such as Trade Representative Zoellick, pursues a far more complex and sophisticated agenda. Theirs is not an ideology of freedom or democracy. It is a system of control. It is an economics of empire.

I was in Bolivia not long ago, and I noticed how every conversation there seemed to turn, inexorably, toward the topics of development and exploitation. Angel Villagomez, a retired state road inspector, told me, "It's very sad. Here in Bolivia we are sitting on a chair of gold—oil, gas, minerals—and yet all the wealth goes to foreigners." Villagomez was sitting outside his house, a simple adobe structure, on a chair of plastic. A vigorous, engaging man, he lives in a dusty *barrio marginal* near the Andean city of Cochabamba.

He was right about Bolivia. Although rich in natural resources, it is the poorest country in South America. Landlocked and thinly populated, it offers a less operatic example, perhaps, of a country struggling with neoliberalism than its neighbor, Argentina, but, in its deep-running underdevelopment and obscurity, a more typical one.

In the early 1980s, Bolivia emerged from many years of military rule in an economically impossible position. It had been looted by the generals. Its foreign debt was overwhelming. In 1985, inflation reached a surreal annual rate of 24,000 percent. The country had no choice but to consent to radical treatment. Advised by Jeffrey Sachs, the young American economist who later became known for designing "shock therapy" plans for countries emerging from Communism, the reformers in Bolivia were led by the minister of planning (later president), Gonzalo Sánchez de Lozada. To halt the inflationary death swoop, they drastically devalued the currency, abolished the minimum wage, and cut state spending to the bone. These measures plunged the economy into severe recession. Wages fell and unemployment skyrocketed. Tin miners, teachers, nurses, and factory workers were especially hard hit. The shock treatment worked, though, in the sense that prices eventually stabilized and the Bolivian government's good relations with its foreign creditors—and, most importantly, with their de facto enforcement arm, the International Monetary Fund—was restored.

There were conditions, of course. The IMF and the World Bank (the Bank's development loans helped keep the country afloat) took effective control of large areas of public policy. Like many poor countries, Bolivia was subjected to what is blandly known as structural adjustment—a set of standardized, far-reaching austerity and "openness" measures that typically include the removal of restrictions on foreign investment, the abolition of public subsidies and labor rights, reduced state spending, deregulation, lower tariffs, tighter credit, the encouragement of export-oriented industries, lower marginal tax rates, currency devaluation, and the sale of major public enterprises. In Bolivia's case, the latter included the national railways, the national airlines, the telephone system, the country's vast tin mines, and a long list of municipal utilities. Many indebted countries have had to be force-fed structural adjustment, but Bolivia turned out to be a model student. The country's small, white, wealthy political class seemed to have come to a quiet understanding with the international bankers. The power of the workers and peasants, once organized and formidable, was clearly broken; all of the major parties were now business aligned. And so the parties began to trade the presidency around every election cycle, and their leaders found that they could collaborate profitably with the international corporations that came in to run the phone company or pump the oil and gas.

Angel Villagomez said, "The politicians here all campaign with their left hands up." He raised his left hand. "But once they get in office, they all turn out to have hearts that beat on the right!" He struck the right side of his chest sharply.

A newspaper editor in Cochabamba put it differently. "The World Bank *is* the government of Bolivia," he said.

Since both the World Bank and the IMF are based in Washington, D.C., and Bolivia's primary overseer in the developed world has long been the United States, it's not surprising that some Bolivians detected that old-time Yankee imperialism in this new globalization regime. It wasn't, to be sure, gunboat diplomacy (except when it came to the war on drugs, an entirely different sore subject in Bolivia), and it wasn't a purely North American operation. The cheap foreign products that flooded the country after 1985 came from all directions, as did the foreign investors.

But the hundreds of local factories that went bankrupt, unable to compete, were, for the most part, Bolivian. And, contemplating what the anthropologist Lesley Gill calls the "imposed disorder" of postshock Bolivia—the havoc and deep social pain caused by structural adjustment—contemplating, especially, the mysterious power of these faceless institutions, the World Bank and the IMF—both ostensibly public agencies dedicated to the reduction of Third World poverty—many Bolivians must have asked one another, echoing those suave gringo outlaws Butch Cassidy and the Sundance Kid (who died, it may be remembered, after robbing a mining company in Bolivia), "Who *are* those guys?"

These pillars of the postwar international financial order were conceived during the later part of World War II at a conference of American, British, and European economists and civil servants held in Bretton

Woods, New Hampshire, and dominated intellectually by John Maynard Keynes. The World Bank was originally intended to help finance the reconstruction of postwar Europe—a project that neither private capital nor shattered states could be expected to undertake. After the Marshall Plan made that purpose redundant, the Bank, looking for a raison d'être, began to concentrate on Asia, Africa, and Latin America, where it loaned money to poor governments, usually for specific projects. Today, the Bank has 9,700 employees, 184 member states, and lends nearly $20 billion a year. The founding purpose of the IMF was to make short-term loans to stabilize currencies and the balance of payments, promote international economic cooperation, and prevent another Depression. It, too, has changed with the times. Now it makes long-term loans as well, functions almost entirely in the developing world, and, by interpreting its mandate to maintain international financial stability as broadly as possible, seeks to actively manage the economies of many poor countries. Because almost all significant aid and loans to poor countries hinge on the IMF's assessment of a nation's financial soundness, the Fund has the leverage to dictate public policy in large areas of the globe. Power within the institutions was originally apportioned among governments according to their relative financial strength and contributions, which meant that the United States had the leading role from the start. Although the managing director of the IMF is traditionally a European, the U.S. is the only country with an effective veto over IMF actions. The president of the World Bank has always been an American. The Bank and the IMF work together closely. They are the two most powerful financial institutions in the world.

During the Cold War, loans were often nakedly political. Anti-Communist dictators—in Uruguay, Ethiopia, the Philippines—were rewarded. Dictatorships in general were viewed as more reliable than democracies, and useful Communists, such as Ceauşescu, in Romania, also became big clients. Even apartheid South Africa got loans from the World Bank. Robert McNamara, having presided over the Vietnam War, became president of the Bank in 1968. He aggressively expanded its operations, pushing poor countries to accept loans to build factories, highways, huge power projects, vast agro-industrial schemes. This development model had fundamental problems. By 1981, when McNamara retired, abandoned megaprojects littered the Third World, together with uprooted populations, ravaged forests and watersheds, countries no longer able to feed themselves, and an ocean of impossible debt.

Both the Bank and the IMF passed through an ideological looking glass in the 1980s. They had been established and run on Keynesian principles—on assumptions that markets need state guidance, whether to stabilize currencies and prevent panics (IMF) or to build infrastructure necessary for economic development (the Bank). But with the ascendance of Reaganite (and Thatcherite) free-market economics in the West—among their rich-country masters, that is—both institutions changed their operating philosophies.* They began pushing laissez-faire policies—what became known as the Washington Consensus.

Unfortunately, they have had even less success with the new philosophy. Financial panics and crises continue to roil the IMF's clients, from East Asia to Argentina. The idea that open markets and increased trade lead invariably to economic gowth may be sound in theory, but it has repeatedly failed the reality test. A recent study found that IMF programs have had, overall, a *negative* effect on economic growth in participating countries. And the World Bank's declared mission of reducing poverty has been a bust so far. More than a billion people are now living on less than one dollar a day—the figure in 1972 was 800 million—while nearly half the world's population is living on less than two dollars a day. When Catherine Caufield began the reporting for her book on the World Bank, *Masters of Illusion*, she asked the Bank to direct her toward some of its most successful projects. The Bank's press officers made repeated promises but produced no list. Finally, as Caufield was leaving for India, which happened to be the Bank's largest client, they came up with the name of one project, the South Bassein Offshore Gas Development Project. Caufield could find no one in India who had heard of it. Later, she discovered that the project was a gas field in the Arabian Sea

---

*The Fund is generally seen as more ideological than the Bank. Certainly that is the view of Joseph Stiglitz, Nobel Prize winner and former chief economist of the World Bank, whose *Globalization and Its Discontents* comprehensively trashes the Fund for its rigidity. "Decisions were made," Stiglitz writes, "on the basis of what seemed a curious blend of ideology and bad economics, dogma that sometimes seemed to be thinly veiling special interests."

and was known in India by a different name. The Bank had loaned $772 million to the project and, because no villagers had needed to be resettled from the open sea, had managed to avoid controversy—this was apparently the successful part. The project had taken twice as long as expected to complete, and, according to Bank records, more than a third of the loan had ultimately been written off "due to misprocurement."

Every generation of Bank officials has vowed to improve this record, to start funding projects that benefit not only big business and local elites but also the poor. And the Bank's efforts to promote access to health care and education—projects undertaken with nongovernmental organizations (NGOs) and other "civil society" groups—have increased. But many Bank contracts are worth millions, and multinational corporations remain their major beneficiaries. Testifying before Congress in 1995, Lawrence Summers, then of the Treasury Department (now president of Harvard), disclosed that American corporations received $1.35 in procurement contracts for each dollar the American government contributed to the World Bank and other multilateral development banks. This was an unusually candid admission by a leading Bank supporter that one of its main activities is, in fact, corporate welfare. Those donated American dollars come, after all, from ordinary American taxpayers—few of whom know anything about what the World Bank does.

The Bank does many things, of course, and employs many people who are undoubtedly devoted to the idea of reducing poverty. (So does the IMF.) It provides technical assistance to poor countries, some of it clearly useful, and even tolerates a degree of internal debate.* But both the Bank and the IMF are locked in unhealthy relationships with their client governments. Governments recognize, obviously, that their poverty is a precondition for the flow of aid, and, for the less scrupulous among them, this can turn the poor themselves into a valuable commodity, their pitifulness a resource not to be squandered through ame-

---

*William Easterly, a senior Bank economist, tested the limits of that tolerance in 2001 when he published *The Elusive Quest for Growth,* a book that chronicled the failed development panaceas the Bank has promoted over the years. In a prologue, Easterly applauded the fact that his employer "encourages gadflies like me to exercise intellectual freedom." In the preface to a paperback edition, published in 2002, however, Easterly was obliged to revise this assessment. In truth, the Bank, he had learned, "encourages gadflies like me to find another job."

lioration. On the donors' side, lending is essential to the continued health of aid bureaucracies and the advancement of careers—not the best environment in which to make wise decisions. Then there is the merry-go-round of fiscal crises and bailouts, aboard which the Bank and the IMF and rich-country bilateral lenders regularly make new loans to deeply indebted countries in order to avoid the embarrassment of non-performing loans. Because it helps condemn the world's poor to a fate of permanent debt, the Bank's self-description as a "pro-poor" development agency is at best self-deluding. (Bolivia, like many other countries, spends more on debt servicing than it spends on health care.) The Bank's core constituencies remain the corporations and the poor-country bureaucrats and politicians whom it enriches.

After 17 years of structural adjustment, Bolivia remains the poorest country in South America. The predicted foreign investment has arrived, largely in the form of multinational corporations taking control of privatized entities. But prosperity has not followed. Inflation is under control, and there has been modest economic growth, but its benefits have been concentrated among the wealthy, exacerbating a centuries-old problem of extreme inequality.

With the labor unions smashed, hundreds of thousands of workers have been thrown into what economists call "the informal sector," which in Bolivia means sweatshops producing knockoffs of brand-name clothing, street peddling in the towns and cities, and coca farming. Peasant farmers, too, have found it increasingly difficult to make ends meet, as prices for their cash crops have fallen under the pressure of foreign competition. The outlook is bleak, as even Jeffrey Sachs, who continues to advise the Bolivian government, concedes. "Belt-tightening is not a development strategy," he recently told *The New York Times,* criticizing IMF policy. Sachs is no fundamentalist. He is not, that is, a fantasist. Regarding Bolivia: "I always told the Bolivians, from the very beginning, that what you have here is a miserable, poor economy with hyperinflation; if you are brave, if you are gutsy, if you do everything right, you will end up with a miserable, poor economy with stable prices."

It is also possible to march backward, though. Some privatizations succeed in improving service. But those that go badly can be catastrophic. Bolivia's national railways were awarded, in a forty-year concession, to a consortium led by a Chilean multinational called Cruz Blanca. The terms of purchase allowed Cruz Blanca to discontinue service on lines it found unprofitable. Accordingly, it soon closed a number of freight and passenger lines, including the line connecting Cochabamba, Bolivia's third-largest city, to La Paz, the capital. (It was the only rail line connecting Cochabamba to anywhere.) Given Bolivia's rugged terrain, and its awful roads, this was a serious blow to the national infrastructure. The closure, moreover, seemed to be indefinite. The Cochabamba train station was turned, willy-nilly, into a vast marketplace, shanties were built over the track bed, and photos began to appear in local papers showing collapsed stretches of track in the mountains. Bolivia's railroads were built a century ago, when superexploited labor made such monumental construction possible. Such railroads will not be built again. Cruz Blanca may abandon as many lines as it chooses, and nonmaintenance for even a few Andean winters will render them irrecoverable. The latest Sánchez de Lozada government, elected in mid-2002, seemed to realize that a historic fiasco was in progress. Within weeks of taking power, the government announced that it planned to reopen the main line from La Paz to Cochabamba. The announcement contained no details, however, and it did not mention Cruz Blanca, and no one seemed to believe a word of it.

The handful of countries that have managed to escape mass poverty since the 1950s are concentrated in East Asia—South Korea, Taiwan, Singapore, and, to a lesser extent, Thailand and Malaysia. South Korea and Taiwan followed strongly *dirigiste* industrial policies. High protective tariffs were raised, for instance, around certain fledgling industries. (This is sometimes known as the "infant industry" strategy.) Some of these industries were selected for their export potential, and when they were ready to compete internationally they quickly found markets. The local standard of living began to rise. This development strategy is similar to what all the Western powers once did to encourage their own industries, but it is anathema under the free-trade dogma of the Washington Consensus, and it could not be implemented by any underdeveloped, indebted country today. It relies heavily on tariffs and state planning, and is thus noxious not only to the IMF and the World Bank but, equally as important, to the World Trade Organization, which is the third Bretton Woods institution. The WTO is dedicated, even more unequivocally than the others, to eliminating "barriers to trade."

South Korea, Taiwan, and Singapore also managed, each in its own way, to turn some of the early waves of the current flood of corporate globalization to their advantage. When manufacturing started fleeing the high-wage nations of the West, opening assembly plants in Latin America and Asia, the countries that came to be known as the Asian Tigers successfully imposed local-content laws (requiring that investors buy locally produced components when possible) and consistently cut better deals for the transfer of technical skills to their own workers than, say, Mexico did. Thus, when the multinationals moved on to Indonesia and Vietnam in search of cheaper labor, Taiwan and South Korea were ready to let the sweatshops go and to assume a higher position in the global production chain.

None of this wise planning meant that the Tigers were immune to pressures from the multilateral financial institutions. The IMF, in particular, was determined that the newly prosperous East Asian countries liberalize their capital markets, and its success in prying open those markets contributed to the devastating regional economic crisis of 1997–98. In the crisis, only Malaysia seriously defied the stern—and, in retrospect, disastrous—advice of the U.S. Treasury Department not to impose capital controls. (These are laws that impede international investors and speculators—what Thomas L. Friedman, the great sloganeer of globalization, calls "the Electronic Herd"—as they move money in or out of a country.) By no coincidence, Malaysia emerged from the wreckage more quickly and less scathed than any of its neighbors. (Chile, which has made more progress against poverty under neoliberalism than any other Latin American country, also uses capital controls.)

China and India, although poor, have the populational heft to ignore many applicatons of Western pressure, which has helped each of them ride the globalization wave at least in the right general direction. China offers foreign corporations some of the world's cheapest labor, particularly in what are called export-processing zones, or free-trade zones. EPZs are tax-free manufacturing zones, where local labor and environmental laws (if any) are often relaxed or suspended in order to attract foreign capital. Today, tens of millions of people in more than seventy countries work in EPZs. They are where the American (and Canadian, and Western European) manufacturing jobs go when they go south. Or, rather, parts of the jobs go there, temporarily, because multinational firms have found that it is often most profitable to distribute the different aspects of production and assembly to different contractors and subcontractors, often in different countries, with the lowest-skilled, most tedious, unhealthy, labor-intensive work typically going to the least developed country. Mobility is essential to this arrangement—the ability to quickly transfer operations from country to country in search of the cheapest production costs and least hassle from local authorities. Thus the facilities in EPZs, the vast prefab sheds and plants, are rarely owned by the contractors who use them, let alone by the multinationals who place the orders. They are leased.

EPZs are not a viable development model. Wages are low, and workers are typically drawn not from local communities but from distant villages and rural areas. With the constant threat that companies will pick up and leave if they are taxed or regulated, local governments rarely profit in any significant way. Local-content laws and knowledge transfer are seldom, if ever, part of the package. A few corrupt officials, along with managers drawn from local elites, profit, certainly, but the great influx of foreign technology and capital that EPZs are supposed to bring rarely materializes.

And this seemingly minor, disappointing fact undermines a crucial assumption, widespread in the West, about the new global division of labor. The assumption is that the developed world is turning into one big postindustrial service economy while the rest of the world industrializes, and that, yes, sweatshops, child labor, egregious pollution, health and safety nightmares, and subsistence-level wages come with industrialization, but that any country that wants to develop must go through all that. *We went through it. So did Western Europe.* This assumption, although not usually stated so crudely, underpins every serious argument for corporate-led globalization. The problem is that the industrialization that Indonesia, Honduras, the Philippines, and dozens of other countries are now experiencing is not the same industrialization that we in the West experienced. It's true that people are moving from farms to factories, and that urbanization is occurring at a rapid pace. But exploitation and immiseration are not development. And unregulated, untaxed foreign ownership, with profits being remitted to faraway investors, will never build good infrastructure. It is simply not clear how, under the current model, the poor majority in most poor countries will ever benefit from globalization.

China has achieved and maintained impressive growth, even in the present world recession. And yet China, although increasingly integrated into the world economy, and recently admitted to the WTO, is following a development path very much its own. It has strict capital controls. It forbids foreigners from owning many forms of stock. It has gone slowly with privatization. (Russia already demonstrated how to do it fast and badly.) The state retains control of the banking system. Still, everybody wants to do business with China, if only because of the size and docility of its labor force and the size of its consumer market, which is expanding swiftly, along with its urban middle class. Politically, China remains, of course, a one-party state—a police state, in fact—nominally Communist, with little interest in human rights, the rule of law, or other democratic niceties that theoretically come with a market economy.

India, the world's largest democracy, has achieved less growth, and it has been racked by battles over some of the main insults of corporate globalization, such as seed patenting and the construction of giant, World Bank–backed dams that have displaced millions of villagers. But the Indian middle class (also growing) has enjoyed the fruits of a technology-led boom, thanks to a thick slice of the world's software programming and back-office work being outsourced to a few Indian firms. The government, meanwhile, has continued to protect many domestic industries—and to use capital controls—basically thumbing its nose at the imprecations of the Bretton Woods institutions to stop.

Most national governments today, though, must struggle in a world economy in which they are dwarfed by global corporations. And those corporations, while gaining power steadily in relation to states (which must compete to lure investment), have also been quietly undergoing a profound self-transformation. This transformation can be seen most easily in two figures: first, the total assets of the one hundred largest multinational corporations increased, between 1980 and 1995, by 697 percent; second, the total direct employment of those same corporations during that same period *decreased* by 8 percent. This was more than mere downsizing. These figures demonstrate, again, that a great many of the jobs that left the rich world over the past 25 years did not, in fact, rematerialize intact elsewhere, in the Global South, where labor is cheaper. Because the question turned out to be, in many cases, again, not where to produce goods but how to produce them, and the answer turned out to be not by owning factories and having employees but by ordering products from contractors and subcontractors and sub-subcontractors in poor countries. EPZs have been instrumental to the success of this strategy.

Bolivia, by the way, has EPZs. Nobody wants to use them, though. Transportation costs alone—in a landlocked country with bad roads and disappearing railroads, far from major markets—deter potential investors. Then there is the country's tradition of labor militancy, which frightens foreign investment and is not a problem in, say, Thailand (and certainly not in China, where independent labor unions are illegal). Bolivian trade ministers end up in the same position as many trade ministers from sub-Saharan Africa. They would be delighted to have foreign corporations come and exploit their people. But the corporations see better opportunities elsewhere.

The market fundamentalist's version of history and economics is both more scriptural and more expedient than it is factual. The idea, for instance, that greater trade leads to greater general prosperity, which is an unshakable conviction not only among true believers but also among liberal globalizers, including most of the American journalistic establishment and the Democratic Party, is in many cases simply untrue. In Latin America, during the 1960s and 1970s—the decades preceding the great trade boom of globalization—per capita income rose 73 percent. During the last two decades, with trade expanding rapidly under neoliberalism, per capita income rose less than 6 percent. The same dismal pattern appears in the United States. Between 1947 and 1973, economic growth averaged 4 percent and nonmanagerial wages—that's the pay of more than 80 percent of American workers—rose 63 percent, in real dollars. Since 1973, with international trade soaring, real wages have fallen 4 percent, while economic growth has averaged 3 percent. Nobody knows precisely what effect trade has had on American wages and growth, but even conservative economists ascribe a significant amount of the long-term American wage stagnation to the effects of globalization. These effects, when they are acknowledged at all by free traders, are, we are assured, only temporary. But they have lasted more than a generation now and, as the Springsteen song says about good jobs, "They ain't comin' back."

Another core belief, that lower taxes promote economic growth by encouraging people to work harder and invest more, is equally unfounded in reality. Neither U.S. history, which shows no correlation between tax rates and growth, nor studies of other countries, which show randomly mixed results, bear out this article of free-market faith. If a government collects high taxes and then spends the revenue unwisely, economic growth will be impeded, obviously. If it spends the money wisely, growth may be enhanced. Of course, different groups in society will be affected differently by the progressivity and specifics of any tax regime—this is why wealthy corporations and individuals tend to be especially enthusiastic about lower marginal tax rates, which reduce their own tax bills.

But even economic growth, which is regarded nearly universally as an overall social good, is not necessarily so. There is growth so unequal that it heightens social conflict and increases repression. There is growth so environmentally destructive that it detracts, in sum, from a community's quality of life. (Trade itself carries vast, and rarely calculated, environmental consequences, with pollution-spreading ships, trucks, and planes rushing goods around the globe.) Then there is the destruction of communities themselves, as nations frantically reshape their economies around exports and specialization—the mass production of those goods that may afford them comparative advantage in the global marketplace. Finally, there is the peculiar way that growth, or gross domestic product, is calculated, which is as a value-free measure of total economic output, one that does not distinguish between costs and benefits. Thus resource extraction is a plus, while resource depletion does not register. Strip-mining, clear-cutting, overfishing, pumping an aquifer (or an oil reserve) dry—these ravages and permanent losses do not figure in the growth equation. Neither is income distribution a factor, meaning that most people may be getting poorer in a context of economic "growth." Medical bills and legal bills all count as growth, leading to an absurdist universe in which, as policy analysts Ted Halstead and Clifford Cobb put it, "the nation's economic hero is a terminal cancer patient who has just gone through a bitterly contested divorce."

This is not to say that the world's poor are not in need of economic growth, in the sense of greater economic opportunity. They are. But the question remains: What policies and incentives will actually provide that opportunity? Increased international trade *can* be beneficial to the poor. *But it is not automatically so.* Markets *can* do great things, and yet they remain flawed, fickle mechanisms that favor those with money, and they must be carefully regulated.

One hears a great deal of piety from the Bush administration about raising global standards of living—and the president has in fact pledged to increase his foreign-aid budget by half—but the U.S. government's primary job is to advance and protect American interests. Our leaders' passion for "free trade" is driven not by altruism but by a desire to open new markets for U.S. firms and products.

How will we respond, though, when our overtures are rejected? There is a popular backlash building against the Washington Consensus throughout Latin America (and elsewhere). The top priority of U.S. policy toward Latin America, meanwhile, is the creation of a hemisphere-wide free-trade zone known as the Free Trade Area of the Americas. If and when it goes into effect, the FTAA, which was first seriously pursued during the Clinton administration, will be a sort of super-NAFTA, including in its embrace 34 of the Western Hemisphere's 35 countries—all but Cuba. Like NAFTA, the FTAA is a brainchild of big business, whose interests it would serve from start to finish. It would virtually eliminate barriers to foreign investment, strengthen investor rights (and gut consumer rights), eliminate tariffs, ban capital controls, and establish secret trade courts in which multinational corporations would be able to sue governments over health, labor, or environmental laws that could be shown to impede profits. The FTAA would actually go beyond NAFTA, with mandatory requirements that national markets be opened to foreign corporations not only for basic services such as banking and insurance but also for public services such as health, education, and water. Within Latin America, there is broad popular and political opposition to the FTAA, which is widely seen as an economic onslaught on national sovereignty. North American firms, it is believed, simply want more access to Latin American markets, on grossly unfair terms. U.S. embassies in the region spend a great deal of time parrying such arguments—presenting the FTAA as a win-win deal, trying to woo local businessmen, politicians, and opinion makers onto the bandwagon.*

Their job would be easier if the United States did not flout the principles it espouses. Last spring, for instance, President Bush, responding to domestic political pressure, imposed steep new tariffs on steel imports. Loud protests came from Europe, East Asia, and Brazil, and complaints were soon being filed with the WTO. The hypocrisy was stark: The U.S. shoves free-trade doctrine down the throat of every country it meets while practicing, when it pleases, protectionism. Even more hypocritical, and economically painful, to dozens of countries in Africa and Latin America has been the latest round of U.S. farm subsidies, which may total as much as $180 billion over the next decade. Most of that windfall goes directly to big agricultural corporations (all of them big political contributors). These subsidies effectively close American markets to many poor-country food producers (we also have tariff barri-

---

*The FTAA even made it onto the Bush National Security Strategy's wish list. Regional and bilateral trade pacts have recently bumped multilateral venues, notably the WTO, from the top of the administration's trade priorities. Bilateral agreements with Jordan, Chile, and Singapore have already been reached. Morocco and Australia are among those next in line. WTO trade rules are, by their global nature, more difficult to control than bilateral agreements with much smaller economies. Indeed, the U.S. has recently violated WTO trade rules so consistently that the organization's top officials have likened American trade unilateralism to Bush's policy toward Iraq.

ers in place, just in case), while allowing U.S. exporters to flood foreign markets with cheap food, often putting poor-country farmers out of business. Global trade rules, as codified in the WTO's Agriculture Agreement, do allow countries to make direct payments to their farmers. But only rich countries, for obvious reasons, have that option. This is one of the many ways that the "level playing field" extolled by free traders does not look level from the Global South.

Our NAFTA partners—Canada and Mexico—are exempt from the new steel tariffs, a fact sometimes pointed out by U.S. diplomats campaigning for the FTAA. The implication is that members of a free-trade pact may actually practice free trade with one another. But since the advent of NAFTA in 1994, the fate of Mexican workers and farmers—especially small corn farmers, the country's rural backbone—has not been confidence-inspiring. Wages have fallen, and a half million families have been driven off their land by a collapse of prices as local markets have been swamped with subsidized corn produced by U.S. agribusiness.

The election, in October, of Luiz Inácio Lula da Silva, a socialist ex-metalworker, as president of Brazil, will likely try the Bush administration's commitment to respecting democratic outcomes. Lula, as he is known, has been a strong critic of neoliberalism and the FTAA, and without Brazil, which has the largest economy in South America, there will be no FTAA. (*Pace* Trade Representative Zoellick, who, in remarks that infuriated Brazilians across the political spectrum, suggested that if the new government did not sign the agreement it would be welcome to trade with Antarctica.) While Lula has vowed not to renege on Brazil's international debt, he has ambitious plans to ease his country's terrible inequality, poverty, and hunger, and international bankers and investors have been loudly nervous about the prospect of his presidency. They caused a plunge in the value of Brazil's currency before Lula was even elected, and it is not too much to say that they retain the power to annul the results of the country's election by pulling out investments and calling in loans. The IMF, especially, with its power to extend or withhold loans, and its even greater power, through its influence, to cut off lines of credit, holds the keys to Brazil's financial stability—which is another way of saying that the U.S. holds those keys. In the Bush administration's quasi-theological version of political economy, democracy and free markets are two halves of a mystical whole. In reality, they can be deadly opponents, when voters decide to go against the markets.

The truth is, no government practices free trade. It is a credo, a chimera, a utopian conceit—a nice idea—as well as a fine club with which to belabor one's political opponents and economic competitors. The E.U. subsidizes its farmers as lavishly as the U.S., and Japan does almost as well by its farmers. The WTO is a tariff-trading bourse, where countries dicker and bicker and hash out compromises under arbitration. Its founding document is more than 27,000 pages long. This is not the yellow brick road to a purified, simplified ("free") global trading system.

But the main problem, from the perspective of poor countries, with the existing system of world finance and trade is simply that the rules drawn up, and the decisions handed down, at the WTO, the IMF, and other international tribunals, are drawn up and handed down almost entirely by the rich countries. They have the negotiators, the expertise, the financial leverage, and in some cases (such as the IMF and the World Bank) the weighted vote to win virtually every dispute. Even when rich countries clearly violate an agreement, their poor-country counterparts may lack the resources (meaning, often, simply the lawyers) to lodge a successful protest.

Lopsided legal contests in trade courts are not tragedies, of course. Those occur, rather, in what international bureaucrats like to call "the field"—when the European Union decides to dump heavily subsidized powdered milk in Jamaica, say, and Jamaican dairy farmers are forced to throw away hundreds of thousands of gallons of fresh milk; or when the United States decides to off-load vast quantities of subsidized rice in Haiti, putting thousands of small rice farmers out of business and causing a regional rise in child malnutrition. Haiti, although the poorest country in the Western Hemisphere, does well, incidentally, on the IMF's trade-openness rankings.

Beyond the egregious incidents, though, there are the structural obstructions. Rich-country tariffs, for instance. They are, in the aggregate, four times higher against the products of poor countries than against the products of other rich countries. Why? Well, what you got to negotiate *with,* mon? Or consider the twist known as "tariff peaks." These charges, levied at rich-country ports, get higher with the amount of processing that an imported product has undergone. Peanuts? We charge you, assuming that this is an American port, *x.* Peanut butter? We charge you *x* plus *132 percent.* Our peanut-butter companies do not appreciate competition, you see. Canada, Japan, and the E.U. all use tariff peaks to keep out processed foods and other manufactured products. The result is to prevent poor countries from adding any value to their raw commodities—to prevent them, that is, from achieving even the primary stages of industrial development.

It's the perennial mismatch of the powerful center and the weak periphery. In economic policy today, though, it plays out in a particularly perverse way. When a poor country is in recession, for instance, it is usually ordered by its paymasters at the IMF to balance its books. This approach to fiscal management went out in the West with Herbert Hoover. In the rich countries, we run deficits during a recession and apply good countercyclical remedies like lowered interest rates. We don't listen to the IMF's ultraorthodox prescriptions because we don't owe the IMF money. Austerity, like free trade, is for us to prescribe and for poor countries to practice. Private enterprises in poor countries are expected to compete with rich multinationals when the interest rates that they must pay to raise capital—pushed dizzyingly high under austerity plans—make fair competition impossible. And all this bitter medicine comes in a bottle labeled Economic Freedom.

I was surprised to learn that the *cocaleros,* Bolivia's coca farmers, have a parliamentary brigade. I went to see its leader, Evo Morales, at his office in La Paz. His office turned out to be a dimly lit room in a high-rise government warren. People clumped in the shadows, and it felt a bit like a NORML meeting, particularly after I told Morales and his aides that I had recently chewed coca to combat altitude sickness on a drive through the high mountains, and they all cackled happily.

Morales is short, dark, handsome, round-faced, with a long pageboy haircut. His father was a peasant potato farmer, he said, and he himself still farmed a coca plot in the Chapare, a jungle district east of Cochabamba. Most of the coca farmers are ex-miners, he said, "on the run from neoliberalism." They had been fighting for years with the Bolivian army, which was being heavily supported by the U.S. in a coca-eradiction effort known as "zero coca." Although the Bolivian government and the U.S. Drug Enforcement Agency were claiming victory, most independent analysts believe the effort is futile, since poor farmers in other parts of South America have always proved willing to raise coca when there is a market for it.

Morales didn't want to discuss the drug business, except to say that in Bolivia it was certainly not a military problem. He preferred to frame the U.S.-Bolivian war on drugs as a war on his people, the Quechua and Aymara, who have been growing coca for thousands of years, and have been suffering attacks from white colonizers for centuries. "Zero coca means zero Quechua and Aymara," he said. "They see us as animals. They enslaved us. When we learned to read, they cut out our eyes."

Evo Morales is a prominent Bolivian politician, but the U.S. Embassy in La Paz assured me that his career had peaked years earlier, and that he would soon be found in the dustbin of local history.

The embassy was wrong. That was in early 2001. In 2002, Morales ran for president, on a socialist ticket. He vowed, if elected, to end Bolivia's participation in the U.S. war on drugs, and to end, moreover, Bolivia's participation in the failed neoliberal experiment. All the industries and utilities that had been privatized? They would be renationalized. To the horror of the local authorities, not to mention the Americans, Morales began to rise in the polls. His radical ideas clearly appealed to a fair number of people. As election day neared, the embassy seemed to panic. Ambassador Manuel Rocha announced that if Morales won the election, the U.S. would have to consider cutting off aid to Bolivia. This threat was taken ill, apparently, by Bolivian voters. Support for Morales surged, and on election day he finished second, behind Gonzalo Sánchez de Lozada. Since no candidate had received a majority of votes, there was a runoff between the top two finishers. Fortunately for Goni, as Sánchez de Lozada is known, the voters in the runoff were not the Indian majority of Bolivians, in which case Morales would probably have won. They were, instead, the Bolivian parliament, whose members overwhelmingly favored the wealthy, well-educated, white man, Goni.

The American presence in Bolivia is less brainlessly imperial than Ambassador Rocha made it seem. The embassy understands, for instance, that the relative success of the coca-eradication program has been a major blow to Bolivia's economy. Jorge Quiroga, Goni's predecessor as president, told me that the income from coca had accounted for more than 8 percent of Bolivia's gross domestic product and 18 percent of exports. "Imagine wiping that out," he said. "All the unemployment and suffering, all the multiplier effects. In the U.S., it would be like wiping out the mining and agricultural sectors combined." The embassy did not dispute these numbers or the analogy (and Quiroga is a *supporter* of eradication). Partly because the war on drugs causes hardship, the U.S. remains by far the largest source of bilateral aid to Bolivia, as well as the prime mover behind the World Bank's local largesse.

The Bank also recognizes the impossible burden that international debt places on nearly all poor countries, and it has lobbied for partial debt relief for poor countries it considers fiscally responsible, including Bolivia. Despite its annexation to the Washington Consensus, the Bank is not a solid bastion of market fundamentalism, and its analysts have seen enough social and financial fallout from hasty privatizations to realize, belatedly, that in many sectors, such as utilities, a strong regulatory framework to protect the public interest is essential to successful privatization. In most poor countries, the modern regulatory body is a novel concept. The Bank has therefore started sponsoring courses to train would-be regulators from countries undergoing structural adjustment. The courses are said to be first-rate, although problems can arise with the students sent to them by client governments. "They always send the minister's nephew," a regulation advocate in Bolivia told me. "Somebody who thinks of regulation the same way he thinks of a job in government, as a way to make money from bribes."

"Structural adjustment," incidentally, has precipitated so many riots in so many countries, caused so much suffering and received so much bad publicity, that it is currently being rebranded, by both the Bank and the IMF, as "development policy support lending," which has a much less procrustean sound.

The U.S. Embassy is not, of course, a charitable organization. It exists to represent U.S. interests, which in Latin America has traditionally meant the interests of U.S. business. This is as true today as ever. Even at the World Bank, and at each of its regional development banks, the United States has, under order of Congress, an officer of the U.S. Commercial Service assigned to look out for U.S. business interests. And the economic big stick is at times still crudely wielded. In late 2002, for instance, the Colombian defense ministry expressed interest in buying forty light attack planes from the leading Brazilian aircraft manufacturer. Columbia, which is racked by civil war, is a major recipient of U.S. military aid. General James T. Hill, head of the U.S. Southern Command, learning of the Columbians' interest in purchasing Brazilian planes, fired off a letter to the Columbian government warning that future U.S. military aid could be jeopardized by the purchase. The Columbian air force should be buying American-made C-130s, the general wrote, mincing no words. When this letter unexpectedly became public, a Southern Command spokesman claimed it was merely a technical evaluation of Columbia's military needs.

It's easy to be cynical about the double binds—the rigged world trade system, to be blunt—faced by poor countries. And the bald contradictions of U.S. policy and preachments suggest, certainly, a degree of official cynicism. But nobody really wants to see economies stultify or implode (nobody except, perhaps, a few financial specialists known as vulture capitalists), and the IMF's great efforts to prevent emerging-economy disasters with emergency bailouts, although frequently unsuccessful, seem basically sincere. The problem lies, rather, with the model.

Even market fundamentalists concede that corporate-led globalization produces both winners and losers. Why should the U.S. government look beyond a strict probusiness definition of the national interest? Because it is *in* our national interest, especially in the longer term, to expand globalization's circle of winners and to throw lifelines to the billions of people struggling to stay afloat in the world economic maelstrom. The U.S. currently enjoys a truly rare global preeminence—

military, economic, pop-cultural. But power is not, obviously, the same as legitimacy. And every overweening, remorseless projection of American power, every unfair trade rule and economic double standard jammed into the global financial architecture, helps erode the legitimacy of American ascendancy in the eyes of the world's poor. This erosion is occurring throughout Latin America, Africa, Asia. At the WTO, in response to worldwide protests against the high prices of AIDS drugs, the United States finally acceded, in November 2001, to a historic decision that public health should, after all, be a consideration in some areas of patent protection. Then, in late 2002, under pressure from the big pharmaceuticals, the Bush administration quietly changed its position and sent Trade Representative Zoellick to kill an agreement allowing poor countries access to generic medicines. Few Americans noticed. But in Africa, and Asia, and all the countries directly injured by this decision, millions noticed.

President Bush had it all wrong about Al Qaeda and world trade, of course. Still, there was the long, horrifying groundswell of popular support for Osama bin Laden and the attacks on New York and Washington that surfaced, mainly in the Muslim world. The depths of hatred that the United States has inspired in some of the world's more oppressed corners may be ultimately unfathomable. But the importance of trying to change that, of trying to inspire something less malignant with policies less rapacious, seems undeniable. As the Bush administration has been discovering in its campaign against Iraq, even empires need allies.

Americans always overestimate the amount of foreign aid we give. In recent national polls, people have guessed, on average, that between 15 and 24 percent of the federal budget goes for foreign aid. In reality, it is less than 1 percent. The UN has set a foreign-aid goal for the rich countries of 0.7 percent of gross national product. A few countries have attained that modest goal, all of them Scandinavian. The U.S. has never come close. Indeed, it comes in dead last, consistently, in the yearly totals of rich-country foreign aid as a percentage of GNP. In 2000, we gave 0.1 percent. President Bush's dramatic proposal, post–September 11, to increase foreign aid to $15 billion looks rather puny next to the $48 billion increase in this year's $379 billion military budget.

Along with our delusions about foreign aid, there persists a more general belief about the rich world trying to help the poor, at least financially. In fact, the net transfer of moneys each year runs the other way—from the poor countries to the rich, mainly in the form of corporate profits and government debt servicing.

But it is simplistic, even misleading, to talk about whole nations as winners or losers under the current globalization regime, since there are, in every country, significant groups of both winners and losers. In China, with its remarkable growth rate and burgeoning middle class, tens of millions of people have been left unemployed and destitute in the upheavals caused by the arrival of capitalism, while millions more find themselves working seven days a week in dangerous, abysmally paid factory jobs. In dozens of countries, a dominant ethnic minority is reaping most, if not all, of the gains of economic integration while working-class and peasant majorities absorb the shocks and bitter downsides of trade liberalization. Even in the U.S., the foremost proponent of free trade and presumably its great beneficiary, there are those millions of good jobs that disappeared with globalization, leaving their former holders working non-union at Wal-Mart. There is a strong argument that the U.S. may be trading itself into oblivion, for it seems that we began, in 1976, running a trade deficit, leading to an international debt that has since ballooned to $2.4 trillion, or roughly 24 percent of GDP. Our major trading partners have yet to call in these debts, but the national balance sheet looks worse every year. With the economy threatening to slip into Japan-style deflation, life as a debtor nation could become quite unpleasant. In that event, globalization, certainly in this corporate-driven form, may start looking like a bad idea to more and more Americans.

Empire is expensive. The finances are tricky. Countries need to be bribed as well as bullied. A government that's solidly in the fold can be sent on many errands: During the first Gulf War, Argentina, neoliberalism's poster child, was the only country in Latin America to contribute troops. That was then. President Bush relies greatly, by his own testimony, on faith—and he does seem to possess the fundamentalist's personal serenity on both the knotty, ambiguous questions of economics and on the far weightier matter of war. But the daily work of increasing American commercial supremacy, while binding the global economy into stronger, more tightly woven webs of intregration, is not for the otherworldly. It's being done quietly, in our name, by trade bureaucrats and proconsuls and "area specialists" even while our leaders speak soothingly of a rising tide of freedom.* Restive countries, awakening to some notion of self-interest, may wander off the reservation, of course. More poignantly, transnational capital always has its own logic and pursues its own ends. While we make the world safe for multinational corporations, it is by no means clear that they intend to return the favor.

Outside the cities in Bolivia, the visitor still enters an unfamiliar world. What are those white flags hanging outside the houses? What does that graffito mean, NO A LA FLEXIBILIZACIÓN? You need a local guide. Drive into the high country and you need a Quechua-speaking guide. In a small town at the base of the mountains, I ask around and find a kid who speaks Quechua and hire him. He's a chubby teenager who makes himself comfortable, then tells me that his ambition is to study radio so that he can make educational programs for *campesinos* who don't speak Spanish and don't see newspapers or TV but listen faithfully to their radios. What are those white flags? Those are *chicherías,* unlicensed taverns selling *chicha,* a homemade corn beer. The flags mean they're open for business. *Chicha* is the people's brew—cheaper than canned beer, which comes from the German brewery. What is *flexibilización*? That was the law that took away labor rights, such as the forty-hour workweek. It was part of structural adjustment and was bitterly opposed by the unions, to no effect.

Everthing feels contested. I ease my rented car through a herd of llamas and try to remember the story. The sale of llama meat, prohibited for centuries, was legalized only in 1994. What was it, besides the power of the big cattle ranchers, that kept llama meat, which is highly nutritious, off the market? "*Discriminación,*" I am told, against the Indian herders.

---

*It's also being done by war planners. *The Wall Street Journal* has reported that the Bush administration's plan to rebuild and administer a conquered Iraq relies not on the UN or other international-development agencies but on American private companies with deep Pentagon connections, such as Bechtel and Kellogg Brown & Root, which have been secretly bidding on contracts since February.

We pass a group of peasant women in beautiful, beribboned, handmade straw hats. Those hats, which are expensive, take months to make, and now they are disappearing, under an avalanche of cheap baseball caps from El Norte. The Indian women in the mountains farther to the west adopted the British bowler hat in the nineteenth century and made it jauntily their own. Somehow nothing similar seems likely to happen today. We come to a village with a brilliant, multicolored, woven flag hanging from a lamppost in the plaza. "That is the *wiphala* of these people." The *wiphala* represents local pride, the organization of local peasants, vehemently distinct from the Bolivian state. It has also become a symbol of resistance to globalization. *Everything feels contested.*

We run low on gas and find ourselves negotiating with a *campesino* in his half-tilled potato field. It's all in Quechua, but I gather he has a can of gas somewhere. He's reluctant to part with it but finally agrees to sell it to us if we'll give him a ride to town. I watch him put away his hoe. His wife comes to the door of their hut and studies me. I've always despised the social-service penchant for classifying hardy peasant self-sufficiency as "poverty." It's such an easy, condescending, incurious, vaguely missionary appropriation of great, unknown worlds of experience and knowledge. This is not a romanticization of peasant life. It's respect. For purposes of analysis and advocacy, of course, the "poverty" classification is useful. I've often been guilty of it myself. The young Quechua woman watches me, unsmiling, as I drive off with her husband down the mountain.

I later find myself at a big commercial *chichería* near a market town, sitting in the garden with a convivial group of local officials. It's a sunny afternoon, and a raucous *ranchera* band plays inside a tile-floored dance hall. Pitchers of cool, earth-tasting *chicha* keep arriving at our table, accompanied by platters of *mote*—huge moist kernels of corn. Drinking *chicha* has its rituals. Four of us share a single drinking bowl, which we pass around, each carefully filling it for the next man. Before each drink, you pour a splash of *chicha* on the ground and then offer a toast to an Andean earth deity called Pachamama. The *chicha* buzz is mild, even after half a dozen pitchers.

A couple of my companions are older men. It turns out that they both fled Bolivia during the days of military dictatorship. One made the mistake of going to Chile, shortly before the military coup that overthrew Salvador Allende. Out of the frying pan, he said, shrugging. He ended up being held for weeks inside the National Stadium in Santiago. Not a nice place to be. We drink a round to civilian rule.

Kissinger, we agree, is a war criminal.

We drink a round to democracy.

Talk turns to the IMF, whose local representative, a U.S.-trained Israeli economist, is in all the papers. It seems he is giving valedictory interviews because his term is up. His parting message to Bolivia? First and foremost, it must solve the corruption problem. That must be done first. Thank you, Señor Kreis.

Seriously, someone asks me, do I think there is any hope for bringing democracy to the World Bank or the IMF? Or, for that matter, to the UN and the WTO? Shouldn't the citizens of the world be electing representatives to these powerful institutions, so that they might be accountable to someone other than wealthy corporations and their allies in the rich countries? I can't think of any reason why not. We drink a round to this brilliant idea. It is only later, back at my hotel—or maybe it's back in New York—that I remember it is only people in countries like Bolivia who know or care what the World Bank or the IMF do. In the West, most of us have other things to worry about.

Only high real estate values are stopping the detonation of America's debt bomb, Jonathan R. Laing of *Barron's* contends. The long history of bubbles was generally fueled each time by a significant buildup in borrowing such as we've recently experienced. A fall in the price of assets, a definite possibility in our current housing market, would have a devastating effect.

Jonathan R. Laing

The Debt Bomb

BUBBLES HAVE LONG BEEN part of the financial firmament. The tulipmania in seventeenth-century Holland and the notorious South Sea Company stock bubble a century later in England are lowlights of economic lore.

History is replete with numerous other examples of financial manias followed almost ineluctably by huge price busts, down to our own era. Japan is still paying the price of deflation and economic narcolepsy a decade after bubbles in its stock and real estate markets popped. Debt collapses in Asia and South America punctuated much of the '90s. The bursting of the U.S. tech-stock bubble in early 2000 led to the vanishing of more than $5 trillion in wealth, at least on paper. Now, many worry that a U.S. housing bubble, lofted by four-decade lows in mortgage rates, could explode, eviscerating consumer spending and economic growth.

Curiously, however, one reads almost nothing about what may be the biggest bubble of them all—the huge ballooning of total debt in the U.S. That measure, an aggregate of the borrowings of all households, businesses, and governments (federal, state, and local), zoomed up from about $4 trillion at the beginning of 1980 to $31 trillion as of 2002's third quarter, according to the latest available Federal Reserve flow-of-funds data.

While some observers see no cause for alarm in these figures, others fear that this debt surge could be edging the U.S. economy toward the abyss of a bust—and then into a depression.

REALITY CHECK

The '90s economic boom boosted wage, profit, and productivity growth, enhancing the ability of consumers and businesses to service debt. Yet, after-the-fact revelations about the accounting shenanigans of that period lead to an important question: How much of the profit boom and productivity miracle was real?

It may have been as much an artificial product of debt leverage as of true internal growth. Credit-market debt now equals 295 percent of gross domestic product, compared with 160 percent in 1980 and less than 150 percent during much of the 1960s. More ominously, debt as a percentage of GDP exceeds the previous record reading of 264 percent from early in the Great Depression—when the aftermath of the Roaring Twenties borrowing binge collided with a sharp economic contraction. And today's debt load is clearly starting to pinch consumers and businesses: Credit-card charge-offs of bad loans exceed 7 percent of total debt outstanding, compared with the previous peak around 5 percent, reached in the mid-1990s, according to Standard & Poor's.

ENGORGED WITH DEBT

U.S. personal bankruptcy filings in the third quarter of 2002 jumped some 12 percent from the level a year earlier. And when 2002's total is in, it will almost certainly eclipse 2001's record 1.43 million.

Meanwhile, mortgage delinquencies are soaring, particularly among less creditworthy borrowers. In the "subprime" market, delinquencies have jumped to 8.07 percent from just 4.5 percent in 1999, according to Loan Performance, a San Francisco tracking firm. This market, which caters to people with checkered credit histories, accounts for about 10 percent of the $5.8 trillion of U.S. mortgage debt currently outstanding. Delinquencies on Federal Housing Administration loans, which make up about 15 percent of the dollar amount of U.S. mortgage debt, are at a thirty-year high of 11.8 percent. The typical FHA borrower is a first-time home buyer with limited funds.

Despite the big home-price jump seen in many regions, soaring mortgage debt and drooping stock prices have severely crimped the net worth of U.S. households. According to the latest Fed numbers, net worth at the end of the third quarter had fallen to just 4.9 times disposable income, about 22 percent below the 6.3 at the end of 1999.

The corporate debt market has seen huge defaults, too, by such formerly investment-grade behemoths as WorldCom and Global Crossing. Defaults in the junk-bond market—which accounts for more than 15 percent of the $5 trillion nonfinancial corporate debt market—have abated somewhat from early fall, when the 12-month default rate spiked to over 18 percent. Yet even with the high mortality rate of the weak and the lame to date, the corporate debt contagion hasn't run its course, warns Moody's chief economist, John Lonski. He contends that the credit cycle can't be deemed to have turned when 88 percent of his company's latest credit actions were downgrades—worse than the previous record, 86 percent, set in 1990 during the Drexel Burnham junk-bond panic.

SLOUCHING TOWARD DEPRESSION?

Ray Dalio, president and chief investment officer of Bridgewater Associates in Greenwich, Connecticut—an outfit that manages around $35 billion in currency and hedge fund assets—believes there's a 30 percent to 40 percent probability of a U.S. depression over the next two to five years.

Dalio notes that, during a recession, interest rates can be lowered to stimulate the economy by making it cheaper for businesses to invest and consumers to buy big-ticket items. Lower interest rates also boost asset prices, by raising the capitalized value of future income streams.

Depressions have a different dynamic. They tend to come after years of debt buildup, when monetary easing no longer works because interest rates are already near zero. Thus, no further debt-service relief is available for overburdened businesses, consumers, or governmental units—especially if deflation causes their incomes to fall. Even if rates hit an irreducible zero, the real burden of debt rises during deflation. Borrowers still have to repay their debts in current dollars while their revenues and collateral fall in value.

In a frenzy to raise cash, debt holders sell assets and cut spending. As a result, the value of the collateral underlying existing debt suffers. Deflationary forces are only exacerbated by businesses cutting prices to stimulate demand in a vain attempt to burnish cash flows. In addition, as unemployment rises, consumer demand falls.

The process is not reversible by normal fiscal or monetary stimulation, as seen in the U.S. during the Great Depression and in Japan since the end of 1989, Dalio avers. The Bridgewater executive is quick to say, however, that the U.S. could avoid depression and simply muddle through the next few years.

Still, a number of questions worry him: Why has the bear market been so impervious to two consecutive years of pedal-to-the-metal monetary easing? Normally, stocks would be on fire after such a span. And what will a Fed out of monetary bullets do if unexpected problems in Iraq or another major terror attack on U.S. soil upset the economy further?

Oft-bearish Morgan Stanley economist Stephen Roach also views the U.S. debt load as a serious problem. "There's no question that we have a debt bomb, but I'm not sure how long the fuse will turn out to be," he says. "It won't detonate if the economy remains strong enough to continue to generate enough real consumer-income growth and corporate cash flow to support the debt. Otherwise, we'll experience the darkest scenario of debt deflation, as a result of the worst set of policy mistakes committed by the Fed since the Great Depression."

One of the first economists to delineate the perils of debt bubbles was Yale's Irving Fisher, who wrote the seminal academic article on the subject in 1933, near the depth of the Great Depression. Apropos of his subject, Fisher had been blindsided by the 1929 stock market crash and subsequent economic collapse; he'd argued in a 1929 magazine piece that the U.S. had achieved a "permanent plateau" of prosperity. To make matters worse, he had lost his personal fortune as well as that of his wife's family in the crash—and would even have lost his house had Yale not bought it from the mortgage-holders and leased it back to him.

In his 1933 article, Fisher asserted that gross "over-indebtedness" lay behind America's three biggest economic calamities to that time— the panics of 1837 and 1873 and the crash of 1929. In each, the debt explosions were sparked by technological developments that transformed the economic landscape (canals in 1837, railroads in 1873, autos and radio in 1929), the advent of new industries, the exciting prospects of new lands or markets (e.g., the Homestead Act's opening of the West in the 1870s), or some combination of these factors. The new developments fired investors' imaginations, Fisher contended, encouraging overconfidence—and greed. Fraudulent claims entice people, too, although there's generally "a very real basis for the 'New Era' psychology before it runs away with its victims," Fisher acidly commented. Sound familiar?

WATCHING FOR THE TIPPING POINT

The tipping point, according to Fisher, comes at a time of "general alarm," when borrowers seeking to get liquid or creditors worried about repayment trigger distress selling. Credit availability contracts, as does monetary turnover. Prices tumble. Businesses fail. Output, trade, and employment career lower. In short, the psychology of derring-do gives way to pessimism and loss of confidence. Finally, deflation causes money's purchasing power to rise sharply, making debt all the more onerous to repay in both real and nominal terms. This, Fisher obsesrved, "is the chief secret of most, if not all, great depressions: The more the debtors pay, the more they owe. The more the economic boat tips, the more it tends to tip."

Of course, there's no inevitability to depressions. Fisher maintained that if Washington had taken immediate steps to reflate the economy—to stimulate it by monetary means—after the 1929 crash, the corrosive debt deflation that ensued might have been avoided. Instead, the Fed raised rates for a time, choking the supply of money and credit in an attempt to balance the budget. Protectionist trade measures compounded the policy bungles.

More recently, notes Martin Barnes, managing editor of the Montreal-based Bank Credit Analyst newsletter, the Bank of Japan kept raising rates for eight months after that nation's stock market peaked in 1990. By the time the central bankers reversed course, stocks were down some 37 percent and deflation was building. Years of subsequent cuts that pushed interest rates below 1 percent still haven't pulled the Japanese out of their funk.

The Fed has only 1.25 percentage points left for cutting short-term rates. In recent speeches, U.S. central bankers have implied their willingness to prime the monetary pump by buying long-dated government and corporate bonds and other assets—and to drive down the dollar's value by selling greenbacks and purchasing assets denominated in foreign currency. The latter moves would be aimed at stimulating the economy by making U.S. exports more competitive while boosting domestic price levels by making imports more expensive.

Nonetheless, economic policy makers are ill-equipped to fight debt deflation, after having spent two decades battling the opposite evil, inflation. Consequently, they've overlooked certain economic imbalances, which have led to economic crises of increasing gravity and frequency. Among them: Japan's post-1990 slump, the 1997 Asian financial crisis, and the 1998 debt crisis in Russia and certain other developing nations. At least that's the contention of a recent working paper by Claudio Borio and Philip Lowe, economists at the Bank for International Settlements in Switzerland.

ASLEEP AT THE WHEEL

In each case, the authors argue, economic authorities, fired with a monomaniacal zeal to crush inflation, virtually ignored a huge buildup in debt—the best indicator of a likely crisis—that created asset-price bubbles. It's ultimately a crash in asset values, be it stocks and real estate in Japan or condos and resort properties in Thailand or Palm Beach, that unleashes the deflationary tidal waves that flatten the workaday economies of goods and services.

First, disinflation (the slowing of increases) in wages and material prices and falling interest rates allow corporate profits to surge. Stocks rise, amplifying consumer demand through the so-called wealth effect. And, the authors assert, the triumph over inflation fosters technological innovation and labor-market liberalization, which make the economic future seem only brighter. Then, belief in unprecedented productivity invariably precedes the fall in asset prices and debt implosions. Finally, policy makers are loath to use monetary policy or other measures to snuff out asset booms, the paper asserts, because such moves aren't politically popular.

The likelihood of the U.S. falling into a deflationary morass seemed so remote until recent years that commentators such as Elliott Wave guru Robert Prechter, economist and Wall Street letter publisher A. Gary Shilling, and Wells Capital economist and investment strategist Jim Paulsen were considered kooks for even broaching the subject.

GLOBAL EXEMPLARS OF DEFLATION

Japan has experienced four years of falling prices, and Germany is on the brink of deflation. U.S. inflation has dropped to an annualized 1 percent or 2 percent, depending on the measure one uses, while U.S. goods' prices have been falling for some months. The annualized rise in service prices, which are less vulnerable to international competitive pressure, has slid to around 3 percent, the smallest increase in decades.

One obvious agent of worldwide deflation is China, with its reservoir of cheap labor, growing manufacturing might, and increased access to global markets by virtue of its recent admission to the World Trade Organization. Ed Yardeni, chief investment strategist of Prudential Securities, recently noted that while the U.S. currently has 16.6 million manufacturing jobs, some 20 million Chinese leave the rural hinterlands each year to seek better-paying manufacturing and construction jobs in their nation's major cities. "China is likely to keep moving up the value chain of production, commoditizing pricing in virtually every low- and high-end product imaginable," he states.

Rising productivity is another deflationary factor. U.S. output per worker-hour has surged 5.7 percent over the past four quarters, largely as a result of efficiencies realized from corporate cost-cutting and delayed benefits from heavy spending on new technology in the late '90s. Productivity improvements have helped U.S. real incomes to rise smartly from the late 1990s until today, despite an unemployment rate of 6 percent.

Yet corporations no longer seem to be reaping the benefits of the productivity boom as they did a few years ago, when profit margins and earnings growth soared. Since then, the same Darwinian price competition that has bolstered consumer purchasing power has hurt corporate revenue and profit growth. "Corporations need to share more in the productivity dividend than they now are [in order] to have a decent recovery," observes Paulsen of Wells Capital. "Maybe it will take a continued slide in the dollar to help corporate bottom lines. With corporate debt levels where they are now, this is not a healthy situation."

DETERMINING THE DETONATOR

At what level does debt turn lethal? No one knows for sure. Some contend that today's debt level of $31 trillion, or 295 percent of the current GDP of $10.5 trillion, is somewhat artificial. About $10 trillion of the debt consists of the borrowings of financial players—banks, savings institutions, finance companies, issuers of asset-backed securities, and government-sponsored enterprises such as Fannie Mae and Freddie Mac. These entities mostly use their borrowings to fund corporate loans, mortgages, auto loans, and credit-card balances. So, in a sense, about a third of today's aggregate debt total is being doubled-counted. That wasn't true in the early '30s, when the ratio of U.S. debt-to-GDP hit its previous high of 264 percent, because the financial sector was far less developed at the time.

"I don't think there's any magic level of debt that's too high," says the Bank Credit Analyst's Barnes. "Much of the jump in current debt levels to GDP is a result of the maturation and democratization of the credit system whereby bankers and other lenders now extend credit to groups that were virtually ignored traditionally. We have more people taking on some debt, rather than some people taking on more debt. A bad recession might cause some severe debt problems, but short of that, the worries about debt are exaggerated."

Current government debt—federal, state, and local—stands at $5 trillion, with Uncle Sam accounting for $3.5 trillion of that. Of course, government borrowing is likely to grow dramatically in the decade ahead as a result of the Bush tax cuts, revenue shortfalls, and the recently announced Bush fiscal-stimulus programs, as well as increased spending on homeland and overseas defense. Some congressional estimates suggest a cumulative deficit of as much as $3 trillion over the period.

Fortunately, however, the federal budget stringency of the past decade and spirited economic growth in the late '90s has driven total U.S. governmental debt down to under 50 percent of total GDP, versus 70 percent in the early '50s and 65 percent in the mid-'90s. The U.S. has a long way to go before governmental debt proves damaging by "crowding out" private credit demand and boosting interest rates. Other developed nations have far higher government debt-to-GDP figures; Japan's is about 150 percent, yet its ten-year government bond yields less than 1 percent.

Meanwhile, the nonfinancial corporate debt market, accounting for $4.9 trillion of the U.S. debt total, has been a charnel house for investors over the past two years. Defaults have skyrocketed, particularly in the wholesale electric-power, telecom, and high-tech sectors. A staggering 18.4 percent of all speculative-grade debt, on a dollar-weighted basis, went into default in the 12 months ended last August 31, Moody's says. Default rates have shrunk some since then, as have the gaps in yields between junk and government bonds. Yet Moody's Lonski says the yield gap is still at an elevated level of nearly 8 percentage points.

Finally, Lonski points out that corporate revenues, the raw material of debt service, have fallen to just 113 percent of corporate debt levels—the second-worst reading in debt-repayment capacity since the Great

Depression. "That revenue-to-debt ratio should be a lot higher—it ran 130 percent to 145 percent in the mid-'90s—for companies to generate sufficient cash flow to handle their debt and maintain the value of the collateral backing their debt," he asserts.

One saving grace: Corporate credit growth has slowed to a crawl of late (it was up 1.8 percent in the third quarter), as companies strive to use internal cash flow to deleverage their balance sheets.

IF THE HOUSING BUBBLE BLOWS . . .

If the U.S. debt bomb ever explodes, the detonator probably will be the residential mortgage market. Home loans account for $5.8 trillion, or nearly 70 percent, of the United States' $8.2 billion in household debt. Academic studies show that changes in home prices have nearly double the impact on consumer spending than does the "wealth effect" from rising or falling stock prices. After all, stock ownership is more concentrated in higher-income groups, and nearly 70 percent of U.S. households own a home.

And home prices have been on a tear, rising nearly 50 percent nationwide over the past six years, bolstered by falling interest rates and looser credit standards. Consumers have tapped this surging equity value through wave after wave of cash-out mortgage refinancings, transforming homes into ATMs. Refinancings have totaled $2.5 trillion over the past two years. In addition, Americans' home-equity loans stand at around $800 billion.

At the same time, Americans' equity in their homes, net of debt, has dwindled to 57 percent, compared with 85 percent a half-century ago, even with the recent powerful surge in home prices. Economist Gary Shilling calculates that 39 percent of U.S. homes are owned free and clear—and that the remaining homeowners have debt burdens exceeding 80 percent of the value of their homes. In other words, many Americans have little margin of safety should home prices level off or should they fall as much as 20 percent, as they did in many overheated areas in the late '80s.

Alan Greenspan and others assert that there's no housing bubble and see no reason why prices shouldn't continue to rise, if at a less torrid pace. Yet Goldman Sachs economist Jan Hatzius sees potential trouble for consumer spending, even if house prices and mortgage rates merely stabilize at current levels. Under such a scenario, refinancing volume is likely to drop markedly, simply because nearly everyone who wants to refinance has already done so.

Hatzius estimates that, in last year's third quarter, on an annualized basis, Americans sucked out $320 billion more in equity from their homes than they reinvested in real estate. This dwarfs the $60 billion in additional outlays the White House says its fiscal stimulus plan could generate this year.

Some of the $320 billion may have flowed into other investments or into savings. But Hatzius thinks that most equity withdrawals went into consumption, given the still-limp consumer-savings rate (now 4 percent, compared with more than 8 percent in the '60s) and poor performance of the stock market. With refinancings slowing, the Goldman economist sees consumer spending rising only 2 percent or less this year.

By his reckoning, home values are at record levels, compared with either rents or median household incomes. Hatzius worries that housing is now highly vulnerable, owing to the likelihood of higher interest rates, rising unemployment, and lower home prices. And if the housing bubble bursts, instead of gently deflating, the nation's economy could be in for a major meltdown. In essence, then, the American home is a bulwark for the economy. As long as housing values stay high, the nation is sheltered from a detonation of the debt bomb.

Public finance can blossom anywhere. A tiny Florida town came up with a plan to rejuvenate itself by issuing more than $1 billion in a wide array of bonds. Noelle Haner-Dorr of the *Orlando Business Journal* tells the quirky story of Moore Haven, "the little city that could." She examines whether its ambitious strategy is legally prudent and justifies all the effort.

Noelle Haner-Dorr

Big Bucks, Small Town, Bond Haven

WELCOME TO MOORE HAVEN, FLORIDA. Population: 1,665. Bonding capacity: $4.5 billion.

Nestled in the heart of Florida's sugarcane country, the sleepy, small south Florida town may not look like a bustling hub of municipal finance.

But in the world of public debt, it is a powerhouse.

Since 1991, Moore Haven has issued more than $1 billion in bonds, funding such far-flung projects as an airport runway in Missouri and two schools in Guam. It financed the sale of student housing for the University of Central Florida.

"It's more than odd," says Richard Lehmann, publisher of *Income Securities Advisor,* a widely read trade publication tracking the health of municipal bonds.

Odder still is that no one—not Moore Haven's mayor, its finance consultant, nor its bond counsel—can say for sure how much money Moore Haven has made from its bond activity.

"At first, [the financial adviser] used to get mad at me because I asked when we would start making money at every meeting he was at," says Moore Haven mayor Harry Ogletree. "I didn't think we were ever going to get anything out of it."

From the stark Town Council Chambers in City Hall, Ogletree can now identify just two concrete benefits from the town's billion-dollar bond deals: a used fire truck and partial financing of a playground.

BONDING RELATIONSHIPS

Moore Haven's bond activity can be traced to its desire for new ways to generate money, without adding to the tax burden of its residents.

Development has come slowly to Moore Haven—an economic fate sealed by the sugarcane barons, cattle ranchers, and dairy farmers that surround the town.

Aging cement block homes line its streets. Per capita income hovers at $15,673. If Moore Haven residents want to shop at Publix or eat at Subway, they have to drive 15 miles to Clewiston. One of the largest local employers is the Moore Haven Correctional Facility—and the prison employs just a little more than two hundred.

However, Moore Haven also had a long-term relationship with Philip Bennett, president of Public Finance Associates Inc. Bennett has been affiliated with Moore Haven since 1971. The tiny town was his first auditing client when he became a certified public accountant.

In 1984, Bennett began working with William Zvara, a Jacksonville-based bond attorney, who was groomed by the bond attorney responsible for the bond issues of another small Florida burg, the Panhandle town of Gulf Breeze.

Gulf Breeze had made fees from issuing certain kinds of bonds designed to fund various projects.

A municipal bond is essentially an IOU—a pledge to repay investors at a later date, with interest.

Such bonds can be issued by cities or towns to fund their own projects, such as roads or other infrastructure projects. In 1991, Moore Haven issued its own water revenue bonds for projects in Glades County.

Bonds can also be sold by quasi-governmental entities known as authorities. For example, the Greater Orlando Aviation Authority, a seven-member panel appointed by the governor, issues bonds to fund projects at Orlando International Airport.

Bonds can also be issued by cities or authorities that agree to act as a conduit: They issue bonds for uses by a company, such as a hospital, in an effort to improve the economic life of a community.

That's what Bennett and Zvara proposed to Moore Haven. They created the Capital Projects Finance Authority, or CAPFA, which could issue tax-exempt municipal bonds if a city or county agreed to act as a conduit.

Revenue-hungry Moore Haven could reap bond fees from such issues.

Even so, the Moore Haven Town Council was a tough sell.

"Primarily, there were legal and financial liability concerns," explains Bennett. "The town wanted to make sure the council and the taxpayers of Moore Haven had absolutely no financial, legal, or moral obligation to any of the bond issues."

Says Ogletree, "I was one of them that was against it at first."

Despite the skepticism, Moore Haven's Town Council eventually agreed to seve as CAPFA's governing board on September 23, 1993.

PECUNIARY POWERHOUSE

Nine years later, Moore Haven is the little town that can. Eleven bond issues totaling more than $1 billion have been issued through CAPFA.

In fact, according to The Bond Buyer's Municipal Issuers Registry, the team of Moore Haven and CAPFA was the fourteenth-largest issuer of bonded debt in all of Florida in the three years ending in 1999.

The projects and places that benefited from the sale of those bonds ran the gamut.

Andersen Air Force Base in Guam got $18.2 million to build an elementary and middle school.

In Missouri, the city of Springfield got $34.4 million to finance the Springfield-Branson Regional Airport's runway and taxiway improvements, a second instrument landing system, and a new airfield electrical vault.

However, more than half of the $1 billion in bonds went into "pools" earmarked for no specific projects. For instance, in 1998, $300 million in bonds were issued to fund unidentified projects for the Florida Hospital Association. In 2000, another $300 million in bonds were sold to fund unspecified projects for the American Association of Airport Executives.

Such bond pools are not unusual. They have gained popularity partly because, as Bennett explains, it is easier and cheaper to do one large bond issue than it is to do ten small bond issues.

However, the bond pools have a potentially troubling tax clause. According to federal law, bond issuers must have a reasonable expectation that at least 95 percent of the proceeds from their bonds will be lent out within a three-year period, or the bonds will run the risk of losing their tax-exempt status.

Further, an undisclosed number of bond pools across the nation—including $330 million issued through the Orange County Health Facilities Authority—recently have come under the scrutiny of the U.S. Internal Revenue Service.

"Any time we see a big loan pool where little or no money is being loaned out, there is a red flag," Charles Anderson, an IRS field agent manager, told *Orlando Business Journal* in an earlier interview. "We have some particularly troubling issues where little or no loans were made."

One of those issues is arbitrage. When bonds are sold at a lower interest rate and the proceeds are invested at a higher interest rate, it may be a violation of the U.S. tax code. Proceeds from the bond sale may become taxable.

Bond pools may raise millions that must be invested until a project is identified, thus rendering them susceptible to arbitrage—and IRS scrutiny. Concern over renewed IRS interest in bond pools is one reason some hospitals declined to borrow money from the Orange County Health Facilities' bond pool.

There were no takers for Moore Haven's hospital bond issue, and those bonds were redeemed last year. So far, only Springfield has jumped at the opportunity to use the town's airport bonds.

MORE MONEY

These issues did make money for the participants, as well.

Those generating such fees are almost always comprised of a select group, according to state records: Zvara is the legal counsel, Bennett's Public Finance Associates is the financial consultant, and the investment banking firm of George K. Baum is identified as the lead underwriter, duties that are sometimes shared with another underwriting firm.

None of those contracts are competitively bid, according to Bennett and Florida's State Division of Bond Finance.

However, exactly how much money was made remains unknown. That's because certain kinds of bond deals are subject to loopholes in state reporting requirements.

Thus, CAPFA's bond issue reports to Florida's Division of Bond Finance are spotty, omitting information about fees paid to financial advisers, attorneys, and underwriters.

Still, it's clear money was made.

Take the $300 million bond pool for the American Association of Airport Executives.

CAPFA, Public Finance Associates—the consulting firm headed by Bennett—underwriters, and a countless number of attorneys shared more than $2 million in fees.

In fact, some were able to earn commissions twice.

According to Bennett, Springfield city officials wanted to remarket their portion of the bonds. As a result, the city's portion of the bonds was reissued. The reissue generated an additional $317,000 for attorneys and underwriters.

The two airport bond issues alone generated more than $900,500 for the Baum firm, based on state records.

Much less clear is how much Moore Haven has made. Even the parties involved are confused.

Ogletree and other city officials look to Bennett for this information.

"I don't have that information, but [Zvara] should," says Bennett.

But, when asked, Zvara says Bennett should have the information on record.

Current estimates of the town's earnings run from $250,000 to $450,000—less than the $600,000 made by co–bond counsels Zvara and Squire, Sanders & Dempsey on the airport bond pool, according to the Division of Bond Finance.

Bennett and town officials say those fees will help finance the implementation of the town's long-term redevelopment plan.

To date, though, city officials can identify just two items funded with proceeds of bond fees.

One was a used fire engine. According to Moore Haven vice mayor Gerry Harris, the fire engine cost the town roughly $250,000.

But even with the proceeds of bond fees, Moore Haven did not buy the fire engine outright. It financed it.

The second project financed with bond fees was a new city park.

But again, the bond fees didn't completely foot the bill. While Moore Haven paid $25,000, that amount was supplemented by matching grants from Glades County and the state.

Even so, town officials are pleased with the outcome thus far.

"I wasn't sure about it at first, but once I got onto the board and saw what it was allowing the city to do, I was convinced," says Harris. "For most cities in Florida, buying a new fire truck is nothing, but here it means something."

Airline industry economics is complex and often inscrutable. Especially galling to travelers are the fares paid by different passengers for identical service. Steve Huettel of the *St. Petersburg Times* analyzed one flight between Tampa and Dallas to help readers better understand the industry-wide dilemma of trying to fill airplanes and make money at the same time.

Steve Huettel

Flight into the Red

TAMPA — CAPTAIN KRAIG BAUM was elated to see his jet filling up with customers for American Airlines' second flight of the day from Tampa to Dallas.

On slow days, he had flown with thirty or forty passengers in the MD-80—so few that most people could have an entire row to themselves. "It was pretty dismal," said Baum, a 17-year veteran of American.

But this sunny December day, nearly three out of four seats on American Airlines Flight 1225 were taken. The first-class cabin was nearly full. Nineteen passengers were flying on pricey full-fare tickets—four times as many as on the average November flight.

Yet, Flight 1225 was another money loser for American, the world's largest airline, which is burning through cash at a rate of $5 million a day.

Too many passengers bought bargain tickets for American to cover its costs for the routine flight connecting a large metropolitan area with its sprawling hub at Dallas–Fort Worth International Airport.

The deal was sweet for passengers such as Kathy Leggiero of Palm Harbor, who landed a $183 round-trip ticket to Kansas City just a week earlier.

But there just weren't enough passengers like Bob Guevremont of suburban Dallas, who had to drop everything to check on a break-in at his parents' Clearwater house and paid $453 the night before for a one-way trip back home.

Revenues fell short of the $13,500 American paid for the 928-mile trip, everything from $4.21 per passenger for food and drinks to $2,900 for the pilots and flight attendants. The airline lost $226.

The story of Flight 1225 explains in a nutshell how the airline industry got into such a financial mess. And a protracted war could push American and other carriers into bankruptcy.

It's a basic problem of supply and demand: too many seats and too few passengers willing to pay full-fare prices. During the last downturn a decade ago, carriers lost more than $13 billion. Since the September 11 terrorist attacks, airlines have lost $18 billion and project a loss of $10.7 billion more this year, counting the effects of a war with Iraq.

That's enough to wipe out the industry's cumulative profits since commercial aviation took wing at the end of World War II.

Ticket demand dropped as the economy weakened in early 2001. Then came the September 11 terrorist attacks. Higher security, insurance, and fuel costs followed. If the war drags on, airlines expect more red ink will flow as people cancel or postpone travel plans.

Economic ups and downs have long plagued commercial aviation. But some problems run deeper and could permanently reduce revenues for major hub-and-spoke airlines.

The expansion of low-fare carriers such as Southwest Airlines, Air-Tran, and JetBlue keep air fares in more and more cities in check. And the growth of travel web sites lets consumers browse thousands of fares, once the exclusive domain of airlines and travel agents.

American and other carriers are testing ways to fix maddeningly complicated fare structures and attract more high-paying business travelers. Their goal: cut the price of the full-fare tickets so more people fly instead of driving or doing business through teleconferencing.

With US Airways and United in Chapter 11 bankruptcy, and American a possible candidate to join them, major hub-and-spoke airlines have taken a knife to costs. Most are leaning on employee unions to cut labor costs, their biggest and fastest-growing expense.

How much worse is it now? The *St. Petersburg Times* looked at the same trip ten years earlier: American Flight 369 from Tampa to Dallas on September 29, 1992, flown with a similar aircraft during the last airline slump.

Flight 1225 cost American $1,100, or 8.8 percent, more to operate than that flight a decade ago. Certain expenses grew much faster. The cost of Flight 1225's crew was $2,900—45 percent higher than the airline paid for the crew of Flight 369.

Flight 1225 taxied away from Gate F77 at Tampa International Airport at 8:30 a.m. on December 11 with 95 passengers in 129 seats of the silver-skinned jet with red, white, and blue stripes down the sides.

Once airborne, coach travelers got a Quaker chewy granola bar. In first class, flight attendant Tina Regalado gave out all seven salsa omelets and served two other passengers cornflakes with mixed fruit.

Most people sipped juice or coffee or sodas. One had a Bloody Mary and two Bailey's Irish Cream liqueurs with coffee.

One in three passengers only went as far as Dallas–Fort Worth. The rest would catch connecting flights to two dozen different destinations, including Tokyo and Tucson, Oakland and Oklahoma City.

If each passenger paid $142.11 for the Tampa–Dallas leg, Flight 1225 would have broken even. But 33 coach passengers were flying on sale or web fares and paid an average of $62 for the flight.

Twelve had AAdvantage frequent-flier award tickets. American books $64 in revenue for each to reflect the amount credit card companies, hotels, and other companies pay for miles they give customers. Five American employees, retirees, or relatives paid only government fees and taxes.

Airlines usually pick up extra cash from what they carry in the plane's belly. But despite Tampa International's steady volume of air cargo—mostly farm-grown tropical fish and human remains—American shut down the local cargo terminal in 2000, saying it was unprofitable.

Carriers also are hurting from post–September 11 rules that prohibit them from accepting U.S. mail weighing more than 16 ounces.

American's diminished load of morning mail on December 11 all went on an earlier Dallas flight. So, the only revenue from the cargo holds on Flight 1225 was $100 that a passenger paid for an extra checked bag.

Still, Flight 1225 had one big advantage: lots of passengers like Wit Ostrenko, director of Tampa's Museum of Science and Industry. Fort Worth's Museum of Natural History hired him as a consultant and supplied a $1,063 full-fare coach ticket.

With businesses reining in travel costs, full-fare travelers are rare. Each time it took off in November, Flight 1225 carried an average of just more than four people paying full fare.

This day, 19 passengers flew on the pricey tickets and paid a combined $6,799. But when American added up revenues from the Tampa-Dallas leg of each passenger's ticket—a process that takes a month—even those big fares couldn't push Flight 1225 into the black.

"It was a good day," said Scott Nason, American's vice president for revenue management. "And we almost broke even."

So, why doesn't American just charge a few dollars more for each ticket?

Because the airline likely would end up losing money if any competitor didn't bump up its own price for the route, Nason said.

Say, for example, that American added $10 each way onto a $200 round-trip ticket and another carrier held firm on its price. That means American would need to get ten people to pay the higher fare to make up for each customer that left for the cheaper carrier.

"It's very easy to believe that at least one in ten people would flee from us because we're $10 more," Nason said. "The idea that we can charge more and be profitable is wrong."

That starts to explain why setting airline fares is such a delicate and complicated art. But filling up a plane with all kinds of different fares during nearly a year takes a computer called Odyssey.

Using historical data, Odyssey estimated how many people will buy tickets between various cities where American flies. The goal is to ensure seats are available for people like Bob Guevremont, the guy who bought the $453 one-way ticket home the night before Flight 1225 took off.

Depending on demand, Odyssey might limit the number of seats for Tampa-Dallas passengers on Flight 1225, keeping space for passengers taking more expensive connections.

"The worst thing would be to let the flight carry a local passenger and not let the Tampa-to-Tokyo passenger on," Nason said. "We want to hold enough seats for the full-fare passenger to Seattle, the full-fare passenger to San Francisco."

Meanwhile, American is continually tweaking fares for as many as twenty thousand combinations of cities where the airline flies. Revenue managers look at how much customers historically paid for each flight, then factor in recent trends and what competitors charge on the same routes.

They set a minimum price for each segment and sell tickets at fare categories that produce at least that amount. If the price for a Tampa-Dallas flight is $120 and for Dallas-Kansas City is $60, American will sell a Tampa-Kansas City ticket for $185 or more.

"Almost from scratch, we say every night, 'What is that seat worth?'" Nason said.

Fares almost always start low and get higher, although American never came close to selling all 140 tickets it could for Flight 1225. (Like all airlines, American oversells flights to compensate for people who cancel reservations or don't show up.)

Three months before Flight 1225, American sold just ten tickets—all at a deep discount. One week before the flight, only two of the 69 seats had been sold at full fare. That included a *Times* reporter's $854 Tampa-Dallas round-trip ticket.

The last seven days almost put Flight 1225 over the top. American filled three full-fare, first-class seats at an average of $476 each for the flight and 14 coach seats at an average of about $330.

But like fresh fruit or seafood, airline seats have a limited shelf life.

American wants to fill every possible seat before a flight leaves the gate. But not in a way that tips off travelers who might pay a high fare to look for bargains a few days before the trip.

So, the airlines sell cheap, last-minute tickets on the internet. American usually does this on "opaque" web sites such as Priceline and Hotwire, where customers can't pick a specific airline or route to their destination.

But specials also leak out elsewhere. A week before Flight 1225, Kathy Leggiero went on the internet to find a flight to Kansas City for a long weekend of scrapbooking and romantic movies with her best friend.

She checked three web sites and scored on Travelocity: a $186 round-trip ticket. "When you call the airlines, it's not as cheap," Leggiero said. "So why bother?"

But airline professionals worry that as more business travelers find bargains on the internet for personal trips, they become more outraged by sky-high full fares.

Returning home to suburban Dallas from a customer conference in Tampa, Microsoft salesman Paul Warren groused about his $520 ticket, which included a corporate discount. The only perk: two open seats beside him.

"I don't think they left them open for me," Warren groused. "But I am going to lie down on them."

Business travel fell off steeply in 2001 and hasn't bounced back, either in the number of passengers or how much they pay.

Companies increasingly shun full-fare tickets that are fully refundable, don't require Saturday night stays, and allow for upgrades to first class, said Kevin Mitchell of the Business Travel Coalition, which represents large buyers of business travel.

In 2000, his clients bought cheaper, nonrefundable tickets just 24 percent of the time. The share last year was 58 percent, he said, and airlines are recognizing the shift could continue after the economy recovers.

"The airlines did not expect to find such a falloff," Mitchell said. "Late last winter, they realized something was fundamentally wrong."

Some of their business switched to low-fare carriers. American's

Flight 1225 has to compete not only with Delta's nonstops from Tampa to Dallas but also with AirTran, which sells round-trip tickets as low as $258 and no higher than $658.

Passengers have to connect in Atlanta, making the trip a lot longer. It's a trade-off more and more businesses don't mind. They make full-fare, nonstop trips off-limits to all but certain top executives.

"The question is when the economy rebounds, will the number of people allowed to fly full-fare, nonstop grow a little or a lot?" Nason said.

In the meantime, American and competitors like Delta, United, and Continental are experimenting with simpler, lower fare structures to see if they stimulate more sales.

American cut full-fare coach rates in November by 40 percent in 23 domestic markets, including Tampa-Dallas. The top coach price dropped from $1,410 to $854.

But the lower fares still cover less than 1 percent of American's routes. The airline isn't ready to declare whether the test is a success, but it recently canceled the discount on all Tampa-Dallas flights.

Richard Halsall usually flies in the front of the plane. But the Airbus A300 captain for UPS is in the back of Flight 1225 this day, pontificating about the financial dilemma facing American and other big, traditional carriers.

In boom times, they've made money by soaking travelers who buy tickets shortly before the flight, Halsall says. But that formula doesn't work in slow times.

Big airlines can't ride out the bad times because of high fixed costs, such as aircraft payments, expensive hubs, and employee contracts that lock in salaries and benefits.

"That's why they adopted this ridiculous fare philosophy," Halsall says. "They're trying to distribute the profitability of this airplane among travelers willing to pay to book at the last minute."

The $13,500 American paid to fly Flight 1225 encompasses a wide range of expenses. The $2,400 in overhead costs includes a slice of the airline's advertising, corporate administration, and airport rental fees at Tampa International.

But the biggest single expense for the two-and-a-half-hour flight, American says, was $2,900 for the flight crew. That was $900 more than the airline paid for the crew of Flight 369 a decade earlier. And that crew had one more crew member: a navigator aboard the Boeing 727.

With nearly 2,600 daily flights, the numbers pile up fast. After targeting $2 billion in other expenses, American in February told unions it needed to cut $1.8 billion a year in salaries, benefits, and work rules to avoid filing for bankruptcy reorganization.

Captain Kraig Baum, the 53-year-old pilot of Flight 1225, has mixed feelings about the airline. He loves the company and his job. But after years of bitter union and company relations, he doubts the airline's financial condition is so dire. Baum and fellow pilots say it's not all their fault.

American wants employees to work more hours. The airline's pilots average only 39 hours of flying a month. At Southwest, pilots average 62 hours, considered the industry's most productive.

American blames restrictive work rules in the pilots' contract. Baum says the airline has about two thousand more pilots than it needs, including many reserve pilots on call to fill in for regulars who are sick or miss connections. Baum thinks pilots and other workers will end up accepting cuts.

Still, he doesn't understand how things went so bad, so fast. In late 2002, experts said American was among the industry's strongest carriers.

"To have the situation go 180 degrees to the point of going into bankruptcy, it's kind of mind-boggling," he says.

—Researcher John Martin contributed to this report.

Forty percent of the uninsured population in the U.S. is under the age of 25, as a weak economy keeps many young people on the fringes of the workforce. This story by Lucette Lagnado of *The Wall Street Journal* about an uninsured young woman who required emergency surgery dramatizes the inequities in current medical billing practices.

Lucette Lagnado

Full Price: A Young Woman, an Appendectomy, and a $19,000 Debt

NEW YORK—Dreams of a bright career in a big city lured Rebekah Nix here from the western plains of Texas two years ago. An appendectomy sent her home.

But not because she was ill. Ms. Nix, 25 years old, was fleeing the nearly $19,200 in medical bills that had piled up on her bedroom dresser. The college graduate and former magazine fact-checker couldn't fathom how two days in a hospital could cost so much, until she learned that people like her—who don't have health insurance—often are expected to pay far more for their medical care than large insurers, health-maintenance organizations, or even the U.S. government.

The hospital where Ms. Nix was treated, New York Methodist in Brooklyn, typically bills HMOs about $2,500 for an appendectomy with a two-day stay, compared with the $14,000—plus doctors' fees— that Ms. Nix was billed. The hospital gets paid about $5,000 from Medicaid, the state and federal health program for the poor, and about

$7,800 from Medicare, the federal program for the elderly, for the same procedure.

"Why does a single person get stuck with the whole bill?" Ms. Nix asks. "An uninsured person would have a lot less money than those government agencies or insurance companies."

Ms. Nix stumbled onto a troubling fact of health care economics: Most major U.S. hospitals are required to set official "charges" for their services, but then agree to discount or even ignore those charges when getting paid by big institutions such as insurance companies or the government. As a result, almost no one but uninsured individuals ever faces the official charges. In some ways, hospital charges are like automobile "list prices" or hotel "rack rates"—posted prices that everybody knows nobody pays. But in the case of hospitals, the pricing disparity isn't publicly known and falls most heavily on the vulnerable. America's 41 million people without health insurance tend to be young, working-class, and unaware that they are being billed more than everyone else for the same services.

At the same time, charges at virtually all hospitals have soared in recent years. That's partly due to the rising costs of new procedures and drugs. Also, deregulation of the hospital industry removed limits on charges in almost all states. But some hospitals say they are raising charges to offset what they view as overly harsh reductions in their reimbursements by HMOs, insurers, and the government. That would mean hospitals are effectively subsidizing their lower income from patients who are insured or have a government safety net by boosting fees paid by the uninsured.

"It is a reflection of the insanity of the system," says Bruce Vladeck, a hospital policy expert who ran Medicare in the 1990s. "The most vulnerable members of society" are being asked to "pay cash at list."

In many areas, hospitals have cranked up their charges far beyond the cost of providing treatment. Before deregulation in 1997, hospital charges in New York state couldn't be more than 30 percent above costs. They now are an average of 87 percent above costs, says the Greater New York Hospital Association, an industry trade group, citing federal data. In California, charges have ballooned to 178 percent above costs. By contrast, in Maryland, where hospital charges are still strictly regulated, charges average only 28 percent above costs, says Hal Cohen, a Maryland health consultant.

At many hospitals, the practice of cutting prices for big insurers, HMOs, and the government has become so routine that the discount is calculated automatically and appears on bills alongside the original charge. The amount of the discount usually depends on how aggressively a particular insurer bargained with the hospital, or on terms struck with a government program, or how much other hospitals in the area are discounting. But uninsured patients aren't told that big institutions get these reduced rates. Some hospitals then retain collection agencies to pursue the uninsured with hard-nosed tactics such as suing, garnisheeing wages, and slapping liens on homes.

"Hospitals have a choice as to who will bear the costs," says Elizabeth Warren, a Harvard Law School professor who is studying the effects of health care costs on the uninsured. "There is someone to negotiate on behalf of the insurance companies. There is someone to negotiate on behalf of the state. . . . But there is no one to negotiate on behalf of people without insurance."

Hospitals say they have no choice but to give steep discounts to powerful payers, even if that means uninsured patients end up being faced with higher bills. Mark Mundy, president and chief executive of New York Methodist, says his private, not-for-profit hospital looks to competitors in setting its charges, and must offer discounts to HMOs and insurers or they won't do business with it. As for the government, it pays whatever it wants. "Pricing makes no sense, we all know that," Mr. Mundy says.

Hospitals also point out that most uninsured patients don't pay their bills—the rate of default varies across the country—yet hospitals are required by law to treat all emergencies. "Anybody that shows up in my ER, the first question isn't, 'Can they pay?' The question is, 'What are we going to do to care for them?'" Mr. Mundy says. "If I had five thousand Ms. Nixes, how do I handle them and keep this place alive?" Mr. Mundy says many uninsured patients, especially those who aren't indigent, could afford insurance and should bear at least some responsibility for their care. He adds that New York Methodist, unlike many hospitals, doesn't charge interest on unpaid bills.

Advocates for the uninsured say poor people without insurance should be charged the same low rates that Medicaid pays. Instead, they are asked to pay "what the Emir of Kuwait pays," says Elisabeth Benjamin, a health attorney with the Legal Aid Society in New York. Royalty and other wealthy foreigners flock to U.S. hospitals, where they're among the few uninsured patients who can afford to pay full freight.

Ms. Nix's billing problems started on a Saturday afternoon last April when she arrived in agony at New York Methodist. The previous night, she had felt stabbing pains in her abdomen while celebrating her twenty-fifth birthday with friends at a Manhattan bar. She had left early, staggered home to Brooklyn, and gone to bed figuring she had food poisoning or the flu. When she awoke to the same unrelenting pain, her boyfriend's mother, a registered nurse, insisted she go to the nearest hospital. As she sat in a hard metal chair in the emergency room, she began to worry: How much was this going to cost?

Ms. Nix had arrived in New York a little less than two years earlier, fresh from graduating Phi Beta Kappa from Southwestern University in Georgetown, Texas. Growing up in Midland, Texas, she saw her hometown as a "desolate wasteland" where social gatherings often revolved around high school football. Her ticket out was a summer internship at *Ms.* magazine in Manhattan, which she loved. "This is the greatest city to be young in," she says. "I had no intention of ever leaving."

But the internship paid just $150 a month. Ms. Nix helped support herself by working as a waitress while sharing a basement apartment that cost her $350 a month in rent. The magazine soon hired Ms. Nix as a full-time fact-checker with an annual salary of $30,000 and health benefits. But it was struggling financially, and Ms. Nix was laid off after the September 11 terrorist attacks. The magazine, as required by law, offered to maintain her health insurance if she paid $330 a month, but Ms. Nix demurred. She figured she couldn't afford it on unemployment payments of $1,122 a month, and thought she could land another job with benefits. Besides, she thought, she was young and had always been healthy.

In the months before her illness, she tried offering her fact-checking services as a freelancer, but jobs were sporadic. She was determined to be independent, so she didn't want to tell her divorced parents that she'd lost health coverage. Her mother, who runs a small medical-supply business she founded near Midland, might have been able to help. Her father, an independent oil consultant, struggles financially. By going without coverage, Ms. Nix became one of the estimated 39 percent of uninsured Americans who are between the ages of 19 and 34, according to the Kaiser Commission on Medicaid and the Uninsured in Washington.

In the emergency room at New York Methodist, someone asked her to collect a urine sample in a paper cup. She kept it at her side for six hours, until at last she was admitted to the clinical area of the emergency room and asked to wait on a gurney. Ms. Nix remembers telling nurses and doctors that she had no money and no insurance. No one seemed to mind, she says. Still, she'd heard horror stories about how costly a hospital could be and decided to try to leave as soon as possible.

When she woke up on Sunday morning, she was still on the emergency-room gurney, and the pain seemed to have subsided. "Maybe I am going to go home," she told a doctor. "I don't have health insurance." According to Ms. Nix, the doctor responded: "It is $1,000 to come to the ER, and it is another $1,000 to come in again." Ms. Nix resigned herself to staying. But while undergoing two CT scans, she recalls telling doctors, "I don't want any extras."

Tests confirmed she had appendicitis. Her surgeon, Piotr Gorecki, removed her appendix using laparoscopy, a method that requires a shorter hospital stay than traditional invasive surgery. The one-hour surgery went smoothly. Ms. Nix was recovering in her room when an attending doctor ordered that she be given a nicotine patch. She regularly used one to control a smoking habit, but she balked at it now, worried about the cost. The doctor insisted, she says.

Ms. Nix left the hospital on Monday afternoon, 42 hours after being admitted. She had a prescription for painkillers but decided not to fill it because of the expense. She also decided to skip a follow-up visit that Dr. Gorecki had recommended. Two weeks later, she received a letter from the hospital offering advice on how she could apply for Medicaid. The letter also gave the first hint as to how much she would be billed: "Note: Hospital bill is $12,973."

In mid-June, she learned that Medicaid had turned her down because her income was too high. New York's Medicaid rules say a single person's income can't exceed $352 a month, unless she's certified as disabled. The hospital urged Ms. Nix to appeal at a hearing before a state administrative law judge, and she arranged to do so.

In July, Ms. Nix received her hospital bill. It showed charges for two days at $1,550 a day, even though she spent the first night on the emergency-room gurney. It also listed operating-room charges of $5,340, a charge of $540 for the recovery room, and a charge of $850 for the emergency room. Every test administered in the emergency room was charged separately. Her two CT scans together came in at $2,120. One charge, which showed up in a more detailed bill, brought a wan smile to her face: $8 for the nicotine patch. Lyn Hill, a spokeswoman for New York Methodist, says Ms. Nix was admitted at 10 p.m. Saturday and remained through Monday, so it was appropriate to charge her for two nights, regardless of where she slept.

The total: $13,110. Soon after, she received $5,000 in separate bills from Dr. Gorecki, an anesthesiologist, and other doctors who had seen her at Methodist. Much like hospitals, some doctors also routinely accept lower payments from insurers, HMOs, and government programs. Dr. Gorecki, whose charge to Ms. Nix was $2,500, says Medicare typically pays him only $589 for a laparoscopic appendectomy, and Medicaid usually pays an even skimpier $160. The New York Health Plan Association, an HMO trade group in Albany, New York, says Brooklyn surgeons get an average of $600 for a laparoscopic appendectomy.

Ms. Nix's bank account held less than $2,000. She tossed some of the bills on her dresser, unopened, and tried not to think about the debt. But often she could think of nothing else. "I knew that I was going to be in major trouble financially," she says.

Her last hope was the Medicaid hearing, which was held on a sweltering July morning at the city's Medicaid headquarters. The building was jammed with applicants standing in lines and sitting in rows of plastic chairs, waiting to see caseworkers. Judge Michael Vass sat at a desk facing Ms. Nix. She recalls his telling her: Your case "is bad, but there are people who come in here and they have cancer and they make too much for Medicaid. Unless you are over 65 or under 18 or deaf or blind, you are not going to get Medicaid." Ms. Nix burst into tears.

She wasn't sure what to do. Her parents offered conflicting advice.

Her mother, whose work has familiarized her with the medical system, told Ms. Nix to get tough with the hospital and negotiate a deal to pay a few dollars a month. Her father told her she should repay the debt she'd incurred, whatever the hardship. Without Methodist's care, he reminded her, she could have died.

In late August, a new hospital bill arrived, listing the total amount due as $14,182. The hospital had added an additional charge of $1,072 earmarked for the Bad Debt and Charity Care Pool, a state fund that compensates hospitals for caring for the uninsured. Ms. Nix was stunned by the irony. "Tack on another grand I can't pay, but use it to help someone else!" she says.

The inequity in health care pricing is rooted in a policy that was designed to prevent it. Rules dating back to the establishment of Medicare in the 1960s require hospitals participating in the program to set uniform charges for all procedures. The idea was to prevent hospitals from charging some classes of patients, such as Medicare beneficiaries, more than others. Hospitals were free to set charges—typically kept on voluminous lists called charge masters—as they wished, depending on costs, local competition, and state regulatory limits.

In the early years of the program, charges roughly correlated to hospitals' costs plus a modest profit, and reimbursements closely tracked charges. Then, in the mid-1980s, Medicare started pegging most payments to standardized diagnostic codes rather than to hospitals' charges. As HMOs became more powerful in the late 1980s and early 1990s, they negotiated their own rates with hospitals.

Ms. Nix contacted the hospital and the doctors who had worked on her, seeking a break. Dr. Gorecki, the surgeon, immediately slashed his fee to $1,000 from $2,500—a break he often gives to the uninsured. Ms. Nix says she has sent him two checks for $20 each. The hospital was somewhat less obliging. It offered to reduce her bill by 20 percent. Ms. Nix says the hospital demanded that she agree to pay within a month or two, but Ms. Hill, the New York Methodist spokeswoman, says the hospital gave Ms. Nix a full year to pay. Under those terms, she would have faced monthly payments greater than $900 a month.

Ms. Hill says three or four uninsured inpatients a month, out of an average of about ninety uninsured inpatients treated, call with concerns about their bills, and they are routinely offered a 20 percent discount off charges before the bill is assigned to a collection agency. Even so, Ms. Hill says, uninsured patients "almost never pay." New York Methodist says that it racked up $50 million last year in "bad debt and charity care," or about 14 percent of its annual budget.

However, those figures are based on the hospital's charges, not its costs. Also, the hospital is able to mitigate some of these losses by tapping into the New York Bad Debt and Charity Care pool. In 2001, the latest year for which figures are available, Methodist collected $13 million to $14 million from the pool. A state health department spokesman says the pool on average reimburses hospitals for their costs at about 50 cents to 70 cents on the dollar.

On October 21, Ms. Nix sent a letter to the hospital. "I understand that I am indebted to Methodist hospital," she wrote. "The staff was so kind to me during my stay." But noting that her bills for the surgery totaled nearly $19,200, she wrote: "This is more money than I will make this year, almost twice as much." She added: "I do not wish to pay nothing for the life-saving services I received," but she said she couldn't pay what Methodist wanted. She had consulted bankruptcy lawyers and was considering returning to Texas.

The hospital didn't respond to the letter. Ms. Nix soon started telling shocked friends that she was leaving. On November 5, she stuffed everything she could into two suitcases and flew home on a ticket her mom had given her.

After *The Wall Street Journal* contacted New York Methodist about Ms. Nix, the hospital told her it would reduce her bill to $5,000—essentially what Medicaid would have paid, says Methodist's Ms. Hill. The hospital also said it would give Ms. Nix one year to pay, provided she pay $3,000 up front, which she has yet to do. She says she hopes to start paying the hospital back within a year.

In Midland, she has taken over her younger brother's old bedroom. Life is slower, and she has gone to some high school football games. "I miss the glamour of the city," she says. For the past few months, she has been working part-time at her mother's medical-supply firm, where she earns $7 an hour for filing and filling out forms. She also has been doing unpaid research for her father. Her mother's company couldn't offer her health benefits because they were too expensive to provide. Two weeks ago, Ms. Nix finally purchased health insurance.

BEHIND THE BILL: WHO PAYS WHAT

Hospitals are required to list official charges for all procedures. But big players such as HMOs, insurance companies, and the government routinely negotiate or demand big discounts. Uninsured patients are almost always faced with full charges. Below, a sampling of charges and discounts for a relatively common procedure: a diagnostic bilateral mammogram.

Hospital (Location)	Official Charge	Medicaid	Medicare	HMOs, Health Plans	Policy on Uninsured
UCLA Medical Center (Los Angeles)	$460	$127	$90	Up to $242	Gives discounts based on individual's ability to pay, says CFO Sergio Melgar
Oregon Health & Science University (Portland)	$240	$65	$59	Average $128	Works with uninsured patients to help them find financial aid; offers sliding scales, payment plans
Jamaica Hospital (Queens, N.Y.)	$351	$50	$96	$40 to $78	Has sliding fee scales for uninsured, says CEO David Rosen
Johns Hopkins Hospital & Health System (Baltimore)	$261	$156	$173	$186	State regulation of charges reduces disparity between bills to insured and uninsured
Grinnell Regional Medical Center (Grinnell, Iowa)	$258	$73	$79	$119 to $190	Works with uninsured to set a payment schedule

Note: Charge includes hospital and physician fees.
Source: the hospitals

When Arthur Andersen accounting closed its doors, it ended a history that began with a solid reputation for getting the numbers right. It finished with a reputation for favoring consulting dollars above all else and a felony conviction for obstructing a federal investigation into Enron. These two articles from a series by the *Chicago Tribune*'s Delroy Alexander, Greg Burns, Robert Manor, Flynn McRoberts, and E. A. Torriero, describe the firm's early years and the conflict between auditing and consulting.

Delroy Alexander, Greg Burns, Robert Manor, Flynn McRoberts, and E. A. Torriero

The Fall of Andersen

TRADING HIS CUSTOMARY DARK SUIT for a pair of jeans, Mike Gagel trudged over pallet after pallet of multicolored bricks in the central Ohio storage yard. The summer heat was stifling as he counted once, then twice. Something was wrong.

Arthur Andersen, the prestigious Chicago accounting firm, had sent the eager young auditor for a routine task: to certify the inventory of a million bricks baking in the sun near Marion. But each time Gagel counted the pallets, he came up 100,000 bricks short.

At first, the factory owner reacted angrily when Gagel confronted him with his findings. He grabbed the phone and asked Gagel's boss why he had sent such a rookie.

The boss told Gagel to count the bricks again. On his third pass, Gagel once again counted 900,000 bricks; only this time, the owner checked into the discrepancy. He discovered that a plant manager had been ripping him off, secretly selling truckloads of bricks out of the back gate at night.

Gagel's brickyard math is a classic example of the vigilance that made the name Arthur Andersen the gold standard of the accounting profession for decades. But the incident occurred in 1969, and it, like Andersen's reputation, is history.

On Saturday, a firm that once stood for trust and accountability ended ninety years as an auditor of publicly traded companies under a cloud of scandal and shame. Its felony conviction for obstructing a federal investigation into Enron Corp., its now-notorious client, cost Andersen the heart of its practice. It will continue with a tiny fraction of the 85,000 employees it spread across the globe just months ago.

Andersen's leaders have portrayed the firm as the innocent victim of overzealous prosecutors and a dishonest client. But a close examination of Andersen's collapse reveals a very different story.

In the 1990s, the firm embarked on a path that valued hefty fees ahead of bluntly honest bookkeeping, eroding Andersen's good name.

Andersen shunted aside accountants who failed to adapt to the firm's new direction. In their place, Andersen promoted a slicker breed who could turn modestly profitable auditing assignments into consulting gold mines.

Repeatedly, Andersen rewarded those involved with the firm's most troubled clients, while guardians of the company's legacy, like Gagel, were shown the door.

In an early-'90s purge, the new leaders forced out roughly one of every ten auditing partners and neutered Andersen's elite corps of in-house ethics watchdogs, who for decades had been the firm's final word on accounting matters large and small. These moves drew scant public attention, but the implications reached far beyond Andersen's headquarters at 33 W. Monroe St. The quiet dilution of standards and the rise of auditor-salesmen at Andersen are central to the scandals that have cost investors billions of dollars, eliminated thousands of jobs, and threatened the retirement security of millions of citizens. Most of all, they have cast suspicion over the financial reports that Americans rely on to judge the health of companies where they work and invest.

As the firm spiraled down during the past year, its leaders contended that conflicts between its auditing and consulting missions had no impact on the quality of its work. And they said Enron should be viewed as an aberration, not part of a disturbing pattern.

To determine how the firm fell so far, so fast, the *Tribune* reviewed volumes of Andersen internal documents, sworn testimony, and congressional hearings. *Tribune* reporters also interviewed scores of Andersen employees—from senior partners to secretaries—as well as federal investigators and industry insiders across a dozen states.

Contrary to Andersen's assertions, what emerges is a cautionary tale, the story of a firm that tried to mix the public interest of an auditing mission with a mercenary consulting culture and botched the job. Even as many of its partners and staff continued to uphold a high standard, others compromised in the interest of generating fees.

"It came down to doing the job as quickly as possible and making the most money. They pushed the edge of the envelope—pushed it too far," said Dean Christensen, who ran Andersen's Columbus, Ohio, office for more than 15 years. "I just think it got out of control. What it ended up being is greed. Total greed."

Andersen's remaining leadership disputed that the firm emphasized the selling of services over audit quality, replacing partners who were strong auditors but didn't generate enough revenue.

"Not true," said Andersen spokesman Patrick Dorton, in a written response. "Work performance and commitment to quality have always been an essential part of our evaluation. No one has ever been dismissed because of their commitment to quality, but personnel have been dismissed for an inadequate commitment to quality."

Neither Dorton nor any other current Andersen official would address what caused the fall of the firm, or whether its own actions contributed to its collapse.

Andersen and other audit firms are supposed to be guardians of the public trust, functioning like the father confessors of the financial world. They know the rules and how to enforce them, defining right and wrong for the corporate flock. If an accounting firm puts its name on a financial statement, it certifies to the public that the company is playing by the rules, and that the numbers conform to minimum standards of conduct.

Consultants, by contrast, are the corporate apostles of change. Few ever got rich advising clients to remain the same. Instead, they battle the status quo, challenging the accepted ways of doing business and offering to fix the problems they identify. At Andersen, that involved selling everything from computer systems to management advice.

The two roles rarely mix well—a fact Arthur Andersen himself warned about as far back as the Great Depression. "To preserve the integrity of the reports, the accountant must insist upon absolute independence of judgment and action," he said in a lecture on ethics at Northwestern University's School of Commerce.

In practice, that meant Andersen sought to always put consulting at the service of auditing. In recent years, however, that principle got turned on its head.

"The culture changed where the auditor was no longer the guy people respected in the '80s and '90s," former Andersen chief executive Harvey Kapnick said in an interview last month, just days before his August 16 death.

Kapnick left Andersen's top job in 1979 after he unsuccessfully sought to address government concerns about conflicts of interest by splitting the audit and consulting practices. "If you were an auditor," he observed, "you were relegated to second-class status. If you were a consultant, you were the top of the heap."

Andersen officials disagree. "Our audit practice, until recently, was the largest component of our business and a critical part of the firm's business strategy and its profitability," said spokesman Dorton.

Through the 1990s, though, Andersen aggressively sold lucrative consulting services to those who relied on them for audits in what turned out to be a profitable strategy. Andersen's top partners tripled their earnings in the '90s, a feat that put them on a par with their Andersen consulting siblings, who had split into their own division in 1989.

But the new strategy also planted the seeds of the firm's downfall.

Suddenly, partners who faced accounting dilemmas with clients had a lot more at stake when deciding whether to reject questionable practices uncovered in audits.

The fallout from those decisions has unfolded in the headlines about shredded documents, restated earnings, shady loans, and financial sleight of hand at Enron, WorldCom Inc., and Waste Management Inc., all Andersen clients beset by accounting scandals.

"THINK STRAIGHT, TALK STRAIGHT"

The story of Andersen—how it went from the self-righteous preacher of the profession to the auditor who couldn't say no—started in 1913, when the son of Norwegian immigrants set up shop on West Monroe Street in Chicago with his partner, Clarence DeLany.

Arthur Andersen's mother had schooled him in a Scandinavian axiom—"Think straight, talk straight"—and he believed a firm that didn't sugarcoat its opinions could earn the respect of clients.

At the time, the accounting profession was dominated by a few big houses with London roots. Andersen wanted to set his firm apart by making money beyond routine bookkeeping. When he sat down to craft the announcement of his firm's opening on December 1, 1913, Andersen also promised to provide "the designing and installing of new systems of financial and cost accounting and organization."

But he insisted that without integrity, the firm would never grow to rival the London behemoths.

Andersen set the tone on a day in 1914 when a railroad executive burst into his cramped reception area, demanding that Andersen bless his corporate ledger. In a distant foreshadowing of WorldCom, the railroad man had inflated his profits by failing to properly record day-to-day expenses.

What followed would be recited to thousands of the firm's trainees for decades to come: Andersen shot back that there was not enough money in the city of Chicago to make him approve the bad bookkeeping.

The small firm lost its big client, but the railroad went bankrupt a few months later, vindicating Andersen and establishing a reputation for independent thinking that would lead to decades of prosperity. Indeed, time and again, Andersen accountants would take bold stands on arcane accounting issues that would anger clients while making Andersen the auditor investors could trust.

No one exemplified the Andersen brand of stern independence more than Leonard Spacek, who succeeded Arthur Andersen after the founder's death in 1947. The firebrand Spacek honed the firm's sense of itself as the financial world's answer to the Marine Corps.

"Everyone should make it a habit to be busy all the time and avoid any appearance of being inactive or unoccupied," he wrote to the Chicago office in 1954. "When walking in the halls, walk briskly."

Spacek's obsession was creating a firm that spoke with a single voice, and that vision had its own iconography: the sturdy set of mahogany doors in Andersen's Chicago headquarters. To him, they represented "confidentiality, privacy, security, and orderliness." Soon, virtually every floor of every Andersen office featured identical doors.

Spacek took his crusade to the tight fraternity of the accounting industry as well.

William Hall, an Andersen accountant who went on to become one of its top ethics watchdogs, remembers learning that firsthand during a 1957 train ride with Spacek in a Chicago-to-Milwaukee parlor car.

"I've got here a blockbuster that I'm going to be delivering tonight," he told Hall, waving a sheaf of papers in the air and sitting down next to the young audit manager. Spacek let him read the speech he would soon deliver to his accounting industry peers, and Hall was impressed by its challenging tone.

Two decades after the Depression ushered in the nation's first modern-day accounting rules, standards had become "a fairyland" for investors, Spacek told the group of corporate controllers gathered in Milwaukee on that winter evening. The railroad industry's bookkeeping was "so bad," and its influence over the debate so pervasive, that no honest principles could be established, he charged.

Peering at the crowd through his thick, horn-rimmed glasses, he asked, "Is our profession so impressed with its ivory tower position in the public mind that we are not hearing these basic criticisms of our work?" Spacek went on to propose an accounting court that would decide once and for all the fair and accurate method for crunching the numbers.

Spacek's tirade had broken the rules of his clubby profession, and leaders of the other major firms decided to pay him back. First, they tried throwing him off a key oversight panel that he had accused of kowtowing to clients. Failing that, they tried unsuccessfully to pull his license for "making comments derogatory to the profession."

By the time he moved from managing partner to chairman in 1963, Andersen was a global enterprise with such heavyweight clients as Walgreens and United Airlines, Occidental Petroleum and Colgate-Palmolive. It had 27 foreign offices and thousands of staffers, up from three hundred when Spacek joined the firm in 1928. His uncompromising reputation attracted clients who believed rigorous auditing would pay off in the long run.

Gagel was among hundreds of bright college graduates the fast-growing firm was recruiting each year. He went through basic training in 1969, staying at the Allerton Hotel on North Michigan Avenue for three weeks to have the Andersen way drilled into him.

At the time, the firm's training guru was a tall, distinguished-looking Texan named Carl Bohne Jr. Partners from Andersen's various field offices ran the training sessions, but Bohne kept a hammerlock on what they passed on to new employees: Each of the presentations had to be rehearsed in front of him.

No detail was left untouched in the effort to standardize how work was done from office to office and country to country. How to do an audit. How to document it. Even what notations had to be used on the final audit reports. The philosophy behind the minutiae was equally consistent. "What you were selling was your opinion," Gagel said. "And if you ever cheapened it or if you gave it away, you lost your birthright as a professional."

Gagel donned the corporate uniform. By the late 1960s, employees no longer had to wear felt hats in winter and straw hats in summer, but conservative suits and white shirts still were expected.

Anyone who didn't hew to that look stuck out. Christensen, Gagel's boss in Columbus, was dubbed Prince Valiant because he sported long sideburns in the 1970s. But like all other Andersen partners, Christensen conformed to the firm's obsessive push to speak with a unified voice.

The keepers of that common culture were a small group of Andersen's most experienced and technically astute partners, which eventually became known as the Professional Standards Group. These ethical sticklers defined Andersen's positions on hundreds of complicated accounting issues, from leasing transactions to depreciation rules.

By the time Gagel joined the firm, the group was headed by George Catlett, whose office was never more than 50 feet away from the head of the firm. At lunchtime, the group's handpicked partners often would assemble at their regular table in the Midday Club atop the First National Bank Building in Chicago's Loop.

They would dig into the usual club sandwiches and iced tea as they steered Andersen through a minefield of laws, regulations, and ethical issues. They made no secret of their high opinions of themselves, but they backed up their self-importance with the clout befitting those who wrote the rules.

"WHO MADE YOU GOD?"

In the late 1970s, companies were snapping up the latest in computer hardware—IBM 360 mainframes. Many were deducting the cost of the machines over a ten-year period.

Then Andersen decided that those computers were obsolete after only five years, so companies would need to spread the cost over the shorter term, which cut into profits. Any company assuming their 360s had an unrealistically long life would get an "adverse" opinion—a red flag to alert investors to potential problems.

Andersen's competitors couldn't believe it. Touche Ross, a rival auditor, had a number of clients with 360s who were writing them off over the longer period. So when word of Andersen's unilateral decision reached them, Touche Ross partners looked at each other and said, "Now what do we do?" recalled Bob Sack, a former partner at Touche Ross who later became chief accounting officer for the SEC's enforcement division.

"They did it without talking to anybody, by themselves," said Sack, now an instructor at the University of Virginia's Darden School of Business. "Andersen effectively set the standard for everyone else to follow.

"In my heart of hearts, I admired them for doing it, because you knew when they went to a client and made that statement, they'd say, 'Who made you God?' Well, Spacek did."

About the same time, a similar spat erupted when the banking industry sought accounting relief from bad loans, arguing that their books needn't take a hit when troubled debtors stopped paying interest.

Art Wyatt, an accounting-principles expert at Andersen, testified to the absurdity of that idea at a tense session of the Financial Accounting Standards Board, the industry's private rule-setting agency. Afterward, an ex-partner from a rival firm stopped him and asked if he realized that Andersen's banking clients surely would dump Andersen.

"We reach our conclusions," Wyatt told him, "and this is our testimony." In the end, no clients fled, and the accounting world years later adopted Andersen's standard on bank loans.

Andersen, in those days, also would walk away from clients based on risk—a policy rooted in a lawsuit filed by angry investors of a former Andersen client. The suit had threatened to wipe out about $80 million, a year's worth of profits.

The firm eventually settled out of court for an undisclosed sum. But that experience in the 1980s—with an oil-and-gas investment venture, Fund of Funds, which had failed back in 1969—persuaded Andersen to take a fresh look at auditing fast-growing businesses.

It began ranking clients according to a complex formula that determined their potential to go bankrupt. Soon, Andersen was shedding those it decided were too likely to drag it into court.

When the savings and loan crisis started unfolding in the 1980s, Andersen partner Bob Kralovetz recognized that "an accident was going to happen." As head of the thrift practice for Andersen, based in Dallas, Kralovetz watched nervously as real estate prices spiraled upward. He spotted the inherent risk in a bubble that would decimate the institutions' loan portfolios once it burst.

Without hesitation, Kralovetz recalled, the firm's leaders decided to drop some of its hottest clients. One was Lincoln Savings & Loan, run by Charles Keating, who was furious about the auditor's decision.

Keating's Lincoln thrift provided roughly 20 percent of the revenues at Andersen's Phoenix office. He first turned to Arthur Young, and later Touche Ross, which bid aggressively for the business Andersen had dumped.

Three years after Andersen ditched Keating in 1986, the thrift collapsed, along with much of the S&L industry, as Andersen had feared.

The failure of Keating's empire cost taxpayers some $2.5 billion. Although Andersen paid damages to investors and regulators for its early role in the Keating account, Arthur Young paid much more.

A HIGHER CALLING

It wasn't just technical rulings and intuition that secured Andersen's reputation. It was so-called line partners like Mike Gagel in Columbus who stood up to clients day in and day out, upholding the strict standards established by the firm's brain trust in Chicago.

During this era, Gagel's career flourished. He was a brilliant auditor, versatile enough to master the accounting details of different industries when other partners specialized in a single client.

Gagel, 59, still sings bass in the choir at St. Brendan's Catholic Church just outside Columbus. Self-effacing and laconic, he is not the sort of person others surround at cocktail parties. But what he lacks in pizzazz, he makes up for in integrity, say friends and colleagues.

He always saw his chosen profession as a higher calling. "You're responsible to the shareholders, not the management," he said.

It was the way Gagel had operated since his youth in a crossroads town of western Ohio called Maria Stein, where he kept the books at his father's hardware store.

Gagel's technical skills served him well for much of his time at Andersen as he and his wife raised three girls in Upper Arlington, a prosperous suburb close to Columbus's downtown. He made his reputation the way Arthur Andersen himself had, as an auditor of public utilities.

But by the time Gagel arrived at Andersen, the firm had moved well beyond simply auditing corporate books. The business world's embrace of computers presented Andersen with a special opportunity to expand, albeit at potential risk to the independence of its core business.

Andersen's computer-consulting experience started outside Louisville in 1954, when a fleet of delivery trucks rolled down the driveway of General Electric Co.'s state-of-the-art appliance plant.

Their 30-ton cargo included more than five thousand glass vacuum tubes, along with enough steel and wire to fill a ballroom. Put it all together, and it formed a single computer. GE had paid an outlandish $1.2 million for its Univac I and was counting on a 40-year-old engineer from Andersen to make the machine do its stuff.

Watching those trucks arrive that January day, Joseph Glickauf Jr. could hardly believe he had convinced his cautious partners to back this venture into the unknown.

Glickauf had built his own portable version of the mysterious "counting machine," taking it on the road to win over skeptics at Andersen's regional offices. He would ask the assembled auditors to start counting along with the flashing lights of his "Glickiac," as it was nicknamed, then crank up the speed. At six hundred calculations a second, the computer beat the bean counters every time.

Spacek, the powerhouse successor to the firm's founder, recognized the potential. He had wooed Glickauf from a research job in the navy to form the firm's three-person administrative services team—the forerunner of its mighty consulting arm. GE was one of the world's first businesses to use a computer, and Andersen became a systems-consulting pioneer.

Even then, Spacek knew the conflict between auditing and consulting could imperil the firm's reputation. Each month as the GE project slowly ground along, Glickauf would fly from Louisville for a private dinner with the boss at the Chicago Athletic Club.

"Don't go overboard," Spacek would tell Glickauf over broiled pompano in the dark confines of the club along Michigan Avenue. "Don't do anything that could possibly influence an audit."

Two decades would pass before Andersen had to confront the full force of such dilemmas. By the early 1970s, American business was clamoring for computers to make itself more efficient. Andersen's consulting arm, expert at computer technology, exploded.

Even smaller accounting firms were scrambling to broaden their work with clients, because audit revenue was stagnant. But the issue held particular interest for Andersen since, by then, nonaudit work provided nearly a third of its revenues.

That was far more than any other Big Eight competitor at the time, largely because Andersen had developed its expertise in computer systems so much earlier.

The Securities and Exchange Commission was concerned how consulting was becoming the main growth business of accounting firms, especially Andersen, said Harold M. Williams, chairman of the SEC from 1977 to 1981.

"I was uncomfortable and concerned that the level of nonaudit services could compromise the independence of the audit," Williams said.

So the SEC proposed a new requirement. When a company went to its shareholders each year to approve the choice of auditors, it would have to disclose the amount and percentage of the auditor's fees that came from consulting.

By 1979, 42 percent of Andersen's $645 million in worldwide fees came from consulting and tax work, as opposed to accounting and auditing. In the U.S., the proportion was greater: More than half its income came from nonaudit services, according to Kapnick, then chairman of the firm.

Andersen's consulting division "was worth a ton of money," Kapnick said, "but it was almost too successful."

Armed with such concerns at the annual partners' meeting that fall, Kapnick declared that he wanted to turn "one great firm into two great firms."

He called for spinning off the fast-growing systems-consulting practice into a separate but related firm, initially headed by him. He sold the idea by suggesting that SEC officials soon would require such a split because of conflict-of-interest concerns.

Like a politician certain he had the votes to win, Kapnick confidently entered the partnership meeting inside a ballroom of the Marriott hotel on North Michigan Avenue. But when he made the proposal from the dais, other senior partners rose to oppose it. The usually staid annual meeting erupted.

Kapnick quickly discovered that Andersen—still dominated by its audit division—wasn't about to let go of its lucrative consulting arm.

On October 14, 1979, he convened a special meeting of the board and stepped down as chairman and chief executive. Not long after, the SEC backed away from its proposed rule requiring disclosure of the consulting interests of auditors. Kapnick's departure sank any thought of splitting the auditing and consulting divisions—at least for a while.

By that time, the firm had grown to more than one thousand partners and eighteen thousand staffers, nearly all through hiring and training its own people rather than through mergers.

As Andersen expanded, so did its influence on the rest of corporate America, not just through its auditing and consulting contracts but by becoming a breeding ground for financial executives and government officials.

The nation's comptroller general, David Walker, was an Andersen partner before he became the nation's chief accountability officer in 1998. A former Andersen CEO runs Unisys Corp.

For nearly thirty years, Andersen employees who audited Waste Management's books could look forward to careers at the trash hauler. Until 1997, every chief financial officer and chief accounting officer in Waste Management's history as a public company had worked as an auditor at Andersen.

Enron, too, had long been a favorite destination for Andersen employees. Sherron Watkins, the Enron executive who warned last August that deceptive accounting might destroy the Houston energy-trading company, came from Andersen. Alumni from the firm also became Enron's president and chief operating officer as well as its chief accounting officer.

As clients like Enron took more prominence at Andersen, consulting was securing its dominance. By 1994, two-thirds of Andersen's $3.3 billion in U.S. revenue came from the consulting side. Coinciding with that shift, the influence of the firm's in-house ethics watchdog dimmed.

Kapnick's successor as managing partner, Duane Kullberg, reorganized the firm to give more representation in management to the consultants who were bringing in so much revenue. Before that, auditors made all the decisions within the firm.

Among other moves, Kullberg divided leadership of the standards group's watchdog role into three parts: accounting, auditing procedures, and professional standards.

The men assigned to those jobs were top-notch, but none had the same unassailable authority as Catlett, who retired in 1980.

When Larry Weinbach took over as managing partner in 1989, he stayed primarily in New York, while the standards group remained in Chicago. Without face-to-face contact, the group leaders lost the opportunity for the spontaneous, closed-door, table-pounding arguments that had served the firm well in the past.

By degrees, the leaders of the group were pushed down the corporate ladder. When Enron's problems emerged, Andersen's most respected technician in recent years—Wyatt's protégé, John Stewart—had seven layers of management between him and the top partner.

Current Andersen officials deny that the influence of the Professional Standards Group has diminished. "Since its creation, the PSG has played an important and central role in providing accounting advice to Andersen engagement teams," said spokesman Dorton. "In fact, until the past couple of months, the firm continued to expand the size and expertise of the PSG."

The standards group was busier than ever throughout the 1990s, as the global ambitions and ever more complicated finances of Andersen's clients posed increasingly difficult questions for them to answer. At the same time, Wall Street's focus on quarterly earnings pressured auditors to go along with "creative accounting" aimed at boosting stock prices by ensuring predictable growth in profits.

"THE GAME IS OVER"

In this atmosphere, the worst fears of Andersen's ethics watchdogs finally came true.

Surrounded by Wyatt's packing boxes prior to his retirement in 1992, Wyatt and Stewart were fuming about the group's future. For the first time in Andersen's history, top management had rejected a key ruling from the group.

Like so much in the business of accounting, the issue in question would seem arcane to an outsider, but the stakes were huge, and they persist today: Should companies start counting stock options as an expense on their balance sheets?

This was the dawn of the 1990s market boom. Enron and hundreds of other corporations were paying their executives and other workers with these paper promises—the right to buy company stock at a set price in the future. Billions of dollars were riding on the answer.

As long as executives kept their companies' stock price rising, they could exercise their options for huge gains. Keeping those options off the books could shroud the true cost to investors and inflate earnings.

The Professional Standards Group had determined the right way to book stock options years earlier, concluding they had to be counted against profits like any other form of compensation.

But this time, Andersen's top management was swayed by the political heat, angry clients, and the risk that government would usurp the industry's right to set its own standards.

The only thing flowing as fast as stock options were political contributions in Washington. Large corporate contributors such as the Business Roundtable were keenly interested. If the Financial Accounting Standards Board ruled that companies had to count stock options as an expense, some powerful politicians were prepared to put the private standards board out of business.

Inside Andersen, the pragmatists carried the day.

"The game is over, John," Wyatt remembers telling Stewart. "You guys are never going to have the authority within the firm that you once had."

Indeed, the standards group would continue making the same pronouncements it always did, but not everyone at Andersen was listening.

Partners throughout the sprawling Andersen empire could see changes coming. Each office was expected to meet higher revenue goals. If they couldn't sell enough services to new or existing clients to support the number of partners, someone would have to go, according to interviews with several Andersen partners.

Current Andersen officials say the reality was more complicated. "Andersen has a comprehensive evaluation process that considers many attributes," said firm spokesman Dorton. "We do not manage our business with such arbitrary quotas."

In 1992, Andersen management was evaluating who could stay and who would go. At the firm's Ohio practice, which included its Columbus office, the answer was there were three too many audit partners, Gagel says he was told. He was one of them.

At a time when Andersen was pushing partners to "develop practice"—Andersen-speak for winning new clients or new fees from existing ones—Gagel was known instead for his auditing acumen.

He was only 50 then, far younger than Andersen's mandatory retirement age of 62 and well short of his own plans. But, like the Professional Standards Group, Gagel was an uneasy fit in the firm's new culture.

So on a dreary Monday morning the week before Thanksgiving, Ed Onderko, Andersen's managing partner in Columbus at the time, spotted Gagel in the hallway. He asked him to come into his office.

"We need to talk," Gagel recalls Onderko telling him. Getting immediately to the point, Onderko said: "The decision's been made that you're going to retire."

At his retirement party a few months later, Gagel's staff presented him with a framed caricature: It showed him passing through Andersen's trademark wooden doors for the last time, briefcase in hand and a white cowboy hat perched above his eyeglasses.

"Mike Gagel," the caption read, "one of the good guys."

• • •

Andersen partners had never seen anything quite like it. Their annual meetings usually exuded the kind of sobriety that America's guardians of financial integrity wore like a merit badge.

But the October 1989 session at the Loews Anatole Hotel in Dallas was something else. As Jim Edwards, the newly minted head of Andersen's U.S. audit division, stood to rally his normally staid partners, the rock anthem "Eye of the Tiger" pounded from speakers. Then a Texas stagehand strode onto the stage with a live tiger on the end of a chain, snarling at the astonished audience.

Andersen's audit division had dramatically boosted its profit in the past year, Edwards told his partners. Doing even better, he said in a rising voice, would "require the eyes of a tiger, eyes that seize opportunities, eyes that are focused on the kill."

"Ladies and gentlemen, the tiger is loose in the Americas," Edwards roared to those assembled in the ballroom, which had been converted into a makeshift sports arena.

"It's the eye of the tiger, it's the thrill of the fight," the speakers blared, as hundreds of partners rose to their feet. "Risin' up to the challenge of our rival."

To an outsider, the gimmicky stunt at this Dallas meeting might seem more appropriate for car salesmen or fast-food franchisees, not partners at one of America's premier accounting firms.

But the dramatic departure from past Andersen meetings exemplified the fundamental change that was sweeping through the old firm. Andersen, the longtime standard setter of the accounting world, was in the throes of a veritable revolution.

Out were the technically adept and fiercely independent auditors who had built the practice from a small office on Monroe Street in Chicago to one of the most influential auditing firms in the world.

In were the "Eye of the Tiger" accountants, a new breed eager to audit the books but also to sell more lucrative services to clients big and small.

The architect of this new Andersen was Edwards's boss, Dick Measelle. He and other Andersen leaders hoped the cultural upheaval would help the firm flourish without compromising its principles.

Instead, it ultimately would destroy the firm's reputation as it built up a rap sheet of bad audits and financial scandals spelled out in a blur of headlines—Enron Corp., WorldCom Inc., Waste Management Inc., and even lesser-known breakdowns like Supercuts, all of them Andersen clients.

By the time it ceased as an auditor of public companies, Andersen had become a central player in financial scandals that cost thousands of Americans their jobs, eroded the pensions of millions more, and led to billions of dollars in losses on Main Street as well as Wall Street. It betrayed not just investors, but also the many Andersen employees who struggled to do honest work.

"The '90s were a go-go period in which the mentality was if you weren't getting rich, you were stupid," said former Andersen chief executive Duane Kullberg, who ran the partnership through much of the 1980s, explaining the feverish quest for profit that consumed his old firm and the profession in general. "I think that permeated Andersen."

Current Andersen leaders dispute the assertion that a salesman culture overwhelmed the firm and undermined its auditing ability. They maintain that personnel decisions, including dismissals, were always based on the quality of a person's work.

The firm remains in business, but Andersen's current partners won't say exactly what they will do with its muddied name, or how many staffers are left to dismantle the final pieces and fight lawsuits.

All that is certain is the firm, which until just months ago had 85,000 people on its payroll serving thousands of companies across 84 countries, is a husk of the Chicago icon it had been for decades.

Arthur Andersen himself likely would be appalled to see the firm he founded devolve into a synonym for failed accounting. A no-nonsense leader, Andersen took bold stands on auditing issues from the outset and made independence as vital to the firm as red and black ink.

If a client threatened to take its business elsewhere because the firm wouldn't sign off on financial statements that contained a sleight of hand, Andersen would bid the client farewell rather than lower his standards.

Nonetheless, the roots of the revolution that would lead to his firm's collapse extend deep into its corporate history. Andersen knew that accountants couldn't live on debits and credits alone. From its inception, the firm also offered business solutions to the problems discovered while scrutinizing a company's books—a precursor to consulting.

As Andersen grew, its leaders made clear that the firm's primary role was that of an auditor, a bluntly honest translator of corporate America's books. Consulting was secondary.

But in the 1980s, that balance began to shift, in part because of Andersen's expertise in information technology. Andersen-installed computer systems worked so well they helped drain the profits out of its core business—checking company financial statements.

As computers flooded the American workplace, the money for

Andersen and its competitors was in consulting. Soon, Andersen became embroiled in a civil war between the auditors, who always had run the firm, and the consultants, who increasingly generated its profits.

The rivalry would color every major decision at the firm for much of its final two decades, from its selection of leaders to its handling of clients.

At the same time, consolidation shrank America's accounting ranks. The largest firms, once known as the Big Eight, became the Big Six, then the Big Five. Fearing they soon would become the Big Three or Two, industry leaders began a frantic search for new lines of business to bolster revenues. Consulting could boost the bottom line.

Scouring the financial landscape for new business and new clients, Andersen accountants had signed up sports car impresario John DeLorean in the late 1970s. The lure of sexy clients like DeLorean—those who held the potential for huge fees—would lead Andersen to underestimate the risks they posed.

STARS IN THEIR EYES

DeLorean often wore his sport shirt open to the waist and jet-setted with model Christina Ferrare. He had a crop of silver hair and a design for a new gull-wing sports car that he promised would rival the finest European automobiles.

His auditors were in awe.

"He was flamboyant," recalled Measelle, who helped woo DeLorean to the firm. "The guy was a movie actor."

Actually, DeLorean was a former General Motors Corp. executive, but his lifestyle seemed more Hollywood than Motown. He charged expenses, no matter how personal, to the company. His houseboy was on the payroll of the DeLorean Motor Co., and DeLorean charged the company for matching Mercedes-Benzes that he got for himself and Ferrare.

Measelle exemplified the new breed of leader emerging at Andersen, more marketer than technical geek, more entrepreneur than bookkeeper.

"His strong suit was probably developing revenue," said Kullberg, a Measelle sponsor, "as opposed to dealing with the tough, scrappy questions that come up in the course of auditing work."

The son of a Ford autoworker, Measelle had joined Andersen's Detroit office in 1961. As a junior accountant, he transferred to the firm's young but growing office in Madrid and immersed himself in the local culture, learning fluent Spanish and even running with the bulls in Pamplona. He wrote an essay for Andersen's in-house publication defending the practice of bullfighting.

By the time he returned to the Detroit office in 1972 as a partner, he had impressed his superiors by finding innovative ways to meet his revenue targets.

DeLorean was a high-profile client for Measelle, who soon became the head of the Detroit office. But the firm's handling of the swashbuckling carmaker would become a template for the problems destined to haunt Andersen in the coming years: the firm's willingness to please a questionable client who held out the possibility of a major payoff in fees.

After DeLorean had been an Andersen client for several years, auditors going over his company's books unearthed the personal expenses. DeLorean's own finance chief called upon Measelle to confront the auto executive with some hard questions.

But DeLorean always had an answer, said Measelle. "Dick, I am 24/7 on this project," Measelle quoted DeLorean as saying. "Everything I do is for this company."

DeLorean's former chief financial officer, Walter Strycker, said he and the auto company's chief accountant spoke to Measelle in late 1979. "We told him we thought John had abused the position of CEO at the DeLorean Motor Co., and that he had taken money that did not belong to him," Strycker said in a recent interview.

Measelle and other Andersen auditors met with DeLorean and then got back to Strycker. "They said they accepted John's explanation," said Strycker, who resigned over the dispute.

DeLorean, in a recent interview, said he didn't remember the Andersen accountant.

The firm's involvement with DeLorean led to a high-profile embarrassment for the firm. At first, bad publicity surfaced. In 1982, the FBI arrested DeLorean for allegedly attempting to buy $24 million worth of cocaine. DeLorean was acquitted of the drug charges.

The bigger problem for Andersen came with tens of millions of dollars in loans and grants the British government made to DeLorean, who had promised to bring much-needed wealth and jobs to troubled Belfast and then failed to deliver.

As his auditor, Andersen's good name was a key factor in helping DeLorean raise funds for the risky project. After the car company collapsed, the British government sued Andersen, contending that the firm should have blown the whistle on DeLorean when numerous partners became suspicious about his financial dealings.

As the lead engagement partner, Measelle had vouched for DeLorean's "experience and entrepreneurial ability" to the British government, according to court documents in the suit. The British accused Measelle and his firm of "negligence, fraud and breach of duty."

After government investigators in the United Kingdom and U.S. uncovered an alleged scheme by DeLorean and his associates to pocket about $17 million of investors' money, the car company's U.S. bankruptcy trustees also sued. They accused Andersen of concealing and delaying the discovery of its own "breaches of duty" as well as "the fraudulent scheme of DeLorean."

DeLorean was acquitted in the U.S. of fraud and racketeering. Andersen paid a total of $62 million to settle the suits by the British and the bankruptcy trustees after juries ruled against the firm. Andersen was barred from auditing government contracts in Britain from 1985 to 1997.

Yet to this day, Measelle stands by Andersen's handling of the job. "The audit work we did on DeLorean was the best audit work that I am aware of," he said. "The firm was totally innocent."

Measelle's career didn't suffer from the DeLorean case. Repeatedly over the years, Andersen partners who managed some of the firm's most troubled clients prospered professionally, and Measelle proved no exception. He was promoted to head Andersen's U.S. audit practice in 1987.

MERCHANT OR SAMURAI

As Measelle took the reins of the firm, the strains that eventually would rip it apart had intensified. Fees from its auditing arm atrophied, while its consulting arm thrived thanks to the information technology revolution sweeping America.

By 1990, consulting accounted for more than half of Andersen's $2 billion in U.S. revenue, and many recruits who joined the staff specialized in consulting.

On average, consultants brought in twice as much in fees for Andersen as audit partners. Yet the top consultants, many of whom had just made partner, had little say in the firm's management or direction.

The auditors under Measelle's leadership were struggling to win new work as the stock market reeled from the Wall Street crash in October 1987. Even more important, traditional ties to corporate clients were eroding, with auditors competing for business more openly than in the past by cutting their audit fees. They scrambled for new direction.

Some audit partners were openly questioning whether the quest for new revenues was depleting Andersen's will to take tough stands with auditing clients. But Measelle—facing a looming financial crisis at Andersen and the rising power demanded by the consultants—decided to act aggressively.

Partners described the struggle that evolved as the "merchant or samurai" question. The merchant impulse would boost profits, while the samurai instinct would protect the firm's reputation. Measelle hoped to balance the two sides. But he never dreamed that striking such a balance would be so hard or lead to such a disaster.

Consultants and accountants inhabit vastly different worlds. Consultants embrace risk-taking and preach innovation. Auditors try to avoid or manage risk. The two disciplines rarely mix well.

"When you've got a gray area, the auditors would always push you toward the white, not the black, closest to the conservative view," said Gresham Brebach, a former head of consulting for Andersen in the 1980s who is now vice chairman of Seurat Co., a marketing management firm affiliated with Chicago-based Frontenac Co.

By contrast, he said, "a consultant is there to influence change, to convince the client to do something different, not to conform or comply. It's a different mindset, a different attitude."

Andersen recruiters had extensive criteria when they visited college campuses to recruit. "In consulting, we were looking for brains, personality, and motivation," said one former Andersen staffer. "On the audit side, we didn't necessarily need all three of those."

Though it wasn't typically flashy work, auditing was crucial to the firm's reputation. Obscured in this season of accounting scandals has been a clear explanation of what those auditors were expected to do day in and day out—and what they were not.

Simply put, they are not investigators. They don't root around a company's books looking for accounting crimes. They're more like a corporate security guard, making sure people are signing in and out. If people are hiding in closets until after closing, or an employee has sold them an extra key, the security guard is unlikely to catch the break-in.

Even in the days before computers, auditors never checked every scrap of paperwork at a company; they took random samples.

Now they may not even do that. At firms with a huge volume of transactions, the auditors may test the computers that handle those invoices. They'll interview executives about their company's methods for recording revenue.

The biggest misconception of all is that accounting is a world of facts, hard numbers, and decimal points adding up to precision. In practice, accounting is more art than science, filled with subjective judgments, guesswork, and interpretation.

Do you account for the wear and tear on a fleet of aging vehicles by reducing their value over five years or ten? When should a business partnership be considered independent, and when should its losses be reflected on its partners' books?

Such are the questions at the heart of some of Andersen's biggest audit embarrassments in recent years. They can be answered conservatively or aggressively.

Too aggressive and, eventually, government regulators, investors, and prosecutors start asking questions. Too conservative and some lucrative clients threaten to go elsewhere.

That was a bluff Andersen always had been willing to call. But by the late 1980s, the leaders of Andersen's audit practice were chafing at that tradition.

"It was unfair to hold our clients to a higher standard of accountancy than the standards that were permitted by others," Measelle said.

His strategy, in effect, mimicked the tactics of his rivals in consulting. For years, Andersen consultants had been showing clients how to cut costs, boost profits, and improve efficiency. He wound up applying some of those same principles to Andersen's own stagnant audit division.

Soon after Measelle got another promotion in 1989—to head Andersen's audit and tax practice worldwide—he and other Andersen leaders took steps that would fatten the firm's bottom line but also would play an important role in Andersen's ultimate fate.

THE HIGH COST OF PROFITS

Measelle and CEO Larry Weinbach turned to Jim Edwards, head of Andersen's U.S. audit practice, to reshape the unit by making it savvier at winning new business.

That was the goal of Edwards's splashy presentation to audit partners in Dallas. Many bought in to the message, seeing it as a much needed jolt for the languishing audit side. "He was trying to boost revenue and remake the firm as the business was changing," said Jim Cunha, who made partner just a few years before the 1989 meeting.

New clients, Cunha said, "weren't going to hire us just because Arthur Andersen founded the firm in 1913."

Edwards and Weinbach did not respond to numerous requests for comment. But other partners described how Measelle and Weinbach urged Edwards to trim the number of partners through early retirement and not-so-friendly encouragement.

Well-respected veterans were out. And if managers didn't make the cuts, they said Edwards badgered them to do it.

"We felt that a partner should handle about 20,000 hours of work a year," including the team of staff accountants and others who reported to each partner, Measelle said. "If there were ten partners in an office handling 100,000 hours, we knew that we had five too many partners."

The new economics played out brutally in many parts of the sprawling Andersen empire, including the West Coast, where senior partners like John Greene viewed the approach as shortsighted.

"I would get a telephone call a day almost, asking what have you done in the last 24 hours," Greene recalled. "I thought their arithmetic was a rather simplistic way of looking at things, and I told them so."

Traditionally, Andersen partners each had a pyramid of employees reporting to them—from rookie accountants to senior audit managers. Partners' compensation was based on the number of shares they owned in the partnership—called "units." The more units you had, the higher your pay. And the easiest way to increase the value of each unit was to limit the number of partners divvying up the profits.

Boosting sales and productivity, of course, is the essence of any successful business. But Andersen wasn't selling widgets; it was selling its expertise and independence. Many at Andersen believed that cost cutting eventually would erode the quality of the work.

Greene was in charge of Andersen's West Coast audit business at the time. He saw the need to reduce costs, and responded by making cuts, as partners were transferred or counseled to look for jobs elsewhere. But "it never seemed to be enough," he said.

In private sessions before a board of partners meeting in February 1988, one of Measelle's lieutenants told regional managing partners to cull four or five partners from their ranks. For Greene, it was worse: They wanted him to cut up to 18 of the 120 partners on the West Coast.

Appalled, Greene argued he already was cutting five or six partners from his cadre. Any more, he said, and "it would be a bloodbath." Greene feared it would cut good technical staff from his ranks and hurt Andersen's auditing work in the long run.

Two days later at a board meeting lunch, Greene said Edwards asked him to pick up his sandwich and join Edwards for a private conversation. We're stripping you of day-to-day control of the West Coast, Greene recalled Edwards telling him. Greene's replacement took over the job of cutting partners.

The tough-minded moves had the desired effect: The remaining partners were making more money. "When I took over Arthur Andersen in 1989, we made $400 a unit," Measelle said. "When I left [in 1997], we made $1,200 a unit, so we tripled the earnings in eight years."

In more concrete terms, the average Andersen partner earned about $130,000 a year in the early 1980s. By 1990, partners were averaging around $200,000. By 2000, they were earning nearly $450,000.

"By asking partners to contribute to the development of work," Measelle said, "the firm and its competitors were only facing up to the fact that they were not immune to the laws of economics."

In many of Andersen's offices, though, employees balked at the new culture. J. Paul Boyer, the former marketing director for the Columbus office of Arthur Andersen, remembers chatting one day with a senior auditor. The man was indignant at how the firm had changed. "I came to Arthur Andersen to be an auditor, not a salesman," he told Boyer. "When I have to start selling, I'm leaving."

Boyer thought to himself, "Should I start planning your going-away party?"

As Measelle and the auditors under his control developed new business, they convinced many clients to let Andersen assume tasks that once were handled by the companies themselves.

One such role that Andersen pioneered at companies like Enron Corp. was internal auditing. Clients traditionally employed their own accountants to review corporate financial operations and had outside auditors double-check the results.

Andersen took over not only the internal audit function, but the staff that went along with it, and continued to act as the outside auditor. The new duties helped boost fees, but they also created situations in which Andersen effectively audited some of its own work.

The rising profits of auditors didn't do anything to stem a bigger problem Measelle faced: Andersen's consulting revenues continued to skyrocket, sustaining an imbalance that made consultants feel like they subsidized the auditors.

With the consultants agitating for greater freedom to strike out on their own, which would have drained the firm of revenue, a bipartisan team of partners in 1989 set out to find common ground. The partners decided to set up two separate business units operating using the Andersen name. Measelle would head the audit and tax partners, and George Shaheen, a Palo Alto–based partner, would head the consultants.

Before the agreement, all Andersen partners were paid from the same pool of funds. The new salary system created two separate pools—one for audit and tax partners, the other for consultants—and a revenue-sharing formula.

Under this formula, auditors feared that if they couldn't boost their own profits, the consultants would have to bail them out. The arrangement effectively served to push the auditors further into the role of salesmen so they could compete with the high-earning consultants.

The feuding only intensified, with some auditors capitalizing on the confusion of having two sets of consultants under the same umbrella. A few of the consulting division's best clients, including Chrysler Corp. and Walt Disney World, were so perplexed that they bought advice from the audit side of the business, thinking it was coming from the consulting arm.

The imbalance in the firm, meanwhile, only grew worse. By the mid-1990s, annual fees generated by Andersen auditors had risen to $1.9 million per partner, but consultants were bringing in $3.7 million per partner.

Within a few years, the consultants would split off entirely and form their own firm, Accenture.

WINNING THE WAR

In Andersen's internal tug-of-war between the merchant and the samurai, the merchant was winning out. Luring new business became imperative if the auditors were to increase revenues and keep their consultant siblings in place.

Andersen was rewarding partners who brought in new business, even when they had been involved with problem audits, such as the Charles Keating account.

The accounting firm actually dropped Keating and his Lincoln Savings & Loan as a client in 1986, before his empire collapsed amid a huge scandal in the thrift industry. But the account eventually cost Andersen more than $22 million to settle with bondholders and federal regulators for allegedly misrepresenting the financial health of Lincoln.

The lead auditor for Lincoln was Jay Ozer, whose career continued to thrive. "I was the rainmaker in the office," Ozer, who retired two years ago, said in a recent interview. "I brought in the new clients and gave them to other partners."

One of the accounts Ozer took over was the Baptist Foundation of Arizona. At $150,000 in audit fees, it was a tiny client for Ozer, who supervised more than $3 million in audit work.

Although Ozer and Andersen signed off on BFA's books, foundation officials were hiding bad real estate investments by transferring the losses to the books of related companies. The accounting trick allowed BFA to lure new investors, mostly fellow Baptists, according to Arizona authorities.

By the time the State of Arizona shut down BFA in 1999, about 11,000 mostly elderly investors had lost $570 million in the scheme. In the ongoing case, three Baptist officials, including its former treasurer and controller, have pleaded guilty to fraud and related charges.

After a newspaper raised questions about BFA's finances, the Arizona State Board of Accountancy opened an investigation and hired an expert to assess Ozer's work. The expert found that "many readily recognizable similarities lead to the conclusion that violations by Ozer in the 1985 Lincoln audit were essentially repeated in the 1995–97 BFA audits."

Ozer disputed that conclusion, noting in the Lincoln case, "We resigned from our largest client, and another firm, Arthur Young, took over the account and issued two clean opinions. I was never sanctioned by any authorities for any of my work related to the Lincoln account."

Arthur Young paid a $400 million settlement for audit problems related to Lincoln and other thrifts.

As for BFA, Ozer and Andersen contended that the firm couldn't uncover the true state of the foundation's finances because its officials lied to them.

"The bottom line is that when there's fraud and collusion by management, you can always get by if you're smart," Ozer said. "It may be found out a couple years later, but when the audit report is filed, it can be covered up."

Andersen settled the BFA case this year by paying $217 million. Andersen admitted no wrongdoing, but Ozer and his audit manager on the BFA account, Ann McGrath, agreed to relinquish their CPA licenses.

BFA wasn't the only Andersen client to encounter trouble in the last decade.

In the early 1990s, another Andersen partner, Robert Kutsenda, led the Andersen team auditing Supercuts, a chain of low-cost hair salons that also ran into accounting problems.

At the time, the company's financial statements portrayed it as growing rapidly. But when a new Supercuts chief financial officer, William Stirlen, came on in the spring of 1993, he quickly discovered Supercuts was not what it appeared to be.

"If you adjusted all the numbers for the aggressive accounting, the company had not grown for three years in a row," Stirlen said. "I was appalled."

Its most unusual accounting tactic was known as the Construction Cut. According to Stirlen, Supercuts' policy was to record revenue from franchise fees the moment a salon opened, whether or not the fee was paid. And they had a curious way of deciding a store was open.

"They would get construction down to a certain point and then give a member of the construction crew a haircut," Stirlen said. In Supercuts' accounting, the salon was open and a moneymaker.

In the short-term thinking of Wall Street and its fixation on quarterly results, the Construction Cuts helped the chain meet expectations for growth, thus attracting more investors.

On a Friday in early 1994, Stirlen said, he told Kutsenda of his suspicions. Kutsenda moved quickly. Over the weekend, "they put together a whole crew of Arthur Andersen personnel," Stirlen said.

That Monday, Supercuts fired Stirlen, who believed the move was in retaliation for raising the accounting issues. Stirlen sued Supercuts and won an undisclosed settlement for wrongful termination.

Kutsenda did not respond to repeated calls for comment.

The problems at Supercuts generated a few negative headlines and eventually the company was sold. Kutsenda moved on too as Andersen bosses promoted him.

WASTE MANAGEMENT FIASCO

In time, Kutsenda would get involved with a much bigger client, Waste Management, whose dealings with Andersen showed how the merchants inside the firm's ranks finally vanquished the samurai.

Like other accounting firms, Andersen encouraged employees, especially those unlikely to make partner, to move on and work for clients or potential clients. The benefit to Andersen was obvious: Networking made it likely that former Andersen employees would keep or hire Andersen as an auditor.

But it could have other effects as well. The closer the relationships, the harder it could be to deliver bad news or say "no" to a client.

Waste Management, the number one U.S. trash hauler, had an internal accounting team colonized by former Andersen auditors. Until 1997, every chief financial officer and every chief accounting officer at Waste Management had worked for Andersen.

For much of that time, Andersen auditors knew Waste Management's financial statements were inaccurate, according to an investigation by the Securities and Exchange Commission, and they repeatedly tried to get the company to mend its ways.

But when Waste Management ignored Andersen's recommendations, the accounting firm went along with its client's wishes rather than resign.

Instead of forcing Waste Management to realistically account for thousands of dumpsters and trucks, for instance, Andersen allowed the company to use simple accounting chicanery that helped inflate the firm's profits, according to the SEC.

In one case, Waste Management assigned a salvage value of $30,000 to worn-out garbage trucks. The true value was closer to $12,000 apiece.

Chicago-based Kutsenda was the regional specialist who had the final say on technical issues. In 1995, according to the SEC, he consulted with the accountants who were auditing Waste Management and agreed to sign off on the company's financial statements.

The lead partner on the account was Robert Allgyer, who had been chosen for the role in 1991 because of his marketing abilities—selling consulting and other non-audit services.

Early on, Andersen's leaders had determined that they were not fully "exploiting Waste Management in terms of its fee-paying capability," as Measelle put it. "Allgyer had a reputation as a businessman who was able to sell," he said.

Sure enough, between 1991 and 1997, Waste Management paid Andersen $7.5 million in audit fees and $11.8 million for consulting and other services. After Allgyer's team took over, Waste Management overstated its pretax income by more than $1 billion from 1992 to 1996, according to federal regulators.

When the trash hauler restated earnings in early 1998, revealing its accounting problems, the SEC investigated the Andersen partners involved.

Alleging that Allgyer "recklessly caused the issuance" of false and misleading audit reports, the SEC in 2001 suspended him from auditing public companies for at least five years. The SEC suspended Kutsenda for one year, stating his conduct resulted "in a violation of applicable professional standards."

Andersen paid the federal government a $7 million fine, without commenting on allegations that it knowingly produced misleading audit reports.

SEC documents also reveal that in 1994 Allgyer told Measelle of the issues at Waste Management.

"What could we do at that point?" Measelle asked, providing an answer a moment later. "We could have resigned."

In March, the SEC accused the trash hauler's former top officers, including founder Dean Buntrock, of a "massive fraud" to inflate profits by $1.7 billion to meet earnings targets.

What happened to Kutsenda? Before the SEC sanctions were announced, Kutsenda was promoted to managing partner of global risk management. Among his new duties: figuring out a way to limit Andersen's exposure to lawsuits.

The problem was simple to diagnose. The mountains of paperwork Andersen generated with every audit had become a gold mine for plaintiffs' lawyers filing investor lawsuits against the firm and its clients.

In February 2000, Kutsenda submitted a new policy on the "organization, retention, and destruction" of client engagement information. "Information gathered or considered in connection with performing client engagements should be evaluated by the engagement partner and manager," it stated, "and only essential information to support our conclusions should be retained."

A year later, Andersen attorney Nancy Temple cited the same policy as the firm struggled to deal with the questionable bookkeeping of one of its most troublesome but well-paying clients—Enron.

"Unconscious" bias may be the primary stumbling block to quality corporate audits. With accounting more an art than a science, audit teams have plenty of reason to come to conclusions that will make clients happy. In this *Harvard Business Review* article, Max H. Bazerman, George Loewenstein, and Don A. Moore analyze problems of the current system and propose an overhaul to underscore the independence of auditors.

Max H. Bazerman, George Loewenstein, and Don A. Moore

Why Good Accountants Do Bad Audits

ON JULY 30, at a ceremony in the East Room of the White House attended by congressional leaders of both parties, President George W. Bush signed into law the Sarbanes-Oxley Act of 2002 addressing corporate accountability. A response to recent financial scandals that had begun to undermine citizens' confidence in U.S. business, the wide-ranging act flew through the House of Representatives and Senate in record time and passed in both chambers by overwhelming majorities. The act places new legal constraints on executives and gives expanded protections to whistle-blowers. Perhaps most important, though, it puts the accounting industry under tightened federal oversight. It creates a regulatory board—with broad powers to punish corruption—to monitor accounting firms, and it establishes stiff criminal penalties, including long jail terms, for accounting fraud. "The era of low standards and false profits is over," Bush proclaimed.

If only it were that easy.

Given the vast scale of recent accounting scandals and their devastating effects on workers and investors, it's not surprising that the government and the public assume that the underlying problems are corruption and criminality—unethical accountants falsifying numbers to protect equally unethical clients. But that's only a small part of the story. Serious accounting problems have long plagued corporate audits, routinely leading to substantial fines for accounting firms. Some of the errors, no doubt, are the result of fraud. But to attribute most errors to deliberate corruption would be to believe that the accounting profession is rife with crooks—a conclusion that anyone who has worked with accountants knows is untrue. The deeper, more pernicious problem with corporate auditing, as it's currently practiced, is its vulnerability to unconscious bias. Because of the often subjective nature of accounting and the tight relationships between accounting firms and their clients, even the most honest and meticulous of auditors can unintentionally distort the numbers in ways that mask a company's true financial status, thereby misleading investors, regulators, and sometimes management. Indeed, even seemingly egregious accounting scandals, such as Andersen's audits of Enron, may have at their core a series of unconsciously biased judgments rather than a deliberate program of criminality.

Unlike conscious corruption, unconscious bias cannot be deterred by threats of jail time. Rooting out bias, or at least tempering its effects, will require more fundamental changes to the way accounting firms and their clients operate. If we are really going to restore trust in the U.S. system of auditing, we will need to go well beyond the provisions of the Sarbanes-Oxley Act. We will need to embrace practices and regulations that recognize the existence of bias and moderate its ill effects. Only then can we be assured of the reliability of the financial reports issued by public companies and ratified by professional accountants.

THE ROOTS OF BIAS

Psychological research shows that our desires powerfully influence the way we interpret information, even when we're trying to be objective and impartial. When we are motivated to reach a particular conclusion, we usually do. That's why most of us think we are better than average drivers, have smarter than average children, and choose stocks or funds that will outperform the market—even if there's clear evidence to the contrary. Without knowing it, we tend to critically scrutinize and then discount facts that contradict the conclusions we want to reach, and we uncritically embrace evidence that supports our positions. Unaware of our skewed information processing, we erroneously conclude that our judgments are free of bias.

Many experiments have demonstrated the power of self-serving bias and shown, for example, how bias can distort legal negotiations. In one series of experiments, which we describe in a 1997 *Sloan Management Review* article, pairs of participants were given police and medical reports, depositions, and other materials from a lawsuit involving a collision between a motorcycle and a car and were assigned to the role of either the motorcyclist plaintiff or the car-driving defendant. They were given the task of negotiating a settlement and were told that if they couldn't reach one, a judge would decide the award amount, and both parties would pay substantial penalties. Finally, before starting the negotiation, each participant was asked to predict the amount the judge would award the plaintiff if negotiations stalled. To further eliminate bias, each member of the pair was assured that the other party wouldn't see his or her estimate and that the estimates would not influence the judge's decision.

The results were striking. Participants playing the motorcyclist plaintiff tended to predict that they'd receive dramatically larger awards than the defendants predicted. This is an example of self-serving bias: Armed with the same information, different people reach different conclusions—ones that favor their own interests. In addition, the degree to which the two hypothetical awards differed was an excellent predictor of the likelihood that the pair would negotiate a settlement. The greater the difference in the negotiators' beliefs, the harder it was for them to come to agreement.

How can such an impulse toward self-serving bias be moderated? In follow-up experiments, the same researchers tried to reduce participants' bias by paying them to accurately predict the amount of the judge's award and having them write essays arguing the other side's point of view. Neither strategy reduced bias; participants consistently thought that the judge would award damages that favored their side. And what about educating the subjects, alerting them that they were likely to reach biased conclusions? That didn't work, either. After teaching participants about bias and testing them to make sure they understood the concept, the researchers found that the participants concluded that their negotiating opponents would be highly biased but refused to believe that they themselves would be.

In yet another of these experiments, participants were presented with 16 arguments—eight favoring the side they had been assigned (plaintiff or defendant) and eight favoring the other—and were asked to predict how a neutral third party would rate the quality of the arguments. In general, study participants found arguments that favored their own positions more convincing than those that supported the other side. But when participants were assigned to the role of plaintiff or defendant only after they'd seen the case materials—and so were unbiased in their evaluation of the data—their degree of bias was significantly less. Taken together, these findings suggest that unconscious bias works by distorting how people interpret information.

ACCOUNTING FOR BAD ACCOUNTING

Professional accountants might seem immune to such biases (after all, they work with hard numbers and are guided by clear-cut standards). But the corporate auditing arena is a particularly fertile ground for self-serving biases. Three structural aspects of accounting create substantial opportunities for bias to influence judgment.

Ambiguity. Bias thrives wherever there is the possibility of interpreting information in different ways. As we saw in the study involving the collision, people tend to reach self-serving conclusions whenever ambiguity surrounds a piece of evidence. While it's true that many accounting decisions are cut-and-dried—establishing a proper conversion rate for British pounds, for instance, entails merely consulting daily foreign exchange rates—many others require interpretations of ambiguous information. Auditors and their clients have considerable leeway, for example, in answering some of the most basic financial questions: What's an investment? What's an expense? When should revenue be recognized? The interpretation and weighing of various types of information are rarely straightforward. As Joseph Berardino, Arthur Andersen's former chief executive, said in his congressional testimony on the Enron collapse, "Many people think accounting is a science, where one number, namely earnings per share, is *the* number, and it's such a precise number that it couldn't be two pennies higher or two pennies lower. I come from a school that says it really is much more of an art."

Attachment. Auditors have strong business reasons to remain in clients' good graces and are thus highly motivated to approve their clients' accounts. Under the current system, auditors are hired and fired by the companies they audit, and it is well known that client companies fire accounting firms that deliver unfavorable audits. Even if an accounting firm is large enough to absorb the loss of one client, individual auditors' jobs and careers may depend on success with specific clients. Moreover, in recent decades, accounting firms have increasingly treated audits as ways to build relationships that allow them to sell their more lucrative consulting services. Thus, from the executive team down to individual accountants, an auditing firm's motivation to provide favorable audits runs deep. As the collision case also showed, once people equate their own interests with another party's, they interpret data to favor that party. Attachment breeds bias.

Approval. An audit ultimately endorses or rejects the client's accounting—in other words, it assesses the judgments that someone in the client firm has already made. Research shows that self-serving biases become even stronger when people are endorsing others' biased judgments—provided those judgments align with their own biases—than when they are making original judgments themselves. In one series of studies, researchers found that people were more willing to endorse an overly generous outcome that favored them than they were to make that judgment themselves. For example, if someone says that you deserve a higher raise than facts might suggest, you are more likely to come to agree with this view than you are to decide on your own that you deserve a higher raise. This kind of thinking implies that an auditor is likely to accept more aggressive accounting from her client than what she might suggest independently.

In addition to these structural elements that promote bias, three aspects of human nature can amplify unconscious biases.

Familiarity. People are more willing to harm strangers than individuals they know, especially when those individuals are paying clients with whom they have ongoing relationships. An auditor who suspects questionable accounting must thus choose, unconsciously perhaps, between potentially harming his client (and himself) by challenging a company's accounts or harming faceless investors by failing to object to the possibly skewed numbers. Given this tension, auditors may unconsciously lean toward approving the dubious accounting. And their biases will grow stronger as their personal ties deepen. The longer an accounting partner serves a particular client, the more biased his judgments will tend to be.

Discounting. People tend to be far more responsive to immediate consequences than delayed ones, especially when the delayed outcomes are uncertain. Many human vices spring from this reflex. We postpone routine dental checkups because of the cost and inconvenience and the largely invisible long-term gain. In the same way, auditors may hesitate to issue critical audit reports because of the adverse immediate consequences—damage to the relationship, potential loss of the contract, and possible unemployment. But the costs of a positive report when a negative report is called for—protecting the accounting firm's reputation or avoiding a lawsuit, for example—are likely to be distant and uncertain.

Escalation. It's natural for people to conceal or explain away minor indiscretions or oversights, sometimes without even realizing that they're doing it. Think of the manager who misses a family dinner and blames the traffic, though he simply lost track of time. Likewise, an auditor's biases may lead her to unknowingly adapt over time to small imperfections in a client's financial practices. Eventually, though, the sum of these small judgments may become large and she may recognize the long-standing bias. But at that point, correcting the bias may require admitting prior errors. Rather than expose the unwitting mistakes, she may decide to conceal the problem. Thus, unconscious bias may evolve into conscious corruption—corruption representing the most visible end of a situation that may have been deteriorating for some time. It's our belief that some of the recent financial disasters we've witnessed began as minor errors of judgment and escalated into corruption. As Charles Niemeier, chief accountant for the SEC's enforcement division, put it: "People who never intend to do something wrong end up finding themselves in situations where they are almost forced to continue to commit fraud once they have started doing this. Otherwise, it will be revealed that they had used improper accounting in the earlier periods."

PUTTING THEORY TO THE TEST

Bias, by its very nature, is typically invisible: You can't review a corporate audit and pick out errors attributable to bias. Often, we can't tell whether an error in auditing is due to bias or corruption. But you can design experiments that reveal how bias can distort accounting decisions. We recently did just that, with telling results.

We gave undergraduate and business students a complex set of information about the potential sale of a fictional company and asked them to estimate the company's value. Participants were assigned different roles: buyer, seller, buyer's auditor, or seller's auditor. All subjects read the same information about the company. As we expected, those who hoped to sell the firm thought the company was worth more than the prospective buyers did. More interesting were the opinions offered by the auditors: Their judgments were strongly biased toward the interests of their clients.

These auditors displayed role-conferred biases in two ways. First, their valuations (judgments) were biased in the clients' favor: The sellers' auditors publicly concluded that the firm was worth more than the buyers' auditors said it was. Second, and more tellingly, their private judgments about the company's value were also biased in their clients' favor: At the end of the experiment, the auditors were asked to estimate the company's true value and were told that they would be rewarded according to how close their private judgments were to those of impartial experts. Despite this incentive for accuracy, the estimates of the sellers' auditors averaged 30 percent higher than those of the buyers' auditors. This exemplifies the persistent influence of self-serving biases: Once participants interpreted information about the target company in a biased way, they were unable to undo the bias later.

Earlier this year, we ran a study with Lloyd Tanlu that focused on professional auditors themselves. The study, of 139 auditors employed full-time by one of the big U.S. accounting firms, illuminated the professionals' vulnerability to bias and their tendency to be influenced by clients' biases. Each participant was given five ambiguous auditing vignettes and asked to judge the accounting for each. Half the participants were asked to suppose that they had been hired by the company they were auditing; the rest were asked to suppose they had been hired by a different company, one that was conducting business with the company that had created the financial statements. In addition, half the participants in each of those two groups generated their own auditing numbers first, then stated whether they believed that the firm's financial reports complied with generally accepted accounting principles (GAAP), while the other half did the two tasks in the reverse order.

For all five vignettes, the auditors were on average 30 percent more likely to find that the accounting behind a company's financial reports complied with GAAP if they were playing the role of auditor for that firm. Furthermore, the participants who generated their own auditing numbers after first passing judgment on the company's financial reports tended to come up with numbers that were closer than the other participants' to the client's numbers. The study showed both that experienced auditors are not immune from bias and that they are more likely to accede to a client's biased accounting numbers than to generate such numbers themselves.

These experiments show that even the suggestion of a hypothetical relationship with a client distorts an auditor's judgments. Imagine the degree of distortion that must exist in a long-standing relationship involving millions of dollars in ongoing revenues.

PROBLEMS WITH PROPOSED REFORMS

Because the reforms in the Sarbanes-Oxley Act and those proposed by others do not address the fundamental problem of bias, they will not solve the crisis in accounting in the United States. Some of the reforms, in fact, may well make it worse.

Consider the provisions dealing with disclosure. They require individual auditors of their firms to reveal conflicts of interest to investors. But to counteract bias, such disclosure must either inhibit bias outright or allow investors to adjust for it. Neither is likely. With regard to inhibiting bias, we saw earlier that a person's conscious efforts to reduce bias have limited effect. And the latter idea, that disclosure would help investors interpret auditors' reports, would be of little benefit unless investors knew *how* a disclosed conflict of interest biased an auditor's judgment. Imagine an investor who reads a positive audit report containing the caveat that the auditor receives $60 million in annual fees from the audited company. By how much should the investor adjust the company's self-reported earnings per share? Without specific guidance, people cannot accurately factor conflict of interest into their investment decisions.

More worrisome is evidence that disclosure could actually increase bias. If auditors suspect that disclosure will lead investors to discount or make adjustments for the auditors' public statements, they may feel less duty bound to be impartial and may make judgments more closely aligned with their personal interests. Research by Daylian Cain, Don Moore, and George Loewenstein paired participants and assigned one member of each pair to the role of estimator and the other to that of adviser. The estimator viewed several jars of coins from a distance, estimated the value of the money in them, and was paid according to how close the estimates were to the jars' true values. The adviser, who could study the jars up close, gave the estimator advice. The adviser, however, was not paid according to the estimator's accuracy but according to how high the estimator's guesses were. In other words, advisers had an incentive to mislead the estimators so that they would guess high.

In addition, we told half of the estimators about the advisers' pay arrangement; we said nothing about it to the rest. Disclosure had two effects. First, advisers whose motives were disclosed provided much more biased guesses (i.e., high estimates of coin jar values) than did advisers whose motives were not disclosed; second, disclosure did *not* cause estimators to substantially discount their advisers' advice. As a result, disclosure led advisers to make much more money and estimators to make much less. Applied to auditing, this finding suggests that auditors who are forced to disclose conflicts might exhibit greater self-serving bias.

One other proposed policy warrants mention: the move to impose stricter accounting standards. This remedy, too, is unlikely to improve the situation. Research shows that it takes very little ambiguity to produce biased judgments. In one study, some participants were asked to imagine that they had worked seven hours on a task and that another person had worked ten hours on the same task. Other participants were asked to imagine the opposite scenario: They'd worked ten hours on the project while the other person worked seven. In each case, it was specified that the person who had worked seven hours would be paid $25; the question was how much the person who had worked ten hours should be paid. Ten-hour participants, on average, thought that they should be paid about $35 for their ten hours of work, while those who had worked seven hours thought that the ten-hour person should receive less—about $30. Here, all it took was a tiny bit of ambiguity—whether the fair solution was equal hourly pay (as the ten-hour people thought) or equal total pay (as the seven-hour people thought)—to produce different self-serving assessments of fairness. Note, too, that the incentives for being biased in this study were awfully weak because the question was hypothetical; in the real world, incentives for bias are far stronger. It seems implausible that stricter accounting rules could eliminate ambiguity—and thus they are unlikely to reduce self-serving bias.

RADICAL REMEDIES

The key to improving audits, clearly, is not to threaten or cajole. It must be to eliminate incentives that create self-serving biases. This means that new policies must reduce an auditor's interest in whether a client is pleased by the results of an audit.

One provision of the Sarbanes-Oxley Act prohibits accounting firms from providing certain consulting services to companies they audit. This is a step in the right direction, but it doesn't go far enough. Clearly, accounting firms that advise their clients on how to boost profits, while at the same time trying to impartially judge their books, face an impossible conflict of interest. This reform both reduces this conflict and eases the pressure on auditors to act as salespeople for their firm's other services. Unfortunately, while the new law limits the consulting services auditing firms can provide, it doesn't prohibit them entirely, and it gives the new oversight board created by the Sarbanes-Oxley Act the option of overriding this provision.

True auditor independence requires, as a start, full divestiture of consulting and tax services. And even then, a fundamental problem will remain: Because auditors are hired and fired by the companies they audit, they are in the position of possibly casting negative judgments on those who hired them—and who can cut them loose. Therefore, even with the elimination of consulting, the fundamental structure of the auditing system virtually ensures biased auditing. To eliminate this source of bias, we must remove the threat of being fired for delivering an unfavorable audit. Auditors must have fixed, limited contract periods during which they cannot be terminated. All fees and other contractual details should be specified at the beginning of the contract and must be unchangeable. In addition, the client must be prohibited from rehiring the auditing firm at the end of the contract; instead, the major accounting firms would be required to rotate clients. Current legislation requires auditor rotation; however, this is defined as a change in the lead partner within an auditing firm. There is no provision to rotate the firms conducting the audit, and there is no provision to prevent a client from firing an auditor. Thus, auditors will continue to have powerful incentives to keep their clients happy.

Audit clients must also be prohibited from hiring individual accountants away from their audit firms. As the Enron scandal unfolded, the common practice of Arthur Andersen employees taking positions within Enron, and vice versa, came to light. Clearly, an auditor can't be impartial when he or she hopes to please a client in order to develop job options. We believe that auditors should be barred from taking positions with the firms they audit for at least five years.

Less tangibly, auditors must come to appreciate the profound impact of self-serving biases on judgment. Professional schools have begun to take ethics seriously in recent years, but teaching auditors about ethics will not have an impact on bias. What's needed is education that helps auditors understand the unconscious errors they make and the reasons they make them. That knowledge alone won't solve the problem, but once members of the auditing profession understand the role of bias in their work, honest and visionary leaders in the profession can help change the conduct of accounting to prevent the conflicts of interest that promote bias. And audit leaders who say that so-called professionalism is a sufficient safeguard against audit error—a claim that's inconsistent with the weight of empirical evidence on human judgment—might abandon that claim if they truly understood the role of bias in auditing.

Our proposals are not perfect. Indeed, it's hard to imagine any practical system that could eliminate all bias. Even with our remedies, for instance, it's still possible that auditors' social contact with clients could introduce subtle biases. But we envision a system in which clients regard auditors as more like tax collectors than partners or advisers—a system that could be expected to at least ameliorate bias. Devising a more robust separation of auditor and client, one that might go further to reduce bias, would require approaches—such as turning over the auditing function to government—that could create problems as serious as those they solve. We see our proposals as both realistic and effective. In the absence of radical and innovative reform, we believe, further accounting disasters are inevitable.

A perk enjoyed by many top executives is free personal tax advice from the accounting firm doing its audit. That's not so great, however, if the legality of investments recommended is attacked by the IRS. This article in *The Wall Street Journal* by Rebecca Blumenstein and Carol Hymowitz traces how a troubled tax shelter and declining stock prices forced a showdown between top Sprint Corp. executives and its longtime auditor. Since this story was originally published, former BellSouth vice chairman Gary Forsee was chosen the new chief executive of Sprint and Ernst & Young agreed to pay a $15 million penalty to the IRS to settle the government investigation of the tax shelters in question.

Rebecca Blumenstein and Carol Hymowitz

Troubling Options—Inside the Tough Call at Sprint

FOR MONTHS, Sprint Corp.'s directors had secretly debated a mounting conflict-of-interest crisis inside the telecommunications giant. Now, it was culminating in an extraordinary showdown as the board met on December 9 to hear its top two executives explain why they shouldn't be fired.

The executives, Chief Executive William T. Esrey and President Ronald LeMay, came into the boardroom of Sprint's headquarters outside Kansas City with a slide presentation to argue their case. At stake for both men: not only their careers but also their vast personal fortunes.

In late 1999, Sprint's auditors Ernst & Young offered the two men and other Sprint executives a lucrative tax shelter. For Messrs. Esrey and LeMay, the maneuver could allow the executives to avoid paying taxes on more than $100 million each in stock-option gains.

But in 2000, the Internal Revenue Service began probing a wide range of tax shelters, including this one. Suddenly it looked as though the two executives had been badly advised by Ernst & Young and would need to pay the taxes after all. The trouble is, the executives no longer had the money since Sprint's stock plunged amid the meltdown of the telecom industry.

The conflict for Sprint's board couldn't have been more acute: The company's two top executives were at war with the auditor the company relied upon to bless its financial results before the public.

How Sprint wound up in this mess is a cautionary tale of flawed executive decisions and corporate governance. Sprint's board helped create the trouble by requiring that its top executives use Ernst & Young to prepare their tax returns and, as a special perk, allowed the executives to consult the company's auditor for personal financial advice. While that practice is common, it has drawn criticism recently because the arrangement has the potential to create a conflict of interest. The boards of some that have used auditors as tax advisers for executives in the past, including Ryder System Inc. and Pfizer Inc., have long barred it.

Moreover, Sprint's board knew about the looming conflict for more than two years before it finally moved to address it. The conflict, and the broader question of who should run Sprint, were the subject of twenty board meetings over the last six months of 2002, say people close to the situation.

Sprint declined to comment on board issues. Messrs. Esrey and LeMay, who have worked as high-ranking executives at the company since the mid-1980s, have not commented beyond statements made last week to employees.

The blowup at Sprint has rocked the tight-knit business world of Kansas City. One of the board's most powerful outside directors, Irvine O. Hockaday, ran Hallmark Cards Inc., one of the city's other preeminent businesses, and is a close friend and neighbor of Mr. Esrey. (Mr. Hockaday also serves on the board of Dow Jones & Co., publisher of *The Wall Street Journal*.) Another director is Louis W. Smith, former chief of the Ewing Marion Kauffman Foundation in Kansas City, built on the fortune of the Marion Labs Drug company.

Mr. Esrey, 63 years old, has been battling lymphatic cancer since last fall. He has said that he could face financial ruin if the IRS rules against the shelters—since he left the proceeds from exercising the options and most of his other personal assets in Sprint shares. "In the event of an extreme adverse outcome . . . future taxes could take up most, if not all, of my assets since I have nearly all my assets in Sprint stock," Mr. Esrey said in a statement to employees last week.

Ernst & Young, which pocketed millions in fees paid by Sprint, initially recommended the shelters as a smart way to take advantage of Sprint's soaring stock price. In 1999, after WorldCom Inc. announced its blockbuster deal to buy Sprint, Sprint accelerated the vesting of options for its executives.

The Sprint executives found themselves with huge potential profits on their options as Mr. LeMay exercised options with a total taxable income of $150 million and Mr. Esrey exercised options with a taxable income of $138 million in 1999 and 2000. The two-part shelter involved several complicated trades that effectively eliminated the multimillion-dollar tax bill that the executives would have owed on the options exchanges.

The first part involved a series of swaps intended to turn the income earned by the executives from the exercise of their options into capital gains, which are taxed at a much lower rate. In the second part the goal was to raise the cost of the asset, in this case the Sprint shares, so that any profit disappears. The planned end result: no tax bill.

Messrs. LeMay and Esrey have said that Ernst & Young assured them that the strategy was legal, and Mr. Esrey obtained an outside legal opinion saying the IRS would likely agree with it.

Soon the IRS stepped up its campaign against aggressive tax shelters. In a notice released in August 2000, the tax agency singled out tax shelters that involved basis shifting, just the type used by the Sprint executives. Saying it had seen a slew of these tactics recently, the IRS warned that because the transaction had no purpose other than to cut taxes it was not valid. "Appropriate penalties may be imposed on participants in these transactions," the IRS warned.

In what would prove to be a fateful mistake, Ernst & Young advised them against putting shares aside to pay for the taxes, say people close to the situation. Ernst & Young has declined to comment.

Also, on the advice of Ernst & Young, to avoid having taxes withheld to cover money owed on their gain from the option exercise, they declared a huge number of exemptions. On one form prepared by Ernst &

Young, Mr. LeMay, 57, claimed tens of thousands of exemptions, say people close to the situation. With that many exemptions, he would owe virtually no tax. Therefore, there would be no need for withholding.

The executives' bets soon went awry. The WorldCom deal ran aground on antitrust concerns in June 2000, tanking Sprint's shares.

By late 2000, Sprint's stock had sunk to $20, as investors worried about its ability to survive the increasingly brutal telecommunications downturn. The company had not been able to bump its share of the long-distance market past 10 percent. Its promising wireless business, now the nation's fourth largest, had racked up $14.5 billion in debt.

Late that year, Messrs. LeMay and Esrey, growing anxious about how their declining stock price affected their shelters, told the board about the problem, say people close to the situation. But they assured board members that Ernst & Young had told them the shelters were perfectly legal. Though increasingly concerned, Mr. LeMay decided not to sell shares to cover the taxes because he thought it would hurt the company, say people close to the situation. "As a matter of principle, while I have been a Sprint employee, I have never sold any of my shares and I continue to hold these shares today," Mr. LeMay said in a statement to employees last week.

The board left the matter alone.

Still the executives and the company were worried enough that in December 2000, Sprint and Ernst & Young together went to the Securities and Exchange Commission to discuss the possibility of undoing their option exercises. They ultimately decided not to because Sprint would have been subject to onerous accounting rules that could have hurt its earnings.

In late 2001, Messrs. LeMay and Esrey, knowing the IRS was increasingly likely to rule against the shelter, alerted the IRS to the possible problem and were granted amnesty for any potential penalties.

In the spring of 2002, directors finally realized they needed to address the situation. Several factors came together: The company's performance was falling. It faced a raft of shareholder suits following its failed plan to merge with WorldCom. And the tax shelter problem, if it leaked, might only add fodder to those suits. In addition, Mr. Esrey approached the board with a request for more compensation to help cover his potential tax liability, which irked some directors, say people close to the situation. The board turned down the request.

Suddenly, board members realized that if they needed to replace Mr. Esrey, Mr. LeMay's tax issues could interfere with his leadership. "They knew the IRS problem wasn't going away," says one informed person.

The tipping point came in June 2002, when the board learned through Messrs. LeMay and Esrey that the IRS was reviewing the shelter they used. These concerns intensified as accounting scandals erupted at numerous companies, including WorldCom. Increasingly anxious about what action they should take, independent directors hired the law firm of Davis Polk & Wardwell that month.

Once they started conferring with Davis Polk over the summer, the directors discussed the looming collision between Sprint's auditors and their two top executives. Directors worried whether it was "a healthy thing to have that kind of tension" between the auditors and the company's leaders, one informed person says. Another tough issue was the embarrassing prospect of having executives at the top of Sprint who were facing possible personal bankruptcy.

By October, Davis Polk made a set of recommendations to the independent directors. Even though many of the directors, including Mr. Hockaday and Stewart Turley, a retired chairman of Eckerd Corp., remained reluctant to consider ousting the top executives, they were advised that might be the most expedient course. If Mr. LeMay was promoted to CEO, for example, the board would have to disclose his tax problems and potential conflict with Ernst & Young, the board was told.

"If it came out, some people might say Mr. LeMay made a mistake, but others might say, 'How could the board pick someone who made such a colossal mistake?'" said one knowledgeable person.

Directors discussed the possibility of firing Ernst & Young, which had recommended the shelters, but worried that firing the auditors would be a public relations disaster.

While the board debated whether they should bypass Mr. LeMay, he sought his own assurances, especially as headhunters were seeking him out for other CEO searches, including WorldCom's. Early in October, Mr. LeMay was told by Sprint's board that he was still the top choice to succeed Mr. Esrey—if they could work out his tax issues. The board told

Mr. LeMay that it would hire a search firm to look at the pool of available talent but that they wouldn't interview any other candidates without first notifying him, according to people familiar with the discussions.

Later in October, Davis Polk, acting on behalf of the outside directors, hired executive recruiters Russell Reynolds Associates Inc. and instructed the firm "to be ready" to launch a CEO search and to draw up a list of possible candidates. The board formed a three-person search committee, whose members were Mr. Hockaday, Linda Koch Lorimer, vice president and secretary of Yale University, and Mr. Smith. "They were all agonizing" over having to look outside the company's ranks, according to one person close to the situation. "They were very uncomfortable."

Among directors, "there were a lot of debates because many of the directors liked and respected Mr. LeMay, and had a tough personal time saying he wasn't the right choice," says another informed person.

Ultimately, the sentiment shifted to ousting the veterans and seeking a new CEO. The directors worried that otherwise Sprint would face constant bad publicity over the tax battle. If, however, they fired the auditors, they might be giving the IRS ammunition in saying Ernst & Young was wrong on its tax-shelter position and even invite an SEC probe of the company.

By the time of the December 9 board meeting, most of the board members were leaning toward firing Messrs. Esrey and LeMay. But they decided to give the executives an opportunity to present their solution to the crisis. During the meeting at Sprint's sprawling headquarters outside Kansas City, Messrs. Esrey and LeMay methodically went through a slide presentation that recommended Sprint fire its auditors after the completion of its 2002 audit. "Sprint does not sacrifice loyal and dedicated employees," they told the board. "The potential for Ernst & Young conflict remains as long as Ernst & Young remains," the executives said, according to a review of their presentation.

A week later, the divided board finally came to a consensus and concluded that it would be preferable to jettison Messrs. Esrey and LeMay than Ernst & Young. Ernst & Young remains Sprint's auditor of 37 years. The company won't comment on whether Ernst & Young is still providing tax advice to executives.

According to an acquaintance, Mr. Hockaday finally concluded that "he couldn't tolerate having a new CEO who would be besmirched" by an IRS probe. "People would say, 'Why did they put a guy in there with a stain on his shirt?'"

But directors were mistaken in thinking their ordeal was behind them.

After news leaked out that Gary Forsee, the number two executive at BellSouth Corp., was Sprint's choice to succeed Mr. Esrey, BellSouth moved to block his exit. The dispute is now held up in court and could be decided as early as today.

While the court weighs Mr. Forsee's future, Sprint's directors are poised to begin considering other CEO candidates.

Take the money and run. That appeared to be the mindset of many Qwest Communications executives whose lucrative stock options offered them a profitable exit. Investors, on the other hand, were burned. Lou Kilzer, David Milstead, and Jeff Smith of the *Rocky Mountain News* examine how an instrument designed to align executives' interests with those of shareholders had the opposite effect. In restating its 2000 and 2001 financial results, Qwest discovered an additional $1 billion in losses. Its accounting practices have been investigated by the Securities and Exchange Commission and the Justice Department.

Lou Kilzer, David Milstead, and Jeff Smith

Wild, Wild Qwest

NINETY PEOPLE WEDGED into the small white house to bid on the 5.8-acre parcel sitting next to the million-dollar estates of the Polo Reserve subdivision.

The owner had once dreamed of building a gabled stone mansion and fishing pond there, but on this autumn day in 1999, he was locked away in a federal prison, convicted of selling bogus bank notes to international customers. Uncle Sam had seized con man Geoffrey Clement's Littleton property and was auctioning it off.

Bids started at $400,000. Five minutes later, a then-unnamed young couple walked away with the prize. The bid: $1.35 million.

Today, the couple has turned that tree farm into an estate that could put to shame even Clement's grandest vision.

The parcel hosts a 16,000-square-foot main house, a 2,900-square-foot garage, and a 1,500-square-foot balcony. In the rear are a 1,300-square-foot guesthouse, a 3,400-square-foot recording studio, and a

64,000-gallon swimming pool with a nearby Jacuzzi, according to county assessor's records.

"How do you appraise it?" asked county appraiser Robert Roy. "There's nothing else like it in Arapahoe County."

Though unidentified at the time, the purchasers of Clement's land, real estate deeds disclosed, were Stephen Jacobsen, then a senior vice president at Qwest Communications, and his wife, Susan.

In many respects, the $9 million estate is a symbol of the vast riches that befell many executives—not just CEOs—in the economic bubble that was the telecom boom of the late '90s.

At the time Jacobsen purchased the land, Qwest, an upstart fiber-optic company with plans to acquire U.S. West, already was creating multimillionaires in its executive ranks. The company gave millions of stock options to managers recruited by then-CEO Joseph Nacchio.

Thanks to Qwest's rocketing share price, the executives below Nacchio's level already had pocketed tens of millions of dollars in 1999.

The completion of the U.S. West merger only accelerated the options-cashout frenzy. By the time the selling ended, 26 executives and insiders racked up an estimated $483 million in profits from options and other sales of stock that Qwest gave them. Of those, at least ten Qwest insiders took home more than $12 million each in profits. Those figures include neither Nacchio's $230 million in profits nor Qwest founder Phil Anschutz's $2 billion in gross sales.

From a high of $66 a share in March 2000, Qwest now trades below $4. The Securities and Exchange Commission and the Justice Department are investigating Qwest's accounting practices, which allegedly inflated revenue to meet Wall Street targets. New CEO Richard Notebaert is forced to dispel talk of bankruptcy.

Investors who stayed with Qwest for the whole ride, or accepted the stock for their shares of U.S. West, were burned. The executives who got in early—and got out quickly—are still rich.

BONUS OR BANE

For years, activists argued that salaried executives lived a golden life, whether their companies' stock flourished or foundered. Ironically, stock options were designed to correct that, to align executives' interests with shareholders'.

A stock option grants an individual the right to buy a stock at a certain price at a specified time. Get a stock option for, say, $10, and you'll make more money if the share price appreciates to $20 rather than $11.

In 1980, only about one-third of the chief executives of public companies had been granted options. But by the mid-1990s, options had become the norm as part of the compensation package of most CEOs. And in many cases, handsome packages of options were granted to entire executive teams, especially at upstart technology companies that otherwise couldn't afford to pay competitive salaries to lure talent.

In theory, options provided the incentive for executives to build a fledgling company into a long-lasting, profitable enterprise.

The problem was that, instead of holding on to the stock, many executives sold it to cash in on the difference between the exercise and market prices.

That "creates the potential for the wrong kind of incentive," said Charles Elson, director of the University of Delaware Center for Corporate Governance. It can create short-term results—and profits for the seller—with a long-term problem for the company.

As long as executives "made their numbers" and hit or beat Wall Street estimates, they could continue to acquire options, cash them in, and take their profits—whether the company stayed healthy over time or not.

THE FEAST

Qwest was no different from other high-tech companies that gorged on stock options.

The company was option-happy from the start. At the time of its

June 1997 initial public offering, Qwest set aside 40 million shares for employee stock options, nearly as much stock as the 62 million shares it sold to the public. Founder Philip Anschutz kept 346 million shares, or nearly 85 percent of the company. (All share numbers and prices have been adjusted for two 2-for-1 splits.)

Qwest gave out nearly 28 million employee stock options in 1997 alone.

By the end of 2000, after assuming 84 million options from the two major companies it acquired, LCI International and U.S. West, the number of outstanding stock options had grown to 130 million. Had employees been able to exercise them, they would have yielded profits of $1.13 billion.

By the end of 2001, Qwest had granted 169.6 million options to its employees in four and a half years.

Thousands of employees ultimately were eligible for options, and Qwest spread them beyond the executive suite. But the options were concentrated at the top, with executive officers and directors getting more than three-quarters of the grants in 1997 and early 1998.

The result: Qwest's policy made multimillionaires of men who'd never had the title of CEO.

The seven top Qwest executives below Nacchio in 1997 received a combined 6.7 million options. The exercise prices ranged from $5.50 to $15 per share, and the options yielded profits (before splits) of $20, $30, and sometimes $80 apiece over the next three-plus years.

Qwest spokesman Tyler Gronbach said the company uses a combination of salary, stock options, and bonuses to compensate executives.

"Executives who joined the company right after the IPO [in 1997] in most cases took a cut in pay in exchange for options. As executives benefited, so did shareholders, who saw the company's stock appreciate more than 700 percent in the first three years the company was public," Gronbach said.

One former Qwest executive who cashed in defended the options, pointing out as Gronbach did that most people took pay cuts and large risk to join Qwest.

The executive, who asked not to be identified, said: "At the time, people looked at it [the venture] and said we were crazy."

In hindsight, crazy like foxes. Qwest executives from the early days rushed through their options as soon as they "vested," or became available to use. Most Qwest option grants vested over four or five years, a structure designed to retain executives and build long-term results.

Each year, as tens or even hundreds of thousands of options vested, Qwest's executives, with few exceptions, dumped all of it on the open market.

Greg Casey, the executive vice president of global wholesale markets, exercised 800,000 options over two years and sold all the stock immediately, never once owning a Qwest share outright. He made $31.4 million.

Lew Wilks, the executive vice president of internet strategy, exercised 1,625,000 options over two years, also selling all his stock immediately. He made $49.3 million in profits.

Options kept making some executives rich after they left Qwest. Brij Khandelwal, the company's first chief information officer, cashed in 490,000 options for $11.2 million in his first three years. When he left in mid-2000 with 910,000 remaining options, he was able to use them for sixty days after departure—and could have added $35.1 million to his profits based on market prices for Qwest stock during that period.

Wilks declined to discuss his stock sales, and Casey and Khandelwal could not be reached.

Executives often timed their departure dates to maximize their payouts. If Qwest employees left the company before options vested, they forfeited them. So executives often said good-bye on vesting day.

Larry Seese, the company's executive vice president of network engineering and operations, and Albert Wandry, the senior vice president of government markets and fiber sales, both left immediately after thousands of options vested.

Wandry did not return telephone calls asking for comment. Seese, an AT&T veteran, said stock options provided the only real financial incentive to join the company.

"I thought it was a good idea and a good opportunity. I built the network, and then Joe [Nacchio] and I decided it was time for me to move on."

Seese, who netted about $19 million from stock sales, left Qwest in

1999 and moved to California, where he now is a partner in a small vineyard in the Napa Valley, and enjoys playing golf and traveling.

"I still have some Qwest stock—for what it's worth, a significant amount," Seese said. "I believed we were going to continue to grow."

Early Qwest executives who stayed through the June 30, 2000, close of the U.S. West merger got the biggest payoff. Because the deal was considered a "change in control" in their employment contracts, all the options vested ahead of schedule.

Three weeks after the merger closed, Qwest executives and board members engaged in an orgy of selling. In 21 days from late July to early August 2000, 13 insiders, including Nacchio, sold 3.75 million shares at prices ranging from $47.50 to $55. The gross proceeds totaled $191 million. In most cases, the shares had just been acquired through options at prices from $3.75 to $15.

Some executives stayed on for the long haul.

Craig Slater, a Qwest director who made $35.7 million in profits from options and other stock awards, helped found the company, structured many successful deals, and is "still hanging in there," said Jim Monaghan, spokesman for the Anschutz Investment Co.

Slater declined to comment.

"He lives within his means. He's not a flashy guy in any sense," Monaghan said. "He makes money the old-fashioned way; he earns it."

But even Nacchio, who made more than $230 million by selling Qwest stock, realized by 2001 that the instant wealth of stock options was giving some executives an incentive to leave.

By then, a number of his top executives had cashed in and given notice. Nacchio, who had created an intense, workaholic culture, was disappointed that the executives didn't feel obligated to stay and build the company, according to a former executive.

At a Goldman Sachs investor conference in October 2001, Nacchio blamed the management turnover on an infirmity he characterized as "they all got very rich."

"I've learned a lot of time that [when this happens] they don't listen to you anymore," Nacchio said. "[They] would rather buy a house in the Cayman Islands or Hawaii."

Yet the wave of options continued. Drake Tempest, the general counsel who started work in October 1998, is today only halfway through a grant of 900,000 options he received upon his arrival. He hasn't touched 400,000 options received in August 1999.

Qwest decided he needed more incentive. The company gave Tempest 600,000 more options in November 2001. He couldn't be reached for comment for this story.

Other executives who joined Qwest in the later years couldn't—or wouldn't—cash out.

President Afshin Mohebbi, who joined Qwest in 1999, has not exercised a single one of the 5.6 million options he's received. Neither did Robin Szeliga, the former chief financial officer, who got 1 million options in 2001.

Many of the options have not vested yet.

A SHOW OF WEALTH

There's no way of knowing exactly what most of the executives and directors did with the money they cashed in from Qwest. In fact, property tax records suggest that some didn't rush out to buy new cars and more expensive houses.

But one employee whose wealth has become far more visible than his colleagues' is Stephen Jacobsen, the owner of the Arapahoe County mansion.

He was one of a line of AT&T employees who in 1997 followed Nacchio to Denver from New Jersey.

Jacobsen's deal was attractive—his salary was $185,000 a year, and he received a relocation allowance of $150,000. But it hardly presaged his soon-to-be multimillion-dollar acquisitions.

A little over a month after beginning his new assignment in spring 1997, Jacobsen and his wife purchased a $665,000 home in the Polo Reserve, right around the corner from their future estate. And they bought a new Chevrolet.

But their Chevy days were numbered.

Qwest gave Jacobsen 1.2 million stock options on June 23, 1997, the day the company went public. The exercise price was $5.50, soon to be a bargain as Qwest investors flocked to the company's shares.

Records show that by 1998, Jacobsen cashed in options for a $2.5 million profit. The following year, Jacobsen's profits totaled $6.5 million; he upgraded to a Jaguar and went bidding on Geoffrey Clement's land.

By 2000, when his option profits were $37.5 million, Jacobsen was building his Littleton estate and buying oceanfront property in southern California.

That property, at 16 Ritz Cove in Dana Point, is assessed at $5.1 million, a computer database of property records says.

By then, Stephen and Susan Jacobsen were mingling in Denver's social elite.

In May 2000, socialites and others gathered at the Cherry Creek mall for the Mask Project Gala to raise money for the Hospice of Metro Denver. A John Elway autographed mask with a 0.8-carat teardrop diamond was expected to bring in the most, and it appeared it had at $20,000.

Then, unexpectedly, Stephen Jacobsen bid $25,000 for a mask offered by Mask Project founder Mickey Ackerman. The Jacobsens were on the society map.

Susan Jacobsen says interest in her family's estate is misplaced.

"This was my dream," she said. "It was not Steve's. . . . I've dreamed this house. I created this house."

For three years, she said, she could barely sleep, coming up with new ideas for the project.

Despite her estate's expanse, she and her husband want to live simple lives. "We want to blend in," she said.

"We didn't know we were going to get to this point in our lives," she said of the risk Stephen took in joining the Qwest team. "We never imagined it."

Jacobsen left Qwest in April 2001, but work continued on pace on his new estate. The pool went in, and a new barn was built in the back.

In the end, the Jacobsens made a statement, intentional or not.

Their main home alone is twice as big as Phil Anschutz's and four times as expensive as Joe Nacchio's New Jersey home.

The Arapahoe county assessor estimates the package is worth $9 million to $10 million.

A couple of neighbors expressed concern that the property might overwhelm others nearby, but neighbor Kristen Brown said it added to the Polo Reserve's value. "It's absolutely beautiful," she said.

"Nobody has ever said anything negative about my property," said Stephen Jacobsen.

As far as his views on Qwest, Jacobsen isn't talking.

"I've been gone from the company for about 19 months now," he said. "I don't know what's happened there recently."

Said Susan Jacobsen: "We're trying to live a quiet life."

The merchandise most coveted by professional shoplifters isn't a fancy leather coat or sparkling jewelry. It is mostly small items most of us would never suspect to be targeted. Joanne Kimberlin, writing in *The Virginian-Pilot*, directs us through a highly organized theft pipeline that's quietly snatching billions of dollars from American retailers.

Joanne Kimberlin

The New Face of Shoplifting

FOR NEARLY TEN YEARS, as often as seven days a week, Chrystine Anne Kelley stole from stores in Hampton Roads.

Kelley was a "booster"—a member of the mushrooming army of professional shoplifters making a career of a petty crime once left to nervous amateurs.

Resourceful, relentless, and ready to fight, the pros are ushering in a new era in the ancient tug-of-war between merchant and thief. Attracted by the lucrative pickings and the light punishment if caught, professional shoplifters have helped turn the old five-finger discount into a $13 billion underground industry.

The nature of this new foe is just dawning on retailers and law enforcement. The pros work for a criminal enterprise so shadowy that it only recently earned an official name: organized retail theft, or ORT.

Its rip-off reaches far beyond the stores. Millions of dollars in sales taxes slip away with the goods. Prices creep ever upward to cover the losses. Jobs disappear when mounting "shrink"—as retailers call it—pushes a store over the financial edge.

More sinister: links between organized shoplifting and terrorist funding.

More personal: a stolen-goods scheme that relabels out-of-date pharmaceuticals and baby formula, gets them back into the wholesale distribution system, then returns them to a store shelf near you.

Boosters like Kelley work the leading edge of the illegal pipeline, stealing specific products they know their fences will buy.

High on their shoplifting list: Tylenol, Visine, vitamins, name-brand nasal sprays, and other over-the-counter medicines. Infant formula. Razor blades. DVDs—especially Disney movies. Film. Batteries. Stop-smoking kits like Nicorette. Cosmetics, home pregnancy tests, and grooming aids.

The targeted products have a few things in common:

They're small enough to be slipped into purses and pockets, or boldly swept from store shelves during an intimidating grab-and-run.

They're pricey enough to be in big demand on black markets in the U.S. and abroad.

They're untraceable, bearing no serial numbers or store ID marks.

Kelley, 36, figures she stole between $3,000 and $5,000 worth of the products nearly every day. In a Norfolk courtroom last year, the sometimes-waitress from Virginia Beach explained that she had a heroin habit to feed, and her fences paid less than 30 cents for every dollar's worth of goods she stole.

Not all boosters are drug addicts like Kelley. Some are simply after a quick buck. Some are foreign nationals sending money home. Some are convicts schooled in prison yards about shoplifting's low-risk/high-reward equation.

Many boosters, however, share Kelley's addictions. When withdrawal made her too sick to shoplift, Kelley's fences would front her the cost of a fix so she could get back to work.

"It's like a slave trade," said S. Clark Daugherty, a deputy commonwealth's attorney in Norfolk. "The fences are the owners and the boosters are the slaves and the drugs are what keeps them in slavery."

MAKING THE CIRCUIT

Kelley's shoplifting circuit stretched from Chesapeake to Yorktown.

Wal-Marts. Kmarts. Eckerds. 7-Elevens. Grocery, hardware, and department stores. Mom-and-pop shops.

"I would generally continuously hit a store until I wore it completely out," Kelley said in court.

She was testifying against four of her accused fences—three men and one woman swept up in FBI-led raids in August 2000. Their arrests were one result of Operation Cold Storage, a sting aimed at busting a Norfolk-based network of retail thieves.

Fed by "the little crabs," as one police officer calls the boosters, the ring operated out of pawn shops, flea markets, liquidation outlets, and warehouses across Hampton Roads. Inventory was reportedly plumped up with tractor-trailer loads hijacked as they traveled through North Carolina.

From Norfolk, the bulk of the stolen merchandise was funneled to Richmond, where it was mingled with legitimate products and sold back to retailers.

Hampton Roads is just one hot spot on a map peppered with ORT bonfires, said William D. Delahoyde, a former federal prosecutor from North Carolina who now runs his own security consulting firm in Raleigh.

Delahoyde says organized retail theft has flared up in cities along both coasts, the Great Lakes, the Gulf of Mexico, and farther inland. Busy port cities, with their heavy cargo traffic, are particularly vulnerable.

"I'd say you have a significant theft problem in your area," Delahoyde said of Hampton Roads, where an estimated $200 million worth of retail goods vanished last year—enough money to build Norfolk a new downtown arena, or Virginia Beach a new convention center.

Operation Cold Storage produced a lull, but it was short-lived.

"There was a temporary reduction in shoplifting afterward, but it didn't last," said Daugherty, the deputy commonwealth's attorney.

Joseph P. McCabe, the vice president of special projects at Phar-Mor headquarters in Ohio, says his company's drugstores are "continuously getting pummeled" in Hampton Roads.

McCabe says Phar-Mor's local losses rival the drain suffered at stores in traditionally tougher towns like Philadelphia.

Perhaps even more alarming, says McCabe, are the increasingly fearless tactics of the area's boosters.

"More and more, it's stop-me-if-you-dare," he said. "They're slamming us in twos and threes, just emptying shelves, grabbing one hundred boxes at a time and running, not even caring if they're seen. People are getting hurt."

McCabe described a confrontation recently captured on security video at a large discount retailer in Hampton Roads.

"These four big guys came in looking like the front line of the Pittsburgh Steelers," McCabe said. "They grabbed a Rubbermaid garbage can, loaded it up, headed for the back exit, and bowled over anybody who got in their way."

A store manager summoned help from an office upstairs. While oblivious shoppers browsed in the aisles out front, store staff faced off with the thieves in the back storage room.

"A ballyhoo ensued," McCabe said. "A huge fight. Right there on the videotape. They battled their way right out of the store."

Such in-your-face tactics are shocking enough to persuade most store employees to step aside and call police later.

At an Operation Cold Storage trial, booster Kevin A. Sherrod put it this way: "We went in there and just took. Completely took."

BILLIONS BOOSTED

U.S. merchants lost $39 billion worth of goods in 2000, according to the latest studies.

Dishonest employees and vendors took nearly half of it.

Another 18 percent is attributed to honest bookkeeping glitches, such as miscounting inventory, or perishable inventories, such as a grocer's spoiled produce.

Shoplifters swiped the remaining 33 percent—or around $13 billion worth.

Impulse, teenage thrills, mental illness, or hard times drive most ordinary shoplifters. No one knows how many of the guilty are propelled by pure profit—the motivation of a professional booster.

Gathering the clues isn't easy. Many shoplifters get away. And retailers are reluctant to discuss their losses publicly.

"Some think it reflects unfavorably on them or makes the bad guys think they're an easy target," said Charles Miller of the Food Marketing Institute, a Washington, D.C.–based grocery trade organization. "They won't even share their numbers with us."

The trade group believes organized retail theft's piece of the shoplifting pie could amount to as much as $10 billion, but only one thing is certain: Despite ever-increasing investments in loss prevention—as the industry calls it—retailers are barely holding the line against thieves.

As a percentage of sales, shrink rates have held relatively steady at around 2 percent in the past decade. In the meantime, more stores have opened, providing more opportunity for thieves and swelling overall retail shrink by nearly a third since 1993, when $30 billion worth of merchandise disappeared off the shelves.

Perhaps even more telling: While the number of shoplifting arrests is down—at least in some areas—individual hits are bigger.

Jack L. Hayes International, Inc., a consulting firm with offices in Florida and Buenos Aires, collects annual shrink reports from thirty department store and mass merchandising chains.

The retailers in Hayes' survey reported 3 percent fewer shoplifting arrests in 2000 than the year before. But the value of the merchandise found on those caught was 4 percent higher. It has climbed 42 percent since Hayes started keeping track in 1994.

"That tells me that all the detection systems and security in the stores is discouraging the amateurs but not the professionals," said Mark R. Doyle, Hayes' vice president.

BLACK-MARKET ECONOMY

The FBI first noticed the new breed of shoplifter in the early 1990s, when the agency began staking out major fencing operations in the

Northeast and Southeast. Phar-Mor's McCabe saw the first wave of boosters in Detroit in the late 1980s.

"We started catching coke addicts with faxed lists of what to steal in their pockets," he said. "So this isn't really so new—just new as far as people really understanding what they're up against these days, and that it's getting more serious."

McCabe blames the black market more than the boosters.

"That's the disease," he said. "Focusing on the boosters is like taking an aspirin for brain cancer."

Black markets exist wherever goods are sold illegally. In the organized retail theft hierarchy, 15 to 20 boosters sell to a single street fence. From there the goods can take many paths.

Some go straight to flea markets, pawn shops, auction houses, or are posted on the internet, where they're offered directly to the public.

Others are sold to upper-level fences, who typically send the merchandise to repackaging operations. Housed in small warehouses or large garages, repack operations "clean" the products.

Price tags are removed with solvents and razor blades. Goods close to their expiration dates get counterfeit labels with new dates, logos, and manufacturer UPC codes. Shrink-wrapped and boxed, they're sent on to crooked wholesalers, who sell them to unsuspecting—or sometimes unscrupulous—retailers.

A portion of the stolen goods are hidden in shipping containers and sent to countries where American products are in demand, but high tariffs, taxes, transportation costs, or embargoes make them scarce and expensive.

"No one thought when we passed NAFTA that it would affect shoplifting," said Richard C. Hollinger, a University of Florida associate professor who directs the annual National Retail Security Survey.

"Everyone just thought free trade would create a demand for Advil in Mexico City," Hollinger said. "Well, it has, but it's also created a demand for more stolen Advil in Mexico City."

Some organized retail theft groups with international ties sell the products in the United States, then smuggle the money overseas. Rings with Middle Eastern connections are particularly worrisome, said former prosecutor Delahoyde.

Uncovered in places like Charlotte, Raleigh, Dallas, Atlanta, New York, and Lexington, Kentucky, such rings are feared to be financing terrorist activity.

The Charlotte, North Carolina, ring, busted with $10 million worth of contraband cigarettes in 2000, had direct links to Hezbollah, a militant Islamic organization listed by the government as a terrorist group.

"It's hard to marshal the kind of evidence you need to really follow the trail upstream," Delahoyde said. "But there's no doubt about where some of this money is going. Organized retail theft is a time bomb for this country, and it's frightening."

"WE'RE THE VICTIMS"

More often than not, law enforcement finds itself frustrated trying to reach higher than the bottom rung. Boosters, who generally have long arrest records, aren't the most credible of witnesses against their fences.

Priority is a problem, too. In overburdened police departments, property crimes take a backseat to violent crimes and drug trafficking.

"It all comes down to money and manpower," said Robert E. Hummel, a detective specializing in property crimes at the Chesapeake Police Department.

Even when convicted, the guilty get relatively easy treatment under sentencing guidelines. Three of Chrystine Kelley's accused fences were found guilty; none was sent to prison.

"Get caught with $25,000 worth of drugs and you might not ever get out of prison," said Robert E. Bradenham II, a federal prosecutor in Newport News. "Get caught with $25,000 worth of stolen goods and there's a good chance you won't do a day."

With many retailers already weakened by lean economic times, organized retail theft is predicted to flourish, said King Rogers, a former vice president of assets protection for the Target Corp.

"Loss prevention is the first budget that gets cut when times are hard," Rogers said. "It's a wicked circle. Shoplifting hurts your profits, so you can't afford to put as many eyes out to watch the floor, which leads to even more shoplifting."

Theft "can be the deciding factor in whether to keep a store open," said Phar-Mor's McCabe. "It can make the difference in whether people have jobs."

Hollinger, at the University of Florida, says shrink losses top car theft, bank robbery, and household burglary combined.

"So the most costly forms of larceny in America are not the street crimes," Hollinger said. "They're the crimes that happen every day in our stores."

He understands that it's "hard for the average consumer to shed crocodile tears about the profitability of some big retailer."

"But in the end, we're the victims. You and me. We're the ones who pay for it."

Memo to music execs: High school kids knew five years ago that your industry was losing its relevancy and was headed for financial trouble. Downloaded music and CD burning by young consumers has turned a fat and sassy industry into one dazed and confused. Charles C. Mann, writing in *Wired* magazine, explains the trends and speculates on the future of the once-great hit-making machine. As 2003 drew to a close, CD prices were being reduced, industry mergers were on the front burner, and one study found that two-thirds of the music on Americans' computers came from illegal file-swapping.

Charles C. Mann

The Year the Music Dies

NOT LONG BEFORE his sudden death from a heart attack, I saw Timothy White at a party in Boston, standing by the bar in his usual bow tie and white bucks. When he waved me over, I was delighted: Timothy was not only the editor of *Billboard* but a respected music critic and biographer. Even the executives he often took to task conceded, with a wince, that he understood the secretive, confusing business better than almost anyone. "How much you want to bet that the entire music industry collapses?" he asked me. "And I mean soon—like five, ten years. Kaboom!"

Truth is, it may happen even sooner. This year could determine whether the music business as we know it survives.

In the first six months of 2002, CD sales fell 11 percent—on top of a 3 percent decline the year before. Sales of blank CDs jumped 40 percent last year, while the users of Kazaa, the biggest online file-trading service, tripled in number. Meanwhile, the labels' new legitimate online music services attracted fewer paying customers than the McDonald's in Times Square.

As recently as ten years ago, the media conglomerates that own record labels regarded them as cash cows—smaller than Hollywood but more reliably profitable. Now all five major labels are either losing money or barely in the black, and the industry's decline is turning into a plunge. In the next year, whether together or separately, the labels will have to set about totally reinventing the way they do business, a horribly difficult task for any institution.

To leap the hurdles posed by digital technology, the industry must find a way to make money selling downloaded music on a per-track basis, allow in-store CD burning, slash recording costs with cheap software and hardware, and change artists' contracts to reflect the new economic reality. Doing any one of these will be next to impossible. Doing all of them would be one of the more amazing turnarounds in business history.

The record labels blame piracy for their woes. And they're right—in part. Before writing this paragraph, I logged on to Kazaa. At ten on a Monday morning, hardly peak time, 3.1 million people were on the network—more simultaneous users than Napster ever had in its heyday.

At least a hundred copies of every song on the *Billboard* Hot 100 were available for download. So were 13 out of 15 tracks on Mariah Carey's new CD, which wouldn't hit stores for another three weeks. And that's not even counting the discs sold on every street corner from the Bronx to Beijing.

The industry rightly believes that if it can make file-swapping more difficult, and legitimate online services easier and less expensive, it can turn the kids on Kazaa into paying customers. Pursuing this two-pronged approach, the companies are spending millions on their own internet services (pressplay from Universal and Sony; MusicNet from BMG, EMI, and Warner), on lawyers to chase away pirates and peer-to-peer networks, and on antipiracy ads featuring the likes of Britney Spears.

But this won't be enough. To survive, the industry will need the active assistance of friends it doesn't have. The labels may be able to kill

Kazaa, but they won't be able to stop even more decentralized networks like Gnutella without help from internet service providers, cable operators, and telephone companies. All their efforts to get DVD-like protection for CDs ultimately depend on the goodwill of hardware manufacturers and Capitol Hill. The online subscription services will flounder without cooperation from performers, songwriters, and record stores. And the ability of Britney to change the hearts and minds of music fans depends on public sympathy.

That sympathy is in short supply. Rightly or wrongly, record companies are detested by politicians (for corrupting youth), by webcasters (for demanding royalties), and by their customers (for inflating prices). Musicians and songwriters are famous for loathing the labels, and many have resisted licensing their songs to MusicNet and pressplay. (Both are under investigation for possible antitrust violations.) Radio and MTV aren't in the industry's corner; the labels, through "independent promotion" programs, effectively have to pay *them* to broadcast music. And the electronics industry's attitude toward the labels is summed up by an Apple slogan: Rip. Mix. Burn. Which, a music executive once told me, translates into "Fuck you, record labels."

Even the music trade's corporate masters are torn. Until the 1980s, most labels were controlled by eccentric, sometimes thuggish entrepreneurs who had their whole lives bound up with selling albums. In the past two decades, every big label has been swept up into one of five major groups: Universal, Warner, Sony, BMG, and EMI, which together control about 75 percent of global recorded-music sales. Despite their dominance, though, the majors are merely duchies in large media empires with other, often conflicting, priorities.

Last year, the Big Five together sold about $20 billion worth of music. Meanwhile, Sony alone saw about $42 billion in electronics and computer sales. If Sony wants to sell MP3-capable cell phones—a big thing in Japan and potentially worldwide—how much attention will it pay to Sony Music's protests?

Similarly, AOL Time Warner is desperately trying to resuscitate AOL by selling high-speed internet access. Yet one of the main uses for high-speed connections is downloading free music—something that Warner Music sees as a deadly threat. Bertelsmann, the German media titan that owns BMG Music, cared so little about its music division that the company invested millions of dollars in Napster, accepting along the way the outraged resignation of its two main music executives.

Worse, at a time when bold thinking is required, the industry, once the province of entrepreneurial risk-takers, is increasingly managed by bean counters focused on short-term survival. Too often, the response to problems is throwing lawyers and money at them, then ducking responsibility.

Why, when most industries are using technology to slash costs, is Michael Jackson running up $30 million in studio bills? Or, rather, why is Sony Music letting him? Career protection. By using the hottest producers and recording studios, executives can deflect failure ("We got the Neptunes, what else could we have done?") and allay their fears artists will blame them for a flop ("That track would've got some air, but the Suits wouldn't shell out $50,000 to clear the Zeppelin sample"). Because the costs are billed against the musicians, there's little incentive to save money.

For years, the safest path to success in the music business has been to hunt the teen market. But by ignoring career artists at the expense of the latest trends, the labels have lost touch with wide swaths of society. Ultimately, Timothy suggested to me that night, the industry as we know it could vanish not so much because of technology but because few people over the age of thirty would care if it did. "I can't believe that the business I've spent my life with could be about to disappear," he said. "And I also can't believe it's happening so fast."

If the industry collapsed, as he predicted, would artists and listeners be better or worse off? After a brutally difficult transition musicians and fans might on the whole benefit. The star-making machinery may crumble, but people will still pay for music, whether it's live, licensed, or digitally delivered (at a competitive price). Look at the bluegrass and gospel circuits, which provide long careers and middle-class lives to some of America's greatest performers. Look at the techno bands that are winning an audience by selling their music to advertisers. And look at artists like Phish, Prince, and Wonderlick, who are trying to use the internet to deal directly with their fans and bypass the middleman.

To be sure, today's middleman does a lot of good, too. Fans taught by two generations of rock and roll to loathe the Suits don't appreciate the enormous contributions of producers and A&R executives (think Ahmet Ertegun or Russell Simmons). And the labels perform the invaluable function of backing young performers financially as they begin their careers. But in a postlabel world, musicians might find other ways to get this help, from the *American Idol* model (building recognition as part of a corporate campaign) to the Broadway show model (getting ad hoc groups of small investors to provide funds). Eliminating the big-label overheads could cut the cost of making music, too, enlarging the pool of contenders and democratizing the process.

All of these models would produce fewer global superstars and more locally successful musicians. We might not see another Michael Jackson circa 1982, but we also wouldn't see another Michael Jackson circa 2002. Not a bad trade-off.

When I made these suggestions to Timothy, a habitual skeptic about the music industry, he wasn't convinced: He didn't think that the people he talked to every day were up for a revolution. It could happen, I argued.

He clapped me on the shoulder agreeably.

"In any case," he said, "we're about to find out."

Here are words of warning for J. K. Rowling of Harry Potter fame: A hit children's book series may have grave financial and personal repercussions. In this story in the *Los Angeles Times*, Meg James describes the long-running legal battle between an 81-year-old widow and the Walt Disney Company over the $1 billion empire of A. A. Milne's Winnie the Pooh. As this book went to press, the legal wrangling was still unresolved.

Meg James

Big Battle for a Silly Old Bear

ONCE UPON A TIME —well, actually 78 years ago—a British playwright named Alan Alexander Milne scribbled some lighthearted verses about a boy and his constant companion, a dim-witted bear who couldn't get enough honey.

Winnie the Pooh was an immediate sensation. Milne spent the rest of his life trying to escape the suffocating shadow of his cuddly creation. Even today, people can't get enough of that silly old bear—or his honey.

Pooh has become a $1 billion-a-year industry for Walt Disney Co., which acquired rights to the Milne characters in 1961. Disney has put Pooh and his forest friends in movies and computer software, on its ABC television network, and on videotapes and DVDs. There's Pooh fruit juice and Tigger telephones. Pooh Beanie Babies dressed in satiny feng shui robes and leatherlike black biker jackets. Piglet cookie jars. Pooh chopsticks. A toaster that plays a Pooh jingle while toasting bread in a pattern that resembles the bear's face.

At Tokyo Disneyland, visitors wait two hours to ride Pooh's Honey Hunt—the park's most popular attraction.

Last year, Disney paid $352 million to buy the remaining Pooh rights from various Milne heirs in England. Yet there remains one threat to the entertainment giant's Pooh empire. Her name is Shirley Slesinger Lasswell.

Lasswell is an 81-year-old widow who lives in Beverly Hills and gets around in a chauffeured silver Mercedes with a 3-foot Pooh doll buckled in beside her. Lasswell and her daughter inherited merchandising rights to Milne's characters half a century ago from Lasswell's first husband, a literary agent.

In 1961, Lasswell turned those rights over to Disney for a share of the merchandising revenue. Since then, she and her daughter, Patricia Slesinger, have collected $66 million in Pooh riches. But they are unhappy. They contend that Disney has cheated them out of at least $200 million in royalties and are asking a court to terminate their Disney contract so they can shop their Pooh rights to other companies.

Their 11-year-old lawsuit, one of the longest-running sagas in Los Angeles Superior Court, is set for trial in March.

For Disney, the stakes are enormous. The company recently warned shareholders that "damages could total as much as several hundred million dollars and adversely impact . . . any future exploitation" of Pooh, Piglet, Tigger, and Eeyore.

It has been a nasty fight. In the early 1990s, Disney workers shredded boxes of old files sought by Lasswell and her daughter, including one labeled "Winnie the Pooh, Legal Problems." Disney says the papers were irrelevant, but a judge last year fined the company $90,000 and ruled that the jury would be told about the destruction of evidence if the case was to go to trial.

Both sides agree that Lasswell and her daughter are entitled to Disney royalties on a wide range of Pooh products. The dispute centers on whether their rights extend to videotapes, DVDs, and computer software featuring the Milne menagerie.

Disney's lead attorney, Daniel Petrocelli, dismisses the case as "overreaching" and "rooted in greed."

Lasswell resents the suggestion that she and her daughter are gold diggers: "We're not grab, grab, grab. We're low-key people," she said.

Back in the '50s, Lasswell marketed upscale Pooh toys and children's clothing to department stores, helping to revive the franchise years before Disney became involved. Lasswell believes that she has been key to developing the Pooh brand.

"We wouldn't be spending all these millions on lawyers all of these years if we just wanted more money," she said. "We just want what we're entitled to: no more, no less."

A BOY'S STUFFED TOYS

A. A. Milne was one of Britain's most popular playwrights in the early 1920s. At one point, five of his comedies were playing at the same time in London and New York.

In 1920, Milne and his wife, Daphne, had their only child, Christopher Robin Milne. They gave him stuffed toys, including a bear, a tiger, a kangaroo, and a donkey whose neck grew limp from the boy's affection. Mother and child would play together, creating stories and voices for the animals. Milne used this as inspiration for a 1924 poem about a boy and his teddy bear, and he later created the cast of *Winnie-the-Pooh,* published in 1926. The book's hero was a boy named Christopher Robin.

The "bear of little brain" and his playmates had personalities and enduring charm. The simple line drawings of Ernest H. Shepard brought the characters to life. The four Pooh books have sold more than 50 million copies in 33 languages.

Milne was smothered by Pooh's success. He fretted about being typecast as a children's writer and grew uneasy about using his son's name in the stories.

One of the first to see Pooh's financial potential was Stephen Slesinger, a young New York literary agent. Slesinger established one of the first successful character licensing firms, acquiring rights to Tarzan and Charlie Chan. He helped create the Red Ryder comics and films and served as the agent for western writer Zane Grey.

In 1930, Slesinger sailed to England to secure from Milne the rights to sell Pooh merchandise in the U.S. and Canada. He agreed to pay Milne a $1,000 advance, plus royalties equal to 3 percent of the merchandising revenue. Two years later, Slesinger acquired the radio and television rights at a time when TV was still just a budding idea among a few engineers. During the Depression, Slesinger licensed Pooh toys and dishes, an RCA record narrated by Jimmy Stewart, and a board game by Parker Bros.

By the mid-1930s, Milne was enjoying steady royalties from his Pooh books as well as Slesinger's merchandise, but his literary career was in a painful slide. His novels and plays about marriage and murder mysteries flopped. Critics suggested that he return to children's verses.

The very mention of Pooh often would make Milne shudder, said his biographer, Ann Thwaite. Milne wrote 530 pages of memoirs and mentioned the Pooh characters on just four.

"He spent five years writing the children's books in a lifetime of being an author—more than fifty years," Thwaite said. "He went on to write marvelous plays and stories, and nobody seemed to be the least bit interested in them."

The Pooh stories also poisoned the relationship between Milne and his son.

Christopher Milne was continually teased for his role in the Pooh books. As an adult, he wrote that his father "had filched from me my good name and had left me with nothing but the empty fame of being his son."

By the time A. A. Milne died in 1956, Christopher had rarely seen his father for years.

To escape his celebrity, Christopher and his wife moved to the English countryside and opened a small bookshop. Only once did he use his famous name—to lead a campaign against a 1980s oil-drilling project that threatened Britain's Ashdown Forest, the real-life setting for Pooh's Hundred Acre Wood. Christopher died in 1996, at 75.

DISNEY SHOWS INTEREST

By the 1940s, Walt Disney's studio was enjoying the success of a string of animated films, including *Snow White and the Seven Dwarfs*, *Fantasia*, and *Bambi*. Disney was scouting for other children's stories to animate and took a keen interest in Pooh.

But Roy O. Disney, Walt's brother and the financial brains of the company, uncovered a problem.

"A. A. Milne has certainly completely balled up his rights in Winnie the Pooh," he wrote in a 1947 memo. "Milne has given to Slesinger not only rights to merchandising, but also rights for radio and television. . . . If we were to attempt to do anything with Winnie the Pooh, Slesinger is in a beautiful spot to either hold us up for an outrageous price or sit back and reap the rewards of our investment."

DISNEY TOOK A PASS ON POOH

About this time, Slesinger had his eye on Shirley Basso, a stunning showgirl twenty years his junior. In 1947, the doe-eyed brunette was a dancer in *Hellzapoppin!* on Broadway. One of the show's producers introduced her to Slesinger.

"He was a little pixie, so sweet and so creative," she recalled.

The couple flew to Las Vegas in 1948 to be married. Silent film actress Clara Bow was the maid of honor. The newlyweds honeymooned at Slesinger's dude ranch in Colorado and split their time between a New York penthouse and a bungalow at the Hotel Bel-Air.

Slesinger died in 1953 while in Los Angeles producing a TV pilot based on the *Blondie* comic strip. He bequeathed his merchandising and licensing business to Shirley and their one-year-old daughter, Patricia.

Within a few years, the stream of royalties began to dwindle. Shirley sold the Colorado ranch. She could no longer afford the Manhattan penthouse.

"I thought, 'Now what do I do?' But it was right there for me," she said. "I decided to promote Pooh."

She reread Milne's books and wrote down verses to use in a new line of products. She designed Pooh postcards, stationery, wall hangings, and oversize coloring books. She fired the Long Island, New York, firm that had been hand-stitching Pooh dolls for twenty years—she thought they weren't "snuggly enough"—and hired other factories to churn out plusher products. She visited buyers at Lord & Taylor and Bonwit Teller in New York, Marshall Field & Co. in Chicago, Filene's in Boston, and Neiman Marcus in Dallas. Soon they were carrying her Pooh line of children's apparel, pink pinafores, and plastic-lined panties with Pooh quotations.

In 1960, Shirley got a call from Disney asking if she was interested in selling her Pooh rights. She was excited by the idea.

"I really went as far as I could go [with Pooh]. It was just me, not some huge company," she said.

She reached a royalty agreement in 1961 with Disney that gave her 4 percent of the revenue on worldwide Pooh sales. Soon after, Shirley said, she met Walt Disney himself at the Waldorf-Astoria hotel in New York.

"He said, 'Shirley, you won't be sorry,'" she recalled.

In 1965, Disney struck a deal with Sears, Roebuck & Co. to sell Pooh merchandise designed by Disney. A year later, Disney released its first Pooh movie, with an Americanized Christopher Robin character. Ernest Shepard, Pooh's original illustrator, pronounced the film "a travesty."

Shirley remarried in 1964, to cartoonist Fred Lasswell, and moved with her husband and daughter to Tampa, Florida, where she drove a Cadillac with a "POOH 1" license plate.

The family's Pooh royalties rose from $13,000 in 1967 to $89,000 by 1981, their attorneys said. Pooh money helped pay for Patricia Slesinger's college education and her art history studies abroad.

Shirley's doubts about Disney surfaced in 1981 while she was on a trip to Disney World in Florida. A self-described Pooh "shopaholic," she went on a buying spree. Later, she compared her haul with Disney's royalty statements and saw that many of the Pooh products were not listed. She hired a lawyer.

By then, Disney had turned Pooh into a global brand and wanted to streamline its character rights. Instead of having separate contracts with the Slesinger and Milne families, Disney wanted to bring all the deals under one contract.

In 1983, Shirley Lasswell, Christopher Milne, and representatives of the Milne estate signed a new Disney contract. The deal trimmed the Slesinger family's Pooh royalties from 4 percent to about 2 percent of what they expected to be a much larger revenue pie. It called for more detailed accounting of what was sold. Disney also paid Lasswell and her daughter $750,000 to resolve the dispute over past royalties.

The peace didn't last long. By the late 1980s, videotapes were the rage, and Disney was busy putting Pooh movies and TV programs on video. In 1987, a lawyer for the Milne estate and Lasswell compared notes about Disney's royalty payments. In one 12-month period, Disney paid the family more than $1 million in royalties on Pooh records and videotapes, plus $17,000 for computer software. Then royalties for those products suddenly dropped. For one six-month period in 1989, according to court records, Disney paid Lasswell and her daughter just $22.37 on software sales.

In 1990, Lasswell hired an auditor to review Disney's books and concluded that the company had failed to keep complete sales records for Pooh merchandise for eight years. She and her daughter sued Disney in 1991. The next year, they received a $2.2 million "catchup" payment to clear up discrepancies uncovered in the audit.

The current court case centers on whether videotapes, DVDs, and software are covered by the 1983 royalty agreement. The family contends that Disney executives promised that videos and other emerging technologies would be included, even if they were not spelled out in the contract.

Disney says the Slesingers tried in 1983 to include videos in the deal and signed even after the company rejected the demand.

"The case boils down to whether they are entitled to be paid for all sorts of uses that are not covered by the contract," said Petrocelli, the Disney attorney. "They say that when Winnie the Pooh is dancing down Main Street and hugs a kid, they ought to get a royalty from that. But the contract never gave them those rights."

While the case dragged on, Pooh's popularity exploded. In 1994, when Disney's merchandise contract with Sears, Roebuck expired, the company launched a "Pooh initiative," rolling out new lines of Pooh products, including wallpaper, bedsheets, snow globes, and a "classic" line of stuffed dolls and novelties that more closely resemble Shepard's original drawings.

Disney's annual Pooh revenue rose from $100 million to more than

$1 billion in just four years, Disney chief executive Michael Eisner told an investment conference in 1998.

Shirley Lasswell and daughter Patricia also have seen their Pooh wealth soar. It took 24 years for their total Pooh earnings to reach $1 million. Since filing their lawsuit, they have received $65 million in royalties.

MILNE ESTATE SELLS RIGHTS

Last year, seeking to tie up legal loose ends in its Pooh royalty agreements, Disney bought all future rights from the Milne estate for $352 million. A Milne family trust distributed the money to four principal beneficiaries.

A London men's club to which A. A. Milne once belonged received $88 million; the members decided to set up a scholarship fund for actors and writers. An additional $88 million went to the British boarding school that Milne attended as a boy. The Royal Literary Fund for struggling writers was given $132 million. The $44 million remaining was put in a trust named for Clare Milne, the author's granddaughter, who has cerebral palsy; the trust pays benefits to her and other disabled people.

Now, the Pooh holdouts are down to Shirley Lasswell and her daughter.

Patricia Slesinger, 49, says the legal battle with Disney has been emotionally draining but also educational.

She has learned about the role her parents played in building the Pooh merchandise empire. Slesinger, who lives in Los Angeles and runs her own business publishing glossy shopping guides for high-end hotels, has spent hours on eBay hunting for treasures licensed by her father or designed by her mother.

Two years ago, Disney published a 176-page coffee-table book about the history of Pooh. Slesinger was offended to find no mention of her family.

"Everybody has done a great job" developing the Pooh brand, she said. "But don't try to erase us out of history."

He came, he saw, he conquered. The late talent agent Lew Wasserman created the Hollywood we know today by cozying up to television rather than shunning it. In short order he built MCA television production into a powerhouse. Connie Bruck, in *The New Yorker,* describes a fast-paced entertainment metamorphosis that received a surprising boost from Ronald Reagan before he became president.

Connie Bruck

The Monopolist

"HOLLYWOOD'S LIKE EGYPT, full of crumbling pyramids," the producer David O. Selznick remarked at the beginning of the 1950s. "It'll never come back. It'll just keep on crumbling until finally the wind blows the last studio prop across the sands." The views of the man who had made *Gone with the Wind* were widely shared in the American film industry. Hollywood, through its unique integration of production, distribution, and exhibition, had dominated the international movie industry since the early 1920s, but in May of 1948 the Supreme Court ruled that the major studios must sell off their theater chains. The studio system began to come apart; studios could no longer afford the vast payrolls required to maintain the stars and directors who had long been employed in multiyear contracts, and many of them left to form independent production companies. Movie attendance had fallen dramatically, and television was commonly viewed as the culprit. The studios could, of course, have made movies for TV, but that was considered heresy. Jack L. Warner, the autocratic head of Warner Bros., ordered that no television set appear in any of his movies, and he was said to be infuriated to discover that Joan Crawford had one in her dressing room.

A young talent agent named Lew Wasserman saw Hollywood's prospects differently, and in the coming years would prove to be the most significant player in the creation of the Hollywood that we know today. The decline of the studio system, the rise of television—all the forces that were eating away at the old Hollywood—would enable Wasserman, in a mere two decades, to build an empire of his own.

Wasserman's parents were Yiddish-speaking Orthodox Jews who had emigrated from Russia to Cleveland. His father worked as a paper cutter, a bookbinder, and a box maker; he opened small restaurants, but they failed. Lew Wasserman, who was born in 1913, went to work at an early age to help support the family. By the time he was 12, he was selling candy in a theater, and at 15 he had a regular job, working as a movie usher from 3 p.m. to midnight, seven days a week. "I wanted to get out of things like gym, so I could work that schedule," Wasserman recalled when I spoke with him in his office at Universal Studios a few years before his death, in June of 2002. "I went to my principal, and I said, 'If I raise enough money for school athletic uniforms, will you let me out?' Yes. So I brought movies to the school, and charged each kid three cents to go. Eight thousand kids times three cents! I knew they'd go. Because what the principal didn't realize and what I did was this: To show movies, it has to be dark. And don't you think kids would pay three cents to sit in the dark? Then I went to my chemistry professor—I've always been pretty good in math—and I said, 'I'll make you a deal. Will you allow me to miss class, so long as I pass every test?' So for two years the only times I went to chemistry class were to take a test."

Wasserman wanted to become a lawyer, but he was unable to obtain a scholarship to go to college; no amount of success would ever erase a lingering self-consciousness about a lack of education. In the summer of 1936, while he was working as a nightclub publicist in Cleveland, Wasserman married Edie Beckerman, the daughter of a local lawyer. Her family had been prosperous in the '20s but had been hard hit by the Depression; since then, her father had been indicted for attempted arson and for embezzlement. He was not convicted in either case, but the cost of his defense had further depleted his funds, and Edie, unlike her older siblings, had also not gone to college. Later that year, Wasserman applied for a job with Jules Stein, the head of the Music Corporation of America. The fastidious Stein gave him a quick appraisal—a tall, spindly 23-year-old in a suit that Stein considered tasteless—and gave him a chance.

The grand-sounding Music Corporation of America was a band-booking agency that Stein had started, 12 years earlier, in Al Capone's Mob-ruled Chicago. By the time Wasserman joined MCA, it was already a force in the entertainment world, controlling about 90 percent of the dance bands in the country. But Stein, realizing that the dance band business had peaked, began representing talent in the motion picture business as well, and in 1936 he moved MCA's headquarters to a neo-Colonial mansion in Beverly Hills. Wasserman, after stints at MCA offices in Chicago and New York, arrived in 1939.

Word soon traveled through Hollywood that there was something exceptional about Wasserman. He was so fast with numbers that, as one associate said, "he was a walking computer before there were computers." He was also inventive—he could devise deals that did something for everyone. He studied tax law, and eventually came up with suggestions about deferred compensation and structuring of transactions which neither Stein nor the company's lawyers had thought of. He was not given to small talk, and yet, when it was necessary, he could win over an actor or a radio sponsor with great charm. He seemed never to tire; the more he worked, the more energized he became.

He even attracted the attention of Louis B. Mayer, who, along with Irving Thalberg, had made MGM into Hollywood's most envied and glamorous studio in the '30s. "I looked up tremendously to L. B. Mayer, because I watched his operation," Wasserman told Steven Spielberg, in an oral history interview. "Mayer's theory was very simple . . . he bought the best. If he thought you were talented, he bought you." Mayer tried to buy him, too, Wasserman recalled: Jules Stein was paying him $350 a week, and Mayer offered him $5,000 a week, but he saw greater opportunity at MCA. "They let me alone at MCA, let me do what I wanted," Wasserman explained.

What he wanted at that point was to build MCA into the most powerful talent agency in the country—by following Mayer's example and buying the best. Wasserman told me that when he first arrived in Hollywood, "Our biggest clients were Ronnie Reagan, Richard Dix, whose career was almost ending, and Hattie McDaniel." MCA, however, was cash-rich, and with Stein's blessing Wasserman began buying up stars' contracts from other agencies, and buying agencies themselves. In 1945, in one bold stroke, he acquired for MCA the Hayward-Deverich agency, with its sterling list of several hundred performers, among them Greta Garbo, Fred Astaire, Joseph Cotten, and Henry Fonda; directors such as Billy Wilder and Joshua Logan; and writers, including Dorothy Parker and Dashiell Hammett. It turned out to be a remarkable deal, and Stein gave him all the credit for it, suddenly realizing that he had a "pupil who was surpassing his teacher." In 1946, Stein made Wasserman, who was only 33, the president of MCA.

In that position, Wasserman wasn't shy about dictating how life within the company was to be lived. It was a tightly controlled environment. The dress code had become rigid: dark suits, white shirts, dark-blue or gray ties. (Wasserman himself had needed instruction in how to dress when he came to MCA, but he was a fast learner.) Now MCA agents, in their somber uniforms, were commonly referred to as the "MCA mafia." Desks were to be left clear at night; if Wasserman and Stein, patrolling, found papers on them, they would sweep them into the wastebasket. "Messy desk, messy mind" was the credo. There were strict rules for the agents' secretaries. They went up the back stairs, while the agents ascended the winding staircases in the front of the building. And there was a prohibition on fraternization. Helen Gurley Brown, who went to work at MCA as a secretary in 1942, recalled how frustrated she and her colleagues were at not being able to date the agents. "I remember for Valentine's Day we decided to wear pink and red—we were a flower house of color in the secretarial pool," she said. "Still, we couldn't attract any attention. The agents were all business." Wasserman provided an example for his troops. "Lew was very attractive, and he could have had anyone," Brown said. "But that didn't seem to interest him." Edie Wasserman had given birth to the couple's only child, a daughter, Lynne, in 1940; but Wasserman seemed almost as uninterested in home life as he was in office dalliances. Brown added, too, that a temper that would become famous was already in evidence; the screams coming from his office could be heard down the hall. Eventually, Brown began having a clandestine affair with MCA's Herman Citron, whose clients included Frank Sinatra. When the relationship was discovered, she was fired.

In those days, the term "corporate culture" had not yet become part of the lexicon, but the guiding spirit at MCA was, unmistakably, survival of the fittest. The agent Shelly Schultz recalled his indoctrination in MCA's Chicago office. "There were two guys in adjacent offices," Schultz said. "They were both selling to nightclubs, and were given the same territory. And you'd hear one of them, on the phone, talking to a customer and saying, about the guy in the next office, 'Don't buy from him! I can give them to you two hundred dollars cheaper!'" It was a brutal arrangement, but it successfully weeded out those who were hampered by personal ethics, or friendship with their colleagues, or the lack of a killer instinct. Thus, MCA agents, by and large, were trained to be as ruthless with one another as they were with outside competitors. They would display their mettle in a kind of gladiatorial combat—shouting and going for one another's throat at company meetings while their boss, presiding, listened quietly, and in the end ruled on the victor.

As the big studios began to decline, it was Wasserman, more than anyone else, who exploited and exacerbated their weaknesses. He advised Olivia de Havilland, who was repeatedly suspended by Warners for refusing roles, that the Hollywood custom of adding suspension time to stars' contracts was probably illegal; de Havilland sued to get out of her contract, and she won, in a 1944 California Supreme Court decision that undercut the power of the studio system. In 1950, Wasserman constructed a revolutionary deal for his client Jimmy Stewart; instead of being paid a salary for his role in *Winchester '73*, Stewart received a percentage of the movie's profits. At a time when postwar income tax rates were as high as 90 percent, the deal was especially advantageous to Stewart, because his income would be spread over the life of the film. Stewart's earnings during the next few years made him Hollywood's best-compensated star. By this time, Wasserman had driven stars' salaries so high that studios grudgingly began to accept this new sliding scale. For the first time, the fact that stars were largely responsible for the success of a movie was reflected in the bottom line. As more and more stars demanded such treatment, their power grew, and the power of the studios diminished. The agent who had shaped this new system (and controlled so much of it, through the talent) was, of course, the most powerful of all.

As gratifying as this shift in the balance of power was to Wasserman, it was only a preliminary goal. He wanted to be the producer as well as the agent. It was not movie production that Wasserman wanted to enter—at least, not yet—but television, the very thing that was anathema to the old studio moguls. Wasserman later said that he had believed in television's potential from the start; he had owned a set in 1940, when, to the best of his knowledge, there was only one other privately owned set in all of California. His was an unprepossessing contraption—a big box with a tiny screen that became a mirror when the lid of the machine was raised. "I would take people up to my office to see this box, and all that was on it was a cartoon, *Aesop's Fables,*" Wasserman recalled. "I'd say, 'Don't you understand it's going to be in your home?' And they'd say, 'Let's go to the projection room.'"

The talent business was well established in Hollywood by the time Wasserman arrived; he had bought up a lot of it, and, eventually, he was able to shape it to his liking. But the television industry was so new that he could almost create it from whole cloth. Even territory claimed during television's infancy now was tantalizingly available. In the late '40s, TV programming—mainly quiz shows, audience participation shows, and talent shows—was still produced and controlled not by the networks but by the advertisers. In 1950, however, Sylvester (Pat) Weaver, who was the head of NBC's new television operations and was eager to improve the quality of programming, decided that advertisers would no longer be allowed to buy an entire program to showcase their commercials but could purchase only short segments. Before long, Weaver's ruling became the norm for other networks as well. This development left a vacuum in the TV-production business. In 1946, there were only around 11,000 TV sets in the United States, but by 1952 there were 14 million.

"The appetite of television is like the great maw of the sperm whale," Milton MacKaye wrote in the *Saturday Evening Post* in January 1952. "Thousands of hours of entertainment must be available to the television public and any guess as to where it will come from is . . . as good as another."

Wasserman wanted it to come largely from MCA. The company started producing television shows in 1950, through a newly formed subsidiary, Revue Productions; but Revue's output was fledgling compared with what Wasserman now had in mind. There was a major hurdle, however. The Screen Actors Guild, one of the actors' unions, had long prohibited talent agencies from producing motion pictures, because of the inherent conflict of interest in simultaneously being the agent and the employer, and it seemed clear that SAG would soon adopt comparable restrictions for TV production. Under the existing regulations, an agent could apply on a case-by-case basis for a waiver to produce a movie, and that, presumably, could be applied to television as well; however, Wasserman wanted untrammeled freedom—a blanket waiver that would allow his talent agency to engage in television production for many years to come. His control of talent would give him an unbeatable advantage in TV production, and his experience with TV production would strengthen his hand with talent; this combination would create a system so powerful that other producers would be unable to compete. As a business model, it had only one weakness, and that lay in its transparency; it was impossible not to see how audacious it was.

In order to win SAG approval, Wasserman needed an influential confederate, and turned to the president of SAG, Ronald Reagan, who had been one of Wasserman's first clients. From the time Wasserman arrived in Los Angeles, before the war, he and Reagan had been friends, and Wasserman guided Reagan through Hollywood's treacherous political thickets. In 1941, Wasserman sought to extend Reagan's deferment from active military duty by writing a letter for Jack Warner to sign. Shortly before Reagan was called up, Wasserman had obtained a seven-year contract for him with Warner Bros., which tripled the salary that Reagan had been earning under his original contract. Immediately after Wasserman concluded this deal, the movie *Kings Row* (in which Reagan uttered his famous line "Where's the rest of me?") opened. Reagan received such praise for his performance that Wasserman succeeded in renegotiating his just-signed contract with Jack Warner. This time, it had one peculiarity: It covered 43 weeks, not the standard 40. As Reagan later told the story, "When all the commas were in place, J. L. said to Lew, 'Now will you tell me why I've just given in to the only 43-week deal in the whole industry?'

"Lew grinned like a kid with a hand in the cookie jar. . . . 'I've never written a million-dollar deal before—so three extra weeks for seven years makes this my first million-dollar sale.'"

During the early months of 1952, Wasserman pursued the SAG waiver in ways so deft and untraceable that even subsequent FBI and grand-jury investigations were unable to fully reconstruct what he had done. No matter how many times they were questioned over the years, Wasserman, Reagan, and the longtime SAG executives Jack Dales and Chester Migden insisted that the waiver was granted solely on the merits of the argument that Wasserman had made—that if MCA were allowed to go into television production in an unlimited way it would create badly needed jobs, and the increase in those jobs in filmed television would mean that SAG would stop losing members to a rival union, the American Federation of Television and Radio Artists, which had jurisdiction over live TV.

Wasserman no doubt made this argument. However, in the late spring of 1952 SAG was also engaged in negotiations with the Association of Television Producers over the issue of "reuse payments"—sums paid to performers when TV programs in which they had appeared were reshown. The idea was blasphemy to producers but not to Wasserman. According to Billy Hunt, a lawyer who for many years worked closely with Wasserman on industry labor matters, Wasserman inaugurated the reuse payments in a secret agreement; he was willing to make the payments when other producers were not. This may have made Wasserman's desired waiver palatable to Reagan; but the waiver still needed to be approved by SAG's board members (who would be unaware of the backroom dealings). Reagan could not appear to be pressuring his board. As the Hollywood labor lawyer Robert Gilbert said, "SAG is not a rubber-stamp board. . . . Reagan couldn't just make the deal one on one with

Lew. They could have an understanding—but someone else would have to bring the board along."

That person was the actor Walter Pidgeon, a SAG vice president "whom everyone loved, he was the father image on that board," Migden told me. Pidgeon was an MCA client, and his long-standing contract at MGM had recently been terminated, as had the contracts of a number of other actors. At a SAG board meeting in July 1952, an angry debate about the waiver's inherent conflict-of-interest issues for talent agents went on for several hours; virtually all the actors vehemently objected to the idea of agents becoming involved in production—agent-producers would inevitably be negotiating, on behalf of their clients, deals with themselves. Migden recounted the debate in an oral history in 1989: "Indeed, the waiver was going down, Reagan didn't say anything, he was in the chair, he was presiding over the debate that was going on. . . . And Walter said, 'Look around, so they want to produce, what do we have to lose? Is anybody working?' He turned to the board members and said, 'Is anybody working? There's no work. Where is this town going to go? How are we going to survive? What am I supposed to do, pack my bag and go to New York and work in live television for beans?' His impassioned speech about what it is they had to lose turned the whole debate around, and suddenly everybody said, 'Somebody wants to create some work, what the hell is wrong with that?'" The board voted, unanimously, to grant the waiver.

The board's action that day arguably changed the history of television. It certainly changed the life of Ronald Reagan. Wasserman had been trying to find Reagan movie jobs, but Reagan's performances spoke for themselves. Las Vegas was just becoming a new mecca for entertainers, and Wasserman tried to place Reagan there, too; but, as the MCA agent George Schlatter, who handled Reagan's engagement at the Frontier casino, said, "He kind of laid an omelette." Now that MCA was not only booking talent but also producing TV shows, however, it had far greater latitude in its search for a successful venue for Reagan. Beginning in 1954, Reagan hosted and often starred in the *General Electric Theatre* drama anthology programs, ultimately becoming a producer of the show as well. There was much talk around Hollywood about how

Reagan had managed to land this new job, which resurrected his career. The connection was hard to miss. Jack Dales, a longtime friend of Reagan's, whom Reagan in later years appointed to state government positions, said, "I think Ronnie did more or less what he thought he should—and then he was rewarded for it, with the GE job."

Billy Hunt was less equivocal: "Lew always told me the waiver was Ronnie Reagan."

With the waiver won, Wasserman launched MCA into the TV production business. He already had a sophisticated understanding of the broadcasting business, and he and other MCA agents had well-established relationships with major advertisers and their advertising agencies. Most important, MCA by and large controlled the talent. Now Wasserman needed only to achieve a liaison with one of the three major TV networks.

MCA already had a relationship with one network. The Columbia Phonograph Broadcasting Company, which was bought by William Paley, the socially ambitious radio magnate, in 1928, had been second to NBC in entertainment programming for roughly twenty years. Starting in 1948, Wasserman and another senior MCA executive, Taft Schreiber, helped Paley raid the other networks for talent by offering pay structures that reduced performers' income tax from 90 percent to 25 percent. Within months, in deals brokered mainly by Wasserman, most of NBC's top entertainers—Burns and Allen, Edgar Bergen, Red Skelton, and Groucho Marx—flocked to CBS. By the end of 1949, CBS Radio had 12 of the top 15 radio programs, and, for the first time, the network was number one in commercial broadcasting—a position it held long into the television era.

Oddly, Wasserman's role in Paley's triumph did not forge a bond between them. Paley knew MCA too well. "Paley did not like the MCA guys," a longtime CBS programming executive named Michael Dann told me. "He wore the gray suit with the perfect tie, and he had the home in Lyford Cay with the French chef, and he had married the most beautiful and elegant woman in the world, and he had his Matisses and Monets and Picassos, perfectly placed. It was quite a jump for a guy from

Philadelphia, whose father was a cigar maker. And the MCA guys embarrassed him. They were too crude, too blatant."

"Paley had a great distrust for just about all agents and everything in Hollywood," said Frank Stanton, who, after being chosen in 1946 to be president of CBS, ran the network with Paley for more than a quarter-century, earning a reputation for his acumen and integrity. Stanton added that he and Paley would occasionally have dinner with Stein and Wasserman, but that "it was strictly for business reasons. There was no rapport." He recalled, though, that after one of these dinners Paley remarked to him how good Wasserman was at handling people—which was no small compliment coming from Paley, a master of the art. "Lew could be very charming—that was part of his effectiveness," Stanton said.

Beneath the charm, though, what Stanton perceived in Wasserman was mainly muscle. "Anything you wanted in the colony, he could get for you. He had all the connections, he knew where all the bodies were. And people had such fear of Lew, because he played rough—blocking careers, pulling talent out of one picture into another. If a producer were reluctant about something, Lew would do something over here"—Stanton gestured, as though pulling at an invisible string—"to make the guy do what he wanted over there." Hollywood might have come under Wasserman's dominion, but in many Easterners' eyes it was indeed merely a "colony," and a shady one at that. CBS, Paley's vaunted "Tiffany network," would never allow Wasserman the kind of propinquity he had in mind.

NBC, in the early '50s, was scarcely more congenial. In 1953, the network's founder, David Sarnoff, a former radio pioneer, who, after serving in the war, liked to be called General Sarnoff, made his son, Robert (Bobby) Sarnoff, NBC's executive vice president, and named Pat Weaver as president. In the aerie of corporate power, Weaver (the father of the actress Sigourney Weaver) was an anomaly—cerebral, unorthodox, highly literate, obsessed with the desire to use new technology for the public good. One of the shows that Weaver created was *Wide Wide World,* the first attempt to capture the American experience live, coast to coast. In a meeting at NBC described by the writer Thomas Whiteside in a 1954 *New Yorker* profile, Weaver was listing the places to be visited in *Wide*

Wide World. Bobby Sarnoff objected that most people might not want to go to Los Angeles's Greek Theatre.

"This show is not just about what the public wants to do but what you want them to do, Bobby," Weaver said. "You *take* the American people to see the Greek drama, you *take* them to see *King Lear* at Stratford, Ontario. . . . I want a show . . . that people will say has enabled us to become more mature, more cultured, and more urbane, and that will be the conversation piece wherever people meet." But Weaver also knew how to produce commercially successful TV. In addition to *Wide Wide World,* he created the *Today* show, the *Tonight Show,* and *Matinee Theatre.* The press gravitated to him, and he became something of a star. That would prove to be his downfall, for he was not meant to outshine Bobby Sarnoff, and he was certainly not meant to outshine the General. In 1955, David Sarnoff made Bobby NBC's president and bumped Weaver up to chairman. A year later, Sarnoff eased Weaver out.

That was the opening Wasserman needed. ABC, which ranked a distant third among the three networks, had recently dismissed its president, Robert Kintner. A former journalist, Kintner was a talented executive, respected particularly for his leadership in broadcast news; but there were rumors that he had a drinking problem. His awkward physiognomy—short, bulky, slightly hunched (he was sometimes called Quasimodo behind his back), with a homely countenance partly obscured by big, thick-lensed glasses—seemed to reflect some inner disproportion as well. At this low point in Kintner's career, Wasserman's associate David (Sonny) Werblin, the leading man in MCA's New York office, came to his rescue.

Werblin was a great raconteur, a devoted sportsman, a man's man in a time when that required no apology—and he held court at "21," entertaining the chairmen of companies like Coca-Cola and AT&T. Werblin had also cultivated a good relationship with General Sarnoff and Bobby. Now he persuaded Bobby that Kintner had the programming savvy that NBC needed, and in early 1957 he joined the network. The following year, Kintner was named president, and Bobby Sarnoff became chairman. For Kintner, it meant that he had been thrown from ABC's executive floor and, miraculously, landed on his feet.

Shortly after Kintner started the new job, Wasserman invited him to a gathering—ostensibly Wasserman's birthday party—in Hollywood. When Kintner arrived, he found himself surrounded by a dazzling array of actors and actresses. Then Wasserman announced to his guests that this was not really his birthday party. "This happens to be a surprise party for my good and true friend Robert Kintner, to celebrate his having taken over the throne at NBC."

The relationship between MCA and NBC quickly became the subject of industry chatter. Most remarkable was its brazenness, which was epitomized in an NBC programming meeting called by Kintner and Bobby Sarnoff in the spring of 1957. After the programming executives were assembled, with a projected season schedule arranged on a magnetic board before them, Werblin strode into the room. This in itself was shocking, since a network's projected scheduling is highly proprietary. And then, instead of banishing him, Kintner declared, "Sonny, look at the schedule for next season; here are the empty slots; you fill them." Werblin proceeded to rearrange the magnetized show squares while the executives watched; when he was finished, he had placed in prime time 14 series that were either produced or sold by MCA. And that became the season's schedule.

MCA occupied a position of such favor and dominance at NBC that there was no true competition. In return, MCA generally treated NBC more favorably than other buyers. "Sonny brought Kintner all MCA's top stuff," the MCA agent Al Rush told me. The situation worked to MCA's advantage in multiple ways. It provided a major, dependable outlet for MCA's production. And it won MCA even more clients, since the common perception was that the best way a producer could get a show on NBC, or an actor could get roles in Revue's constant flow of productions, was to be represented by MCA. Once these clients signed on with MCA, moreover, they were tied to the agency for the long term. Clients had to sign an "omnibus" contract, giving MCA the right to represent them in all facets of show business for many years.

The MCA-NBC relationship was unique, but by the late '50s MCA could impose its will on other networks, too—even, surprisingly, on CBS. Unlike NBC, which produced very few of its own shows, CBS prided itself on its in-house production, and its executives routinely derided MCA, whose Revue staple was formulaic Westerns, as a "sausage factory." It was well known within CBS that Paley had no interest in buying MCA-produced shows, and would never countenance the kind of surrender that NBC had made. "We didn't want to deal with those guys, we wanted to control our own destiny," Salvatore Ianucci, a lawyer at CBS in the '50s and '60s, said. "Lew's method was intimidation. But we had the power, we didn't need their productions." What they did need, however, was MCA talent.

Not all radio stars had been able to make a successful transition to television, but Jack Benny, an MCA client, certainly had—his show was one of the highest-rated TV programs at CBS in the '50s. Wasserman, therefore, had enormous leverage when he went to CBS to renegotiate Benny's deals. According to both Ianucci and Mike Dann, Wasserman demanded not only a specific time slot for the Benny show but, even more remarkably, another specific time slot, for another season-long show. "He'd say, 'Jack must have another hour'—it would be for some unnamed project," Dann said. "And of course it wasn't Jack who had to have it; it was Lew. Power leads to power."

As the president of MCA, Wasserman was in a position to put director, star, story, and supporting talent in a single deal, and to demand a 10 percent commission on the whole package. Before long, he carried this idea even further. MCA would demand its commission on the cost of an entire show—including all above-the-line (talent) costs and below-the-line (facilities, production) costs—even when the network itself was supplying much of the talent, and producing the show. The company demanded its 10 percent on the whole thing as if it were responsible for every element—becoming, in a sense, a virtual packager. As Al Rush said, grinning, "We took our commission on everything—above the line, below the line, and sideways! If the whole show cost three hundred thousand dollars, we got thirty thousand."

MCA could make up the rules because no one in the commercial television world was strong enough to challenge it. By the 1959–60 season, MCA was producing or coproducing more television series than any other company; and it got a cut from about 45 percent of all network evening shows. Among those it produced were *Wagon Train, General Electric Theatre,* and *Bachelor Father.* It was the agent for many shows made by independent producers, including *Alfred Hitchcock Presents,*

Tales of Wells Fargo, and *Ford Startime.* Wasserman had devised a system that produced a perpetual stream of money, flowing from multiple sources to MCA. Although the agency prized secrecy—it would not divulge which television series it represented, or even how many series it handled—*Fortune,* in 1960, attempted to offer a glimpse of MCA's TV economics.

Fortune calculated that MCA was likely to earn $7 million from a 39-week, half-hour TV series that it produced at its Revue studios. And for a successful hour-long show, the magazine estimated, MCA would earn much more. The first three years of *Wagon Train,* budgeted at $100,000 a week, would probably bring MCA about $17 million. By now, it was easy to understand why Wasserman had been so determined to enter the production end of the business. To earn $17 million as an agent, MCA would have to collect a $170 million of client salaries—an astronomical sum, notwithstanding all that Wasserman had done to drive up stars' earnings.

Although NBC was vital to MCA, there was no question about which was the dominant partner. This dynamic was illustrated in the story of Revue's *Wagon Train,* a one-hour Western that had become a great hit at NBC, garnering top ratings for four years. MCA wanted NBC to buy not only more new episodes but a package of old ones, as reruns. The network had a contractual right of first refusal (the right to bid on renewing the show before it could be sold elsewhere), and, according to Don Durgin, a network executive, NBC fully intended to make the deal. But Durgin and his colleagues learned that Wasserman had sold the package to ABC. "Wasserman just took it away!" Durgin said. "And when we screamed he said, 'You didn't act.'

"We said, 'Wrong! Wrong!'

"So he said, 'Look, in our opinion, you didn't act. Anyway, it's gone. But now we're going to do a show, *The Virginian,* and it's going to be great, and you can have it.'"

Dealing with Wasserman was unlike anything Durgin had experienced in his network career. "I had been used to dealing with honest guys," he said. "But Lew would misrepresent and let you draw a conclusion at your peril. Anything he had a legal duty to disclose he'd disclose in full detail. That would make you feel he was honest, and maybe let your guard down. But then you'd discover later that the package had shifted—and if you complained he'd say, 'O.K., forget it! We'll take it back!' " In retrospect, Durgin continued, it seemed that he and his colleagues were "little boys in kindergarten dealing with Darth Vader." Wasserman was the smartest executive he had ever known. He had a way of negotiating which let you know he had assessed his advantage to the decimal point ("If he thought he had a 50.1 percent advantage, he would be merciless, threatening, nasty—though not in a vulgar way"), and he was always willing to walk away. "He never had any briefcase, never any notes," Durgin recalled. "Dark suit, white shirt. A handkerchief in his breast pocket, another in his back pocket. He would pat his forehead occasionally, though he was never perspiring—it was just a habit. He was so finished. A very attractive man. I didn't like him, because he was such a shark—but it was a shark you almost had to admire as he circled you."

Speculation about some lucre in the MCA-NBC relationship was endemic in the industry. "Let's be realistic," Sal Ianucci, of CBS, said. "Agents did whatever it took—girls, money. I know, because as an executive I was offered it." Alan Livingston, who joined NBC in 1955 as vice president in charge of programming, told me, "There was a lot of speculation that Kintner got payoffs. But did they just flatter him? All I know is that they controlled NBC." Livingston added that executives at NBC in those days were not very highly paid. Then he said, "There are different ways of paying off, too. A vacation? A car? A case of Scotch every week?" Certainly, MCA was known for its extravagance in gift-giving. Harris Katleman, who was an MCA agent in the '50s, told me, "At Christmastime, so much money was spent you could have run a small country. There were 'A,' 'B,' and 'C' lists. The 'A' list got cars, mainly Cadillacs."

However much comment MCA's dispensing of favors provoked, it was only a small part of the system that Wasserman had engineered. "Lew was an entertainment mogul without peer," Mike Dann said. "I don't think he was a great recognizer of talent, but he knew how to acquire it and implement it and negotiate for it. Part of the problem was that network executives—me included—were novices about dealing with talent." Dann added that the television industry was largely a Wasp preserve, populated by executives who had graduated from prep schools and Ivy League colleges—and they were no match for MCA. "The MCA guys did not play by the Marquis of Queensberry rules," Dann said. "They had started out in the nightclubs, and you know who owned *them*. The early days of MCA's existence left an imprint on the personality of the company—and it was very different from William Morris, for example. The MCA agents always wore the white shirts and the black suits, but underneath they were guys who were much too smart, too aggressive, too streetwise for most broadcasting executives.

"As a unit, they were the shrewdest people in the history of the entertainment world," Dann went on. "You wouldn't want to take a Greyhound bus trip with them, or model your children after them—but they could deliver for themselves."

Wasserman had become the very personification of the maxim that information is power. His appetite was insatiable, ranging from quotas and currency restrictions and tax provisions in the overseas market to the latest merchandising revenues on *Laramie;* and to his men his retentive capacity seemed preternatural. "He had a truly photographic memory," the MCA agent Freddie Fields said. "Therefore, he always knew where every man in the company was, what his deal was, who his clients were. He'd read lists of all this on the plane going back and forth between New York and L.A., and he'd retain it all."

Everyone in the company dressed like Wasserman, Fields said. "You had to wear a white shirt and a dark tie—you didn't have to wear a black *knit* tie! You didn't have to wear loafers—" Fields broke off and, decades after having left MCA and its dress code behind, swung a loafer-clad foot out from beneath the table. "Everyone in the company who stayed either admired or feared him. A guy like Sonny Werblin, for example. He was smart-ass, tough, competitive—but he was scared to death of Lew. He would never take him on. No one would. You might disagree about a deal or something—but you'd never take him on. He had an aura," Fields concluded. "He was my god."

As awestruck as some of his subordinates were, Wasserman remained down-to-earth, laconic, seemingly indifferent to the extravagant, if inchoate, feelings he inspired. Virtually everything about him was spare. He never exercised, but remained thin. He did not often exert himself to smile; he had a dry sense of humor, but he tended to stay poker-faced as he delivered his sallies. His clothes were so uniform that he could don them without thinking—dark suit, dark tie, dark raincoat, even dark bathrobe. Fueled by his work, he seemed to be otherwise self-sustaining; he appeared to require little respite, little sleep, little human connection. With those who worked for him, he was famous for never admitting that he had made a mistake and for not dispensing praise. Sometimes employees would think they could detect a hidden compliment in something he said, but they could never be sure. Hungry for any sign, they became grateful for a gesture. ("He was always cool, aloof, but he knew how to handle people—he'd put his arm on your shoulder," Al Rush recalled. "Guys lived for a pat on the back.")

Wasserman's rules for his employees, too, evinced economy: Tend to the client, dress appropriately, divulge no information about MCA, commit very little to paper, never leave the office without returning every call, always do your homework. Doing one's homework meant, among other things, paying close attention to detail. Once, when advertising executives who were sponsoring an MCA television series were about to arrive for a cocktail party at Wasserman's home, Wasserman asked the MCA publicist working on the event whether he had checked which cigarette accounts the company had. He had not, but he was able to find out and to change all the cigarettes in the cigarette holders, moments before the guests arrived.

Wasserman's most important commandment to his employees was that they should never mislead him. Those who did found that the only aspect of Wasserman that was not spare was his rage. His tirades were legendary. When he removed his watch, it was a sure sign that the storm was coming; at its peak, he would scream, shake, even froth at the mouth as though he were having a seizure. Some of his victims burst into tears or fainted. It was such a wild, eccentric display that one might assume it was beyond his control, but these rages—like virtually everything he did—served a purpose. Discipline was enforced, certain executives were made into object lessons, and fear was kept fresh.

Yet Wasserman made it a habit to give credit to his troops rather than claiming it for himself; this made them more devoted to him, and, since it bolstered their standing with clients, freed him to do other things. "He wanted to build manpower—if he felt you were capable of representing someone he was involved with, he would gladly let you do it," recalled Jay Kanter, who had started in the MCA mailroom when he was 21 and eventually became an agent, representing stars like Marlon Brando and Marilyn Monroe. "I'd hear him on the phone with studio heads—'I don't know, Marlon won't answer my phone calls, you have to call Jay Kanter.'

"We were going out to Universal one day," Kanter continued. "Lew was going to make a deal for Jimmy Stewart to do *Winchester '73,* and he was meeting with Leo Spitz and Bill Goetz, the heads of Universal at the time. After discussing this deal, Lew said, 'I don't know, I don't think it is going to work out.' And we left. I said, 'Lew, why? That's a great deal!' He said, 'You call them back in a few hours and tell them you worked it out—and you'll never have trouble getting them on the phone again.'"

The agent Irving (Swifty) Lazar, who worked at MCA for a time in the '30s and again in the mid-'40s, observed that the culture of MCA bore no small resemblance to the Mafia's; and that likeness became only more pronounced once Wasserman was fully in charge. Loyalty to the MCA family was a supreme value, and it was duly rewarded. An executive might be eviscerated by Wasserman time and again, but, if he died while in the employ of MCA, his family would be quietly taken care of. Sometimes if an agent could not afford to buy the private shares of MCA stock which were allotted to him, the company advanced the money. If someone wronged one of Wasserman's people, Wasserman would exact retribution. An MCA agent recalled a situation involving two of his colleagues at the time. One was only a mid-level employee—he worked in the nightclub division, which had become a relatively unimportant venue for MCA, and he had a gambling problem besides. The other was a crackerjack TV agent. "The first agent walked into his apartment and found the TV agent screwing his wife. Lew called the TV agent and said, 'I want you out of the building today'—despite the fact that he was a major piece of manpower. That was Lew," this agent said. "His loyalty to loyalty was incredible."

Disloyalty, however, was a capital crime, and, when a valued employee chose to leave MCA, it was perceived as a consummately disloyal act. Edie Wasserman was notorious for severing connections with former friends decisively and cleanly. When Wasserman encountered people who had left MCA, he would be more civil than his wife; but they knew that for him, too, they had ceased to exist in any meaningful way.

Wasserman himself had a fondness for gambling. The combination of his extraordinary memory and his numerical wizardry made him a formidable cardplayer, and in his early years in Los Angeles he played a great deal. Many of the moguls did. Sam Goldwyn was a compulsive gambler, given to cheating and famous for his losses (in one session, he lost $150,000, the equivalent today of about $2 million). Gambling allowed Wasserman to test himself against these men. "There used to be big card games," Wasserman told me. "It started with pinochle, then moved to bridge—that was too complicated for some people—then gin rummy and poker. The first time I met Sam Goldwyn, it was at his house, four of us playing gin rummy for money. The next time I was there, he wanted me to play. I said, 'No, Sam, I will not play you for money, I'm going to beat you and I don't want to take your money.' He was furious, yelling. When he stopped, Frances"—Goldwyn's wife—"said to him, 'Listen to Lew, Sam. He's the only one who's your friend.'"

One of Wasserman's favorite gambling anecdotes involved a trip he made in 1956 to Cuba with Alfred Hitchcock. Of all the actors, writers, directors, and producers Wasserman cultivated, Hitchcock was probably the most important to him. By the '50s—the decade in which Hitchcock's productions included *Strangers on a Train, Rear Window, Vertigo,* and *North by Northwest*—it was plain that he was one of the most gifted directors ever to work in movies. And he was probably the best known as well—in large part because Wasserman had persuaded him to produce and host *Alfred Hitchcock Presents,* which went on the air in 1955 and became one of the biggest shows on television. It was a triumph for both men. Hitchcock had disdained television at first; but Wasserman had been so decisive that he succumbed. One day, when he was in Wasserman's office, a passerby made some derogatory comment about TV, and

Hitchcock responded, "Go away and don't bother us. We're busy count-ing our money."

There was a great deal of it to count. According to his friends, Hitchcock had a complicated relationship with Wasserman, who he felt took advantage of him financially—which he resented—but upon whom he also felt quite dependent. Hitchcock commissioned Bernard Buffet to do a portrait of Wasserman as a gift. Curiously, the portrait, which hung in the foyer of the Wassermans' home, has a slightly sinister air; Wasser-man is wearing a black suit, and is seated, his hands—clawlike—resting on his knees. "His hands looked like black-widow spiders!" a former MCA executive said. "I said to Hitch, 'How could you do that?' And he gave me that enigmatic smile."

On the 1956 trip to Cuba, the Wassermans spent Christmas with Hitchcock and his wife, Alma, at the gambling tables in Havana. Wasserman's underworld friends Moe Dalitz, known as "the godfather of Las Vegas," and Sam (Sambo) Tucker, in league with Meyer Lansky, had got into the hotel business there. By paying off Fulgencio Batista, the Cuban dictator, Lansky had built up one of the world's most luxurious casinos, at the Hotel Nacional. Wasserman explained, "So these guys owned all the hotels. They took us to dinner in a great restaurant. We're sitting there—Hitch, Alma, Edie, Lansky, and the rest. Hitchcock at that point was the biggest TV star, with *Hitchcock Presents.* Lansky says to my wife, 'Is that *Alfred Hitchcock?*' And Hitch says to me, 'Is that *Meyer Lansky?*'

"We went to the Hotel Nacional casino to gamble. Sambo takes out this enormous wad—it must have been tens of thousands of dollars. Hitch gives Alma fifty dollars. And she can't win a bet! They wanted her to win, but she kept losing. We were walking back to our hotel, about five in the morning, and I said to Moe, 'Why are you guys here? You own Las Vegas, and here you risk losing it all.' Castro was already in the hills, it was reported. And he said, 'Sambo loves to fish, and this is the best fishing in the world. But, then, there was nothing to do at night—so we built the casinos.'" Wasserman paused. Then, with a small smile, he added, "Do you know that when Batista bet he *never* lost?"

Wasserman had known Dalitz for many years, and the two seemed

436 THE BEST BUSINESS STORIES OF THE YEAR: 2004 EDITION

almost familial. Dalitz was tall and engaging, with a keen business sense and an avuncular manner; there was nothing hard-edged visible to a casual observer. He and Wasserman spoke the same language, and their rapport, natural as it seemed, also served a business purpose for MCA. The group of Lansky, Dalitz, et al., was a kind of highly select social club; and, as in any such organization, the connections provided could be highly beneficial. The relationship between Dalitz and Lansky had been formed during Prohibition, when they set up a national bootlegging network. Dalitz had got to know the young Jimmy Hoffa, the future Teamsters leader, in Detroit in the 1920s. It was through Dalitz that Hoffa met Lansky. Now Hoffa was becoming the most powerful and feared labor boss in the country—and someone crucial to Wasserman, since the Teamsters could cripple his production business.

Probably nothing was quite as helpful to Wasserman as his friendship with the well-spoken Mob lawyer Sidney Korshak. It had begun, Wasserman told me, when they met in Los Angeles in 1939, shortly after Wasserman arrived in town. Wasserman, Korshak, and Reagan had quickly become friends. "In those days," Wasserman recalled, "money was not something people talked about. It didn't matter that Reagan was making two hundred dollars a week, I was making about three hundred, and Sidney much more." Wasserman paused, seeming to consider. "We didn't know just what Sidney was making, or what he was doing. He was a lawyer, very accepted in the community. And he was a good friend of mine for fifty years."

Korshak, a personable and clever young attorney, had got his start in Chicago, advising gangsters; Al Capone was an early client, according to one of Korshak's friends. During the '30s and '40s, Korshak had proved his mettle to the Mob in various ways, and he had risen in the hierarchy. From these early days in Chicago, he embarked on a practice that became his hallmark, winning entrée into establishment business circles at the same time that he was operating as the Mob's trusted consigliere. His efficacy as a "labor consultant" initially opened most corporate doors. Many business executives were caught in a dilemma: they wanted to resist attempts by honest labor unions to organize their employees, since that would be costly; but they did not want to deal personally with Mob-dominated unions. Korshak was the perfect intermediary.

The unions with which Korshak dealt—especially giant organizations like the Teamsters and the hotel and restaurant unions—recognized the power behind him. He operated in close league with Murray (the Camel) Humphreys, a quick-witted, charming Welshman who had organized protection rackets under Capone, and was widely viewed as the mastermind of the Mob's infiltration of labor unions. Korshak also enjoyed a strong bond with Hoffa, which had been forged when Hoffa was a young man, trying to fight his way up in the Teamsters. "Sid was the closest person to Hoffa," said Leo Geffner, a lawyer in Los Angeles who dealt with Korshak in racetrack labor negotiations in later years, and became his friend. "He was close to people all the way up and down the line in the Teamsters. He made cash payoffs to business agents— $5,000 here, $3,000 there. That's the way it was—to keep labor peace, you'd find a corrupt business agent and pay him off."

By the '50s, Korshak had moved from Chicago to Los Angeles with his wife, Bernice, and their two small boys. In California, his professional existence seemed almost chimerical. He never took the state bar exam, so he was not licensed to practice law. At first, he worked out of the office of a talent agency in which he had an interest, then at the Beverly Hills office of Las Vegas's Riviera casino, and occasionally at the law office of one of his friends. He took no notes; at most, he might scribble a number on a torn piece of paper or a matchbook cover. (He told reporters once, with lawyerly precision, "My records will show I never represented any of the hoodlums.") He was said to run his phone lines through friends' offices. Even so, he used the phone only guardedly. An MCA agent who was a good friend of Korshak's recalled, "He would never talk to you on the phone. 'C'mon, let's take a walk,' he'd say, whenever he had something to talk about. And we'd walk through the streets of Beverly Hills."

As a Mob emissary in Hollywood, Korshak achieved a level of recognition and respect that was different not only in degree but in kind from that of his predecessors. The fact that he was a lawyer gave him a patina of legitimacy, particularly for those who wanted to rationalize their association with him, but legitimacy really was not the coin of the realm. Korshak had presence ("When he entered, it shook up the room," an acquaintance recalled), and in this community that counted for nearly everything. Although his physical attributes were hardly notable—he was tall, with regular, if rather fleshy features, and an undistinguished countenance—Korshak had perfected, and subtly conveyed, the intimation of power (and dark power, at that). He exhibited none of the clichéd attributes of his compatriots, in their white ties and white shirts, with their icy eyes, bejeweled hands, and hair-trigger tempers. Korshak, one felt, wouldn't deign to raise his voice; his kind of threat was "I wouldn't do that if I were you," uttered ever so quietly. He was debonair, wore hand-tailored suits, and was so smooth that the boys in Chicago called him Mr. Silk Stockings.

Several people who knew the two men asserted that Korshak was Wasserman's closest friend. Certainly, Korshak was his most useful friend, providing him with a valuable connection to the Teamsters. And once MCA moved into TV production the Teamsters' cooperation was critical. In the tightly scheduled television business—much more than in the movie business—a strike could be devastating. The Teamsters controlled everything that had to be driven to and from a set: props, food, portable toilets, the film itself. Moreover, they were so feared that few would attempt to cross their picket lines, and in a labor war their support could be invaluable. It was almost like having a private army at your disposal.

"Sidney Korshak controlled the Teamsters," the MCA agent Harris Katleman, who knew Korshak, told me. He recalled an incident when Korshak went to Los Angeles's Hollywood Park racetrack, which was owned by Marjorie Everett, a longtime Korshak adversary from Chicago. "He went to the Turf Club, and Marge Everett threw him out—because he was a gangster. The Teamsters struck the next day and closed down Hollywood Park. She called and apologized to Sidney, and the Teamsters quit the strike." (Everett denied this incident and refused to comment on Korshak.) According to Andy Anderson, who was head of the Western Conference of Teamsters for ten years, beginning in 1974, "The Teamsters never struck Lew. And it was because of Sidney."

Korshak's power wasn't limited to the Teamsters. For those who enjoyed his protection, many of life's problems would simply disappear. Richard Gully, a well-born Englishman who had once been an assistant to Jack Warner, was in a car accident, and the other motorist sued him; Gully told Korshak, and the suit was dropped. Performers like Tony Martin incurred big gambling debts in Las Vegas; Korshak had them cleared. Mickey Rudin, Frank Sinatra's lawyer (and someone with no mean connections himself), had tried to get his wife on a ship to Europe when there were no more cabins. He asked Korshak, and, Rudin said, "They gave her one of the officers' cabins. And after they got her on the ship I got a call from the travel agent—'Would you please let the person to whom it was important know that it has been done.'" Rudin added that Korshak "was very close to Giancana"—Sam Giancana, the long-time head of the Chicago Mob.

For most of his friends, Korshak did the occasional favor, but with Wasserman he seemed to be almost on call—a uniquely proficient kind of *chef de bureau.* "Lew and Sidney were joined at the hip in the '50s," Katleman said. "Sidney did whatever Lew needed." Wasserman had a range of problems that tested even Korshak's versatility. "Korshak was a fixer," Chester Migden, the former SAG executive director, said. "The studios had a lot of money invested in actors, writers, directors. And, when those people got in trouble, they needed fixers." Korshak's reach into the judicial system was not always illicit; among his good friends were some of the most powerful lawyers and judges in Los Angeles. Sometimes, though, it was Korshak's contacts in a different world that were required. MCA was once shooting a movie in a Mafia-dominated neighborhood in Boston; the script was set in the '20s, and TV aerials were a jarring anachronism, but the producer had had no success in trying to persuade the residents to take them down. Wasserman called Korshak; within hours, the aerials were down, according to an MCA executive. And there were some situations—say, a deal that was difficult for MCA—in which Korshak's mere presence might win the day. "When Sidney was brought in to negotiate, it was very powerful," Ted Raynor, a Los Angeles attorney who had first known Korshak in Chicago, said. "Dealing with him, you never knew what the consequences would be."

The SAG waiver that allowed MCA to be at once agent and TV producer had enabled the company, in the space of a few years, to dominate TV production. But its very success made MCA vulnerable. Wasserman knew that SAG would not be able to withstand much longer the criticism of its unique dispensation; and the Justice Department was beginning to scrutinize MCA's operations. If Wasserman was forced to choose between the agency and the production businesses, his preference was unmistakable: it was for the business *he* had started. And by the late '50s—though there was no public hint that MCA might one day leave the agency business—Wasserman had begun positioning the company to do just that.

In 1957, Wasserman set out to acquire Paramount's library of pre-1948 films. Barney Balaban, the studio head, failed to anticipate the significance of losing control of these old movies, and became persuaded to sell them for the seemingly steep price of $50 million. The deal was widely viewed at the time as a blunder by Wasserman, but his critics did not know what an associate of Wasserman's told me—that Wasserman had about $80 million in sales commitments before the deal closed. With his experience in television, Wasserman no doubt had a keener appreciation of the values of distribution than most studio executives. But probably not even he could imagine just how valuable film libraries would become decades later, when the original TV appetite ("like the great maw of the sperm whale," as Milton MacKaye had written) would be enlarged by ever multiplying channels of distribution (cable, video-cassettes, DVDs). According to Wasserman, MCA eventually made more than a billion dollars on its $50 million investment. "Not a bad return," he commented, with thinly disguised pleasure.

Wasserman quickly followed this coup with another. MCA had been leasing space at Republic Studios for Revue's TV production, but Wasserman was now ready for MCA to have a studio lot of its own. He negotiated a deal with Milton Rackmil, the president of Decca Records, which controlled Universal Pictures Company. MCA would pay $11.2 million for all the land and facilities of Universal—and then Universal would lease back studio facilities for ten years, at a rental of a million dollars a year. Universal was, in effect, covering the cost of MCA's acquisition of it. It was pronounced by Stein "one of the greatest deals Lew ever conceived and made for MCA."

Moving to further solidify MCA's strength as a production company, Wasserman began adding to his store of "product." In 1959, MCA owned about 1,650 shows outright; as a coproducer, it also owned, on average, a 50 percent interest in about 525 additional programs. For years, MCA had been setting its clients up in corporations for tax purposes, often financing those corporations, and then advising the clients that their companies should back other shows. (For example, Jack Benny created J&M Productions at MCA's urging. Then MCA told Benny to add new properties to his corporation: *Checkmate, Ichabod and Me, The Marge and Gower Champion Show, The Gisele MacKenzie Show.*) Now MCA was trying to buy outright some of these companies, in order to gain the rights to their programs. Irving Fein, Jack Benny's manager, who also had an interest in J&M, recalled that MCA bought J&M in 1961, in a stock-for-stock transaction that earned Benny about $3 million. "We owned about 86 filmed shows at that time, and we were making 27 shows a year," Fein said. "We had two years to go on our contract at CBS, so we could have had many more shows, and sold it for much, much more. It was a terrible mistake—but MCA convinced Jack to do it."

Larry White, an NBC programming executive, told me that it was hard for many people to refuse to be bought by MCA: "If you didn't sell, they'd kill you. Economically, I mean. They'd tear your guts out." But when MCA approached White about buying his shows he had been a willing seller. He had been producing a series of circus shows for television; Sonny Werblin, acting as his agent, had sold the shows to Kintner, in a 13-show package to be aired on NBC. "They wanted to buy me out," White said. "They wanted to own all the residual rights to the programs. They were doing the Jack Benny deals at that time; it fit into that pattern. I was willing. One day, they stopped negotiating. The next thing I knew, they were selling the shows in syndication, without asking me." By this time, another MCA agent, Herb Rosenthal, was handling the account. "I said to Herb, 'How can you do this?'

"'We got the rights.'

"'How did you get the rights?'

"'Lew gave your partner a hundred thousand.'"

White's partner was Joe Cates, who had produced the $64,000 *Question* quiz show, which ended in scandal. "Cates never told me!" White said. "They had been talking about a deal worth several million dollars—and then they got it for a hundred thousand! I could have sued—but I wasn't capable of doing it. Lew *knew* that. He was so nice to me after that." White paused. "I felt awful, really, that I was so passive. The worst of it is that I knew what was going on and I never said anything. But you couldn't go to the government. MCA had what I call 'scare power.' It was as bad as McCarthy. Lew could put you through the wringer, and ruin your career."

By 1961, it was evident to Wasserman and Stein that time was running out for them in the agency business. Three years earlier, the Justice Department's Antitrust Division had commenced an investigation of MCA, and the new attorney general, Robert F. Kennedy, was taking an interest in the case. Stein always insisted that Kennedy's involvement had been sparked by Frank Sinatra, with whom Wasserman had clashed and ultimately "fired" as a client, and who, Stein believed, was carrying out a vendetta against MCA. But one did not have to resort to conspiracy thinking to explain why the Justice Department was focused on MCA; indeed, the more appropriate question was why no fewer than eight investigations of the company by the Antitrust Division had been aborted since 1941.

During the fall and winter of 1960, a young Justice Department attorney named Leonard Posner had begun conducting interviews in New York. Among many others, he had spoken with Pat Weaver, the former president of NBC. Weaver, who described MCA as "tough and efficient," told Posner about the company's use of "packaging," which was a version of an old practice known in antitrust language as a "tie-in"—that is, using one's power over one product to sell another. The practice is illegal, because it prevents companies that do not have power over the most desirable products from breaking into the market. "NBC had production facilities and was ready to go ahead with top scripts, writers, and directors, and had its own facilities in Burbank, California, and merely wanted a star from MCA," Posner recalled Weaver's telling him. "MCA would agree to furnish Phil Silvers, but only if it got a commission not only on Silvers but also on the salary of all producers, directors, writers, etc., employed in the show. If NBC remonstrated that it wanted the best writers, and that some of the best writers were not those in the MCA stable, MCA would simply say, 'That's the deal; that's the way it's got to be.'" Not only were such practices anticompetitive; they could also result in MCA's serving its own interest to the detriment of its clients'. An independent producer might be prepared to pay a star $10,000 for a show. But if MCA were to demand 10 percent of all the above-the-line costs—say $25,000—despite the fact that the independent producer had already arranged for a director and other talent, the producer would have to pay $35,000 for a star worth only $10,000. And that might well mean that the producer could not afford to hire the star.

Mike Dann, the CBS executive who had been Weaver's assistant at NBC, was also interviewed by Posner, and elaborated on what Weaver had told him. Posner recalled Dann's saying, "General Sarnoff would frequently bellow in rage at the idea of paying tremendous commissions to MCA for packaging the show when NBC did its own packaging." Dann had been inspired by Weaver's almost messianic conviction that television, properly developed, could become a force to transform people's lives. Instead, it had become a pedestrian medium, which Dann attributed in part to the pervasive influence of MCA. He argued that creativity was being stifled because MCA had appropriated the production business to such an extent that there was a dearth of other programming sources, and that MCA was "merely interested in money, not creativity, and hence wants only shows which are in the standard-format design, to bring in the biggest ratings by appealing to the largest mass audience."

In February 1961, Posner wrote a lengthy memorandum describing what he believed to be MCA's antitrust violations. He acknowledged that some of the allegations were based on hearsay but said that he considered the overall picture "generally reliable." Among the many elements were tie-ins, exclusive contracts, packaging, demanding packaging commissions even when MCA had not done the packaging, conflicts of interest, omnibus contracts, coercive dealings, blacklists, bribes, procuring women, luring talent from other agencies with houses, cars, and huge sums of money, and withholding top talent from competitors. "Each dominant position feeds and reinforces MCA's control of other facets,"

Posner wrote. "The totality of control, through all these facets, is such that MCA wields monopoly power."

The government investigation continued for nearly 18 months. During that time, Bobby Kennedy repeatedly asked in internal memorandums to be informed of the progress of the investigation, and he urged "faster action." On one occasion early in the investigation, Posner explained that "it would be important to try to have a grand jury in the MCA matter, because the witnesses were frightened to death and we wouldn't expect to be able to get any specific direct evidence without the cloak of secrecy of a grand jury." He also said that there was no likelihood of obtaining any direct evidence from MCA; he had been told that "MCA is not only cleansing its files but has actually maintained specific records in anticipation of our forthcoming antitrust suit."

On August 31, 1961, Lee Loevinger, the assistant attorney general in charge of the Antitrust Division, wrote a memo to J. Edgar Hoover, the director of the FBI, requesting an FBI investigation of MCA. He placed particular emphasis on MCA's relationship with NBC, saying that many in the television industry believed it was a "captive market" of MCA, and that Robert Kintner "may have entered into a secret agreement (written or oral) with MCA providing for a continuous flow of programs." Summarizing the thrust of the government's investigation, Loevinger stated that MCA's drive to monopolize television production appeared to be built on two pillars: the waiver from SAG and an exclusive agreement with NBC. He was asking the FBI to look for evidence of conspiracy in both.

A few days later, the Justice Department requests for a grand jury and an FBI investigation were authorized. Almost immediately, articles appeared in the trade press stating that MCA was planning to divest its talent agency from its production business. The Screen Actors Guild, furthermore, announced that at the end of 1961 it would revoke production waivers for talent agencies, with no extensions beyond June 1962. It was surely a collaborative decision—"Lew knew it couldn't go on, it had got too big," SAG's Migden told me—that Wasserman and Stein thought would likely short-circuit the government's plans. In traditional MCA style, Stein had also been active on another front. Shortly after President John F. Kennedy took office in January 1961, Jacqueline

Kennedy had decided to conduct a major restoration of the White House. Doris and Jules Stein (notwithstanding the fact that Jules was a right-wing Republican) volunteered to contribute. And on May 11, 1961, Jacqueline had sent them a handwritten note:

> It is a wonderful thing that anyone would be so generous—and I'm so happy it is you—as all I hear from everyone is how beautiful—and perfectly arranged your collection is—and what great taste you have. . . .
>
> There was never any Chippendale or Queen Anne in the White House, which breaks my heart as I love it the most. . . . There is one other place I would be so grateful for your help. . . . It is the 2nd floor hall (outside our yellow oval room—I'm sure you saw it with Tish [Letitia Baldrige, her social secretary]. It is just a sad collection of tired old mismatched stuffed chairs and department store tables and lamps. It looks like the lobby of a rather dreary hotel. . . . The reason this hall is so important is that all the important visitors the President brings upstairs pass through it and wait in it. It is where foreign dignitaries assemble before state dinners. All it has now worth keeping are 3 lovely old crystal chandeliers—and the Catlin paintings of Indians I have borrowed from the Smithsonian, which they may loan to us permanently.

Now, though, Justice Department officials told Baldrige that the Steins' intended gifts could not be accepted. And Bobby Kennedy agreed with his prosecutors' decision to move aggressively with their grand-jury and FBI investigations. MCA's plans to divest itself voluntarily of the agency had not had the desired effect. Posner was convinced that, unless the divestiture was supervised by a court, the possibility of behind-the-scenes cooperation between the talent agency and the production company would remain.

The government decided to focus on the MCA relationship with SAG, not with NBC. "The case was twofold," Gordon Spivack, a Justice Department lawyer who ultimately made the recommendation to Bobby Kennedy on the disposition of this case, told me. "Did they bribe someone to get the waiver? And did they do these tie-ins? The waiver looked like they must have bribed someone. But we put Reagan in front of the grand jury, and he said he got nothing—and we weren't able to find any checks. And as for the tie-ins—we won't give you this actor unless you take this package, or we won't give you this show unless you take these—we had a lot of smoke but no fire. People either would say it hadn't happened or, if they did feel coerced, you'd ask why, and they'd say, 'Well, he didn't say you have to do X, it was more of a feeling,' or 'I understood I had to.'"

Spivack concluded that the evidence was not strong enough to bring a criminal case. Posner and other staff attorneys believed that MCA should be indicted, and they were afraid that the company's power would somehow prevent that from happening.

While the government was weighing its options, MCA attempted to seize the initiative. On June 18, MCA acquired Decca Records and its subsidiary, Universal Pictures—thus fulfilling Wasserman's goal of becoming a diversified entertainment company, dedicated to television and movie production, and to music, too. Universal also had an international distribution system, which would be vital to MCA as it moved into film production. At the same time, Wasserman was proceeding with his plan to spin off the talent agency, by selling it to two trusted senior MCA agents, Larry Barnett and George Chasin, who were to pay MCA a million dollars a year for ten years. But on July 13 the government intervened. The Justice Department brought a civil antitrust suit against MCA, and named the Screen Actors Guild as a coconspirator; it charged the company with a series of violations and asked for court orders to halt them. Most critically, the suit asked that MCA be required to divest itself of Decca Records and Universal Pictures. It also asked that the company be ordered to dissolve—not spin off—the talent agency.

After the suit was filed, Stein recalled, MCA's lawyers were negotiating with the government lawyers, "and they were getting no place. And I finally said to Wasserman, 'Lew, you go to Washington and you stay there until you make a settlement.'"

Wasserman went, and stayed for four days; by the time he returned to Los Angeles, the outlines of the settlement were plain. Spivack remembered telling Wasserman that MCA simply could not be in a position to control both the production business and the agency, even indirectly. "And he said, 'I'll get out!'" Spivack recalled. Wasserman was willing to dissolve the agency, rather than pass it along, intact, to Barnett and Chasin. Thus, ten days after the government filed its suit, the Justice Department announced that MCA had agreed to the agency's dissolution. It took two more months for the terms of MCA's consent decree to be ironed out, but the major elements had been decided during Wasserman's trip to Washington. And, while MCA ultimately accepted certain restrictions on its dealings, the dissolution of the agency was the only major concession it had to make. What Wasserman cared most about— the acquisition of Decca and Universal, and his ability to become a full-scale entertainment conglomerate—was preserved. Spivack told me that he and Harry Sklarsky, the Justice Department's chief of field operations, negotiated the settlement with Wasserman. "After that, Wasserman would do little things for Sklarsky," Spivack said. "Not money—but Wasserman arranged some tour, when Harry went to Israel. Things like that. Harry would call Wasserman."

The resolution of the government's antitrust case was an unmitigated triumph for Wasserman. The agency had become his albatross; he had to be rid of it. To spin it off, however, carried several disadvantages. Although it would be run by those loyal to him, they could not really do his bidding without arousing objections from the government. And, if they didn't do his bidding, he would find himself on the wrong side of the equation that he had created. After all, when Wasserman had come on the scene, the biggest stars were salaried employees of the studios; he had driven their salaries so high that studios finally found it more economical to give them a share in their movies; and then Wasserman had set the stars up as producers. He had changed the economy of Hollywood, but now that he—a producer himself—would have to deal with the mammoth agency he had created, it could all come back to bite him. He could not have dissolved the agency voluntarily; the talent that he would want to hire for his movies would be outraged at being summarily abandoned. If the government was forcing his hand, however, no one could blame him. Finally, in dissolving the agency, Wasserman decided that MCA would demand a split commission (5 percent) on everything related to deals that the company had negotiated for its clients—which would continue for many years. As Wasserman said to me, "If we had sold it, we would have gotten about $10 million; this way, we got about $100 million."

The outcome was so advantageous that many who knew Wasserman remained convinced that the government had done for him what he could not do for himself. Wasserman declined to shed any light on how this resolution was achieved, saying, "No one but me knows how I solved it." What he did volunteer, however, was this: "Some people—even people not in the government—believed we had a monopoly. . . . Well, I plead the Fifth."

The general perception that all had ended happily for MCA with regard to the antitrust settlement was underscored by a note from Jackie Kennedy to Doris and Jules Stein in March 1963. By this time, the prohibition on gifts from the Steins had been lifted; they were contributing substantially to her White House restoration project, and they were also guests for a dinner at the White House. (After the dinner, they sent a gift of a whale-tooth box, mounted in vermeil, which, Jackie wrote, thanking them, "is my husband's favorite thing in the world. He collects them with a passion. . . . May I also say that it is the only whale's tooth I have found beautiful, too!") Though Jackie rejected two of their breakfronts, she declared herself thrilled with their other offerings: two English eighteenth-century mirrors and a rare English eighteenth-century octagonal pedestal writing desk, inlaid with satinwood. "The superb eagle mirrors and the octagonal desk would be marvelous for the Long Hall. I always loved them more than anything," she wrote. And, referring to the antitrust case, she continued:

> You know this whole thing upset me terribly—and I felt so badly and upset for you and Mrs. Stein. In the beginning no one wanted to give anything to the White House—and you were among the very first to come forward—and give so generously of your time and offer us such beautiful things.
>
>   Then came the anti-trust suit—and the enormous wheels of government started to grind. I felt rather like a fly trapped in a machine and kept saying I don't care—I don't even know

what an anti-trust suit is. All I care about is to behave as graciously towards the Steins as they have to me. And months went on and we all lost track. . . . As it turned out, I suppose it was best to have waited, though that never was my opinion. Because you won your suit—which I am so happy about and now nobody can tell us what we can or can't do any more.

The day after MCA's consent decree was filed in federal court, in September 1962, earthmoving equipment on MCA's Universal lot went into action, preparing a foundation for a 15-story office building, the largest ever constructed at a studio. There was no mistaking that this would be Wasserman's building—a forbidding black structure, in a radical counterpoint to Stein's beloved neo-Colonial mansion, now shuttered—and that this, more than ever, was now Wasserman's company. Once again, he was plotting his own rather contrarian course. While the other studios were selling off much of their property, and filming was increasingly being done abroad, Wasserman was betting that movies could be made more efficiently in a properly run Hollywood studio, as long as it was operated at close to full capacity. That September, in an interview with Murray Schumach in the *Times,* Wasserman gave his rejoinder to Selznick's gloomy prophecies of a decade earlier, declaring, "Now, we will see if Hollywood will become a desert. I don't think so." Then he added, with the ease of a man who knows that the record suggests otherwise, "But I could be wrong."

In June of 1963, Wasserman and Kintner struck what was called "the biggest and perhaps most significant deal in TV annals." MCA would produce a full season of two-hour feature films for weekly showing on NBC during the 1964–65 season; simultaneously, these films would be shown in movie theaters abroad, and later it was planned that they would have a second run, in American movie theaters. It remained to be seen how successful the made-for-TV movie might be, but the immediate impact of the agreement was unequivocal; it made Universal Hollywood's largest movie producer.

This deal, moreover, was only a test run. Two years later, in October 1965, reports appeared in the trade press that MCA and NBC had consummated the largest single film deal in the history of television, estimated to approach $60 million. It was thought to include sixty Universal films for network showing, at about half a million dollars each; forty for showing on the network's owned-and-operated stations, at about $100,000 each; and an uncertain number of made-for-TV feature films, for an estimated subtotal of $15 million. An MCA official was quoted as saying that the press reports were "essentially correct."

Not long before his death, however, Wasserman—now frail, his once striding gait hobbled—told me proudly that it had been not a $60 million but a $200 million agreement, one that included sixty first runs and two hundred made-for-TV movies. The deal had been negotiated directly between Kintner and Wasserman; their subordinates met later to draft the papers. The format of the two-hour TV movies was not new, but Wasserman provided a kind of inaugural fillip by coining the term "World Premiere" movies. "This deal was really the basis for our being able to dominate TV production," Frank Price, a TV executive at MCA during the years the deal was in effect, said. "With that contract, you could get the most important writers, directors, producers in town. That's how we were able to acquire this stable of talent. One of the things that eliminated the contract system in the old Hollywood was that no one could afford to carry all those people. So this was, in TV, a return to the old contract system. It gave you a way to pick up people whose series weren't yet on the air and carry them. No one else was able to do what MCA was doing then, because no one had got that kind of order before—and no one has since."

Thus, Wasserman was able to create his own version of the contract system he had once helped destroy. When he left the agency business to become a producer, many wondered how he would cope with the soaring production expenses he had helped to create, which were crippling other studios. One way was by running Universal like a factory—the most computerized in show business—prizing efficiency, cost-effectiveness, and fully utilized facilities. His deal with Kintner helped accomplish that, with its guaranteed stream of production. The TV movies, moreover, had budgets that were said to average only about a million dollars. The top twenty box-office stars, therefore, who demanded the salaries Wasserman had engendered, were out of reach. But Universal was building a roster of youthful, affordable contract players, and was also loaning them out to other studios—as Wasserman's predecessors had done in the heyday of the studio system.

Recalling his early years in Hollywood, Wasserman once remarked to me, with discernible admiration in his voice, "MGM owned this town—they had all the best actors, writers, directors." Much as he had fueled the forces that had undermined MGM, that studio, at its height, had long been his icon, and he now was intent on emulating it, to a greater degree than ever before. But he would fashion his model with the financial sophistication that had always set him apart from the old moguls. For, while NBC had paid $200 million for these movies, Universal retained the rights for syndication sales, foreign television, foreign theaters, and conceivably, domestic theaters. In 1966, upon the debut of the first of the movies, *Fame Is the Name of the Game,* starring Jill St. John, Wasserman spoke to Charles Champlin of the *Los Angeles Times.* Although all the World Premiere movies might not be suitable for all these markets, Wasserman was convinced that the potential revenue was great. He had reason to trust his instincts; they had brought him to this high place, where, gazing out through the black-glass windows of his fifteenth-story office, he could survey his 400-acre domain—the humming soundstages, and the trams of the Universal City tours wending their way through the vast lot, and the sites where plans called for a second black tower, and two hotels, to be built. This was the city within a city that Wasserman had envisioned when he first steered MCA into film production. It would grow even beyond his original design, becoming not only the largest Hollywood studio but, for a time, a paragon of corporate success and stability in an industry characterized by flux, turmoil, and periodic weakness. From this formidable base, Wasserman would reign for decades.

CEOs have felt the admiration and the hatred of the American people. Lately, the emphasis is heavily on the latter. Jerry Useem of *Fortune* magazine writes that many corporate leaders, under the banner of "shareholder value," have deftly manipulated circumstances for their personal gain. As a result, it's high time for the CEOs themselves to rebuild their fallen reputations, Useem contends.

Jerry Useem

From Heroes to Goats . . . and Back Again?

THE FOOD WAS GOOD. The weather was heavenly. But the Greenbrier resort in West Virginia was not an especially joyous place in early October as 68 chief executives converged for a meeting of the super-exclusive Business Council. Alone for once, shielded from the media, CEOs normally relish the opportunity to mingle with their peers and bask in one another's reflected glory. But this was the year of the disgraced CEO, and as a panel on corporate governance got under way, the participants spoke reservedly. There were the predictable comments about a few bad apples. There was frustration that everyone was being punished for the sins of a few. There was agreement that most chief executives were not criminals.

But then the discussion took an unexpected turn, according to two people present. All CEOs, declared the chief of a big European manufacturer, were in some sense responsible. It wasn't just a few bad seeds who were taking unjustifiable salaries or pushing accounting rules to their limits, he said. Everyone needed to take a look in the mirror. With that, the head of a financial services giant took the floor and issued an appeal: CEOs needed to break their public silence and forcefully condemn the business practices that had led to the scandals. Otherwise, their image as crooks would linger.

If the discussion veered from self-exoneration to something resembling a Maoist self-criticism session, take it as a measure of CEOs' confusion—confusion about how to respond to their sudden transformation from visionary giants to moral midgets. For there was a time, believe it or not, when CEOs weren't regarded as a threat to children. Bookstores brimmed with titles like *How to Become a CEO, How to Act like a CEO, The Mind of the CEO,* and, oh, yes, *CEO Logic: How to Think and Act like a Chief Executive.* We got ourselves a whole White House full of CEOs. And what fun it was to be one! As Jack Welch observed in his autobiography, "Being a CEO is the nuts!"

Now many feel they'd be nuts to take the job. A recent Burson-Marsteller poll found that the proportion of senior executives answering "no" to the question "Would you want to be a CEO today?" doubled in just one year, from 26 percent to 54 percent. While CEOs have become fodder for editorial cartoonists, the TV network Pax has launched a new series, *Just Cause,* in which a morally supercharged paralegal goes around whup-assing Ken Lay types. (Tagline: "Cleaning up America . . . one crooked CEO at a time.") It's demoralizing enough that some real-life CEOs have started sounding like Stuart Smalley. "I'm proud to be a CEO," one *Fortune* 1,000 chief affirmed to himself (and me) a few months back. "It's an honor." And doggone it, people *like* me.

The embattled CEO is the focus of this special issue, and the scandal fallout is only part of the story. Chief executives simultaneously face a reeling stock market, a go-nowhere economy, and their own very personal battles. Yet they're all working under a heightened scrutiny born of one thing: lack of trust.

How did CEOs get themselves into this fix? And why are they having such difficulty getting out of it? The answer to both questions can be traced to two words: shareholder value. Today the CEO talking solemnly about shareholder value has become such a cultural fixture that, like the pro athlete who just wants to give 110 percent, it's hard to imagine that things weren't always thus. But they weren't. A generation ago the leading CEOs were public-minded statesmen who were comfortable addressing big questions about business's role in society, government, the solar system, and so forth. Shareholders were only one concern—and not the central one at that. General Electric's Reginald Jones, for instance, spoke in terms that today's CEOs wouldn't touch with a 10,000-foot pole: "Too many managers feel under pressure to concentrate on the short term in order to satisfy the financial community and the owners of the enterprise—the stockholders," he told *U.S. News & World Report* shortly after retiring in 1981. "Boards of directors have to understand that they must shelter management from these pressures." They should do it, Jones added, "in the interest of the nation."

The nation, no less!

The week that *U.S. News* interview appeared, another article was sitting on the newsstands. It was penned by accounting professor Alfred Rappaport in the *Harvard Business Review,* and it popularized the term "shareholder value."

The first to pick up on it were corporate raiders like T. Boone Pickens, who wielded the phrase as an intellectual cudgel in their attacks on entrenched managers. Terrorized CEOs eventually found ways to defeat the raiders. But by then boards of directors had begun acting like raiders themselves, ousting CEOs who failed to deliver—you guessed it—shareholder value. CEOs began to catch on: If they wanted to keep their jobs, they had better start talking about shareholder value too.

While their embrace of their persecutors' religion was at first grudging, CEOs soon found the enemy faith had a major upside. One of its main tenets was to "align" managers' interests with shareholders' interests through the use of stock options. A noble idea in theory. Yet in a twist the theoreticians hadn't foreseen, CEOs began taking options grants worth not thousands or millions but tens and even hundreds of millions. CEOs' interests, it seemed, just needed more and more aligning.

Soon some of the biggest shareholder-value tub-thumpers were taking the lead in gaming the system. Instead of treating the stock price as the natural by-product of building a successful company, they began pursuing it as an end in itself, boosting their own net worth but often crippling the company's long-term prospects in the process. This narrow conception of shareholder value no longer had much to do with valuing shareholders, and in all too many cases familiar today—Global Crossing, Enron, WorldCom, Sunbeam—it turned them into bag holders.

Having co-opted the rhetoric of shareholder value and perverted it to their own ends, CEOs as a class now find themselves friendless. During the downsizing debates of the early and mid-1990s, they had been criticized for giving shareholders too privileged a position in relation to other groups, notably employees and communities. Now the very people in whose name CEOs had acted—shareholders—feel betrayed as well.

Which brings us to the paralysis part. Now seems the time for corporate leaders to step forward and repair public trust through an open airing of the issues: What are the internal conflicts and pressures that contributed to the system's failure? How might they be fixed? Yet with a few courageous exceptions—Goldman Sachs's Hank Paulson, Intel's Andy Grove, Warren Buffett—the overwhelming response has been . . . silence. "Where are the business leaders?" asks Warren Bennis, the dean of leadership experts. "Why aren't they speaking out?"

In part, CEOs are prisoners of their own rhetoric. Having chanted the shareholder-value mantra for so long, they seem to have forgotten how to talk about anything else. Not that anyone's suggesting a return to the days when CEOs could blithely ignore their stockholders. But it's gotten to the point where anyone who dares set aside parochial interests to address, say, the public interest risks mockery as a chump or a hypocrite. "CEOs complain to me, 'We've lost all credibility. We've lost all trust,'" recounts James O'Toole, a leadership professor at the University of Southern California, "So I ask, 'What are you going to do about it?' And they don't answer. Maybe they just don't know."

Even a collective organization like the Business Roundtable, which doesn't have to worry about where it stands at the closing bell, has failed the test of public leadership. During this year's debates over stock options and corporate governance, it chose to work behind the scenes—and then mostly to water down reforms.

The result, Yale School of Management professor Jeffrey Sonnenfeld has written, is that "the American CEO community has become largely a spectator group as its reputation and its destiny are debated by others."

Yes, they've lost control of their reputation. The trust is gone. But their *destiny*? That will be a function of something else: power.

The assumption thus far has been that CEOs' clout will shrink to match their stature: The fall of the "imperial CEO" has been declared everywhere from *The New York Times* to the *Green Bay Press Gazette*. This magazine, too, ran a cover story entitled "The King Is Dead," announcing that "the imperial CEO has had his day" and quoted Paul O'Neill as saying, "The imperial CEO is doomed." The difference, though, is that this story ran in January 1993.

Then, as now, shareholders were in revolt; CEOs were losing their heads; the media were in a lather over executive pay; and Congress was considering curbs on corporate excess. Yet as we know now, the imperial CEO was not only alive and well but very much on the upslope of his career.

What to make of this? One interpretation is that *Fortune* had it all wrong and that nothing ever changes. But in fact a lot did change a decade ago: CEOs lost the job security they had long enjoyed and had to start paying ritual obeisance to the shareholder.

Here's a more likely interpretation: The more things change, the more creative CEOs get at turning circumstances to their advantage. In other words, they've got the power. It's a problem foreseen as far back as 1932, when Adolph Berle and Gardiner Means observed that corporate ownership had become widely diffused among scattered shareholders. Shareholders didn't come to the office every day. Neither did board members. That left the CEO with a chokehold on information and, therefore, a position as the ultimate advantaged insider.

So is it possible the imperial CEO will survive a second round of eulogies?

Those who answer "no" point out, rightly, that the current backlash dwarfs anything that has come before it. In 1992 no CEOs were paraded around in handcuffs. The Senate was not passing tough new corporate governance rules 97 to 0. And no one had yet thought of paying $15,000 for a poodle-shaped umbrella stand. (That awaited Dennis Kozlowski, God bless him.) Perhaps most crucially, the stock market soon continued on its merry way north.

But let's consider the forces arrayed against the imperial boss. Rules, while important, are unlikely to do the trick all by themselves. In a recent study of *Fortune*'s list of Most Admired Companies, Yale's Son-nenfeld found that when it came to the standard measures of good governance—the independence, attendance, and financial acumen of directors—the least admired companies stacked up just as well as the most admired. (Enron's board had only two insiders, for instance, while that of one highly admired company was packed with relatives and asso-ciates of its CEO, Warren Buffett.) If quantity of rules ensured quality of behavior, Sonnenfeld might have added, GAAP would be the most air-tight accounting system in the world.

Public outrage isn't likely to topple the imperial CEO either. When polls show that just 16 percent of Americans trust business executives, you'd think an enraged citizenry would be mobilizing for change. Yet not too much happened back in 1996, when the figure stood at 17 per-cent. (Even during the height of the boom, the number never exceeded 25 percent.) And the executive-pay flap of 1991–92, when everyone from 60 *Minutes* to *Time* to *Nightline* was on the attack, suggests that Americans have trouble converting disgust into action: CEO pay has shot up another fourfold since. "People say, 'I'm mad. I'm not going to take it anymore,'" notes the executive-compensation critic Graef Crys-tal. "But they'll take it."

The thinkers I canvassed were thus uniformly skeptical about the incredible shrinking CEO. As *Good to Great* author Jim Collins put it, "When you have weak corrective mechanisms and you have Caesar, Cae-sar wins."

So is there any real possibility that CEOs will change their act? Many commentators have concluded that the only hope lies in a funda-mental change in values. But before we go recruiting CEOs from divin-ity schools, maybe we could simply rethink what kind of leadership we value.

Over the past decade we've inflated the myth of the savior CEO, the chest-beating action figure who could single-handedly save or sink billion-dollar organizations. The notion was mostly a crock—in truth, a company's fate depends on everything from market trends to an organi-zation's history to pure luck. But neither are CEOs irrelevant. So what might the postheroic CEO look like? Not a return to the statesmen of old who, for all their fine rhetoric, often forgot they were running actual companies. Rather, picture a humbler sort dedicated to creating great companies, not Everest-like stock charts.

In crafting an agenda for CEOs, however, more candor would be a good place to start. For their own sake, it's time to break radio silence and declare their positions on what practices are proper and how the improper ones should be fixed. "It would take only a dozen major CEOs to give the business community a good chance of rebuilding its reputation," says Jeffrey Garten, dean of the Yale School of Management and author of *The Politics of Fortune: A New Agenda for Business Leaders.* Yet the onus shouldn't rest on CEOs alone. Investors, boards, and the media must learn to see them as something other than quarterly-earnings machines. Only by expecting less of CEOs in that sense can we realistically expect more of them in the other.

If we ignore these lessons, the imperial CEO will eventually return to wreak an entirely new kind of havoc. If we heed them, well, just imagine an episode of *Just Cause* in which the CEO appoints a model board, keeps his hand out of the options jar, goes bargain-hunting for umbrella stands, and never, ever takes the words "shareholder value" in vain.

Wouldn't *that* be the nuts?

The traits of trust, honesty, and decency are compatible with the capitalist system. James Surowiecki, writing in *Forbes* magazine, points to
the exemplary early business dealings of the Quakers to illustrate that
honesty is indeed the best policy, leading to respect and financial success. Though recent scandals may have clouded our vision of business,
we should remember that rewarding the right things can make a positive difference.

James Surowiecki

A Virtuous Cycle

IN EIGHTEENTH- and early-nineteenth-century Britain a sizable chunk of the nation's economy was run by members of the religious
sect known as the Quakers. Quakers owned more than half of the country's ironworks. They were key players in banking (both Barclays and
Lloyds were Quaker institutions). They dominated consumer businesses
like chocolate and biscuits. And they were instrumental in facilitating
the transatlantic trade between Britain and America.

Initially their success was built around the benefits Quakers got
from trading with one another. Because they dissented from the Church
of England, members of the sect were barred from the professions and as
a result gravitated toward business. When Quakers went looking for
credit or for trade, then, they found it easy to partner with fellow believers. Their common faith facilitated trust, allowing a Quaker tradesman
in London to ship goods across the ocean and be certain that he would be
paid when they arrived in Philadelphia.

Quaker prosperity did not go unnoticed by the outside world. They were well known already for their personal emphasis on absolute honesty, and as businessmen they were famously rigorous and careful in their recordkeeping. They also introduced innovations like fixed prices, which stressed transparency over sharp dealing. All of this clean living, as it were, paid off. Soon, people outside the sect began to seek out Quakers as trading partners, suppliers, and sellers. And as Quaker prosperity grew, people drew a connection between that prosperity and the sect's reputation for reliability and trustworthiness. In the long run, observant businessmen came to see, being trustworthy was more lucrative than being Machiavellian. Honesty was the best policy.

Or so it once seemed. In the wake of the corporate scandals of the past year, the idea that trustworthiness and business success go hand in hand now appears almost painfully naive. We've grown used to the spectacle of chief executives looting companies and walking away with tens or hundreds of millions of dollars while leaving their shareholders, their employees, and their creditors with little or nothing. And the idea has taken hold that the Enrons and WorldComs are not aberrations, but rather the inevitable by-products of a system that plays to people's worst impulses: greed, cynicism, and selfishness. What happened at Enron, the argument goes, was a perfect expression of capitalism and its excesses.

This argument sounds plausible, if only because capitalist rhetoric so often stresses the need to destroy the other guy and the virtues of what "Chainsaw Al" Dunlap liked to call "mean business." But this popular image of capitalism bears little resemblance to its reality, and if you wanted to find a real example of how the system works, you'd be better off picking one of those Quaker tradesmen than you would Jeffrey Skilling. Over time, in fact, the evolution of capitalism has been in the direction of more trust and transparency, and less self-serving behavior; not coincidentally, this evolution has brought with it greater productivity and economic growth.

That evolution, of course, has not taken place because capitalists are naturally good people. Instead, it's taken place because the benefits of trust—that is, of being trusting and of being trustworthy—are potentially immense and because a successful market system teaches people to recognize those benefits. At this point, it's been well demonstrated that flourishing economies require a healthy level of trust in the reliability and fairness of everyday transactions. If you assumed every potential deal was a rip-off or that the products you were buying were probably going to be lemons, then very little business would get done. More important, the costs of the transactions that did take place would be exorbitant, since you'd have to do enormous work to investigate each deal and you'd have to rely on the threat of legal action to enforce every contract. For an economy to prosper, what's needed is not a Pollyannaish faith that everyone else has your best interests at heart—"caveat emptor" remains an important truth—but a basic confidence in the promises and commitments that people make about their products and services.

Establishing that confidence, then, has been a central part of the history of capitalism. In the medieval period people found that confidence primarily within their particular group. Historian Avner Greif has shown how the Maghribi built a trading system across the Mediterranean in the eleventh century by creating a system of collective sanctions to punish those who violated their commercial codes. Trade among groups, meanwhile, depended on rules that applied to the group as a whole. If one Genoese trader ripped off someone in France, all Genoese traders paid the price. This may not have been exactly fair, but it had the virtue of creating conditions under which interstate trading could flourish, since it obliged trading communities to enforce internal discipline to encourage fair dealing. On the flip side of this, merchant guilds—most notably the German Hanseatic League—protected their members against unfair treatment from city-states by imposing collective trade embargoes against cities that seized merchant property.

As the Quaker example suggests, intragroup trust remained important for centuries. (For that matter, it remains important today—look at the success of ethnic Chinese entrepreneurs in Southeast Asia.) But in England, at least, contract law evolved to emphasize individual responsibility for agreements and, more important, the idea of that responsibility began to take hold among businessmen more generally. As one observer put it in 1717, "To support and maintain a man's private credit, 'tis absolutely necessary that the world have a fixed opinion of the honesty and integrity, as well as ability of a person." About the same time Daniel Defoe famously wrote, "An honest tradesman is a jewel indeed, and is valued wherever he is found."

Still, Defoe's very emphasis on how valuable people found an honest businessman is probably evidence that there weren't that many of them. And the Quakers, after all, became known for their reliability precisely because it seemed exceptional. It's certainly true that the benefits of honesty and the relationship between trust and healthy commerce were recognized. Adam Smith, in *The Wealth of Nations,* wrote, "When the greater part of people are merchants they always bring probity and punctuality into fashion," while Montesquieu wrote of the way commerce "polishes and softens" men. But it wasn't until the nineteenth century—not coincidentally, the moment when capitalism as we know it flowered—that trust became, as it were, institutionalized.

As the historian Richard Tilly has shown in his study of business practices in Britain and Germany, it was during the 1800s that businessmen started to see that honesty might actually be profitable. In America, as John Mueller has shown in his wonderful book, *Capitalism, Democracy, and Ralph's Pretty Good Grocery,* P. T. Barnum—whom we all know as the victimizer of suckers—in fact pioneered modern ideas of customer service, while around the same time John Wanamaker was making fixed retail prices a new standard. And the end of the nineteenth century saw the creation of independent institutions like the Underwriters Laboratory and the Better Business Bureau, all of which were intended to foster a general climate of trust in everyday transactions. On Wall Street, meanwhile, J. P. Morgan built a lucrative business by assuring investors that companies with a Morgan man on the board were reliable and solid investments.

At the heart of this shift was a far greater emphasis on the accumulation of capital over the long run as opposed to merely short-term profit, an emphasis that is arguably a defining characteristic of modern capitalism. As Tilly puts it, businessmen started to see "individual transactions as links in a larger chain of profitable business ventures," instead of just "one-time opportunities to be exploited to the utmost." If your prosperity in the long run depends on return business, word-of-mouth recommendations, and ongoing relationships with suppliers and partners, the value of fair dealing rises. The lubrication of commerce that trust provides became more than desirable. It became necessary.

The important thing about this new idea of trust is that it was, in some sense, impersonal. Reputation had, of course, been important as long as intergroup commerce had been around. But previously, trust had been the product only of a personal relationship—I trust this guy because I know him—rather than a more general assumption upon which you could do business. The real triumph of capitalism in the nineteenth and twentieth centuries was that trust was woven into the basic fabric of everyday business. Buying and selling were no longer about a personal connection. It was now about the virtue of mutual exchange.

As it happens, the impersonality of capitalism is usually seen as one of its unfortunate, if inescapable, costs. In place of relationships founded on blood or affection, capitalism creates relationships founded solely on what Marx called the money nexus. But from a certain angle this impersonality should instead be seen as a virtue, because it advocates the fair treatment of people not on the basis of consanguinity or proximity, but just because they're, well, people. Capitalism, ultimately, widens horizons, because it makes the idea of trusting only people within your particular ethnic or geographic group seem outmoded. At its core, the system is cosmopolitan, since you should be willing to trade with anyone who can offer a good deal.

But it's possible that capitalism's impact was not limited just to making merchants treat one another fairly. The historian Thomas Haskell has argued convincingly that the rise of modern capitalism was instrumental in the emergence of what you might call the humanitarian sensibility, as exemplified by the campaign to abolish slavery in the British colonies. Historians have always noted that the key figures in the abolitionist movement of the late eighteenth and early nineteenth centuries were Quakers and that the Quakers were also, as we've seen, key figures in business at the time. Traditionally, this connection has been seen either as a historical curiosity or as an anomaly that had to be explained away via theories of "ideological hegemony" and "class interest." Haskell, though, suggests that the connection is not an anomaly and that it was logical that the people most enmeshed in the capitalist system would also be the people most likely to act to alter the lives of people living thousands of miles away, even though they had no personal relationship to them.

Haskell's point is not that being good capitalists made the Quakers saints. (Their religious convictions were at the root of their abolitionist sentiments.) Instead he argues that being good capitalists made the Quakers more able to think about the long-term and long-distance consequences of their actions, and gave them what he calls "recipes for intervention." Humanitarianism depends on the idea that we are connected to—and, in some sense, responsible for—people who live a long way away from us and who have no familial or national connection to us. More than that, though, humanitarianism also requires a long-term perspective—you act now in the hope of achieving something in the distant future—and a faith that successful change is possible. Today we take all of these things pretty much for granted. But in the eighteenth century they were relatively new concepts, and the people who understood them best were businessmen.

Capitalism, after all, encouraged universalism over provincialism. It demanded a willingness to make and keep promises—often to strangers and foreigners—deep into the future. It fostered a sense of individual, rather than group, responsibility, and encouraged a more strict accounting of the relationship between action and consequence. And it also, as Haskell argues, widened the sense of possibility by demonstrating that people were able to rationally judge risk and reward and deal intelligently with problems that were thousands of miles away or years into the future. In the case of slavery this meant that instead of simply dismissing it as something irrelevant or unchangeable, the Quakers were able to see it as their problem and as a problem they could do something about.

The relationship between capitalism and humanitarianism is essentially invisible now: The ideas it depends on have become part of the background of everyday life. The same is true of the commonplace workings of a healthy capitalist system. I can walk into a store nearly anywhere in America and be guaranteed that I'm going to get pretty good service and that whatever product I buy—a product that, in all likelihood, will have been made in a country 9,000 miles away—will probably work pretty well. And this is true even though I may never walk into that store again. At this point we take both the reliability of the store and my trust in that reliability for granted. But in fact they're remarkable achievements. And without them the kind of economic growth and standard of living that Americans have grown accustomed to would not be possible. In the end a successful capitalist system succeeds because it makes people more trusting. It encourages people to believe that most transactions will go off without a hitch, not because of the law or possible sanctions, but because that's the way for everyone to prosper. When the system is working right, it creates a virtuous cycle, in which an everyday level of trustworthiness breeds an everyday level of trust.

Of course, we're still confronted with the reality of recent business crimes. If capitalism is actually a system that fosters trust and rewards good behavior, what went wrong?

Part of what happened was certainly a function of the giddiness of the bull market. Capitalism may rely on trust, but its motto is probably closer to "Trust, but occasionally verify." (We buy on eBay, but we rely on the rating system, and we read *Consumer Reports* or CNET before buying that new DVD player.) And there's little doubt that stock market investors stopped bothering to verify because they were so intoxicated with the money they were making. At the same time, and more important, the self-organized institutions whose job is to verify—Wall Street firms and accountants—simply abandoned their roles as what economist Daniel Klein calls "independent knowers," sacrificing their reputations as providers of objective analysis in exchange for the fat fees that the companies they shilled for could offer them.

Perhaps the most important fact, though, was simply that the money to be made from sketchy or dubious behavior was so immense that the discipline imposed by the market vanished. At its heart capitalism works because success depends on repetition. My commitments are believable today because they need to be if I want to stay in business tomorrow. Even if you and I will never trade again, I treat you honorably because my reputation demands it, and because whatever gain I might reap from sharp dealing doesn't outweigh the possible damage to my future. And my experience as a businessman has taught me that fair dealing really is the best recipe for long-term success.

In the case of the executives at companies like Enron and Tyco, though, the short-term gains from self-interested and corrupt behavior were so immense—because they had so many stock options and because the boards of directors turned a blind eye—that any long-term considerations must have paled by comparison. In the case of Dennis Koz-lowski, for instance, it's hard to see how he could have made $600 million honestly if he had stayed chief executive of Tyco. But dishonestly, it suddenly became possible (if the accusations against him prove out). Capitalism is supposed to be a non-zero-sum game, in that every trans-action takes place only if both sides feel they're gaining—otherwise, the deal wouldn't get made. But in more than a few boardrooms in the late 1990s the game was zero-sum: The chief executive's gain was, ultimately, everyone else's loss. In that sense, someone like Kozlowski was not so much the archetypical capitalist as he was a kind of feudal lord, milking his demesne for all it was worth without worrying about the long-term health of his enterprise.

The problem, of course, is that though the scandals themselves will be short-lived, their impact will endure. When capitalism is working well it encourages people to trust one another; when things go wrong it encourages people to be skeptical and cynical. Some of that skepticism is appropriate. (If more investors had scrutinized balance sheets in the last decade, we'd all be better off.) But too much of it will throw sand in the wheels, raising the cost of capital and making everyday transactions more arduous and more expensive. The simple answer to what's hap-pened on Wall Street and in the executive suites of America is, of course, the same answer that capitalism has proffered for the last two hundred years: transparency. But along with that, corporations need to do a much better job of ensuring that the right things get rewarded. The history of capitalism shows the value of trust and fair dealing. But it's a lesson that capitalists periodically need to learn all over again.

PERMISSIONS ACKNOWLEDGMENTS